UNIVERSITY OF
WOLVERHAMPTON

LR/LEND/001

Dudley Learning Centre

Castle View
Dudley DY1 3HR

Wolverhampton (01902) 323559

Telephone Renewals: 01902 321333
This item may be recalled at any time. Keeping it after it has
been recalled or beyond the date stamped may result in a fine.
See tariff of fines displayed at the counter.

THE CASE FOR THE RIGHT TO SILENCE

Biographical note
Susan M. Easton, B,Sc.(Econ), LL.M., Ph.D., Barrister (Inner Temple)

Susan M. Easton is a Senior Lecturer in Law at Brunel University. She has previously lectured at the Universities of Sheffield and Sussex. She is the editor of the *International Journal of Discrimination and the Law* and author of *The Problem of Pornography: Regulation and the Right to Free Speech* as well as books and papers on jurisprudence and criminal evidence.

For Esmond and Clementine

The Case for the Right to Silence

Second edition

SUSAN EASTON

Ashgate

Aldershot · Brookfield USA · Singapore · Sydney

Published by
Ashgate Publishing Ltd
Gower House
Croft Road
Aldershot
Hants GU11 3HR
England

Ashgate Publishing Company
Old Post Road
Brookfield
Vermont 05036
USA

British Library Cataloguing in Publication Data
Easton, Susan, 1951-
  The case for the right to silence. - (Avebury series in philosophy)
  1. Science (Law) - England 2. Science (Law) - Wales 3. Police questioning - England 4. Police questioning - Wales
  5. Self-incrimination - England 6.Self-incrimination - Wales
  7. Law - Philosophy
  I. Title
  345.4 ' 2 ' 056

Library of Congress Catalog Card Number: 98-70150

ISBN 1 85972 186 9

Printed in Great Britain by Galliard (Printers) Ltd, Great Yarmouth

Contents

Acknowledgements

I would like to thank Liz Nolan for editorial assistance and Jane Winter for assistance in obtaining materials. I am grateful to Sweet and Maxwell for permission to include a revised version of a paper 'Bodily Samples and the Privilege against Self-Incrimination' originally published in the *Criminal Law Review* in 1991.

Preface

Since *The Right to Silence* was published in 1991 there have been several important developments culminating in the effective abolition of the right to silence by the Criminal Justice and Public Order Act 1994. Following revelations of miscarriages of justice, the Royal Commission on Criminal Justice was set up in 1991 to review the criminal justice system. It recommended retention of the right to silence in principle, although modified by a new system of advance defence disclosure. In reaching that decision it commissioned a number of research projects on detention and interrogation of suspects, and access to legal advice and related topics which had a direct bearing on the right to silence. Despite the reservations of the Commission and other bodies regarding substantial change, the Criminal Justice and Public Order Act 1994 allowed the court or jury to draw adverse inferences from silence during interrogation and at trial in the circumstances specified in the Act. The effect of this legislation has been to undermine the right to silence and to shift the balance between prosecution and defence in favour of the prosecution. This also entailed changes to the PACE Codes on detention and questioning which came into effect in April 1995. New legislation has changed the appeals process and grounds for appeal, introduced defence disclosure and established a new body to deal with alleged miscarriages of justice. Since 1991 there have been further challenges to the loss of the right to silence in Northern Ireland which have now reached the European Court of Human Rights.

The Case for the Right to Silence documents and reviews these changes and considers the debate on the right to silence in its political and historical context. In the light of both the empirical research and matters of principle, it argues strongly for the restoration of the right to silence.

Introduction

Critiques of the right to silence have been advanced by a wide range of groups, including the Police Federation and senior police officers, the Royal Ulster Constabulary, the Criminal Law Revision Committee[1] and the Home Office Working Group on the Right of Silence[2] as well as academics including Sir Rupert Cross.[3] Arguments for abolition and modification of the right to silence have a long ancestry and may be found in the work of the nineteenth century philosopher and jurist, Jeremy Bentham, in his work on the principles of criminal evidence.[4] Critics of the right to silence were rewarded finally with new legislation which purported to deal with the 'problem' of abuse of the right to silence by permitting the court or jury to draw adverse inferences from silence during interrogation and at trial in the circumstances which fell within the scope of the Criminal Justice and Public Order Act 1994.

Although the term 'abolitionist' is used to describe critics of the right to silence, many critics favour a modified form of the right to silence rather than abolition, although as we shall see civil libertarians have argued that a diluted version of the right to silence constitutes a *de facto* abolition. Moreover, while it is true that no one can be forced to speak, and in this sense the suspect still possesses a 'right' to silence, clearly the way in which silence is constructed by the court and the inferences which may be drawn from silence will be crucial in determining the suspect's decision whether or not to exercise his right and whether we can talk meaningfully of the existence of that right.

Criticism of the right to silence embraces a range of views. For example, many critics are sceptical regarding the value of a right to silence at the pre-trial stage and would see the safeguards provided by the Police and Criminal Evidence Act 1984 which protect the suspect during interrogation, as offering sufficient security to the suspect in the absence of the right to silence, but would prefer to retain the right to silence during the trial stage. But others would support the loss of the right to silence at the trial stage where the accused is in a public setting in open court, with representation, having heard the full details of the prosecution's case against him, but not at the pre-trial stage, where the suspect is detained in the seclusion of the police station.

Dennis,[5] for example, argues that the claim to equality of treatment and the requirements of natural justice, including the right to be informed of the full case against the accused and the right to an impartial tribunal, which are recognised at the trial stage, cannot be met in the context of pre-trial police interrogation. For this reason he finds the criticism of the right to silence at the trial stage, where the defendant participates in the trial, as more persuasive. Judicial questioning does not give rise to the risks of unreliability and abuse of power found in interrogation.

Support for abolition of the right to silence may depend on whether one views the ultimate aim of the law of evidence as facilitating police efficiency or furthering the goal of rectitude of decision-making. Bentham[6] was principally concerned with removal of the right to testify in court while the CLRC[7] favoured changes at both stages, using similar arguments in each case. Although not adopted at the time these proposals were influential in shaping the subsequent changes in Northern Ireland embodied in the Criminal Evidence Order and in the drafting of the Criminal Justice and Public Order Act 1994 although there were some differences.[8] The Home Office Working Group, considered ways of implementing modification of the right to silence at both pre-trial and trial stages including measures to encourage advance disclosure and more robust comment on the accused's silence.[9] The Royal Commission on Criminal Justice favoured retention of the right to silence at the trial stage but recommended the introduction of advance disclosure at the pre-trial stage.[10] The Criminal Justice and Public Order Act effectively abolished the right to silence at both stages of the criminal process in specified circumstances.

Criticism of the right to silence rests on a number of distinct arguments but they have not always been carefully distinguished and it is often unclear which stage of the criminal justice process is being considered. Bentham's arguments regarding the desirability of abolishing the right to silence in court, for example, often have been incorrectly cited in support of arguments to abolish the right to silence at the pre-trial stage. The implications of dilution of the right to silence at each stage may differ because of the vulnerability of the accused in interrogation, especially if he does not have a solicitor present, in contrast to the trial stage where the prosecution's case is presented in a public context with representation.[11]

These arguments for change have been vigorously challenged by those who favour retention of the right to silence. The original proposals of the Criminal Law Revision Committee attracted substantial criticism from a wide range of groups and individuals including Lord Devlin, Lord Salmon, the Bar Council and civil libertarians. Manfred Simon, who gave evidence to the CLRC, described these proposals as 'the first step to dismantle the fortress built by generations of British lawyers to protect the innocent'.[12] The Report of the Thomson Committee on Criminal Procedure[13] in 1975 in Scotland did not follow the CLRC recommendations and the Royal Commission on Criminal Procedure,[14] which reported in 1981 opposed changes to the right to silence. The proposals of the Home Office Working Group have also received criticism from academic lawyers, practitioners and civil libertarians.[15] The Runciman Commission split on the issue of the right to silence. The majority favoured retention of the right to silence, arguing that the potential increase in convictions of the guilty was outweighed by the risk that extra pressure on suspects to talk during interrogation and allowing adverse inferences to be drawn from silence might result in more convictions of the innocent.[16] The Commission also questioned the necessity for change given that the right to silence was rarely exercised in practice. The research conducted for the Royal Commission on Criminal Justice provided empirical evidence to inform the debate.

The Criminal Justice and Public Order Act aroused widespread criticism and gave rise to a vigorous public campaign against it. It was one of the few pieces of legislation in the post-war period to generate public demonstrations and disturbances. Although this was due in part to provisions on trespass and raves, the right to silence provisions also generated considerable protest. The attack on silence in court was criticised by the Bar Council, the Criminal Bar Association, the Law Society, Liberty, Justice, Lord Taylor, the Lord Chief Justice and Viscount Runciman. Although the bill was amended in response to criticism from senior members of the judiciary,[17] it still constituted the strongest attack on the right to silence in recent history.

The right to silence has been seen as having a symbolic significance in affirming the presumption of innocence and the placing of the legal burden of proof on the prosecution to prove its case against the accused; it defines the nature of the delicate relationship between the individual citizen and the state, which has been carefully drawn over the past three centuries, even if that right is for the most part not exercised in practice. But it also has had a real value in protecting innocent suspects from being wrongfully convicted and has been of substantial significance when the suspect is vulnerable because of learning disabilities, age or mental disorders.

Between the two poles of the debate, total abolition and restoration of the right to silence, lie a range of views. For example, a compromise may be sought by arguing that weakening of the right to silence should be contemplated only if existing procedural safeguards are strengthened and fairness is guaranteed.[18] These safeguards might be extended and fortified by further measures such as mandatory video recording of interviews and access to legal advice before silence can be construed as having any evidential significance.

Arguments for and against the right to silence have often been presented in terms of the contrast between rights-based and utilitarian arguments. This is partly due to the fact that the right to silence has become the site in which conflicts between the police and civil libertarians have been fought out during the past twenty-five years. Defenders of the right to silence have usually appealed to fundamental principles such as the presumption of innocence and the *Woolmington* principle.[19] But even if one wishes to rest the case for the right to silence on a purely rights-based foundation, utilitarian arguments need to be considered and met as they have largely determined the parameters of discussion in recent debates. It is also important to note that consequentialist arguments may be used in defence of the right to silence if utility can be shown to favour the continued granting of such a right. It will be argued that the value of empirical evidence should not be under-estimated even if it is not determinative of the issue to those who hold strong views. Of course matters of principle and fundamental rights arguments need to be recognised but at the same time, empirical evidence concerning police practice, the behaviour of suspects in custody and perceptions of silence by the police, the courts and the public, has a useful role to play in assessing arguments for abolition and restoration and should not be dismissed too readily. The research commissioned by the Runciman Commission and studies of policing and defence lawyers over the past five years means that a substantial body of qualitative and quantitative research is now available from which to assess the workings of the criminal justice system and to judge whether abolition of the right to silence was either necessary or desirable.[20]

The debate on the right to silence also reflects the conflict between due process and crime control.[21] As we shall see defenders of the right see it as crucial to the protection of the accused within the criminal justice system, reflecting values of fairness and the presumption of innocence. Conversely those who adopt the crime control model would argue that the right protects the guilty and facilitates the manipulation of the criminal justice system by professional criminals.

The conflict between rights-based and utilitarian approaches will provide the framework for an assessment of the arguments for and against the right to silence. The underlying philosophical issues will be addressed in the context of a review of the current law and recent changes.

Chapter 1 will consider the history and development of the law on the right to silence. This will be followed in chapter 2 by an examination of recommendations for reform. Chapter 3 will consider the impact of changes to the right to silence in Northern Ireland in the context of the peace process. Chapters 4 and 5 will critically assess the claims that the right to silence is anachronistic and that it primarily protects the guilty. Rights-based and consequentialist arguments concerning the right to silence are examined in chapter 6, with reference to the work of Bentham and Dworkin. The evidential significance of silence in the United States is discussed in chapter 7. The rationality of excluding bodily samples from the scope of the privilege against self-incrimination is reviewed in chapter 8 where it is argued that the distinction between speech and bodily samples rests on a crude version of Cartesian dualism.

The statutory and common law limitations on the right to silence are examined in chapter 9. Attention is also given to the reasons why the right to silence has usually been waived in practice. Chapter 10 identifies the factors involved in recent miscarriages of justice and considers the problems which arise when the pressure on suspects to speak is increased.

Notes

1. Criminal Law Revision Committee (1972) *Eleventh Report, Evidence, General*, HMSO, Cmnd 4991.
2. Report of the Working Group on the Right of Silence, Home Office, C Division, London, July 13, 1989.
3. R. Cross [1973] 'The Evidence Report: Sense or Nonsense - A Very Wicked Animal Defends the Eleventh Report of the Criminal Law Revision Committee', Crim LR 329.
4. J. Bentham (1825) *A Treatise on Judicial Evidence*, London; (1843) *Rationale of Judicial Evidence, The Works of Jeremy Bentham*, Bowring edition, Edinburgh, William Tait.
5. I. Dennis (1989) 'Reconstructing the Law of Criminal Evidence', Current Legal Problems 21; (1995) 'Instrumental Protection, Human Right or Functional Necessity? Reassessing the privilege against self-incrimination', Cambridge Law Journal, 54(2), 342.
6. J. Bentham, *Rationale of Judicial Evidence*.
7. CLRC, *op.cit.*
8. The CJPOA for the most part followed the original proposals of the CLRC except that the accused's counsel is asked if he understands the implications of a failure to testify and no reference is made to corroboration in the CJPOA, unlike the Criminal Evidence Order which follows the CLRC recommendations more closely. Clause 1 of the CLRC's Draft Bill aimed to intensify pressures on the accused to speak during interrogation and Clause 5 proposed that if the court considers that there is a case to answer, it shall call on him to give evidence, and if he then refuses to do so, the court or jury may draw such inferences as appear proper and may also treat his silence as corroboration of any evidence against him. The court would advise the accused at the end of the prosecution case that he would be called on to give evidence and be advised of the effects of his refusal. The Criminal Evidence (Northern Ireland) Order 1988 follows the CLRC's bill in treating silence as corroboration of other evidence against the accused. Changes were implemented initially in Northern Ireland six years before being introduced in England and Wales.

9. Report of the Working Group on the Right of Silence (July 13 1989) Home Office C Division, London. The Working Group did not go as far as the CLRC on the issue of corroboration. See chapter 2, below.

10. Report of the Royal Commission on Criminal Justice (1993) London, HMSO, Cmnd 2263.

11. See I. Dennis (1995) *op.cit.*

12. M. Simon [1972] letter to *The Times*, 5 October.

13. Thomson Committee (1975) Criminal Procedure in Scotland (Second Report) London, HMSO, Cmnd 6218.

14. Report of the Royal Commission on Criminal Procedure (1981) London, HMSO, Cmnd 8092.

15. Report of the Working Group on the Right of Silence: Response of the Legal Action Group, January 1990.

16. RCCJ Report, para. 4.22.

17. Lord Taylor, giving the Tom Sargant Memorial Lecture (1994) 144 NLJ 125, argued that the original clause based on the Criminal Evidence (Northern Ireland) Order in which the judge warned the defendant of the adverse effects of failure to testify entailed a more inquisitorial role for the judge, and this was amended; schedule 10 para.1 of the CJPOA amends Article 4.

18. See, for example, A. Zuckerman (1989) *The Principles of Criminal Evidence*, Oxford, Clarendon; [1989] 'Trial by Unfair Means - the Report of the Working Group on the Right to Silence', Crim LR 855; (1990) 'The privilege against self-incrimination and procedural fairness' in S. Greer and R. Morgan (eds.) *The Right to Silence Debate*, Bristol Centre for Criminal Justice, 28-30; (1994) 'Bias and Suggestibility: Is there an alternative to the right to silence?' in D. Morgan and G. Stephenson (eds.) *Suspicion and Silence*, London, Blackstone, pp 117-40.

19. *Woolmington v DPP* [1935] AC 462.

20. See, for example, R. Leng (1993) *The Right to Silence in Police Interrogation*, RCCJ Research Study, no. 10, M. McConville and J. Hodgson (1993) *Custodial Legal Advice and the Right to Silence*, RCCJ Research Study no. 16, London, HMSO.

21. H.L. Packer (1968) *The Limits of the Criminal Sanction*, Stanford University Press.

1 The history and development of the law on the right to silence

The right to silence in English and American law has been shaped by policy issues, questions of utility and moral principles. Consequently, any challenge to what is seen in some jurisdictions as a fundamental right, written into the constitution, inevitably raises considerable debate. Although in the following discussion, the right to silence will be considered in the specific context of the criminal trial, in the law of evidence generally the right has been much more broadly conceived as both a right and a privilege, a privilege against self-incrimination which developed in the late sixteenth and seventeenth centuries. The privilege in this broader sense has embraced both the right of the defendant not to testify at his own trial and also the decision of third party witnesses not to disclose self-incriminating knowledge. The right has also been invoked in civil trials relating to possession of incriminating evidence in infringement actions, although this was curtailed by s 72 of the Supreme Court Act 1981. In the United States the privilege has been used in civil and criminal trials but also in cases held before grand juries, legislative committees and administrative tribunals. Efforts have also been made to extend the right to the refusal to supply bodily samples, although in both jurisdictions these have been strongly resisted.[1]

The privilege against self-incrimination gained acceptance in the seventeenth century in response to the forced interrogations and arbitrary power of the Star Chamber, the prerogative Court of the King, Charles I, and to the ecclesiastic court of the High Commission.[2] Methods used by the Star Chamber included torture, mutilations, the pillory and imprisonment. The Star Chamber was used to censor political works and unorthodox religious ideas, to detect heretical opinions, both religious and political, and to identify dissidents. The objects of attention included members of the professional classes and aristocracy. Both courts were abolished in 1641 and by 1660 the common law courts had established their supremacy. It was in this political context that the privilege against self-incrimination developed, crystallising a general abhorrence and condemnation of Stuart practices of the period, culminating in the English Revolution. One of the most pernicious features of the Star Chamber and the High Commission was the use of interrogation as a fishing expedition: instead of being confronted with a particular charge by a complainant, the 'accused' might be encouraged to speak on oath before being charged, in the hope that he would come forth with an incriminating statement. Initially seen as a protection against the excesses of the ecclesiastic courts and against courts using improper procedures, the commitment to the principle that no one should be forced to incriminate himself on oath in the witness box, was extended to common law courts, and to courts using proper procedures. Although the right to silence has strong historical associations with notoriously iniquitous tribunals, pressures on the defendant to testify are by no means confined to such extreme examples.

While the principle that no man should be compelled to give evidence against himself, often referred to as the *nemo debet* principle,[3] was initially construed in terms of formulating the first accusation against himself, this eventually broadened to prohibit all questioning of the accused without his agreement to testify. So the Fifth Amendment in the United States does not prohibit all self-incrimination but only compelled self-incrimination.

The acceptance of the new privilege by the judiciary was by no means rapid or enthusiastic. As Wigmore[4] points out, the tradition of the vigorous questioning of the accused did not disappear until the eighteenth century had begun and the English Revolution had been firmly established. In the parliamentary declarations and petitions leading up to the expulsion of the Stuarts, the privilege was rarely mentioned and did not achieve the prominence it received in discussions of the American constitution and Bill of Rights in the 1787-1789 period. Wigmore talks of privilege 'creeping' into English life rather than being seen as a major constitutional landmark as it was in the United States and it may be that this lukewarm acceptance is one reason why the right to silence has been more strongly guarded in the United States than in Britain. Support for Wigmore's argument may also be found in the fact that a procedural reform Digest published in 1845 did not even mention the right to silence. Zuckerman[5] has described the undermining of the privilege against self-incrimination in both English and American law as 'a process of attrition' but it might be seen rather as a process of adjustment. For as concessions have been made to strengthen the position of the suspect, a *quid pro quo* has usually been given to the interrogating police in the form of certain exceptions to the privilege. In the United States it has been vigorously defended and its importance as a focus for the protection of political freedom was emphasised in the McCarthy trials of the 1950s. Although attacks on the privilege were launched both then and again in the 1980s, nonetheless it has survived in a stronger form than in England.

As the Federal and State constitutions of the United States have afforded little assistance in construing the meaning of the privilege, considerable argument has

2

been generated concerning the best interpretation of its scope and application, in which both rights and policy considerations have figured. The Fifth Amendment to the Federal Constitution gave the defendant in a criminal trial the right not to incriminate himself and embraced the right not to be forced to give evidence at his trial. The zealous defence of the privilege was also reflected in statutes in Washington and Indiana, prohibiting any reference to the accused's silence in instructing the jury and in some states prohibiting jurors from discussing the subject of the defendant's silence among themselves. In *The State v Rambo*[6] a verdict was set aside because the jurors did not comply with such a statute, while in *Canales v State*[7] a new trial was granted when the jurors admitted that they had discussed the defendant's failure to testify.

In England a number of technical devices and exclusionary rules developed during the eighteenth and nineteenth centuries, under the long shadow cast by the Star Chamber, including limits on the competence of witnesses on the grounds of interest. The defendant was deemed incompetent to testify in his own defence until 1851 in civil proceedings and until 1898 in criminal proceedings, although in the nineteenth century the accused was allowed to make an unsworn statement from the dock. In *Smith v Director of SFO*[8] Lord Mustill described the right to silence as 'a disparate group of immunities, which differ in nature, origin, incidence and importance, and also as to the extent to which they have already been encroached upon by statute.'[9] It includes (i) the immunity from being compelled on pain of punishment, to answer questions posed by other persons or bodies, (ii) the general immunity from being compelled to answer questions to which the answers may be incriminating, (iii) the immunity of persons suspected of criminal responsibility from being compelled to answer questions by police officers, (iv) the immunity from being compelled to answer questions in the dock, (vi) the immunity of persons charged with criminal offences from being being asked questions by the police and (vii) the immunity of persons being tried from being subjected to adverse comment on their failure to answer questions before the trial or to give evidence at trial. It is the final immunity which is removed by the Criminal Justice and Public Order Act but it will be argued that the other immunities are also weakened by the impact of the Act.

In charting the course of the right of silence since the seventeenth century three major landmarks may be identified, the establishment of a professional police force which principally affects the pre-trial stage, the enactment of the Criminal Evidence Act in 1898 which gave the right to silence at trial a statutory basis and the Criminal Justice and Public Order Act 1994 (CJPOA) which radically contracted the right to silence.

The development of the professional police force

The desire for order and predictability, necessary for the smooth functioning of the new industrial society undergoing rapid social and economic change, extended to crime control and to the desire for protection of moveable chattels as wealth was no longer primarily land-based, and in the face of urban unrest. With the development of the Metropolitan Police in 1829, and the subsequent creation of a national police force, came the demand for orderly law enforcement with clear rules of procedure. The development of criminal procedure was fashioned by the concern to strike a balance between the rights of the individual citizen and the authority of the state in the ideological milieu of laissez-faire liberalism when aversion to strong state control was at its height. Like the privilege itself, criminal procedure developed slowly and unevenly as the need to control police discretion in conducting interrogations became clear. While the debate on the reliability and voluntariness of admissions had formerly been focused on the trial, it now shifted to the pre-trial stage, to police interrogation, as the judiciary came to question the treatment and interrogation of suspects. The suspect in the isolation of the interview-room was exposed, not only to the risk of threats of physical harm but also to the danger that any statements he made could be distorted or inaccurately recorded. But while the privacy of the police station contains greater potential for abuse of citizens than the public context of the courtroom, the public and the judiciary have been unwilling to impose very strict controls on the process of interrogation, on the ground that the police would be hampered in their work. While paying lip service to the right to silence, in practice the courts seemed to take the view that if all suspects exercised their right to silence valuable information would be lost, which would undermine the fight against crime. They therefore allowed the police considerable discretion in the interrogation of suspects. Eventually a form of control was set up in the Judges' Rules initially drawn up in 1912 but subsequently revised and amended. These rules have been described as the 'first conscious effort within the pre-trial procedure to set out a considered balance between the need to protect the rights of the individual suspect and the need to give the police sufficient powers to carry out their task.'[10] Although these rules were criticised for not going far enough, in the sense that they were administrative directions and rules of practice rather than rules of law, they did constitute progress in the regulation of interrogation. In addition, rules relating to the admissibility of confession evidence at common law gradually developed. The rule requiring that admissions made to the police were obtained voluntarily rather than through fear or hope of advantage, enunciated in *Ibrahim*,[11] influenced the subsequent development of the Judges' Rules and the Codes of Practice accompanying the Police and Criminal Evidence Act (PACE).

The Judges' Rules, with appropriate amendments, set out the procedures for interrogation until they were replaced by the provisions of the Police and

Criminal Evidence Act in 1984 and the accompanying Codes of Practice. If the Act or its Codes are breached and an admission is obtained then it may be excluded at trial on the ground of oppressiveness and unreliability under s 76, unfairness under s 78 of PACE or under the court's general exclusionary discretion preserved in s 82(3) of PACE.

In practice it had been difficult to enforce the Judges' Rules because of the inability to control discretion during interrogation which occured in the seclusion of the police station and without any reliable means of verifying the accuracy of the contents of the statement. Although the PACE provisions ensured greater control over the process of interrogation and included tape recording of interviews, it has been argued that without appropriate remedies for breaches of the Codes of Practice accompanying the Act, these controls offer insufficient protection.[12] If the discretion to exclude is exercised in favour of the police and against the suspect, the disciplinary effect of the exclusionary discretion is weakened if it is known that some breaches will be tolerated by the courts. The Royal Commission on Criminal Procedure[13] reviewing the need for control of the police in obtaining confessions, viewed police disciplinary procedures as the appropriate way of dealing with breaches of rules relating to the treatment and interrogation of suspects. However, exclusionary discretion has been used, as we shall see, to protect suspects and to discipline the police.[14]

The Codes of Practice concerning the detention, treatment and questioning of persons by police officers, which accompanied the Police and Criminal Evidence Act and which were issued under s 66, came into force on 31 December 1985. These now govern the treatment and interrogation of the accused. They were revised in 1991 in the light of empirical research and criticism of the operation of the Codes[15] and revised further in 1995 to take account of changes in the Criminal Justice and Public Order Act 1994. The tape recording of interviews with suspects is covered by Code E which specifies when tape recording should be used, the type of interviews which should not be recorded and procedures for recording.[16] The suspect has the right to examine the Codes of Practice. Section 56 of PACE gives the arrested person the right to have someone informed of his arrest and of where he is being detained and s 58 gives him the right to legal advice. He is also advised that this right is a continuing one and that he may consult a solicitor at any time while in custody and that the advice will be free.

PACE itself does not refer specifically to the right to silence but it arguably underpins the Act and is referred to in the Codes, although the Codes have been amended as the right to silence has been weakened. The Codes reflect the Royal Commission's desire to strike a balance between citizens' rights, including the right to silence and police powers. In considering the right to silence in police interrogation the situation before and after the enactment of the Criminal Justice and Public Order Act 1994 needs to be considered as it fundamentally changes both the right to silence and the caution given to the suspect.

Silence in interrogation: (i) 1984-1994

The original PACE Codes on detention and questioning of suspects required that the suspect should be told before questioning that: 'You do not have to say anything unless you wish to do so but what you say may be given in evidence.'[17] If he is unclear on the meaning of the caution, it should be explained to him that he 'need not answer any questions or provide any information which might tend to incriminate him, and that no adverse inferences from this silence may be drawn at any trial that takes place.'[18] This caution was used until the new PACE Codes came into effect on 10 April 1995.

The caution should be repeated at the resumption of questioning following any breaks. In *Furnival*[19] the trial judge directed the jury to acquit Furnival on a charge of the murder of his step-mother after hearing that the police had cautioned him at the beginning of the interview but did not warn him of his right to silence when they changed the tape. The judge directed the jury that there was no further evidence to justify continuing the trial.

Traditionally, the duty to help the police with their inquiries has been seen as a moral rather than a legal duty as Lord Parker stressed in *Rice v Connolly*:

> It seems to me quite clear that though every citizen has a moral duty, or if you like, a social duty to assist the police, there is no legal duty to that effect, and indeed the whole basis of the common law is that right of the individual to refuse to answer questions put to him by persons in authority. In my judgement there is all the difference in the world between deliberately telling a false story, something which on no view a citizen has a right to do, and preserving silence or refusing to answer, something which he has every right to do.[20]

Simply exercising the right to silence was insufficient to allow an adverse inference to be drawn. But the failure to advance defences when first questioned was still admissible and the fact of initial silence was part of the whole picture of the case the jury was assessing. The jury could not be prevented from drawing its own conclusions. But certain forms of judicial comment were prohibited. The judge was prohibited from commenting in a way which encouraged the jury to equate silence with guilt or to draw any adverse inferences from the accused's exercise of his right to silence or to treat silence in response to police questioning as corroboration of evidence against the accused.[21] However, even before the passing of the Criminal Justice and Public Order Act, some judges had stretched the boundaries of comment to question the innocence of silence in certain circumstances.

In *Leckey*[22] the trial judge had commented on the accused's silence when cautioned by the police, that an innocent man might be expected to deny the charge, but the Court of Criminal Appeal quashed his conviction because the comment was prejudicial and unacceptable. If such comment were permitted, the caution would be meaningless. Similarly, in *Hoare*[23] the trial judge had said 'members of the jury, what would you have done if you were an innocent man?' and this kind of comment was deemed unacceptable.

If the accused answered some questions during the police interview but refused to answer others, then the jury was still not entitled to draw adverse inferences from his selective silence.[24] In *Raviraj* the court said that 'where suspicious circumstances appear to demand an explanation and no explanation is given... the lack of any explanation may warrant an inference of guilty knowledge in the defendant.'[25] The appropriate comment on out of court silence was considered in *Sullivan*.[26] Sullivan had been jointly charged with an associate, Dredge, with smuggling 1,000 Swiss watches. The watches had been found in Dredge's bag. Dredge's telephone number and a cable from Geneva addressed to Sullivan, signed 'Everything ready regards Rudi', had been found at Sullivan's home. Sullivan refused to answer questions put to him by customs officers. In summing up, the trial judge had said:

> Sullivan refused to answer any questions. Of course bear in mind that he was fully entitled to refuse to answer questions, he has an absolute right to refuse to do just that. But you might well think that if a man is innocent he would be anxious to answer questions. Now, members of the jury that is what it really amounts to.[27]

This was held to be a misdirection, although it was noted that this is precisely what members of the jury must have been saying to themselves if they were guided by common sense. But even if common sense leads one to think that a person would want to speak if innocent, the jury must not be told that if the accused were innocent he would have answered the questions. At the same time silence could not be ignored, as part of the whole mass of evidence in the case, but it was not of itself evidence of guilt. Reviewing the earlier authorities on this issue, the court said that sometimes comment on the defendant's silence was unfair, although that was not the case here. On the state of the law at that time, the court felt compelled to hold the trial judge's comments a misdirection but as it did not constitute a miscarriage of justice, Sullivan's appeal was dismissed. This common sense approach to silence was later applied in Northern Ireland in drawing inferences from silence under the Criminal Evidence Order in cases such as *Murray*[28] and *Martin*[29] and is likely to figure in interpretations of the Criminal Justice and Public Order Act.

The construction of pre-trial silence also arose in relation to ambush defences, that is, where the accused exercises his right to silence in the context of police interrogation, only to later give an account which takes the prosecution by surprise, by which time it is too late for the prosecution to undermine that defence effectively. The alleged use of these defences has been a recurring argument in the attack on the right to silence, for the fact that an explanation was given late could not be used against the accused although the lateness of the explanation was a matter the jury could take account of in assessing the weight to attach to that explanation. In *Ryan*[30] it was decided that if the accused does remain silent during interrogation and fails to mention a defence he later relies on, his failure to speak initially could be used to undermine the credibility of that defence. This has now been given a statutory form in s 34 of the CJPOA. Prior to the 1994 Act the courts had shown increasing dissatisfaction with the right of silence and had tried to push the boundaries of comment to their limit. In this respect the attack on the right to silence in 1994 can be seen as the culmination of a long-standing campaign against the right.

Before 1967 the issue of ambushes arose principally in relation to tactical alibi defences at trials on indictment, that is, alibi defences made only at trial so that the police could not investigate them fully. Section 11 of the 1967 Criminal Justice Act aimed to prevent defendants producing alibi evidence at trial leaving the prosecution insufficient time to verify the veracity of the alibi. The accused was obliged to give notice to the prosecution of his intention to adduce evidence in support of an alibi, within 7 days of the end of committal proceedings although alibis out of time could be permitted at the judge's discretion. This effectively curtailed the tactical use of ambushes relying on alibis. The alibi had to be very specific: a vague sequence of events happening over the period of a month, for example, would be insufficent to invoke s 11 according to *Hassan*.[31]

The Court of Appeal, consisting of Viscount Dilhorne, Lord Scarman and Mr. Justice Jupp, considered the issue of pre-trial silence in *Gilbert*.[32] Gilbert was convicted for murder. Although when arrested, he spoke of his relationship to the victim, he stayed silent when questioned about the incident, an argument on a building site, which ended in the victim's death. At trial he argued for the first time that the stabbing had been in self-defence and due to provocation. The trial judge commented that Gilbert was entitled to remain silent but that he had not mentioned self-defence in his statement to the police. On appeal it was argued, *inter alia*, that the direction on self-defence was insufficient. The Court of Appeal found that the judge had misdirected the jury when he said:

> Bear in mind we have heard of this matter of self-defence for the first time. Ask yourselves the question, if it is the real explanation of what happened, do you or do you not think it remarkable that when making the statement, the accused says nothing whatever about it. That may help you, applying your common sense to test the substance of the matter of self-defence, which he has now gone into in some detail in the witness box.[33]

8

The Court of Appeal considered whether this amounted to a serious error and reviewed the previous cases on this issue. While noting that not all the earlier authorities could be reconciled, and while expressing some misgivings with the current law, the court sought to clarify the boundaries of commment:

> In our view it may not be a misdirection to say simply 'This defence was first put forward at this trial' or words to that effect, but if more is said, it may give rise to the inference that a jury is being invited to disregard the defence put forward because the accused exercised his right of silence, in which case a conviction will be placed in jeopardy... No accused can be compelled to speak before, or for that matter, at his trial. But it is another thing to say that if he chooses to exercise his right of silence, that must not be the subject of any comment adverse to the accused. A judge is entitled to comment on his failure to give evidence. As the law now stands, he must not comment adversely on the accused's failure to make a statement.[34]

Viscount Dilhorne stated that:

> As the law now stands, although it may appear obvious to the jury in the exercise of their common sense that an innocent man would speak and not be silent, they must be told that they must not draw the inference of guilt from his silence.[35]

Acknowledging that the law seemed in some cases, 'inconsistent with the exercise of common sense,'[36] and that for this reason Bentham and others were critical of the right to silence, nonetheless the court asserted firmly that:

> It is in our opinion now clearly established...that to invite a jury to form an adverse opinion against an accused on account of his exercise of his right to silence is a misdirection.[37]

These comments in *Gilbert* constituted a powerful restatement of the right to silence by two Law Lords and a puisne judge notwithstanding their dissatisfaction with it.

The right to silence did not depend on the fact of being cautioned so that if for some reason the suspect had not been cautioned, he could still be seen as exercising his right, according to the Privy Council in *Hall*.[38] Here it was stressed that the caution only reminds him of a right he already has rather than giving him the right. As Lord Diplock said:

9

The caution merely serves to remind the accused of a right which he already possesses at common law. The fact that in a particular case he has not been reminded of it is no ground for inferring that his silence was not in exercise of that right, but was an acknowledgement of the truth of the accusation.[39]

Lord Diplock reaffirmed the appropriate construction of silence:

> It is a clear and widely-known principle of the common law in Jamaica, as in England, that a person is entitled to refrain from answering a question put to him for the purpose of discovering whether he has committed a criminal offence. *A fortiori* he is under no obligation to comment when he is informed that someone else has accused him of an offence. It may be that in very exceptional circumstances an inference may be drawn from a failure to give an explanation or a disclaimer, but in their Lordships' view silence alone on being informed by a police officer that someone else has made an accusation against him cannot give rise to an inference that the person to whom this information is communicated accepts the truth of the accusation.[40]

Silence in interrogation (ii) the effect of the Criminal Justice and Public Order Act

The Criminal Justice and Public Order Act has a number of implications for the PACE provisions and new codes were issued in 1995 to take account of these changes. The Codes govern stop and search powers, searching of premises and seizures of property found on persons or premises, the detention, treatment and questioning of persons by police officers and identification of persons by police officers and tape recording. Sections 34, 36 and 37 of the CJPOA cover silence in the pre-trial stage and s 35 deals with silence at trial. The Act permits the court or jury to draw the inferences from silence as appear proper in the circumstances specified in the Act.

Section 34 states:

(1)   Where, in any proceedings against a person for an offence, evidence is given that the accused -

(a)   at any time before he was charged with the offence, on being questioned under caution by a constable trying to discover whether or by whom the offence had been committed, failed to mention any fact relied on in his defence in those proceedings; or

(b)   on being charged with the offence or officially informed that he might be prosecuted for it, failed to mention any such fact, being a fact which in the circumstances existing at the time the accused could reasonably have been expected to mention when so questioned, charged or informed, as the case may be, subsection (2) below applies.

(2)   Where this subsection applies -

(a)   a magistrates' court, in deciding whether to grant an application for dismissal made by the accused under section 6 of the Magistrates' Courts Act 1980...

(b)   a judge, in deciding whether to grant an application made by the accused under -
(i)   section 6 of the Criminal Justice Act 1987...
(ii)   paragraph 5 of Schedule 6 to the Criminal Justice Act 1991...

(c)   the court, in determining whether there is a case to answer, and

(d)   the court or jury, in determining whether the accused is guilty of the offence charged, may draw such inferences from the failure as appear proper.

The caution had to be amended so the suspect is now reminded of his right to silence while at the same time warned that silence may be subject to adverse comment at trial by the judge and prosecution who may now invite the jury to draw adverse inferences from his silence. The new caution states that:

You do not have to say anything. But it may harm your defence if you do not mention when questioned something which you later rely on in court. Anything you do say may be given in evidence.[41]

The Code states that minor deviations from this wording would not constitute a breach as long as the sense of the caution is preserved. At the beginning of the interview at the police station, the interviewing officer should refer to any significant statement or silence in response to questions prior to interview and ask him whether he confirms or denies his earlier silence or statement and whether he wishes to add anything to it.[42]

If there is a break in questioning, it should be made clear to him that he is still under caution and if there is any doubt then he should be cautioned again. If the suspect does not understand the caution the officer may explain it in his own words. He is still not under a legal obligation to answer, but runs the risk of adverse inferences being drawn from his initial silence if he fails to mention a fact which he later relies on in his defence.

A person suspected of an offence should be cautioned before being asked any questions about it if his answers, or his silence, may be given in evidence to a court.[43] He must be cautioned upon arrest for an offence unless it is impracticable to do so or he has already been cautioned.[44]

Section 36 of the CJPOA concerns the effect of the accused's failure to account for objects, substances or marks:

(1)   Where -

    (a)   a person is arrested by a constable, and there is -

        (i)   on his person; or

        (ii)   in or on his clothing or footwear, or

        (iii)   in any place in which he is at the time of his arrest, any object, substance or mark, or there is any mark on any such object; and

    (b)   that or another constable investigating the case reasonably believes that the presence of the object, substance or mark may be attributable to the participation of the person arrested in the commission of an offence specified by the constable; and

    (c)   the constable informs the person arrested that he so believes, and requests him to account for the presence of the object, substance or mark; and

    (d)   the person fails or refuses to do so...

(2)   (c)   the court, in determining whether there is a case to answer; and

    (d)   the court or jury, in determining whether the accused is guilty of the offence charged, may draw such inferences from the failure as appear proper.

He must be warned in ordinary language what the consequence is of his failure to answer questions. He must be told by the officer what offence is being investigated, what fact he is being asked to account for and told that the officer believes this fact to be due to the suspect's involvement in the offence and that a court may draw inferences from his silence and that his silence may be given in evidence. Section 36 applies only if he is under arrest at the time he fails to give an account.

Section 37 covers the effect of the accused's failure or refusal to account for his presence at a particular place:

(1)   Where -
     (a)   a person arrested by a constable was found by him at a place at or about the time the offence for which he was arrested is alleged to have been committed; and
     (b)   that or another constable investigating the offence reasonably believes that the presence of the person at that place and at that time may be attributable to his participation in the commission of the offence; and
     (c)   the constable informs the person that he so believes, and requests him to account for that presence; and
     (d)   the person fails or refuses to do so, ...

(2)   Where this subsection applies-
     (c)   the court, in determining whether there is a case to answer ; and
     (d)   the court or jury, in determining whether the accused is guilty of the offence charged, may draw such inferences from the failure or refusal as appear proper.

The accused must be told in ordinary language what the effect of 1(c) would be if he refuses or fails to comply with the request.

To draw an inference under s 34 the fact that the accused fails to mention must be relevant to the defence, so failure to mention a fact which is irrelevant to it, cannot justify drawing an adverse inference. Whether he could reasonably have been expected to mention the fact will depend on the circumstances and on the characteristics of the suspect, for example, his knowledge of the circumstances in which the offence was allegedly committed, his awareness and mental state, and his understanding of the offence with which he is charged.

If the accused remains silent during questioning or refuses to answer some questions, then for an inference to be drawn under ss 36 and 37 of the Criminal Justice and Public Order Act, the interviewing officer must tell the suspect 'in ordinary language', the following points: what offence he is investigating, what fact he is asking the suspect to account for, that he believes this fact may be due to the suspect's taking part in the commission of the offence in question, that a court may draw a proper inference if he fails or refuses to account for the fact about which he is being questioned, that a record is being made of the interview and that it may be given in evidence if he is brought to trial.[45]

Sections 34, 36 and 37 do not preclude the drawing of inferences from the failure to speak which could be drawn apart from these sections, so the common law position on silence in response to third party accusations would still apply. At common law adverse inferences may not be drawn from silence unless the suspect is on even terms with the person questioning him and in circumstances in which it is reasonable to expect a denial of an accusation made in the presence of the accused.[46] However, attempts have been made to erode the even terms principle by applying the rule to the context of the police station interrogation where a solicitor is present.[47]

Sections 36(6) and 37(5) allow the drawing of any other inferences which could be drawn apart from the sections, so possession of incriminating objects or presence at the crime scene would, in any case, constitute circumstantial evidence against the accused but its weight will be increased by the silence when asked to explain that possession or presence.

Section 38(3) states that a conviction or decision to transfer proceedings cannot be based just on an infererence permitted by ss 34(2), 35(2), 36(2) and 37(2). The court still retains its discretion to exclude evidence: s 38(6) provides that 'Nothing in sections 34, 35, 36 or 37 prejudices any power of a court, in any proceedings, to exclude evidence (whether by preventing questions being put or otherwise) at its discretion.' Inferences which might be drawn under those sections could still be excluded by the trial judge. If there is concern regarding the propriety of police behaviour the judge could direct the jury not to draw any adverse inferences from silence. Otherwise it is the task of the jury to determine what inference to draw, using common sense.

In considering appeals under these sections of the Act the Court of Appeal will be looking to the interpretation of the similarly worded Criminal Evidence Order in Northern Ireland, although the fact that many of the Northern Irish decisions are non-jury cases will need to be taken into account. It also seems likely that the original thinking expressed in the report of the Criminal Law Revision Committee[48] will be used in future cases. For example, the CLRC said that the inference drawn will depend on the circumstances and that there may be reasons compatible with innocence and the court or jury will decide depending on the circumstances whether an adverse inference is appropriate. The type of person would also be relevant, for example, if the person is vulnerable, young, or unused to criminal proceedings. If the accused is silent during interrogation and he argues that this is because the police had not disclosed fully the case against him, then the court may exercise its exclusionary discretion under s 78 to prevent adverse inferences being drawn from silence.[49]

Some of the problems in implementing the new Act may be gauged from the experience of applying the Criminal Evidence Order in Northern Ireland, as well as the experience of other jurisdictions which have enacted the original recommendations of the Criminal Law Revision Committee. In Northern Ireland problems have been raised for practitioners in determining the appropriate advice to clients. Lawyers may be called on to give evidence at the client's trial regarding the advice given earlier. Notes must be kept of any requests made by the police, whether the client appears to understand the significance of speaking or remaining silent, how the caution was worded and the reasons why the lawyer advised the client to speak or refrain from speaking. The legal adviser needs to be clear that the client understands the implications of speaking or silence. The lawyer also needs to carefully assess the relevant facts of the case and its strength to consider whether to advise silence in those circumstances, whether speaking is more hazardous than silence, notwithstanding the risk of adverse inferences. Problems may also arise for juries, as they have for judges in the Diplock courts, in determining the point at which silence becomes evidentially significant.

Given the wording of s 34 there may be arguments concerning whether a fact is being relied on subsequently and whether it was reasonable to mention it earlier when being interviewed. There are likely to be disputes over whether facts which did not appear to the defendant to be material early on in the investigation are now material. Questions of relevance and materiality will still need to be argued at trial. What might seem a peripheral factor in the early stage and not mentioned, could later transpire to be crucial to the defence in the light of new knowledge or witness testimony. The suspect may not even know at the initial stage on which facts he will be relying, especially if he has not yet received legal advice or does not know the full details of the prosecution's case against him. In Northern Ireland the equivalent provision has been used even where the accused does not testify at trial. Clearly when evidential significance is formally attached to silence, access to legal advice is crucial but this access is by no means guaranteed. But even with a solicitor present, the accused is being questioned before he has heard the full case against him and may make rash statements which will be prejudicial.

The Law Society[50] has advised that the lawyer should state at the interview whether or not he is advising his client to answer questions and if he is advising silence, to state his reasons clearly at that stage, so that if the client decides to remain silent there will be no doubt at trial that the client was following his lawyer's advice. The reasons might include the fact that the lawyer is not satisfied with the quantity of information provided by the police, or he believes that the full facts have not been disclosed, or because the client is afraid of reprisals. If these reasons are clearly stated at the interview stage it will assist the court in determining whether adverse inferences should be drawn. Also if the client does not feel able to speak he could draft a brief statement of the key facts to give to the police instead, to protect himself at trial. It is also important that the lawyer is assertive. In response to criticism of the quality of legal advice, improvements have been made to the training of advisers and the accreditation scheme.

Zander[51] questions whether the abolition of the right to silence will have the unintended consequence that solicitors are more likely to advise their clients to remain silent, so that at trial it can be argued that silence followed from legal advice and that therefore no adverse inference should be drawn. If the solicitor's advice is subsequently perceived by the court to be the wrong advice it would seem unfair to penalise the client. But in Northern Ireland the fact that the accused remained silent on the basis of legal advice was seen in *Martin*[52] as unreasonable. It is unlikely that the court will see the fact of following legal advice as sufficient to preclude the drawing of adverse inferences from silence.

But this view may not be shared by the European Court of Human Rights. In *Murray* the Court stressed that the privilege against self-incrimination and the right to remain silent during police interrogation are 'generally recognised international standards which lie at the heart of the notion of a fair procedure under article 6.'[53] As Munday observes:

> If a suspect, having been granted his " minimum right" under Article 6(3)(i) of the Convention of legal assistance, is informed by his legal adviser that the right of silence is a "generally recognised international standard which lie(s) at the heart of the notion of a fair procedure" under the European Convention on Human Rights, it might appear peculiar to say that adverse inferences can then reasonably be drawn from the accused's failure to answer questions.[54]

The situation where the the defendant refuses to speak on the basis of legal advice was not considered by the court in *Murray*. But it is possible, Munday argues, that such inferences might be considered unfair and unreasonable under European human rights law.

But there may, in any case, be more appeals concerning the veracity of confessions, and police behaviour in interviews and arguments over the meaning of the new caution and whether it was fully grasped by the client as many suspects find difficulty in understanding it and some police officers and lawyers are confused by it, as well as arguments over whether the defendant was silent and, if so, in response to which particular questions. While tape recording and transcripts of interviews may resolve some of these arguments, there may well be arguments about interviews outside the police station. Access to legal advice and the presence of an adviser during interrogation may be seen as a precondition of drawing adverse inferences following the decision of the European Court of Human Rights in *Murray*. This is likely to form the basis of future cases on the CJPOA taken to the European Court.

The question of legal advice and s 34 was considered by the Court of Appeal in *Condron and Condron*.[55] The appellants were convicted of supplying and possessing heroin. When interviewed at the police station they did not answer questions, acting on their solicitor's advice. The solicitor thought that their drug withdrawal problems rendered them unfit to be interviewed but the police medical examiner declared them fit. The trial judge directed the jury that it was open to them to draw inferences from the appellants' failure to mention at interview facts which they could reasonably have been expected to mention at that time and upon which they subsequently relied in their defence. The appellants argued that if silence was based on legal advice given for non-tactical reasons, such as health grounds, then no-comment interviews should be excluded. The appellants further argued that the trial judge's direction, which broadly followed the Judicial Studies Board Specimen Direction, did not go far enough in warning the jury about the limits of the inferences they may draw. The Specimen Direction states that where the accused fails to mention when questioned a fact which he could reasonably have been expected to mention the jury should be told:

> The law is that you may draw such inferences as appear proper from his failure to mention it at that time. You do not have to hold it against him. It is for you to decide whether it is proper to do so. Failure to mention such a fact at that time cannot, on its own, prove guilt, but depending on the circumstances, you may hold that failure against him when deciding whether he is guilty, that is, take it into account as some additional support for the prosecution's case. It is for you to decide whether it is fair to do so.

The appellants argued that the jury should have been told not to draw an adverse inference unless they thought that the failure to mention relevant matters could only be attributed to the fact that the appellants must have fabricated the evidence at a later date.

The Appeal Court rejected both arguments, dismissing their appeal, noting that the police doctor had certified them fit to be interviewed, they had been cautioned and had received legal advice. It was a matter for the jury to decide whether the appellants should have mentioned earlier facts relating to the purchase of heroin in small wraps and innocent explanations of items found at the flat. The Appeal Court also endorsed the use of the direction given in *Cowan*,[56] relating to s 35 of the CJPOA, as being appropriate to s 34. Under the *Cowan* direction the jury should be told that if they can sensibly attribute the defendant's silence only to having no answer or one which would not withstand cross-examination, they may draw an adverse inference. The Court of Appeal in *Condron* also considered the question of privilege. If the accused gives as his reason for not answering questions that he was advised to do so by his lawyer, this does not *per se* amount to a waiver of privilege. However, this alone is unlikely to be seen as a sufficient reason for not mentioning factors relevant to the defence. The accused will need to state the reasons for the advice if he wishes to ask the court not to draw an adverse inference and he will be deemed to waive his privilege if he gives evidence of the nature of the advice and the trial judge should warn him of this.

In *Argent*[57] the Court of Appeal set out the circumstances in which an inference may be drawn under s 34 and reference was made to advice as one factor to consider. The Court of Appeal stressed in *Argent* that the jury is not concerned with the correctness of the solicitor's advice, or whether it complies with Law

Society guidelines, but rather with the reasonableness of the appellant's conduct in all the circumstances which the jury have found to exist. These circumstances may include the solicitor's advice, but neither the Law Society nor the solicitor can preclude consideration by the jury of the issue which Parliament has left to the jury to determine.

In *Argent* the defendant was convicted of manslaughter. The prosecution claimed that he stabbed the victim outside a nightclub because he had asked his wife to dance. Argent was identified by witnesses as present when the victim was killed and positively identified at an identity parade. At trial the defence denied any contact between the defendant and the victim. Argent claimed that he and his wife had left the club before the attack, they walked home intending to eat in a restaurant on the way home but it was closed, so they returned home and spoke to the baby-sitter but knew nothing of the incident until interviewed by the police.

At the first interview on the day of the killing Argent was interviewed and declined to speak. At a second interview three months later, he also declined to comment. The trial judge excluded the first interview as there were no circumstances existing at the time which required the accused to say anything as all the police had was an anonymous telephone call identifying Argent as the perpetrator. However, he allowed in the second interview which was preceded by a positive identification as by that time the accused could reasonably have been expected to mention facts which were or might be relevant. The Court of Appeal dismissed Argent's appeal. The Lord Chief Justice said there were six formal conditions to be met before the jury could draw inferences under s 34:

1. There had to be proceedings against a person for an offence.
2. The alleged failure to mention a fact later relied on had to occur before a defendant was charged.
3. The alleged failure had to occur during questioning under caution by a constable or any other person within s 34(4).
4. The questioning had to be directed to trying to discover whether or by whom the alleged offence had been committed.
5. The alleged failure by the defendant had to be to mention any fact relied on in his defence in those proceedings. This raises two questions of fact: (a) Was there some fact which the defendant had relied on in his defence? (b) Did the defendant, when he was being questioned in accordance with s 34, fail to mention it? These factual questions are for the jury to resolve. In Argent's case there were matters on which he relied in his defence such as the fact that he did not quarrel with the deceased at the club, or the fact that he left the club early and that he was not carrying a knife and had not been involved in a fight in the street where the victim was killed, that he went to a restaurant but it was closed and that he returned home and spoke to the baby-sitter.

18

6.   The fact the appellant failed to mention was a fact which, in the circumstances existing at the time, he could reasonably have been expected to mention when so questioned. The relevant time was the time of questioning and account had to be taken of all the relevant circumstances existing at that time.

The Court of Appeal stressed in *Argent* that the court should not construe 'in the circumstances' restrictively; it could include a number of matters including the time of day, legal advice, the defendant's age and experience, his mental capacity, state of health, sobriety, tiredness, and personality. The Court also emphasised that attention should be addressed to the actual accused with the qualities, knowledge, apprehensions and advice he was shown to have had at the time, rather than a hypothetical reasonable accused of ordinary fortitude. The Court of Appeal emphasised that the above questions were for the jury to resolve in the exercise of their 'collective common sense, experience and understanding of human nature.'[58] The drawing of appropriate inferences is a matter for the jury although there will be circumstances in which a judge should warn a jury against drawing inferences.

The accused as a witness: silence at trial

In considering silence in court again we need to distinguish the situation before and after the Criminal Justice and Public Order Act.

The Criminal Evidence Act 1898

The Criminal Evidence Act was a major landmark, which made the defendant a competent, but not compellable, witness in his own defence. The subsequent case law clarified and delimited the boundaries of judicial comment on the silence of the defendant in court. At common law there had been a general rule of incompetence from interest, that is, parties with a direct interest in the case were precluded from giving evidence. This bar was removed from witnesses in 1843 and from the parties to most civil cases in 1851. At common law the defendant, in criminal cases, before the 1898 Act, was not competent to testify on oath at his own trial. This reflected the long-standing aversion to the forced interrogation and use of torture of the Star Chamber and fears that the unprepossessing or inarticulate defendant would create a bad impression if he testified and would be exposed to the risk of wrongful conviction. However, critics argued that incompetence benefitted the guilty in so far as counsel could argue that if only their clients were permitted to go into the witness box, they could easily prove their innocence but were being unreasonably prevented from doing so. Judges softened the prohibition by allowing the accused to make an unsworn statement from the dock but this carried little weight as it was not on oath. To reinforce the principle that the burden of proof still remains squarely on the prosecution, the Criminal Evidence Act made the accused a competent witness for the defence but not for the Crown. Under the Act, the accused is not compellable for the defence or prosecution and the prosecution is prohibited from commenting on the defendant's exercise of his right to silence. Section 1 states:

> Every person charged with an offence shall be a competent witness for the defence at every stage of the proceedings, whether the person so charged is charged solely or jointly with any other person. Provided as follows:
> (a) A person so charged shall not be called as a witness in pursuance of this Act except upon his own application;
> (b) The failure of any person charged with an offence to give evidence shall not be made the subject of any comment by the prosecution;
> (c) Nothing in this Act shall affect the right of the person charged to make a statement without being sworn.

The Act gave the defendant three choices: to give sworn evidence, to stay silent, or to make an unsworn statement from the dock. The last option was abolished by s 72(1) of the 1982 Criminal Justice Act, subject to certain exceptions. The choice open to the defendant was either to avail himself of his right to silence or to give evidence on oath. He could defer his decision until the close of the prosecution case, to assess its strength, although if he did not testify, he could of course still be convicted and obviously the jury would be aware of his silence. It is clear from the wording of the Act that testifying by the defendant was seen as a right rather than a duty. If the accused is jointly charged with a co-defendant, he cannot call his co-defendant to give evidence for him unless the co-defendant consents. In *R v Everitt, R v Riley*[59] the Court of Appeal said that the prosecution should not comment on the defendant's failure to give evidence even if the comment is not unfavourable. If an accused was charged with more than one count, he could not elect to testify on one count but not others. Once he had elected to testify, he could be cross-examined on all counts.[60]

Furthermore, the Act did not prohibit counsel for the co-accused from making comments on the defendant's failure to testify. The Court of Appeal held in *Wickham*[61] that the judge had no discretion to prevent such comment. This comment would be important, for example, where co-defendants put forward a cut-throat defence blaming each other.

Although the Criminal Evidence Act made clear that the accused does have a right to silence, clearly the exercise of the right may be limited by judicial comment. While the Act did not refer to the boundaries of judicial comment on the accused's silence, the subsequent case law clarified this point.

20

The issue of judicial comment on the accused's failure to testify under the 1898 Act was addressed in *Rhodes*[62] in 1899. Here Lord Russell of Killowen argued that it was impossible to lay down a rule on the extent and type of comment because of the wide range of cases, so that it must be seen as a matter of judicial discretion:

> There are some cases in which it would be unwise to make any comment at all; there are others in which it would be absolutely necessary in the interests of justice that such comments should be made. This is a question entirely for the discretion of the judge.[63]

After *Rhodes* the judiciary was more adventurous in charting the boundaries of acceptable comment. In *Waugh*,[64] for example, the trial judge referred to the accused's failure to give evidence nine times. The Privy Council criticised the trial judge, saying that his comments could have led the jury to think that no innocent man would fail to testify. If the judge wished to comment, he should simply have said that the accused was not bound to give evidence and reminded the jury that the prosecution bore the burden of proof.

The proviso to the 1898 Act was also considered by Lord Goddard in *Jackson*,[65] where he said that the aim of the proviso was to prevent the prosecution exploiting the accused's silence and undermining the 'free choice' of the accused whether to speak or not. The case also established that silence could not be treated as corroboration of evidence against the accused, although it was a matter which could be taken account of by the jury.

A formulation of the appropriate direction was given by Lord Parker in *Bathurst*.[66] This direction was subsequently seen as appropriate in most cases. He stated that:

> The accepted form of comment is to inform the jury that, of course, he is not bound to give evidence, that he can sit back and see if the prosecution have proved their case, and that while the jury have been deprived of the opportunity of hearing his story tested in cross-examination, the one thing they must not do is to assume that he is guilty because he has not gone into the witness box.[67]

In *Mutch*[68] it was made clear by the Court of Appeal that in most cases the direction should follow the direction of Lord Parker in *Bathurst*. The Court of Appeal took the opportunity to review these earlier authorities in *Sparrow*[69] and to clarify the principles which would guide judges in the future. An attempt was also made to identify the exceptional cases in which a stronger comment might be justified. Sparrow, with his co-defendant, Skingle, had been charged with the murder of a police officer. Skingle had fired the shot while they were engaged on a joint enterprise. Although Sparrow gave no evidence his counsel denied that he was involved in a joint plan to use loaded guns. Sparrow was convicted and appealed on the ground of the judge's misdirection on his silence. The trial judge had said to the jury that:

> ...if there was a real belief in his mind that he never contemplated for the moment that any shooting was going to take place, is it not essential that he should go into the witness box himself and tell you that himself and be subject to cross-examination about it? Well he did not do so and there it is.[70]

The Court of Appeal concluded that the *Bathurst* direction was sufficient in most cases, but that in the interests of justice stronger comment may be required in certain cases: the judge must not suggest or imply that silence can be seen as corroboration or that it can bolster a weak case against the accused; nor should he suggest to the jury that the defence cannot succeed unless the accused testifies or imply that silence may be equated with guilt. But he may comment on silence more than once if he thinks it appropriate and in certain cases the judge has a duty to comment. In Sparrow's case strong comment was warranted but the reference to 'essential' had gone beyond the bounds of acceptable comment.

Where the defendant does elect to remain silent at trial, he may still be able to give evidence on the voir dire, for example, to challenge the admissibility of a confession.[71] If the defendant is faced with a number of counts on the indictment and is willing to testify on some counts but not others, the trial judge is not obliged to grant separate trials.[72]

The *Bathurst* direction was reaffirmed in *R v Martinez-Tobon* in 1994 just before the CJPOA was enacted:

(1) The judge should give the jury a direction along the lines of the Judicial Studies Board specimen direction based on *R v Bathurst* [1968] 2 QB 99 at 107, [1968] 1 All ER 1175 at 1178.

(2) The essentials of that direction are that the defendant is under no obligation to testify and the jury should not assume he is guilty because he had not given evidence.

(3) Provided those essentials are complied with, the judge may think it appropriate to make a stronger comment where the defence case involves alleged facts which (a) are at variance with prosecution evidence or additional to it and exculpatory, and

(b) must, if true, be within the knowledge of the defendant.

(4)   The nature and strength of such comment must be a matter for the discretion of the judge and will depend upon the circumstances of the individual case. However, it must not be such as to contradict or nullify the essentials of the conventional direction.[73]

The specimen direction of the Judicial Studies Board referred to by the Lord Chief Justice states that:

> The defendant does not have to give evidence. He is entitled to sit in the dock and require the prosecution to prove its case. You must not assume that he is guilty because he has not given evidence. The fact that he has not given evidence proves nothing one way or the other. It does nothing to establish his guilt. On the other hand, it means that there is no evidence from the defendant to undermine, contradict, or explain the evidence put before you by the prosecution.

The Court also noted in *Berry*[74] that in his summing up the judge should not prejudice the defendant's right to silence by commenting adversely on the problems his decision not to testify may raise for him. In *Taylor*[75] and *Fullerton*[76] the *Bathurst* direction was treated as mandatory.

Failure to testify under the Criminal Justice and Public Order Act

The 1898 Criminal Evidence Act governed silence in court for nearly a century but the crucial sections on silence in court were repealed by the 1994 Criminal Justice and Public Order Act. Before the CJPOA the prosecution were not allowed to comment on the defendant's silence in court, but the co-accused's counsel could comment. Judicial comment was confined to the boundaries discussed above and any suggestion that silence may be equated with guilt constituted a misdirection. Now the interpretation of silence is much broader and silence in court may be used as evidence against the accused. Under the CJPOA the accused is still competent and non-compellable and he may not be committed for contempt if he does not testify.[77] However, the pressure to speak has increased considerably by permitting the court or jury to draw the proper inferences from silence without good cause. Comment on silence in court as well as pre-trial silence, in certain circumstances, is now governed by the CJPOA. Section 1(b) of the Criminal Evidence Act 1898 is repealed by schedule X of the CJPOA. The prosecution as well as the judge may comment and no doubt the

23

prosecution will use this new freedom to suggest appropriate adverse inferences to the jury. Section 38(3) makes clear that the accused cannot be convicted on silence alone but there must be some evidence against him. The accused cannot be convicted solely on the basis of an inference drawn under ss 34–37. The Act itself does not specify the appropriate direction to be given by the trial judge. Silence at trial is addressed by s 35 of the CJPOA which provides that:

(1)   At the trial of any person who has attained the age of fourteen years for an offence, subsections (2) and (3) below apply unless –

(a)   the accused's guilt is not in issue; or

(b)   it appears to the court that the physical or mental condition of the accused makes it undesirable for him to give evidence...

(2)   Where this subsection applies, the court shall, at the conclusion of the evidence for the prosecution, satisfy itself (in the case of proceedings on indictment, in the presence of the jury) that the accused is aware that the stage has been reached at which evidence can be given for the defence and that he can, if he wishes, give evidence and that, if he chooses not to give evidence, or having been sworn, without good cause refuses to answer any question, it will be permissible for the court or jury to draw such inferences as appear proper from his failure to give evidence or his refusal, without good cause, to answer any question.

(3)   Where this subsection applies, the court or jury in determining whether the accused is guilty of the offence charged, may draw such inferences as appear proper from the failure of the accused to give evidence or his refusal, without good cause, to answer any question.

(4)   This section does not render the accused compellable to give evidence on his own behalf, and he shall accordingly not be guilty of contempt of court by reason of a failure to do so.

(5)   For the purposes of this section a person who, having been sworn, refuses to answer any question shall be taken to do so without good cause unless –

(a)   he is entitled to refuse to answer the question by virtue of any enactment, whenever passed or made, or on the ground of privilege; or

(b)   the court in the exercise of its general discretion
           excuses him from answering it...

So the court may still exercise its discretion to excuse silence and the accused
may still not be obliged to answer under statute, for example, under s 1(f) of the
Criminal Evidence Act 1898, regarding previous offences or bad character.
Section 35(1) states that subsections (2) and (3) do not apply if it appears to the
court that the accused's physical or mental condition makes it undesirable for him
to give evidence. They also do not apply if the accused is under 14. The Act
says that inferences may be drawn rather than must be drawn, so even without
good cause, the jury is not obliged to draw adverse inferences. However the
concern is that other innocent reasons for silence may be overlooked.[78]

Section 35 follows the CLRC recommendation that once a prima facie case has
been made against the accused he should be required to give evidence and if he
does not, both the judge and prosecution should be entitled to comment on his
failure to testify.[79] The Act does not include guidelines for appropriate comments
or directions to the jury or for appropriate interpretations of silence in the new
circumstances, but the experience of the Criminal Evidence (Northern Ireland)
Order may be instructive. As the limits of judicial comment are not specified,
judicial comment may well follow the approach of the courts in Northern Ireland,
namely a common sense approach, and this also will be stressed in prosecutorial
comment.

The 1995 Practice Note sets out the procedure to be followed at trial.[80] Here the
Lord Chief Justice gave direction on how the courts should satisfy themselves
that the defendant was aware of the opportunity to testify and the effect of
choosing not to do so, under s 35, before inviting the jury to draw an adverse
inference. If the defendant is represented and chooses to testify, his lawyer
should state this to the court and the trial proceeds in the usual way. If the court
is told that the defendant does not intend to speak, then the judge, in front of the
jury, should ask the lawyer the following:

> Have you advised your client that the stage has now been
> reached at which he may give evidence and if he chooses not
> to do so or, having been sworn, without good cause refuses to
> answer any questions, the jury may draw such inferences as
> appear proper from his failure to do so?

If the legal representative tells the judge that his client has been so advised, the
case proceeds. If he says he has not yet been advised, the case will be adjourned
by the judge for the advice to be given. In the unlikely event that he is
unrepresented, the judge at the end of the prosecution's case, would say to the
accused in the presence of the jury the following:

25

You have heard the evidence against you. Now is the time for you to make your defence. You may give evidence on oath, and be cross-examined like any other witness. If you do not give evidence, or having been sworn, without good cause refuse to answer any question the jury may draw such inferences as appear proper. That means they may hold it against you. You may also call any witness or witnesses whom you have arranged to attend court. Afterwards you may also, if you wish, address the jury by arguing your case from the dock. But you cannot at that stage give evidence. Do you now intend to give evidence?

Section 35 will not be activated if the accused is under 14 or his physical or mental condition is such that it makes it undesirable for him to give evidence. Both before and after the Act, if the failure to testify is due to the mental state of the accused then it would be wrong for the trial judge to direct the jury to draw adverse inferences from silence. Section 38(6) preserves the court's exclusionary discretion: nothing in ss 34-37 prejudices the court's power to exclude evidence at its discretion.

In *R v Cowan, Gayle and Ricciardi*[81] the Court of Appeal considered whether the discretion to draw inferences from silence under s 35 applied generally or only in exceptional cases and what directions the judge should give. The court stressed that the right of silence remains and rejected the view that the burden of proof is altered by s 35 as the accused cannot be convicted solely on silence, and the issue of the failure to testify can be raised only after the prosecution has established a prima facie case against the accused.

The three appellants had been convicted of unrelated offences. The trial judge had directed the jury that they could draw adverse inferences from their silence in court. They argued, on appeal, that the trial judge should have exercised his discretion under s 35 to direct the jury that they could draw adverse inferences from silence only in an exceptional case where there was no reasonable possibility of an innocent explanation for silence.

The Court of Appeal held that the wording of s 35 did not confine it to exceptional cases. On the contrary there had to be an exceptional factor or some evidential basis before the court could decline to draw an adverse inference from silence at trial or before the judge could advise the jury against drawing such an inference. Certainly the possibility that the defendant could be cross-examined on his previous convictions, which arose in Cowan and Gayle's cases, was not a good reason to direct the jury against drawing such an inference. The trial judge had a broad discretion whether any proper inference was capable of being drawn by the jury, and if not, he should tell them so, otherwise it was for the jury to decide whether an inference should properly be drawn. Mandatory exceptions are provided for in s 35(1) including situations where the accused's mental or physical state makes it undesirable for him to give evidence. In addition the court could direct the jury against drawing an adverse inference where the circumstances of the case justify this.

A specimen direction has been given by the Judicial Studies Board to guide judges on the wording of the direction:

> The defendant has not given evidence. That is his right. But, as he has been told, the law is that you may draw such inferences as appear proper from his failure to do so. Failure to give evidence on its own cannot prove guilt but depending on the circumstances, you may hold his failure against him when deciding whether he is guilty. [There is evidence before you on the basis of which the defendant's advocate invites you not to hold it against the defendant that he has not given evidence before you namely...If you think that because of this evidence you should not hold it against the defendant that he has not given evidence, do not do so. But if the evidence he relies on presents no adequate explanation for his absence from the witness box then you may hold his failure to give evidence against him. You do not have to do so.] What proper inferences can you draw from the defendant's decision not to give evidence before you? If you conclude that there is a case for him to answer, you may think that the defendant would have gone into the witness box to give you an explanation for or an answer to the case against him. If the only sensible explanation for his decision not to give evidence is that he has no answer to the case against him, or none that could have stood up to cross-examination, then it would be open to you to hold against him his failure to give evidence. It is for you to decide whether it is fair to do so.

The trial judge should tell the jury that:

1.   the burden of proof remains on the prosecution throughout and what the required standard is;
2.   the defendant is entitled to remain silent;
3.   as expressly provided by s 38(3) of the 1994 Act, an inference from failure to give evidence cannot on its own prove guilt;
4.   the jury must be satisfied that the prosecution has established a case to answer before drawing any inferences from the defendant's silence;
5.   if, despite any evidence relied on to explain his silence or in the absence of any such evidence, the jury conclude the silence can only sensibly be

27

attributed to the defendant's having no answer or none that would stand up to cross-examination, they may draw an adverse inference.

The Court of Appeal approved the remarks of Kelly LJ in *R v McLernon*[82] that the court has a complete discretion whether inferences should be drawn or not and if it decides to draw inferences what their nature, extent and degree of adversity, if any, may be. Although *McLernon* was a Diplock case the Court of Appeal saw these comments applying equally to the directions a judge would give to the jury. While a Diplock judge was obliged to set out reasons for drawing inferences, a jury could be properly directed on when they may draw inferences. However it is questionable whether a jury would be assisted by this direction. The innocent reasons for silence may not be brought to the jury's attention, especially if they are personal or embarrassing, so drawing the appropriate inference may be difficult.

The Court of Appeal in *Cowan* made clear that it would not lightly interfere with the judge's exercise of discretion to direct or advise the jury regarding the drawing of inferences from silence, or the nature, extent and degree of such inferences. The Court rejected the view that the procedure set out in the Practice Note violates professional lawyer-client privilege as asking the lawyer what he has advised his client here does not reveal anything confidential.

Cowan's appeal was allowed because the judge had failed to tell the jury that they could not infer guilt solely from silence and did not warn the jury that the condition for holding a defendant's silence at trial against him was that the only sensible explanation for silence was that he had no answer to the case against him or none that could have stood up to cross-examination. Without such directions the jury could have attached undue importance to his absence from the witness box. *Gayle's* appeal was allowed because the judge did not tell the jury that the accused had the right to remain silent and had given the impression that the right to silence no longer existed. *Ricciardi's* appeal was dismissed because he had not advanced any reason to the judge why he should not give an adverse inference direction to the jury and therefore the judge had been entitled to give such a direction. It was not incumbent on a judge or appropriate for him to embark, or invite the jury to embark, on possible speculative reasons consistent with innocence which might theoretically prompt a defendant to remain silent.[83] The Judicial Studies Board specimen direction had been followed in his case. The standard direction referred to in *Cowan* was approved in *Napper*.[84]

The Court in *Cowan* did not find it necessary to refer to the European Commission's opinion in *Murray v UK*[85] as there was no ambiguity in s 35. But the Court of Appeal's emphasis on discretion and on the fact that only in exceptional cases should the judge direct the jury that it should not draw adverse inferences, argues Munday, may fall foul of the European Court.[86] The court in *Murray* focused directly on the particular circumstances in Murray's case but it may be that the CJPOA will be treated less favourably when future cases reach the Court. The court stressed that while limits might be placed on the right to silence it would be incompatible with Article 6 of the European Convention on Human Rights to base a conviction on silence alone. While this is precluded by the CJPOA, Munday[87] argues that it is possible that a conviction could be based mainly on inferences from silence, following *Cowan*, if the jury in considering the strength of the case against the accused in the light of his refusal to testify under s 35, also took account of the failure to respond to police questions under ss 34(2), 36(2)(d) and 37(2)(d), and that this would be likely to breach Article 6.

Silence in response to questioning by third parties where the parties are on even terms

A further context of silence needs to be considered, namely silence in response to questioning by persons other than police officers or those in authority. The common law rule regarding the evidential significance of silence in such cases was that where an individual was accused of a crime by someone on even terms with him, then the fact of his silence could be admitted to show his acceptance of the charge made. One of the earliest reported cases on this issue was *Cramp*[88] where a man was accused of administering a noxious thing to a woman with intent to cause miscarriage. When the woman's father accused Cramp he did not deny it and it was held that the absence of a denial was capable of corroborating the woman's evidence. The circumstances must be such that it would be natural to reply and the parties must be on even terms if evidence of the silence is to be admissible.

This was followed by *Mitchell*[89] which firmly established the principle of equality of the parties determining the reasonableness of the expectation of a reaction. As Cave J. argued:

> Undoubtedly, when persons are speaking on even terms, and a charge is made, and the person charged says nothing and expresses no indignation, and does nothing to repel the charge, that is some evidence to show that he admits the charge to be true.[90]

Mitchell was approved and applied in *Parkes*[91] where the appellant, Parkes, was convicted of the murder of a girl. When the mother of the victim accused him of stabbing her daughter, he was silent. When she tried to detain him until the police arrived, he tried to stab her. The Privy Council applied the *Mitchell* test and concluded that the trial judge was not in error when he directed the jury that Parkes' reactions to the accusation - his silence and the attempted stabbing - were matters from which they could, if they saw fit, infer that he had accepted the truth of the accusation. *Parkes* would seem to be the paradigm case of the type of situation Cave J. had in mind in *Mitchell* where the response, on common sense grounds, might seem to constitute an admission of the truth of the statement. Moreover Parkes' response included stabbing and silence, rather than silence alone and occurred outside a police station. Lord Diplock referred to Cave J.'s rule in *Mitchell* and argued that the trial judge in *Parkes* had been right to direct the jury that the accused's reactions, including silence, were matters they were entitled to take into account in determining his guilt. Only if a reply could be reasonably expected in the circumstances, can silence properly be taken account of by the jury.

But even if an answer might reasonably be expected, it does not of course follow that silence is a sure sign of guilt as it may be due to a number of factors, including anxiety, embarrassment and surprise, and these factors have been strongly emphasised by defenders of the right to silence.

Silence in the face of questioning where the parties are on even terms, would have the same effect after the CJPOA. The common law rule would still apply. This is made clear in s 34(5) which states that s 34 does not:

(a)   prejudice the admissibility in evidence of the silence or other reaction of the accused in the face of anything said in his presence relating to the conduct in respect of which he is charged, in so far as evidence thereof would be admissible apart from this section; or

(b)   preclude the drawing of any inference from any such silence or other reaction of the accused which could properly be drawn apart from this section.

So s 34(5) preserves the common law position that inferences could be drawn from silence when a person is confronted by another person on even terms, or from a denial or other reaction.

An attempt to broaden the scope of the even terms principle to police interrogations was made in *Chandler*[92] where it was held that the *Hall* principle did not apply to situations where the accused has his solicitor with him during questioning. The reasoning behind the decision was that the presence of the solicitor places the parties on equal terms. The Court of Appeal in *Chandler* said that the accused and the police officer could be seen as talking on equal terms because the solicitor could advise his client and also testify in court to the questions and answers given during interrogation. Lawton LJ stressed that the fact of police interrogation does not itself imply inequality for a police officer might be at a disadvantage when, for example, questioning a local dignitary.

While Lord Diplock had stressed in *Hall*[93] that silence during police interrogation cannot of itself give rise to the inference of acceptance of the statement, Lawton LJ seems to allow that it could be evidence to support an accusation. He criticised Lord Diplock's comments in *Hall* which he saw as unsatisfactory because they conflicted with earlier authorities such as *Christie*.[94] Lawton, LJ argued that:

> The law has long accepted that an accused person is not bound to incriminate himself; but it does not follow that a failure to answer an accusation or question when an answer could reasonably be expected may not provide some evidence in support of an accusation. Whether it does will depend on the circumstances.[95]

But the reasoning in *Chandler* is flawed for the inequalities between the suspect and the police are not eradicated simply by the presence of a solicitor, given the psychological effects of detention in the surroundings of a police station. But even if the solicitor is present it could be argued that as a fundamental principle of English law the right to silence should not be varied according to the presence or absence of a solicitor, any more than it should depend on the fact of being cautioned. In any event, the fact that the accused does have his solicitor with him during questioning could demonstrate his resolution to exercise his right, rather than to relinquish it. The exercise of the right to silence may of course be the result of legal advice. The implication of access to legal advice for the question of the appropriate comment on the accused's exercise of the right to silence was considered in *Alladice*.[96] Here Lord Lane, the then Lord Chief Justice, argued that the effect of s 58 of PACE, which gives the suspect the right to legal advice, shifted the balance between prosecution and defence in favour of the suspect and that a change in the law to allow adverse comment on silence would redress this. He said that the effect of s 58 was such that the balance between prosecution and defence cannot be maintained 'unless proper comment is permitted on the defendant's silence in such circumstances. It is high time that such comment should be permitted together with the necessary alteration to the words of the caution.'[97] A change in the permitted judicial comment on silence was needed to prevent ambush defences and this was effected by the CJPOA. Section 34 which governs silence in interrogation can be seen as reflecting the view found in earlier decisions, including *Chandler*, that the lawyer's presence compensates for inequalities and brings the parties closer to an even terms relationship. But even with a solicitor present, as Dennis notes, there is still 'no guarantee that the rules of natural justice are observed'[98] and the situation is far removed from the public context of the trial. For this reason many would see the loss of the right to silence at the earlier stage as more troublesome than at the trial stage.

It is also questionable whether there is a conflict between the approaches to silence in *Christie* and *Hall*, referred to by Lawton LJ, because in *Christie* the issue was not silence but rather the denial of an accusation. In *Christie* a boy had been indecently assaulted and the boy approached Christie in the presence of his mother and touched him saying 'that is the man' and described the assault. Christie replied 'I am innocent'. The Court of Appeal quashed Christie's conviction on the ground that the evidence of the mother had been improperly admitted. It was held by the House of Lords that this denial could be capable of being an admission and was properly proved against him. However, their Lordships also stressed that the value of a denial was likely to be limited and that it should not normally be admitted in a criminal case, although there was no rule of law excluding it:

> the rule of law undoubtedly is that a statement made in the presence of an accused person, even upon an occasion which should be expected reasonably to call for some explanation or denial from him, is not evidence against him of the facts stated save so far as he accepts the statement, so as to make it, in effect, his own.[99]

Lord Atkinson noted that:

> He may accept the statement by word or conduct, action or demeanour, and it is the function of the jury which tries the case to determine whether his words, action, conduct or demeanour at the time when a statement was made amounts to an acceptance of it in whole or in part.[100]

He also made clear that a denial of the facts in the statement would not necessarily be inadmissible:

> because he may deny the statement in such a manner and under such circumstances as may lead a jury to disbelieve him, and constitute evidence from which an acknowledgement may be inferred by them.[101]

The facts of *Christie* and the issues in question are thus quite distinct from those in *Hall*. It is therefore difficult to see why Lord Diplock's statement in *Hall* was seen as problematic in *Chandler*. Nonetheless, on the basis of *Chandler* it would seem that if a solicitor is present during police interrogation he will be hesitant in advising his client to exercise his right to silence in certain circumstances as to do so may expose him to the risk of adverse inferences being drawn. The court in *Chandler* is converging silence in police interrogations with the line of cases on accusations by third parties. If a solicitor is present and the accused remains silent on the basis of his lawyer's advice, this can hardly be seen as an acceptance that the accusation is true.

Notwithstanding these problems *Chandler* was followed by the Court of Appeal in *Horne*.[102] If the accused is interviewed by a police officer with his solicitor present the parties may be construed as being on even terms, said the Court of Appeal, because the presence of a solicitor is deemed to 'equalise' the balance of power. Yet the research for the Royal Commission on Criminal Justice and other studies have shown that the quality of legal advice may be variable and in the past advice has often been given by poorly qualified and untrained staff.[103] The behaviour of defence solicitors has been criticised as a factor contributing to miscarriages of justice.[104]

The claim that access to legal advice provides an adequate safeguard for the suspect in the absence of the right to silence will be considered following a discussion of the campaign against the right to silence and the abolition of the right to silence in Northern Ireland.

Notes

1.   S. Easton [1991] 'Bodily samples and the privilege against self-incrimination', Crim LR 18; see chapter 8 below.
2.   C. Hill (1974) *Change and Continuity in Seventeenth Century England*, London, Weidenfeld and Nicolson.
3.   *'Nemo debet prodere se ipsum'*; see Lord Diplock in *R v Sang* [1980] AC 402 at 436.
4.   J. Wigmore (1961) *Evidence*, 8, McNaughten rev.ed.
5.   A. Zuckerman (1989) *The Principles of Criminal Evidence*, Oxford, Clarendon.
6.   69 Kan 77 Pac 563 (1904).
7.   Tex Crim 198 221 SW 2d 950 (1948).
8.   [1992] 3 All ER 456.
9.   at 463.
10.   Report of the Royal Commission on Criminal Procedure (1981) London, HMS0, Cmnd 8092, para. 1.21.
11.   [1914] AC 599.
12.   A. Sanders [1988] 'Rights, Remedies and the Police and Criminal Evidence Act', Crim LR 802.
13.   RCCP, *op.cit.*
14.   See chapter 4 below.
15.   See D. Wolchover and A. Heaton-Armstrong [1990] 'The questioning code revised and the flaws which persist', 140 NLJ 320, 369, 407; F. Fairweather and H. Levenson [November 1990] 'The new PACE Codes of Practice,' Legal Action, 21.
16.   Code E 4.3.13.
17.   Code C 10.4.

18. Code C 10.D. (1985)
19. [1990] The Independent, 7 February.
20. [1966] 2 QB 414.
21. See *R v Whitehead* [1929] 1 KB 99; *R v Keeling* [1942] 1 All ER 507.
22. [1944] KB 80.
23. (1965) 50 Cr App Rep 50.
24. See *R v Henry* [1990] Crim LR 574.
25. (1987) 85 Cr App Rep 93. The relationship of the right to silence to the doctrine of recent possession is considered in that case.
26. (1966) 51 Cr App Rep 102.
27. *Ibid*, pp 104-5.
28. [1994] 1 WLR 1.
29. Belfast Crown Court, May 8 1991; [1992] 5 NIJB 40.
30. (1966) Cr App Rep 144.
31. [1970] 1 QB 423. Section 11 has now been repealed by s 5(7) of the Criminal Procedure and Investigations Act 1996 which requires the defence to provide details of alibi witnesses to the prosecution prior to trial. See chapter 2 below.
32. (1977) 66 Cr App Rep 237.
33. *Ibid.*
34. *Ibid*, at 244-5.
35. *Ibid*, at 243.
36. *Ibid.*
37. *Ibid*, at 244.
38. [1971] 1 WLR 298.
39. *Ibid*, at 301.
40. *Ibid.*
41. Code C 10.4 (1995)
42. Code C 112A.
43. Code C 10.1.
44. Code C 10.3.
45. Code C 10.5B.
46. See *R v Mitchell* [1892] 17 Cox C.C. 503.
47. See *R v Chandler* [1976] 1 WLR 585.
48. See Criminal Law Revision Committee (1972) *Eleventh Report, Evidence (General)*, London, HMSO, Cmnd 4991.
49. See, for example, A. Zuckerman (1994) 'Bias and suggestibility: is there an alternative to the right to silence?', in D. Morgan and G. Stephenson (eds.) *Suspicion and Silence*, London, Blackstone, pp 117-140.
50. 'Changes in the Law Relating to Silence: Advice to Practitioners from the Criminal Law Committee of the Law Society', Criminal Practicioners Newsletter, October 9, 1994.; see also E. Cape, 'The right

to silence: defending at the police station under the new regime', Legal Action, April 1995, pp 12-14.

51.   See M. Zander, 'Abolition of the right to silence 1972-1994' in D. Morgan and G. Stephenson, *op.cit.*, pp 141-55.

52.   See *R v Martin*, Belfast Crown Court, May 8, 1991; [1992] 5 NIJB 40.

53.   [1996] Times, 9 February; case no. 411994/480/570, para. 45.

54.   R. Munday [1996] 'Inferences from Silence and European Human Rights Law', Crim LR, 370 at p 380.

55.   (1996) 161 JP 1.

56.   [1995] 4 All ER 939.

57.   *R v Argent* [1996] Times 19 December.

58.   *Ibid.*

59.   (1990) 91 Cr App Rep 208.

60.   See *R v Phillips* (1987) 86 Cr App Rep 18.

61.   (1971) 55 Cr App Rep 199.

62.   [1899] 1 QB 177

63.   *Ibid*, at 177.

64.   [1950] AC 203.

65.   [1955] 1 WLR 591.

66.   [1968] 2 QB 107.

67.   *Ibid*, at 108.

68.   [1973] 1 All ER 178.

69.   [1973] 1 WLR 488.

70.   *Ibid.*

71.   See *Wong Kam-Ming v R* [1980] AC 247.

72.   See *R v Phillips* (1987) 86 Cr App Rep 18.

73.   *R v Martinez-Tobon* [1992] 2 All ER 90, at 98.

74.   [1993] Crim LR 973.

75.   [1993] Crim LR 223.

76.   [1994] Crim LR 63.

77.   See *R v Ackinlose* [1996] Crim LR 747.

78.   S 80(8) of PACE which forbids comment by the prosecution on the failure of an accused's spouse to testify was not repealed by the CJPOA.

79.   CLRC, *op.cit.*, para.110.

80.   Practice Note (Crown Court: Evidence: Advice to Defendant) [1995] 2 All ER 499 [1995] Times, 12 April, *sub.nom.* Practice Direction [1995] 1 WLR 657.

81.   [1995] 4 All ER 939.

82.   [1990] 10 NIJB 91, at 102.

83.   *R v Cowan, Gayle and Ricciardi* [1995] 4 All ER 939, at 949.

84.   [1996] Crim LR 591.

85.   18 EHRR CD 1.

86.   R. Munday, *op.cit.*

87.   *Ibid*, at 376.
88.   [1880] 14 Cox CC 390.
89.   [1892] 17 Cox CC 503.
90.   *Ibid*, at 508.
91.   [1976] 1 WLR 1252.
92.   [1976] 1 WLR 585.
93.   [1981] 1 WLR 298.
94.   [1914] AC 545.
95.   *R v Chandler* [1976] 1 WLR 585, at 589.
96.   (1988) 87 Cr App Rep 380.
97.   *Ibid*, at 385.
98.   See I. Dennis (1989) 'Reconstructing the Law of Criminal Evidence', *Current Legal Problems* 21; (1995) 'Instrumental Protection, Human Right or Functional Necessity: Reassessing the privilege against self-incrimination', Camb LJ 54(2) 342.
99.   [1914] AC 545, at 554.
100. *Ibid.*
101. *Ibid.*
102. [1990] Crim LR 188.
103. See chapter 4 below.
104. See *R v Paris, Abdullah and Miller* (1993) 97 Cr App Rep 99; see also chapter 10 below.

2 Proposals for reform: the debate on the right to silence

Arguments for and against the right to silence were considered by the Criminal Law Revision Committee,[1] the Royal Commission on Criminal Procedure,[2] the Home Office Working Group[3] and the Royal Commission on Criminal Justice.[4] Changes to the right to silence in Northern Ireland were implemented in 1988 and changes to the right to silence in England and Wales were introduced by the Criminal Justice and Public Order Act 1994. The implications of these changes have also been considered by the European Court of Human Rights.[5] In the post-war period there have been several reviews of the right to silence which will now be examined.

The Criminal Law Revision Committee's Eleventh Report

The report of the Committee published in 1972 expressed strong dissatisfaction with the law governing the construction of silence at that time. The Committee considered the right to silence at the pre-trial and trial stages. The belief that only the guilty would want to withhold an explanation while the innocent are anxious to account for their position underpinned the CLRC proposals for dealing with ambush defences. To prohibit an adverse inference to be drawn in such cases, the Committee argued, 'seems contrary to commonsense.'[6] The Court of Appeal's criticism of the existing law in *Sullivan*[7] was cited in support of this point. The Committee shared the court's view of this rule and Clause 1 of the Draft Bill was designed to allow for the drawing of such inferences as appear proper to the jury where the accused fails to mention a fact in interrogation later relied on at trial. Where there are no reasons for withholding such an inference, then it should properly and readily be drawn. Clause 1 stated that where the accused relies in his defence on a fact he failed to mention when charged, the

37

court or jury should be able to draw such inferences as appear proper and treat his initial silence as corroboration of evidence given against him, where the failure to mention is material and the fact relied on is one that it would have been reasonable for him to mention earlier. He should be cautioned accordingly.

The accused's failure to testify in court was also scrutinised by the Committee and similar arguments were advanced. The same kinds of adverse inferences 'as common sense dictates'[8] should apply as in the case of failure to mention a fact relied on in interrogation. In fact the Committee saw the arguments for allowing an adverse inference to be drawn from a failure to give evidence as stronger than in the pre-trial case. But it made clear that this was dependent on a prima facie case being established. Where the case was weak, the failure to speak would be of little significance, 'but the stronger the case is the more significant will be the failure to give evidence.'[9] Moreover, the Committee argued that in such circumstances, where the prosecution has adduced enough evidence for the case to be put to the jury, then the accused's failure to give evidence should be capable of corroborating that evidence against him. The Committee proposed a procedure whereby the accused would be told in court that he will be called and the effects of his failure to testify. However, the Committee made clear that in situations where the defendant suffers from a physical or mental condition which makes it 'undesirable' for him to give evidence, for example, where pleading insanity or diminished responsibility, then this procedure would not be followed. In clause 5 of the Draft Bill the Committee proposed that if the court considers that there is a case to answer, then it shall call on the accused to give evidence. If he then refuses to do so, 'without good cause', the court or jury may draw such inferences from his refusal as seem proper and treat his refusal as corroboration against him. In other words, this would in effect have removed the shield in s 1(b) of the Criminal Evidence Act 1898.

These proposals aroused strong criticism and the Committee's proposals were not implemented at that time, although they were made use of subsequently in Northern Ireland and in Malaysia and eventually in England in 1994. The right to silence at the pre-trial and trial stages was abolished in Singapore by the Criminal Procedure Code (Amendment) Act in 1976. Although the Act was found initially to have little impact on the numbers of suspects speaking in interrogation or at trial,[10] it is now being used more frequently. The CLRC's report also stimulated the debate in the Republic of Ireland on abolition of the right to silence and changes were introduced in the Republic by the Criminal Justice Act 1984.[11] The next major review of criminal procedure reached quite different conclusions on the value of the right to silence in protecting the civil liberties of suspects.

The Royal Commission on Criminal Procedure

The Royal Commission on Criminal Procedure, chaired by Sir Cyril Philips, was set up in 1978 in the light of public concern over rising crime rates and the abuse of police powers. The inquiry into the circumstances leading to the trial and conviction of three youths for the murder of Maxwell Confait had raised further misgivings about the treatment of juveniles by the police.[12] The Commission surveyed criminal procedure from initial investigation to trial and reported in 1981. Although it included a discussion of the right to silence it offered a broader analysis. Many of its proposals to safeguard the rights of the suspect during interrogation and the need for special protection for vulnerable groups, were subsequently implemented in the Police and Criminal Evidence Act 1984. When considering the CLRC recommendations regarding the right to silence, however, it advanced a view diametrically opposed to that of the CLRC and argued for retention of the right to silence during police interrogation and at trial. This was partly a result of the perspective it adopted, namely striking a balance between the conflicting interests of the community in fighting crime and punishing the guilty, and the rights of the individual embodied in the presumption of innocence and the burden of proof, a perspective it saw as missing from earlier reports on criminal procedure. In focusing on the defence of civil liberties, the Royal Commission was guided by what Ashworth[13] has described as the protective principle which compensates the individual for infringements of his liberties and ensures that he is not disadvantaged by them, but the Commission also took account of the reliability principle. What was required, the Commission argued, was an approach which 'constructed as firm a factual base as possible and undertook the analysis of existing procedures and proposals for change within a framework of general principles.'[14]

Only from this standpoint could a fair assessment of the problems in the existing law and possible alternatives be mounted. One criticism of the CLRC report had been that many of its assumptions, such as the exploitation of the right to silence by professional criminals, had not been based on any sound empirical evidence and the Commission therefore initiated research into the dynamics of interrogation.[15] The Commission identified the problems which could arise if the CLRC proposals to allow adverse inferences to be drawn from silence during police questioning were implemented and concluded that the right to silence when being questioned by the police after cautioning should be retained.[16]

The right of silence at trial was considered by the Commission. It acknowledged that the failure to testify raises different issues from the pre-trial stage. The defendant is in a stronger position at trial, having heard the evidence against him and having had time to consider his defence and with immediate access to counsel. But nonetheless similar justifications apply to both stages. The majority of the Commission concluded that:

any modification to the present law of evidence which aimed at requiring the accused to answer a *prima facie* case established by the prosecution would be likely to weaken the initial burden of proof that the accusatorial system at trial places upon the prosecution. The accused should not be obliged, indeed, in the ultimate event, cannot be obliged, either to enter the witness box, or to mount any defence. Comment on the lines at present allowed should be enough to enable a jury to form a sensible judgement on the significance of that failure, such as it is.[17]

The majority of the Commission also favoured retention of the right to silence in police interrogation. Although the Commission did not resolve the problem of balancing civil liberties against the public interest in convicting the guilty, not least because of the difficulties of weighing rights in the balance, it did dampen for a few years the demands for abolition of the right to silence and the introduction of PACE provided a breathing space. But the demand for change resurfaced in 1987 and reached fruition in 1994.

The report of the Home Office Working Group

In the late nineteen eighties, the issue of the right to silence came under scrutiny again when the Home Secretary, Douglas Hurd, announced in a lecture to the Police Federation in July 1987, that a further review of the right to silence was now deemed necessary.[18] In May 1988 he set up a Working Group to investigate any problems prior to the introduction of legislation and to receive submissions and recommendations from interested groups.[19] He made it clear to the Group that he wanted advice on how to change the law, especially the precise changes in the law required to achieve the purpose of combatting ambush defences and measures to encourage early disclosure of defences and not an examination of the desirability or justifiability of the change. It was already apparent that the views of the CLRC, rather than those of the Royal Commission, had found favour with the Thatcher administration. In October 1988 he laid before Parliament the draft Order in Council amending the right to silence in Northern Ireland and said that he intended to bring forward legislation on the subject for England and Wales, at the earliest opportunity following the Working Group's Report:

> Although the timing of the change will inevitably be different in the two jurisdictions the Government see a clear need for substantial changes to be made in both if the law is to be effectively enforced.[20]

In the eighties and nineties the focus was on how change might be implemented rather than with matters of principle. Moreover with the introduction of PACE, improved access to legal advice, and tape recording of interviews, critics of the right to silence argued that there was now an appropriate framework of safeguards to protect the suspect, which was not in place at the time of the CLRC Report and which would compensate for the abolition of the right to silence.

The Criminal Evidence (Northern Ireland) Order, which came into effect in November 1988, amended the evidence in criminal proceedings in Northern Ireland, including the inferences to be drawn from the silence of the accused. The proposals of the CLRC on the right to silence were implemented in Northern Ireland despite the misgivings of the Royal Commission and were supplemented by provisions modelled on ss 18 and 19 of the Republic of Ireland's Criminal Justice Act 1984. Section 18 of that Act stipulates that where a person has substances or marks on his person, clothing, footwear or in his possession, the court may draw such inferences as appear proper and failure to account or refusal may be treated as counting as corroboration. The Gardai must tell the accused in ordinary language what the effect of a failure or refusal could be. Section 19 of the Act contains similar provisions relating to presence at a particular place or time. The right not to testify at trial remains in the Republic and the scope of judicial comment on failure to give evidence is limited and normally juries would be directed in terms similar to the *Bathurst*[21] direction.

The Home Secretary announced in October 1988 that it was the Government's intention to extend these changes to England and Wales, to solve the problem of ambush defences, by allowing adverse inferences to be drawn from silence during interrogation. These proposals were welcomed by the police and some senior judges. The police had been concerned about the right to silence for some time, especially in the light of the Court of Appeal's adventurous use of s 78 to PACE to exclude evidence. In addition the Lord Chief Justice, Lord Lane, had argued in *Alladice* for the need to change the law in view of the benefits accorded to the accused by PACE.[22] Many of the arguments from the seventies were resuscitated and considered afresh in the light of the effects of PACE. Although the debate had been defined by the Home Secretary as addressing practicalities rather than the desirability of change, nonetheless defenders of the right to silence sought to recapture this lost ground in their submissions to the Working Group.[23]

The Home Office Working Group recommended in its report in July 1990 that inferences should be permitted to be drawn from silence during questioning, subject to certain safeguards. Like the CLRC, the Working Group expressed concern that experienced criminals were using the existing system to their advantage.[24] The Working Group examined the failure to answer questions and ways of encouraging early disclosure of the defence. A number of modifications were proposed to facilitate the change and to satisfy the demands for safeguards for the suspect, but the Group's proposals were not as radical as those enacted in Northern Ireland.

The concern of the Working Group reflects an interest in the practicalities of implementing change rather than issues of principle. The Working Group's task was to examine:

> the precise form of the change in the law which would best achieve our purposes given the significant changes in police and criminal procedure in England and Wales in recent years, and of any warning given by the police to suspects before commencing interviews; the practical implications, both for police interviews and in court; and the relevance of other measures to encourage early disclosure of the defence case.[25]

The major recommendations of the Working Group were as follows:

> [1] Statutory guidelines for the courts setting out the factors to be taken into account, in relation to which inferences may be drawn.[26]

> [2] In the Crown court, the prosecution, defence and trial judge should be able to comment on the defendant's failure to mention a fact on which he subsequently relies in his defence and the prosecution should be able to cross-examine him about his failure to do so.[27]

> [3] The judge should be required to guide the jury regarding the factors, set out in the guidelines, which members of the jury should take into account in assessing the veracity of the evidence addressed at the trial. The magistrates should direct themselves in accordance with the guidelines.[28]

> [4] A new caution was recommended by the Group to advise the suspect of the effects of silence:

> You do not have to say anything. A record will be made of anything you do say and it may be given in evidence. So may your refusal to answer any questions. If there is any fact on which you intend to rely in your defence in court, it would be best to mention it now. If you hold it back until you go to court you may be less likely to be believed.[29]

> [5] The primary inference which may be drawn from the defendant's previous failure to answer questions or to mention a fact subsequently relied on at trial, is that the subsequent line

42

of defence is untrue and that it may also have an adverse effect on his general credibility.[30] Failure to answer questions or to mention such a fact should not be capable of amounting to corroboration or constitute positive evidence of guilt. In this respect the Group's proposal diverged from the CLRC recommendations and from the provisions of the Criminal Evidence Order in Northern Ireland.

[6] The Group also looked at measures to encourage early disclosure and concluded that there should be no requirement for advance disclosure of the defence case in the Magistrates' Court, but that in the Crown Court advance disclosure should be required where there is a risk of an ambush defence and that it should be modelled on section 9 of the Criminal Justice Act 1987.[31] A pilot study was proposed, with advance disclosure being limited to serious or complex cases in view of the resource implications. The introduction of advance disclosure should be progressive and closely monitored. When selecting cases, the judge should have the power to order disclosure on his own initiative or on application from the prosecution or the defence. The Group made recommendations regarding the appropriate procedure for advance disclosure.[32]

The Working Group also considered silence in court and proposed that in the Crown Court, the prosecution should be able to comment on the defendant's failure to give evidence or to answer questions at his trial in terms similar to those in which judges were already able to do so and that judges themselves should make more frequent and robust use of the existing right of comment.
The Group's proposals included the issuing of a rule of conduct to counsel and defence lawyers, namely, to warn the defendant of the possibility of adverse judicial comment if he fails to give evidence or refuses to answer questions at his trial.
The Working Group's report was criticised for not making clear how silence based on legal advice should be treated by the court. Its proposals were seen as adding to the length and complexity of trials and increasing the burden on the defence.
When the Report of the Working Group was published the Home Secretary, Douglas Hurd, said the report offered one way of reducing the scope for unfair exploitation by a suspect of his right to decline to answer questions from the police or to give evidence in court. He announced that he wanted to study the effectiveness of Northern Ireland's provisions and to hear further views before taking a decision.

Although the changes had originally been expected to be incorporated into the 1990-91 Criminal Justice Act, the Government deferred the implementation of the Working Group's proposals to await the outcome of the May Inquiry into the Woolwich and Guildford Bombings and to allow time for further reflection. The Government made it clear that the right to silence was still under close scrutiny, despite concern over the miscarriages of justice and the vulnerability of the suspect in police custody. However, the revelations of miscarriages of justice prompted the Government to set up a Royal Commission to review the criminal justice system in general and to consider whether changes should be made to the right to silence.

The Royal Commission on Criminal Justice

The Royal Commission was appointed in 1991 and reported in 1993. Its terms of reference were 'to examine the effectiveness of the criminal justice system in England and Wales in securing the conviction of those guilty of criminal offences and the acquittal of those who are innocent, having regard to the efficient use of resources.'[33] So the cost implications of existing procedures and any proposed changes were essential to the Commission's enquiry. It was set up in the context of miscarriages of justice, after the Birmingham Six were released, although it was criticised for failing to give sufficient attention to this in its final report.[34]

It was asked to consider whether changes were needed 'in the opportunities available for the accused to state his position on the matters charged and the extent to which the courts might draw proper inferences from the primary facts, the conduct of the accused and any failure on his part to take advantage of the opportunity to state his position.'[35] So notwithstanding the context in which the Commission was set up, the experience of wrongful convictions and the problems of confession evidence, it was clear that the possibility of abolition of the right to silence was on the agenda, although in the end the Commission rejected abolition.

The Commission considered the arguments for and against retention of the right to silence, including the fears for vulnerable suspects, the risk of false confessions arising from adverse comment and the problem of innocent reasons for silence. Two members of the Commission argued that adverse comment should be permitted at trial and the caution amended to address the problem of professional criminals sheltering behind the right to silence. However, the majority took the view that 'the possibility of an increase in the convictions of the guilty is outweighed by the risk that the extra pressure on suspects to talk in the police station and the adverse inferences invited if they do not may result in more convictions of the innocent.'[36] In view of this the Commission supported retention of the right to silence and no changes to the caution and trial direction then in use.

The Commission found that 'There are too many cases of improper pressures being brought to bear on suspects in police custody, even where the safeguards of PACE and the codes of practice have been supposedly in force, for the majority to regard this with equanimity.'[37] Given that some people will confess to offences they did not commit, the threat of adverse comment at trial may increase the risk of vulnerable suspects making false confessions.

While acknowledging the frustration police officers feel confronted with silence, the majority doubted whether the opportunity to make adverse comment would make a difference: 'The experienced professional criminals who wish to remain silent are likely to continue to do so and will justify their silence by stating at trial that their solicitors have advised them to say nothing at least until the allegations against them have been fully disclosed.'[38] Although there might be an increase in convictions of the guilty where silence is subject to adverse comment, the majority thought that the number would be slight, while 'It is the less experienced and more vulnerable suspects against whom the threat of adverse comment would be likely to be more damaging.'[39]

The Commission found that the right to silence was exercised only in a minority of cases, although it may tend to be used in the more serious cases and on legal advice. It could find no evidence to show that silence in interrogation was used disproportionately by professional criminals or that it increased the chance of acquittal:[40] 'Most of those who are silent in the police station either plead guilty or are subsequently found guilty.'[41] But if the judge or prosecution were permitted to suggest to the jury, that silence can amount to supporting evidence of guilt, then 'some who are silent and are now acquitted might rightly or wrongly be convicted.'[42]

The Commission pointed to existing cases where improper pressure is exerted on suspects despite the protections of PACE. It supported the view of the earlier Philips Commission that adverse inferences would put strong pressure on some suspects to answer without knowing the case against them which may well increase the risk of the innocent making damaging statements. Since publication of the Report Lord Runciman has criticised the decision of the Government to limit the right to silence and highlighted the increased pressure on vulnerable suspects and the risk of increasing the conviction of the innocent.

However the Commission proposed a form of advance disclosure of the general substance of the defence once the prosecution case has been disclosed, thereby weakening the force of its argument. It recommended that when the prosecution's case has been fully disclosed defendants should be required to answer the charges made against them at the risk of adverse comment at trial on any new defence they then disclose, or any departure from the defence previously disclosed:[43]

it is when but only when the prosecution case has been fully disclosed that defendants should be required to offer an answer to the charges made against them at the risk of adverse comment at trial on any new defence they then disclose or on any departure from the defence which they previously disclosed. They may still choose to run the risk of such comment, or indeed to remain silent throughout their trial. But if they do, it will be in the knowledge that their hope of an acquittal rests on the ability of defending counsel either to convince the jury that there is a reasonable explanation for the departure or, where silence is maintained throughout, to discredit the prosecution evidence in the jury's eyes...it should be open to the judge, as now in serious fraud cases, to comment on any new defence or any departure from an earlier line of defence.[44]

The Commission also supported a pre-trial review of cases before the Crown Court[45] and the continuing admissibility of confession evidence, provided that the tests in PACE are met, and rejected a corroboration requirement.

Other recommendations included enhanced police powers in apprehending suspects, improved training in interrogation techniques and supervision of the police, changes to the classification of bodily samples,[46] abolition of the accused's right to elect jury trial in triable either way offences and a new body, the Criminal Cases Review Authority, to deal with miscarriages of justice and better training of officers to deal with interrogation.[47] It also supported a formal system of plea-bargaining and a sentence canvass. It advocated transferring a large number of cases from the Crown Court to the magistrates' courts and supported the Law Commission's recommendation to abolish corroboration rules.

Underpinning the Royal Commission's report is the desire to establish value for money and achieve cost-effectiveness in the criminal justice system. It also recommended that the police be permitted to continue questioning suspects after they have been charged, until the first court appearance or the transfer of the file to the CPS. In return the suspect would have free legal advice and the opportunity for a solicitor to be present during questioning. It recommended further research on video-taping of interviews, and the revision of the PACE Codes to remove confusion over what constitutes an interview for the purposes of the Code.[48]

The Commission's report was criticised on a number of grounds. Its proposal to remove the right of defendants in triable either way offences to elect jury trial was criticised by civil libertarians[49] for undermining due process rights and for adding to the delays in going to trial in the magistrates' courts. McConville argued that the Report 'is not empirically grounded, deploys defective reasoning in support of its recommendations, is based upon a flawed understanding of the organising principles of criminal justice, and often amounts, to coin a phrase, to little more than opinion and assertion.'[50] He criticised the Commission for failing to undertake research on key issues such as the quality of justice, the reliability of guilty pleas, the quality of defence services or miscarriages of justice. He also argues that it misapplies already published research including research commissioned by itself. He has in mind Leng's[51] study of ambush defences which showed that the claims of an ambush problem cannot be substantiated, yet the Commission nonetheless recommended advance defence disclosure. The overall effect of the recommendations, he argues, is to undermine the burden of proof.

The Report was widely criticised for focusing on cost-effectiveness rather than matters of principle. Northern Ireland should have been included in its remit, given that so many miscarriages of justice involved Irish suspects and conditions of detention under the PTA and EPA also needed urgent examination. Attention also should have been paid to the role of racism in miscarriages of justice. The Commission did not consider the problems with the magistrates' courts where most cases are heard. It failed to support a corroboration requirement for confession evidence. But Zander,[52] a member of the Commission, has defended its Report and argues that the majority of its findings will strengthen the position of the suspect and prevent conviction of the innocent. Several of the Commission's research studies do address issues relevant to miscarriages of justice and many of its recommendations have now been implemented.

The Criminal Justice and Public Order Act

Similar provisions to those in Northern Ireland were introduced into Parliament in December 1993 by Michael Howard as part of the Criminal Justice and Public Order Bill. Earlier that year at the Conservative Party Conference he had attacked the right to silence claiming that 'The so-called right to silence is ruthlessly exploited by terrorists. What fools they must think we are. It's time to call a halt to this charade. The so-called right to silence will be abolished.' In the House of Commons he justified the need for such provisions because the 'present system is abused by hardened criminals.'[53] He referred to a study by the Association of Chief Police Officers which showed frequent use of the right to silence and also cited the Northern Ireland changes as an example of successful limits on silence.[54]

The Government decided to follow for the most part the Northern Ireland and Criminal Law Revision Committee's model rather than the Working Group's proposal. However, there was a significant difference between the bill and the Criminal Evidence Order, namely that in Northern Ireland silence can be treated as corroborating other evidence but this is missing from the Criminal Justice and Public Order Act.

The Criminal Justice and Public Order Act can be seen as the culmination of an attack on the right to silence over the past 23 years beginning with the CLRC Report in 1972. The provisions on the right to silence in the Act fail to take account of the views of the Runciman Commission in 1993, based on its own research studies, that the chance of an increase in convictions of the guilty was outweighed by the increased pressure on suspects to speak during interrogation and that permitting adverse inferences from silence may result in an increase in convictions of the innocent.

The caution initially proposed under the draft codes to accompany the Criminal Justice and Public Order Bill stated that:

> You do not have to say anything. But if you do not mention now something which you later use in your defence, the Court may decide that your failure to mention it now strengthens the case against you. A record will be made of anything you say and it may be given in evidence if you are brought to trial.

This was widely criticised for being long-winded and confusing and likely to be challenged in the courts. The caution finally formulated in the Codes was shorter, but it also raises problems of comprehension. The suspect is now told:

> You do not have to say anything. But it may harm your defence if you do not mention when questioned something which you later rely on in court. Anything you do say may be given in evidence.[55]

Advance disclosure

One dimension of the attack on the right to silence has been the demand for disclosure of the defence case to deal with ambush defences. A framework for advance disclosure of the defence case already existed within PACE in the provisions relating to expert evidence, and in the Criminal Justice Act 1967, in the provisions pertaining to alibi evidence. Advance disclosure was further extended by sections 9 and 10 of the Criminal Justice Act 1987 used in complex fraud cases. The Home Office Working Group examined advance disclosure as one way of dealing with the problem of ambushing. It recommended the use of advance disclosure in the Crown Court modelled on s 9 of the Criminal Justice Act 1987.[56] The feasibility of extending these provisions beyond fraud cases to all criminal trials on indictment, with disclosure required at the point of committal or immediately afterwards, has been accepted by a number of groups. The Law Society,[57] for example, acknowledged that ambushing may be a problem in relation to serious offences. It mooted the possibility of extending pre-trial disclosure by the defence in such cases and introducing pre-trial reviews for serious arrestable offences.

The majority of the Royal Commission favoured extending the obligations on the defence to provide advance disclosure. The majority argued that advance disclosure would not undermine the privilege against self- incrimination, as the defendant could still remain silent at trial and that it is wrong in principle that the defence should be able to withhold information until trial. The defence should be obliged to disclose the substance of the defence in advance or the trial or to indicate that they will not be calling any evidence but simply arguing that the prosecution has failed to make out its case.[58] If the prosecution think that insufficient information has been provided it may ask for clarification and if the defence do not comply, the prosecution may apply to the court for a ruling on the matter.

The Commission advocated a statutory framework for disclosure which included advance disclosure by the defence and prosecution to speed up case preparation and resolution:

> In most cases disclosure of the defence should be a matter capable of being handled by the defendant's solicitor (in the same way that alibi notices are usually dealt with at present). Standard forms would be drawn up to cover the most common offences, with the solicitor having only to tick one or more of a list of possibilities, such as "accident", "self-defence", ... and so on.[59]

The names and addresses of witnesses would not need to be disclosed. If at trial, the defence then wished to change his defence, the prosecution, with the leave of the judge, could invite the jury to draw adverse inferences and the judge could also comment on this. The defence could give its reasons for a late defence or change its defence and it would be up to the jury to decide whether to accept those reasons. In cases where there were good reasons for departing from a defence it would be open to the court to rule that no adverse comment by the prosecution would be permitted.[60]

The new system of disclosure would also embrace the prosecution: in indictable and triable either way cases, the Commission advocated a statutory basis for full prosecution disclosure of all material relevant to the offence, and the accused and the surrounding circumstances of the case. Codes of Practice would be used to supplement the primary legislation. It also favoured a system of pre-trial review. The defence would be sent a form, after delivery of the papers from the CPS, to indicate if the defendant is pleading guilty to all or some of the charges or offering a plea to a lesser defence, the CPS would state if it found this acceptable and a date for the hearing would be fixed. The Commission emphasised that defence disclosure would rest on full prosecution disclosure. It advocated a statutory duty on the police to disclose and preserve evidence, and on the prosecution to disclose material relevant to the offence or offender, regardless of whether it was to be relied on and disclosure of schedules of other material. This would benefit the defence, as the secrecy of the police and prosecution has been crucial to some miscarriages of justice.

The Commission stressed the importance of balancing the duties of the prosecution and the rights of the defence. The prosecution should be under a duty to supply to the defence copies of all material relevant to the offence or offender or to the surrounding circumstances of the case, whether or not the prosecution intended to rely upon that material, for example, material concerning the defendant's mental state or suggestibility.[61] The prosecution should inform the defence of any other material obtained in the course of its inquiry. The defence should then disclose the substance of its own case. Following this it can request further documents relevant to its defence. If the prosecution does not accept the relevance of the document in question, the matter, if the defence insist, can be referred to the court.[62] The Commission thought that for sensitive material a different procedure could apply and approved the approach in *Johnson, Davis and Rowe*.[63]

The Home Office published a Consultation Document on disclosure in 1995 and legislation was introduced following this.[64] The aim of the new regime is to identify and clarify issues before trial and to improve the management of trials. The Home Office viewed the extension of disclosure in *Ward*[65] as imposing too heavy a burden on the prosecution and was concerned over the problem of disclosing sensitive material. In *Ward* the Court of Appeal criticised the failure of the prosecution to disclose material which tended to weaken the prosecution case, or strengthen the defence, and said that it was not simply a matter for the prosecution that evidence should be withheld on grounds of sensitivity or public interest immunity. But subsequently the prosecution decided in some cases that it would not prosecute if revealing sensitive information would put lives at risk. In *Johnson, Davies and Rowe*[66] the Court of Appeal thought that the *Ward* judgement had gone too far and favoured using *ex parte* applications in such cases. In *Johnson* the Court of Appeal said that it might be appropriate for a court to hear *ex parte* an application by the Crown not to disclose sensitive material on the ground of public interest immunity. But in the course of the trial the public interest in nondisclosure may be outweighed by the need to disclose, in fairness to the accused, and the Crown would either have to disclose or to offer no further evidence. In *Keane* the Lord Chief Justice emphasised the test of materiality which he expounded as follows:

> I would judge to be material in the realm of disclosure that
> which can be seen on a sensible appraisal by the prosecution:
> (1) to be relevant or possibly relevant to an issue in the case;
> (2) to raise or possibly to raise a new issue whose existence is

not apparent from the evidence the prosecution proposes to use;
(3) to hold out a real (as opposed to fanciful) prospect of
providing a lead on evidence which goes to (1) or (2).[67]

The Government accepted the general approach of the Runciman Commission on disclosure but thought that it did not go far enough in dealing with the problems of the existing regime.[68] The Government argued that:

> the prosecution should not have an open-ended obligation to
> disclose all material which might conceivably be relevant to
> any defence; otherwise the scheme would differ little from the
> current and unsatisfactory disclosure regime. The Government
> believes that, although the burden of proof must remain with
> the prosecution, the defence should also have a responsibility
> to help ensure that justice is done by narrowing the issues in
> dispute, and should not be able to exploit the rules in a way
> which obstructs the identification of the truth.[69]

The regime proposed was that the investigator would be under a statutory duty to preserve material, to make it available to the prosecutor and to retain it until the conclusion of criminal proceedings. A Code of Practice would define the material to be preserved and govern the handling of sensitive material. The investigator would not be under a duty to disclose all material to the prosecution at the initial stage but should make available material expected to form the basis of the prosecution case and material falling in certain categories, including results of forensic tests and expert witness material, and other material which may undermine the prosecution case, for example, a negative test showing that fingerprints on the crime weapon did not match those of the accused, or that it is in possession of a psychiatric report showing that its main witness has a history of psychiatric disorder with a tendency to fantasise. The prosecutor would not be obliged to disclose sensitive information which does not undermine the prosecution case and the defence at that stage would not be able to ask for material other than that which is disclosed by the prosecution. The aim here is to preclude fishing expeditions by the defence.

Following this, the defence would be required to supply sufficient particulars of its case to identify the issues in dispute, including names and addresses of witnesses to be called, written statements of expert evidence or evidence supporting for example, a defence of consent, duress or self-defence. If the defence does not comply or presents a different defence at trial, the prosecution may bring the fact of non-compliance to the attention of the court and the court may decide what inferences, if any, to draw from it. So it would still be possible to present a last minute defence provided that the defendant is prepared to risk adverse comment. However the accused could not be convicted solely on the inference drawn from his response at that stage.

The defence disclosure will trigger a secondary disclosure by the prosecution of unused material which might reasonably assist the particular line of argument disclosed. If the prosecution refused to disclose specific material requested by the defence, the defence can renew its application before a court. The court would grant the application only if it is satisfied that the material in question would assist the defence case and the court, to determine this, would need to see the material. Sensitive material should be disclosed only if it undermines the prosecution case or assists a line of argument advanced by the defence. If the prosecution wish to withhold it, then the procedures set out in *Johnson, Davis and Rowe*[70] should be followed and in addition the Court would consider the balance of interests.

A disclosure bill was introduced in the 1995-6 Parliamentary session. The provisions on disclosure apply to all trials except non-contested trials in the magistrates' courts. The legislation reflected the reasoning in the Consultation Document. Section 23 of the Criminal Procedure and Investigations Act 1996 stipulates that the Secretary of State shall prepare a Code of Practice concerning the recording, detention and disclosure of material. Following the new Act prosecution counsel will be required to disclose to the defence any prosecution material which might undermine the case for the prosecution. If there is no such material he should give the defence a written statement to that effect. Otherwise he should supply details of material relating to the defence which has not been disclosed to the accused and which the prosecutor believes is not sensitive and supply copies to the defence or allow inspection.

After the prosecution has complied with the requirement of primary disclosure, there will be a duty on the defence to disclose the defence in general terms. The defence statement should set out the general terms and nature of the accused's defence, the matters on which he takes issue with the prosecution and reasons for this, and details of alibi witnesses.[71] Section 11 of the Criminal Justice Act 1967 concerning notice of alibi is repealed by s 74 of the Criminal Procedure and Investigations Act and alibi evidence is now governed by ss 5(7) and 5(8) of the Criminal Procedure and Investigations Act: if the defence statement discloses an alibi defence the accused must give particulars of the alibi including names and addresses of any witnesses whom he thinks can support his alibi or information which will help to find such witnesses.

If the defence does not respond to the requirement for disclosure, gives mutually inconsistent defences, or gives a defence at trial different from that disclosed pre-trial, or adduces evidence in support of an alibi without giving particulars of the alibi in his statement, failure to disclose the defence or to give details of his alibi could be the subject of adverse comment at trial and the court or jury would be entitled to draw such inferences as appear proper in deciding whether he is guilty of the offence charged.[72] Moreover, there will be no obligation in such cases for secondary prosecution disclosure of any further material which might assist the defence disclosed by the defendant. This was intended to combat ambush defences even though the Royal Commission research found no evidence of an ambush problem.[73] In any case s 34 of the CJPOA allows the court to draw adverse inferences from the failure to mention a fact later relied on and this was expected to solve the problem of ambush defences.

The Criminal Procedure and Investigations Act has been criticised on a number of grounds. It is possible for the prosecution to withhold material supporting a potential defence because the defence has not raised it. It may be hard to put some defences until the defence has seen the relevant prosecution material, but the prosecution may not reveal it until the defence has been given. The Act also gives judges the right to make binding rulings on the admissibility of evidence at a preparatory hearing if it appears that substantial benefits are likely to accrue. So arguments about the admissibility of evidence are likely at both stages before two different judges. The Act gives judges discretion to hold preparatory hearings in lengthy or complex cases, similar to those already used in serious and complex fraud trials, if it appears to the court that this will lead to substantial benefits. As serious fraud cases present problems of unusual complexity which baffle juries, such concessions might be justified but are less justifiable in relation to simple property offences or offences against the person. The fact that inroads have already been made into the right to silence, by the various advance disclosure provisions, should not be used to legitimise further losses.

Zander[74] dissented from the proposals of the majority of the Royal Commission because they still undermine the principle that the burden is on the prosecution to prove its case without the help of the defence. He also saw them as unnecessary because ambush defences are exceptional. Disclosure will be of little value to the prosecution because they will be told relatively little; the proposed scheme will be hard to enforce and will lead to delays. He argued that advance disclosure is wrong in principle: 'the defendant should be required to respond to the case the prosecution makes, not to the case it says it is going to make...it is not the job of the defendant to be helpful either to the prosecution or to the system. His task, if he chooses to put the prosecution to proof, is simply to defend himself.'[75]

It is also harder for the defendant to resist testifying at trial once the pre-trial disclosures are submitted as part of the prosecution's case, particularly as the Criminal Justice and Public Order Act now permits the prosecution to comment on the defendant's silence in court.

The disclosure regime must be set in the context of the much greater resources of the prosecution compared to the defendant relying on legal aid or defending himself. Once the prosecution knows what the defence case is, it is in a better position to undermine it, simply because of its greater access to resources, records and forensic laboratories, including the DNA databank, while the legally-aided defendant will be in a relatively disadvantaged position without

53

automatic access to those resources and constrained by budgetary considerations. Furthermore, the unrepresented defendant denied bail would find it extremely difficult to cope with the paperwork involved while on remand.[76] Advance disclosure exposes the defence to the danger that the prosecution can shape or adjust its evidence in the light of its knowledge of the defence case. A careful selection of witnesses and material could be made, again strengthening the prosecution's hand. Advance disclosure of the defence case was criticised by the Legal Action Group because it 'will increase the temptation to "lose" evidence favourable to the defendant'[77] whereas fears of the defendant interfering with the prosecution witnesses can easily be assuaged by the denial of bail. Examples of cases where documents and items in police possession have been 'lost' are cited by the Group. Advance disclosure of the defence case can only increase the risk of the occurrence of such practices. The evidence which disappeared in the investigation of the Guildford Bombings and the disbanding of the West Midlands Serious Crime Squad, render the advance disclosure proposals less attractive. Apart from deliberate loss of items of evidence, there is a danger of selecting and shaping evidence to meet the defence case.

The Roskill Committee,[78] which investigated the problem of advance disclosure in fraud cases, thought that the prosecution case should be fixed before the disclosure by the defence to solve this problem, but this recommendation was not enacted. Amendment of the indictment by the prosecution could be prohibited but this would not deal with the problem of the tailoring of the evidence. While pre-trial exchanges of information might be appropriate in civil actions, to save court time and resources, the issues are quite distinct in a criminal case, raising issues of fundamental rights and due process, so those practical benefits cannot justify a shifting of the burden of proof.

Advance disclosure, whether modelled on the alibi or fraud provisions, provided a ready-made model for reform, which targets ambush defences. But while advance disclosure by the defence was seen initially as an alternative to abolition of the right to silence, it has now been used to supplement the loss of the right to silence. The validity of the case for abolition will be considered following a discussion of the removal of the right to silence in Northern Ireland.

Notes

1. Criminal Law Revision Committee (1972) *Eleventh Report, Evidence, General*, London, HMSO Cmnd 4991.
2. Report of the Royal Commission on Criminal Procedure (1981) London, HMSO, Cmnd 8092.
3. Report of the Working Group on the Right of Silence, Home Office, C Division, London, July 13, 1989.

4. Report of the Royal Commission on Criminal Justice (1993) London, HMSO, Cmnd 2263.

5. See *Murray v UK* [1996] Times, 9 February.

6. Criminal Law Revision Committee, *op.cit.*, para. 30.

7. *R v Sullivan* (1956) 51 Cr App Rep 102.

8. Criminal Law Revision Committee, *op.cit.*, para.110.

9. *Ibid.*

10. The impact of the changes in the Criminal Procedure Code on the decision to speak were assessed by Meng Heong Yeo [1983] 'Diminishing the Right to Silence: The Singapore Experience' Crim LR 89. The changes were modelled on the CLRC recommendations. The new Code provided that if the accused failed to mention a fact he later relied on and which he could reasonably have been expected to reveal when charged, the court may draw 'such inferences from his failure as appear proper' and may treat his failure as corroboration of any evidence against him to which the failure is material. The Code also changed the position of the defendant at trial; if he refuses to testify, the judge may now draw those inferences as 'appear proper' and is required to give the accused a warning to this effect.

Considering the pre-trial stage, Yeo compared a sample of cases before and after the amendment designed to encourage suspects to respond to police questioning. He found that the impact of the change was insubstantial because the majority of suspects were already speaking during interrogation before the amendment was enacted. In the earlier sample, in 57 of the 61 cases examined, the suspect spoke during interrogation, while in the later period, all the suspects spoke in a sample of 58 suspects. He also considered the impact of changes at the trial stage, where the changes were aimed at inducing the defendant to testify. He found that the percentage of cases where the accused did testify was actually slightly higher in the pre-amendment period than the post-amendment period, although this needs to be adjusted in view of the fact that the accused lost his right to make an unsworn statement. Yeo's findings suggest that the amendment did not have the desired effect of encouraging defendants to testify and that the judges' new power to comment adversely had little impact. One possible reason to account for this, as he points out, is that the accused was already aware that inferences might be drawn from silence, so the fact of being warned by the judge of the adverse inferences which may be drawn from silence, may make little difference. While the judges do now have the power to make adverse inferences and to comment on silence, in none of the post-Amendment cases Yeo studied did the judges appear to exercise that power by expressly commenting on or expressly drawing inferences from the failure to testify. Yeo argues that the judiciary should be more 'explicit' if they exercise this power, to facilitate the development of guidelines for future use. The new Code on silence did not assist the police force or the prosecution in fighting crime. The use of the amendments in the context of pre-trial silence appears for the first time in the reported decision of *Ng Chong Teck v PP* [1992] 1 SLR 863. Recent studies suggest that it is now being used more frequently. See A. Khee-Jin-Tan [1997] Crim LR 471.

Although the Singaporean example is of interest jury trials were abolished in Singapore in 1969 and it is questionable whether the inferences formulated by a judge cognisant with the law of evidence and its problems, would necessarily be drawn in the same way in a court with a division of function between judge and jury, as in England. The case of Singapore may be particularly relevant, however, in considering the impact of change on the Diplock courts in Northern Ireland. The Singapore provisions also need to be considered in the context of the debate on due process rights. See M. Hor [1995] 'The presumption of innocence - a constitutional discourse for Singapore', Singapore Journal of Legal Studies 365. See also M. Hor [1993], The privilege against self-incrimination, fairness and the accused', Singapore Journal of Legal Studies, 35 for discussion of the implications for the burden of proof in criminal cases.

11.   The changes in the Republic, like those in Northern Ireland, were stimulated by concern over the breakdown of law and order, the actions of para-military groups and narcotics traffickers and by discussion of the CLRC's report. At the same time there was concern over the treatment of detained suspects under emergency provisions and the publication of a report by Amnesty. The O'Briain Committee (Report of the Committee to recommend certain safeguards for persons in custody and for members of the Garda Siochana, Prl.158.) which examined safeguards and which reported in 1978, included an addendum which recommended modification of the right to silence but this reflected the minority view; the majority refrained from making recommendations on silence.

The Bill was introduced in 1983 and enacted by 6th December 1984 in the face of considerable opposition by civil libertarians. The sections on silence were reserved until a Complaints Board had been set up so that the relevant sections were finally brought into effect on 1st July, 1987 and covered failure to account for substances or marks on one's person, clothing or possession (s 18) and failure to account for one's presence at a particular place or time (s 19). Section 15 of the Act created an offence of failing or refusing, without reasonable excuse, to give the Gardai information or giving false information in relation to how one came by firearms or ammunition. Section 16 contains a similar provision relating to money or property which the Gardai believe is derived from an offence. The offence is punishable by fine and imprisonment for wilful failure or refusal to give information, in addition to the penalty relating to the substantive offence. These sections can also be used before and after arrest. Provisions relating to ambush defences which had originally appeared in clause 16 of the Criminal Justice Bill were withdrawn in the face of strong opposition.

Although the right to silence was an established feature of the common law of Ireland, and retained in the Irish Free State in 1921 and the Republic in 1937, nonetheless since the 1930s it has been curtailed by the Constitution (Amendment No. 17) Act 1931 s 15(1) and *The State (McCarthy) v Lennon* [1936] IR 485. Section 52 of the Offences against the State Act 1939 stipulates that when detained in custody any member of the Gardai may demand a full account of the person's action during any specified period and information relating to the commission or intended commission of an offence; a refusal to provide information or giving false information means that he is guilty of an offence under the section and liable on summary conviction to imprisonment up to six months. In *The People (DPP) v Doyle* [1977] IR 336 it was stated that s 52 must be construed as limiting or restricting what would otherwise be the right of a person to remain silent in certain circumstances and particularly not to incriminate himself.

12.   Report of an Inquiry by the Hon. Sir Henry Fisher into the circumstances leading to the trial of three persons on charges arising out of the death of Maxwell Confait and the fire at 27 Doggett Road, London S.E.6 (1997) London, HMSO.

13.   A.J. Ashworth [1977] 'Excluding Evidence as Protecting Rights', Crim LR 723.

14.   RCCP Report.

15.   P. Softley (1980) *Police Interrogation: an Observational Study in Four Police Stations*, RCCP Research Study no.4, London, HMSO; B. Irving and L. Hilgendorf (1980) *Police Interrogation: The Psychological Approach*, RCCP Research Study no. 2, London, HMSO.

16.   RCCP Report, para. 4.53.

17.   *Ibid*, para. 4.66.

18.   Lecture, Police Foundation, 30 July 1987.

19.   HC Debs Vol.133 col. 466 (18 May 1988)

20.   Speech, Bow Group, 25 October 1988.

21.   *R v Bathurst* [1968] 2 QB 99.

22.   See *Alladice* (1988) 87 Cr App Rep at 385.

23.   Response of the Legal Action Group to the Home Office Working Group on the Right of Silence Consultation Paper (November 1988) London.

24.   Home Office Working Group, *op.cit.*, para. 57.

25.   Working Group on the Right of Silence (1988) Consultation Paper, Home Office, para. 2.

26.   Report of the Home Office Working Group, para. 64, 126(i); appendix D.

27.   *Ibid*, paras. 65, 126(ii).

28.   *Ibid*, paras. 65, 67, 126(iii), 126(iv).

29.   *Ibid*, paras. 71, 126(v)

30.   *Ibid*, paras. 86, 126(vii).

31.   *Ibid*, paras. 102, 127(xi).

32.   *Ibid*, paras. 103, 106, 107, 127 (xiii - xxi).

33.   RCCJ Report, p i.

34.   See, for example, Legal Action Group (1993) *Preventing Miscarriages of Justice*, London.

35.   RCCJ Report, p ii.

36.   *Ibid*, para. 4.12.

37.   *Ibid*, para. 4.23.

38.   *Ibid*, para. 4.22.

39.   *Ibid*, para. 4.23.

40.   *Ibid*, para. 4.19.

41.   *Ibid*, para. 4.19.

42.   *Ibid*, para. 4.19.

43.   *Ibid*, para. 4.30.

44.   *Ibid*, para. 4.24.

45.   *Ibid*, para. 7.18.

46.   See chapter 8 below.

47.   See chapter 10 below.

48.   RCCJ (1993) para. 3.10.

49.   See Legal Action Group (1993) *Preventing Miscarriages of Justice*.

50.   M. McConville, 'An error of judgment', *Legal Action*, September 1993, 6-7.

51.   R. Leng (1993) *The Right To Silence in Police Interrogation*, RCCJ Research Study no. 10., London, HMSO.

52.   M. Zander (1995) 'Reform of the Criminal Justice System: The Report of the Runciman Royal Commission', in *Criminal Justice*, ed. E. Attwooll and D. Goldberg, Stuttgart, Steiner, pp 9-26; (November, 1993) 'An error of judgment?' Legal Action, pp 6-7.

53.   Hansard 11.1.94, col. 26.

54.   Association of Chief Police Officers (1993) *The Right of Silence: Briefing Paper*, London, ACPO.

55.   PACE Code C 10.4 (1995).

56.   Report of the Working Group on the Right to Silence (1989).

57.   Law Society (1988) Submission to the Home Office Working Group on the Right to Silence; see also Criminal Bar Association (1988) Comment of the Criminal Bar Association on the Consultation Paper.

58.   RCCJ Report, para. 66.6.

59.   *Ibid*, para. 6.68.

60.   *Ibid*, para. 6.70.

61.   RCCJ Report, para. 6.51.

62.   *Ibid*, para. 6.52.

63.   [1993] Crim LR 689.

64.   Home Office (1995) A Consultation Document on Disclosure, London, HMSO, Cmnd 2864.

65.   (1993) 96 Cr App Rep 1.

66.   *R v Johnson, Davis and Rowe* [1993] Crim LR 689

67.   [1994] 2 All ER 478.

68.   Home Office (1995) A Consultation Document on Disclosure.

69.   *Ibid*, para. 26.

70.   [1993] Crim LR 689.

71.   S 5(4)

72.   S 11

73.   See R. Leng, *op.cit.* and RCCJ Report (1993).

74.   M. Zander (1993) Note of Dissent, Report of the Royal Commission on Criminal Justice, London, HMSO Cmnd 2263, pp 221-35.

75.   *Ibid*, p 221.

76.   See, for example, Report of the Working Group on the Right of Silence: Response of the Legal Action Group, London (January, 1990).

77.   Legal Action Group (1988) Response of the Legal Action Group to the Home Office Working Group on the Right of Silence Consultation Paper.

78.   E.W. Roskill (1986) *Improving the Presentation of Information to Juries in Fraud Trials*, London, HMSO.

3 The right to silence in Northern Ireland

The debates of the early seventies focused on the 'abuse' of the right to silence by professional criminals, but by the late eighties this concern was overshadowed by anxieties over professional terrorists, such as members of the Irish Republican Army and other sectarian para-military groups. While the two groups may share a familiarity with criminal procedure and experience of dealing with the police and prosecution, there are important differences, namely that in Northern Ireland, extensive emergency legislation already existed which meant that there was even less justification for the loss of the right to silence in the province. A discussion of Northern Ireland is important because similar arguments relating to the 'abuse' of the right to silence were advanced to support the recent changes for England and Wales. The right to silence was lost for all criminal offences in Northern Ireland following the Criminal Evidence (Northern Ireland) Order 1988 which was used as a model for the Criminal Justice and Public Order Act 1994. The interpretation of the CJPOA is likely to follow the Northern Ireland courts' interpretation of the Criminal Evidence Order. These decisions are persuasive, not binding, but are likely to be very influential. The loss of the right to silence in Northern Ireland has been challenged in the European Court of Human Rights as a violation of the European Convention on Human Rights, specifically Articles 6(1), the right to a fair trial, and 6(2) the presumption of innocence, in the case of *Murray v UK*.[1]

The CJPOA amends the Criminal Evidence Order to bring it in line with the English provisions.[2] Adverse inferences may be drawn from silence in interrogation only if the suspect has been properly cautioned. Section 61(3)(b) changes the trial procedure for dealing with the decision to testify. Under the Order the defendant was called into the witness box and asked to testify and advised of the effects of a failure to do so. But the procedure now follows the English procedure, of asking the defendant's legal representative if he has advised his client of the implications of silence.[3] However, silence in Northern Ireland can corroborate any evidence against the accused in relation to which the failure or refusal is material but no reference to silence as corroboration is made in the CJPOA.[4]

The provisions of the Order will be outlined before examining the political context of change and the problems which have arisen in applying the new law in the province. Examining the use of the provisions in Northern Ireland may indicate the problems which may arise in England. Challenges to the Criminal Evidence Order will be useful in mounting challenges to the CJPOA, although most of the cases on the Order are Diplock cases. The judgement of the European Court of Human Rights in *Murray v UK* has implications for the court's approach to the CJPOA as the Act is largely modelled on the Criminal Evidence Order. The experience of Northern Ireland also has implications for the role of the legal adviser.

The Provisions of the Criminal Evidence Order

The Criminal Evidence (Northern Ireland) Order 1988 amended the evidence in all criminal proceedings in Northern Ireland, and was not confined to terrorist offences.[5] It specified the nature of the inferences to be drawn from the silence of the accused and the situations in which those inferences may be drawn. The modifications to the right were confined to these specific circumstances but the effect was nonetheless quite substantial. It reflects the recommendations of the CLRC report[6] and sections 18 and 19 of the Republic of Ireland's Criminal Justice Act 1984. It was designed to enable the courts to draw whatever inferences would be proper from the fact that an accused remained silent in four situations: (i) the ambush defence, where an explanation of conduct is offered for the first time at trial but the accused could reasonably have been expected to mention it earlier; (ii) the failure to testify at trial; (iii) the failure or refusal to explain the presence of substances or marks on his clothing and (iv) the failure or refusal to explain his presence at a particular place. These provisions are not exclusive. They can all be applied in appropriate circumstances.

Article 2

Article 2(2) of the Criminal Evidence Order draws the boundaries of the scope of the Order. It stipulates that 'A person shall not be committed for trial, have a case to answer or be convicted of an offence solely on an inference drawn from such a failure or refusal as is mentioned in Article 3(2), 4(4), 5(2) or 6(2).' The Order does not prejudice the operation of existing statutory provisions, which provide that any answer or evidence given in specified circumstances shall not be admissible in evidence against him or some other person in any other proceedings, or the court's power to exclude evidence, for example, by preventing questions being put, at its discretion. Articles 3, 4, 5 and 6 allow the court to treat silence as or capable of amounting to corroboration of any evidence against the accused to which his silence is material.

Article 3

Article 3, modelled on the CLRC proposals, was designed to combat ambush defences. If evidence is given that the accused on being questioned to see whether an offence has been committed, or when he has been charged with an offence or on being informed that he might be prosecuted, failed to mention any fact relied on in his defence which in the circumstances he could reasonably have been expected to mention, then the court or jury in determining whether to commit him to trial or whether there is a case to answer or in determining his guilt, may draw such inferences from the failure as appear proper. Prior to the Order this would have been permitted at common law when the parties were on even terms. The court or jury may, 'on the basis of such inferences treat the failure as, or as capable of amounting to, corroboration of any evidence given against the accused to which the failure is material.' But once the jury or court focuses on the issue of reasonableness, problems may arise. As Jackson[7] has noted, it is unclear whether reasonableness should be construed subjectively or objectively, that is, whether it should be judged from the perspective of the accused himself, who might be hostile to the police and therefore might not be expected to cooperate with them, or from the standpoint of a reasonable person in the circumstances of the accused at that time. Determining reasonableness would require sufficient information on the relevant circumstances which might not be available to the court, for example, if the accused does not himself testify or if the full details of the interview are not available. Although routine tape recording of interviews was introduced in the Province under the PACE Order, interviews with terrorist suspects in Northern Ireland are not normally tape recorded, although they are in England, so a crucial protection for the suspect is lost. This also means considerable delay in the trial process as court time is taken up with arguments over what was said in interrogation and whether confession evidence should be admitted.

Moreover, for suspects detained under the Northern Ireland (Emergency Provisions) Act 1991 access to a solicitor can be deferred initially for 48 hours and renewed further for up to an additional 48 hours and solicitors are not permitted to be present during interviews. So the decision to remain silent will normally be taken without a solicitor present and before access to legal advice.[8] Suspects detained under the PTA in England may have their access to legal advice deferred for 48 hours, but this is rare in practice with access to a lawyer seldom being delayed for more than six hours. Solicitors normally remain with their clients during interviews under the PTA in England, in contrast to detainees in Northern Ireland where solicitors are excluded.

Even if a tape recording of an ordinary interview is available, to assess the question of reasonableness, the jury will need to ascertain how much the defendant knew of the details of the case, whether the caution was properly administered and whether he had access to legal advice. It might be argued that it is reasonable not to mention the fact until the solicitor has been consulted or to refrain from mentioning it on the basis of a solicitor's advice and that suspects should be advised to inform the police that they will remain silent until they have exercised their right to see a solicitor and that if a suspect refers to the fact that he was advised not to mention it by his solicitor, he should not be seen as acting unreasonably.[9] Jackson[10] argues that the problem with the Order is that it leaves too much discretion to the court. Article 2(2) specifies that the suspect could not be convicted or committed or have a case to answer solely on the basis of the inferences drawn from his failure to mention the fact, but the inference could be seen as undermining the credibility of his account. If the inference is that the newly submitted account is untrue, then this might corroborate allegations against the accused made by an accomplice or complainant. Drawing the appropriate inferences would also be difficult given the range of possible reasons for initial silence which might exist. The original Order did not require a caution in relation to the effects of failing to mention a fact later relied on but a caution was specified in the subsequent Guidance and is now contained in the Code of Practice on Police Detention and Questioning under the PACE Order 1989 and in the Emergency Powers Guidance with the cautions for Articles 4, 5 and 6.

Article 3 is equivalent to s 34 of the CJPOA which is also aimed at ambush defences. Under s 34 if the accused fails to mention a fact relied on in his defence when being questioned under caution or on being charged, if the fact was one which in the circumstances existing at the time he could reasonably have been expected to mention, then the court or jury may draw such inferences as appear proper. But the nature of the inferences which may be drawn is not specified in the Order or the Act, and in Northern Ireland this has been treated as a matter of common sense.[11]

Article 4

Article 4 deals with failure to testify at trial. When the Order was enacted the procedure was as follows: before any evidence is given for the defence, the court shall tell the accused that he will be called on to give evidence in his defence and tell him the effect of Article 4 if, when called, he refuses to be sworn or having been sworn, 'without good cause, refuses to answer any question.' If the accused then refuses to be sworn or having been sworn, without good cause, refuses to

63

answer any question, then the court or jury in determining whether he is guilty of the offence charged, may draw such inferences from the refusal as appear proper. On the basis of such inferences, the court or jury may treat his refusal as, or capable of, amounting to corroboration of any evidence given against him to which that refusal is material. This went further than the recommendations of the Home Office Working Group for changes in England and Wales.[12] It repealed s (1)(b) of the Criminal Evidence Act (Northern Ireland) 1923 so that the prosecution and judge may comment on the silence of the accused.

When the Criminal Evidence Order was enacted the defendant was warned by the judge of the adverse effects of silence if he did not testify. This provision was also in the Criminal Justice and Public Order Bill but amended, following strong opposition, to the judge being satisfied that the defendant was aware of the consequences. The Criminal Evidence Order was subsequently amended to follow this procedure.[13] The Practice Notes on silence issued on 10 April 1995 by the Lord Chief Justices for Northern Ireland and for England and Wales stipulate that the judge should ask defence counsel, in the presence of the jury, if he or she has advised his client that the stage in the trial has now been reached where the defendant can give evidence and that inferences may be drawn from a failure to testify. If defence counsel says this advice has not yet been given, the judge must direct counsel to do so and the trial will be adjourned to allow for this.

Section 35 of the CJPOA follows Article 4: the court or jury in determining whether the accused is guilty of the offence charged may draw such inferences as appear proper from the failure of the defendant to give evidence or his refusal, without good cause, to answer any questions. However the appropriate warning to the jury is not specified in s 35.

A suspect in Northern Ireland retains the right to silence in the sense that he cannot be forced to speak, but clearly is under pressure to do so, if he is warned in front of the jury of the effects of his refusal to testify. The construction of 'without good cause' is given in Article 4(6) which states that the refusal will be seen as without good cause unless he is entitled to remain silent by virtue of a statutory provision, on grounds of privilege or because the court has exercised its general discretion to allow him to refuse to answer. Determining the proper inferences to be drawn would also seem problematic here if the defendant is silent, for a full knowledge of the circumstances may be needed to answer this question. These problems also highlight the difficulty of achieving the Benthamite goal of rectitude by infringing the right to silence. It is impossible to compel the accused to speak and Article 4(5) makes clear that the Article does not render him compellable to give evidence. But if the right to silence is limited by the pressures to speak contained within the provisions of the Order, then the jury may nonetheless find itself relying on vague and ill-informed speculations in drawing inferences. The unintended consequence of the weakening of the right to silence could be a decrease in rectitude of outcome.

Article 5

Article 5 deals with the situation where a person is arrested and there is found on him, his clothing or footwear, or otherwise in his possession, or found in any place in which he is at the time of his arrest, an object, substance or mark, and the constable reasonably believes that the presence of the object, substance or mark may be attributable to his participation in the commission of an offence. If the constable then informs him of that belief and requests him to account for the presence of the object, substance or mark and he fails or refuses to do so, then the court in determining whether to commit him for trial or that there is a case to answer, and the court or jury in determining whether he is guilty of the offence charged, may draw such inferences from the failure or refusal as appear proper. On the basis of those inferences, the court or jury may treat the failure or refusal as, or as capable of amounting to, corroboration of any evidence given against him in relation to which the failure is material. The provisions of Article 5 do not apply unless a warning is given at the time of the request by the constable advising of the effects of failure or refusal.

Article 5 is the equivalent of s 36 of the CJPOA. It permits the court or jury to draw such inferences as appear proper from the failure of the accused to account for the presence of objects, substances or marks on his person, clothing or possessions or in any place in which he is at the time of his arrest, when a constable reasonably believes that these are attributable to his participation in an offence and he is asked to account for them.

Article 6

Article 6 specifies the inferences which may be drawn from the failure or refusal to account for one's presence at a particular place. If the person is arrested at a place or about the time the offence for which he was arrested is alleged to have been committed, and the constable reasonably believes that his presence at that place and at that time may be attributable to his participation in the commission of the offence and the constable informs him that he so believes and requests him to account for that presence and he fails or refuses to do so, then the court in determining whether to commit him for trial or whether there is a case to answer, and the court or jury in determining whether he is guilty of the offence charged, may draw such inferences as appear proper. On the basis of such inferences, the court or jury may treat the failure or refusal as, or as capable of amounting to, corroboration of any evidence against the accused in relation to which the failure or refusal is material. The provisions of the article would apply only if the accused is advised of the effect of a failure or refusal at the time the request is made. Again, problems may arise in drawing the proper inferences in the absence of a full knowledge of the relevant circumstances and the range of possible reasons, unrelated to guilt, for nonco-operation. As Jackson[14] has argued, the less responsive the accused is, the harder it becomes to make any inference which the jury or court can be confident is the correct one. Instead it may draw an inference based on vague assumptions about what a person in that situation might do, and it may be that the jury will be reluctant to draw inferences without that information. Juries do find it difficult, in any case, to know how to interpret silence, but the Order does not lessen that confusion.

Article 6 is the equivalent of s 37 of the CJPOA. Section 37 permits a court or jury to draw such inferences as appear proper from the failure of an accused to account to a constable for his presence at a particular place at or about the time an offence for which he has been arrested is alleged to have been committed and which presence the constable reasonably believes to be attributable to his participation in the offence. The difference is that silence can constitute corroboration in Northern Ireland but not in England and Wales. Failure to provide an explanation of an object, substances or marks, found on his person or clothing can amount to corroboration under Article 5 as can failure to account for his presence at the crime scene under Article 6. Articles 5 and 6 of the Criminal Evidence Order cannot be used unless the accused has been told by the police officer in making the request, in 'ordinary language' what the effect would be if he failed or refused to comply with the request.[15] He must be cautioned that his failure or refusal to account may be given in evidence and the court may draw such inferences from his failure or refusal as appear proper.

In *R v Martin and others* the Northern Ireland Court of Appeal said 'that the word "inference", like the phrase "I infer" is common place in the vocabulary of the community. It is part of everyday language frequently used and readily understood.'[16] It would be hard, said the court to find an equivalent phrase which did not lose its meaning. But it may be difficult for suspects or juries to appreciate the precise meaning of 'inference' or the type of inference which is appropriate.

The caution

When the Order came into effect in 1988 the Judges' Rules were replaced by the Guidance issued by the Secretary of State to the Chief Constable. It explained the terms of the Order and the appropriate procedures to be followed during questioning. There were problems with the caution issued under the Guidance in relation to Article 3. When a police constable was questioning a person to discover whether an offence has been committed, or by him, or where he had reasonable grounds for suspecting that he has committed an offence, he had to caution the suspect as follows:

You do not have to say anything unless you wish to do so, but I must warn you that if you fail to mention any fact which you wish to rely on in your defence in Court your failure to take this opportunity to mention it may be taken as supporting any relevant evidence against you. If you wish to say anything, what you say may be given in evidence.[17]

The wording of the original Northern Ireland caution was criticised for its lack of clarity. The Standing Advisory Commission on Human Rights expressed concern over whether the wording of the caution would be fully understood by all suspects.[18] The reference to 'your defence in court', for example, could suggest that the suspect has already been charged when this is not the case. The caution referred to 'support' rather than corroboration and the inexperienced suspect may not appreciate the evidential significance of remaining silent.[19] The suspect may be reaching a decision without having the benefit of legal advice. The right to legal advice was improved by s 15 of the Emergency Provisions Act 1987 which gave a statutory right to access to legal advice to terrorist suspects and to ordinary suspects under s 59 of the PACE Order, but with powers to delay that access. This does not guarantee that one will be requested or granted and there is no statutory duty solicitor scheme in Northern Ireland.

The Guidance was subsequently replaced by the Police and Criminal Evidence (Northern Ireland) Order which came into force on January 1st 1990 and which encompassed all criminal procedures. Given that the Codes of Practice for Northern Ireland were being drafted at the time the Draft Order was passed, it would have been more appropriate to wait until they had been published before initiating change. A Code of Practice on Detention and Questioning was issued under Article 65 of the PACE (Northern Ireland) Order 1989.

The Codes, while mirroring, in most respects, the provisions for England and Wales, contained a caution different from that used in England and Wales at that time. Code C(10) specifies the cautions to be used in relation to the relevant articles of the Criminal Evidence Order, which should be given before questioning. The suspect is advised that he does not have to speak, but warned of the significance of failing to mention facts, or failing to account for objects or marks or his presence in a particular place, using the same caution as formerly used in the Guidance.

Research published by Justice and the Committee on the Administration of Justice[20] in 1994 on the new caution in Northern Ireland showed that there was little understanding of its meaning by suspects. The police often backed up the caution with comments such as 'You have to speak to us now or we'll charge you.' or 'Now is the time to speak'. In the opinion of the solicitors they interviewed, only a small minority of suspects understand the significance of the caution, even when they claim to understand. Most clients thought that they were obliged to answer any question, which may lead to detainees telling lies to protect others. The lawyers were critical of some officers for 'misrepresenting' the effect of the Order. Indeed, it is difficult for many solicitors to understand the precise meaning. Earlier studies of the caution being used in England and Wales at that time, 'You do not have to say anything unless you wish to do so, but what you say may be given in evidence', showed that only 42% of suspects understood it fully and the general level of understanding of disadvantaged people, in some cases, was inadequate to grasp it and that it needed to be simplified into everyday language.[21] From the legal adviser's standpoint, it is clearly important to keep meticulous records of how the accused was cautioned, his response and reasons for the advice given.

The caution in Northern Ireland has been amended to follow the caution used in England and Wales since April 1995.[22] The English caution states that: You do not have to say anything. But it may harm your defence if you do not mention when questioned something which you later rely on in court. Anything you say may be given in evidence.[23] The two cautions have now been brought into line by the CJPOA and the new PACE Codes.

The wording of the caution is still ambiguous and consequently suspects may be unsure what the precise consequences of silence might be. The suspect's decision to speak may be taken without fully understanding the meaning of the caution or knowing the full details of the case against him, or without the benefit of legal advice. Similarly the wording of the request to testify is likely to encourage the accused to relinquish his right to silence.

The enactment of the Criminal Evidence Order

The Criminal Evidence Order was enacted with great haste by delegated legislation, using an Order in Council. This precluded a full Parliamentary discussion of the principles underpinning the changes, and scrutiny by the Joint Select Committee on Statutory Instruments. Amendments to the proposals were also prohibited. Although there is an established pre-Parliamentary procedure for Orders in Council, which involves advance circulation of the proposals to allow for comment and amendments, albeit within a mere six weeks, as Hadfield[24] points out, this was not used in relation to the Criminal Evidence Order. The lack of consultation was strongly criticised by the Standing Advisory Commission on Human Rights. It argued that it was denied an opportunity to make effective comments on the Order even though it had direct implications for human rights and the Commission was created specifically to advise the Secretary of State on human rights matters.[25] The use of the procedure could not be justified on emergency grounds and its use would seem to rest on either the low significance attached to the change or the desire to circumvent public debate. The right to silence, which symbolised the assertion of the common law and Parliamentary sovereignty against the use of prerogative power, in the seventeenth century, was effectively extinguished by this procedure and its use has further undermined confidence in the administration of justice in the province.[26]

The changes in Northern Ireland attracted far less criticism than the proposals for changes to the right to silence for England and Wales. Moreover, given that the Home Office Working Group did include a representative of the Northern Ireland Office, it would have been possible to defer a full decision on the changes in Northern Ireland until that Group had reported. It would have been prudent to await the introduction of the PACE Codes and the results of research on the operation of the relevant sections of the Republic of Ireland's Criminal Justice Act 1984, which came into effect in 1987,[27] to see whether the erosion of the right to silence was necessary. Normally changes relating to criminal procedure in Northern Ireland would be modelled on established legislation for England and Wales rather than introduced in advance of such legislation. It was also expected that any changes to the right to silence in Northern Ireland at the time would be incorporated into emergency legislation, and restricted to terrorist offences, rather than becoming part of the ordinary criminal law. This would have been feasible. The Prevention of Terrorism (Temporary Provisions) Bill was being considered by Parliament in November 1988 and it would have been possible to insert clauses relating to the right to silence, thereby limiting their effect to terrorist offences. However, even with the peace process it seems unlikely that this route will be taken now that the curtailment of the right to silence is a feature of the English criminal justice system applicable to all suspects.

The merits and problems of these changes were consequently never fully aired either inside or outside Parliament. The original announcement of the Order was made in October 1988 and by November 14th it had become law.

The arguments for change in Northern Ireland

What was unique, of course, to the case for abolition of the right to silence in Northern Ireland was the concern with the problem of terrorism. Terrorists were seen as most prone to 'exploit' the right to silence whereas in the 1970s attention was focused on professional criminals. Prior to the change, the Royal Ulster Constabulary proposed abolition of the right to silence, expressing its concern over the exploitation of the right to silence by terrorist suspects trained to resist interrogation.[28] The police had been demanding changes for some time on the ground that they were experiencing problems extracting information from suspects. Republican newspapers had been advising silence during police questioning.[29] Efforts to use supergrasses in the early eighties had ultimately proved unsuccessful, as convictions were overturned on appeal, and internment had been abolished.[30] But the right to silence had not been on the agenda in the discussions on emergency powers in the seventies.[31] The Diplock Commission[32] was set up to consider possible arrangements 'for the administration of justice which might be made to deal more effectively with terrorist organisations'[33] other than by internment. It provided the foundation for emergency powers legislation and did not refer to the right to silence as contributing to problems in convicting the guilty. The Gardiner Committee,[34] which reported in 1975, reviewed the workings of the Northern Ireland (Emergency Provisions) Act and its implications for civil liberties, but did not contemplate changes to the right to silence.

However, by the late 1980s the issue was beginning to emerge in the debates on emergency powers. Viscount Colville,[35] in his review of the Prevention of Terrorism Act in 1987, advocated abolition of the right to silence and reference was made to the concerns of the RUC on this issue. The police in Northern Ireland, as in England and Wales, have repeatedly expressed dissatisfaction with the use of the right to silence and their fears that if the right is fully exercised, police investigations will be hampered. Viscount Colville pointed out that unless the RUC catch a terrorist in the act 'they find great obstacles in the way which leads to successful conviction'[36] because detainees detained on suspicion of terrorist offences increasingly rely on the right to silence. Reference has been made to the special training given to members of para-military groups to withstand interrogation, to construct a 'wall of silence' and to resist the psychological pressures to speak which suspects experience in detention. Colville referred to the advice given in terrorist training manuals to help the detainee resist answering even the most innocuous questions. He therefore argued that as detainees held on suspicion of terrorist offences increasingly made use of silence, anti-terrorist legislation should be strengthened by abolishing this right, otherwise the use of the right by suspected terrorists could undermine the rule of law. If an individual is caught in incriminating circumstances and chooses to stay silent, he argued, the court should be entitled to draw adverse inferences from his silence as they were able to do in the Republic of Ireland.[37]

By the late 1980s the police were particularly concerned with racketeering which was being used to raise money for para-military purposes, and the fact that these racketeers and terrorist suspects were refusing to speak. During the Parliamentary debates on the Order, the Secretary of State for Northern Ireland, Tom King, referred to the fact that the Royal Commission figure of 4% of suspects refusing to answer questions did not apply to Northern Ireland.[38] When asked for figures, he replied:

> The RUC informs me that of all those detained for questioning in connection with serious crimes, including terrorist offences in Northern Ireland, just under half refuse to answer any substantive questions while in police custody. Many of those people will not answer any questions. It is quite clear that in too many cases justice is being thwarted.[39]

The identification of the right to silence as a problem intensified against the background of a wave of bombing attacks on targets in England and an increase in terrorist violence in the summer of 1988. The announcement of the Order and the dissemination of the belief that the guilty were hiding behind a wall of silence also coincided with the trial of the Winchester Three, McCann, Cullen and Shanahan, for conspiring to murder Tom King. All three exercised their right to silence. During a Parliamentary debate on the Criminal Evidence Order in November 1988 Tom King had referred to the exploitation of the right to silence by the guilty and by hardened criminals and similar comments had been made in television interviews. On appeal, it was recognised by the Appeal Court that these comments were highly prejudicial to the appellants in suggesting that silence was an indication of guilt and could have affected the outcome of the trial. Their convictions were quashed in 1990.

In assessing the case for change in Northern Ireland, it is difficult to evaluate whether these changes were justified in the absence of strong empirical evidence of the 'abuse' of the right by the guilty. The evidence on which the figure of 'just under half', referred to by Tom King, is based has never been revealed or published. It is therefore difficult to verify or challenge this assertion. Even if the numbers using the right to silence were high, which was never conclusively established, this may have been attributable to factors other than guilt. In the context of political violence, of retributive measures such as 'knee-capping' and 'breeze-blocking' used against informers, fear for one's own well-being or that of one's family, might well discourage the innocent detainee from speaking. Responding to questioning by silence in such circumstances may be a rational and intelligible response of the innocent rather than an indication of guilt. Even before the Order was passed suspects may well have weighed up the possibility of adverse inferences being drawn from silence in reaching a decision and may still consider the risks are outweighed by the dangers of waiving the right. Conversely, sophisticated terrorists may be more likely to be prepared for interrogation with a clear-cut alibi.

The right to silence had already been circumscribed in a number of ways, so that the opportunities for 'exploitation' of the right were already limited. Although the Prevention of Terrorism Act did not expressly strip the right to silence from detainees, it did give extensive powers of detention to the police, in the expectation that detention would induce the detainee to speak. Furthermore, s 11 of the Prevention of Terrorism Act 1984, reenacted in s 18 of the Prevention of Terrorism Act 1989, provided that it is an offence for a person who has information which he knows or believes might be material in preventing the commission of a terrorist act by another person or ensuring their capture, prosecution or conviction, for the commission or preparation of a terrorist act connected to Northern Irish affairs, to withhold that information. The Act has been renewed annually since 1989 despite the peace process and the ceasefire. In addition, the statutory limitations to the right to silence in England and Wales

71

have also been applied to Northern Ireland, for example, the duty to disclose an alibi and the special arrangements for advance disclosure of defences at pre-trial hearings for serious fraud cases. Exercising the right to silence may be seen as suspicious in the context of procedures for the granting of exclusion orders. If an application by the police to the Secretary of State for an exclusion order follows a period of detention during which the detainee has exercised his right to silence, he may be assessed as a terrorist trained in anti-interrogation techniques.[40]

The Criminal Evidence Order was an indiscriminate measure which denied the right to silence to all criminal suspects, not just to terrorist suspects. The proportionality[41] argument clearly applied to the Northern Irish context, when all criminal suspects, and not just those accused of terrorist activities, lost their right to silence. This is pertinent in view of the fact that large numbers of people interrogated in Northern Ireland are eventually released without charge.[42] From 1990 to 1994 the number of people arrested under the PTA and released without charge in Northern Ireland ranged from 75% to 77%.[43] Northern Ireland has not enjoyed the benefit of a major review of its criminal justice system, unlike England and Wales, as it was excluded from the remit of the Royal Commission on Criminal Justice and no research was undertaken on it. The Order also needs to be considered in the context of the treatment of Irish suspects and miscarriages of justice, such as the Maguire Seven, the Birmingham Six and the Guildford Four. The fact that the right has been curtailed for all suspects in the UK by the CJPOA demonstrates that once inroads are made into a right it is very difficult to prevent further infringements.

When the Order was introduced fears were expressed that vulnerable suspects would be at risk. The Order also raised practical problems of cautioning suspects appropriately and in determining what is evidence material to the defence and also effectively shifted the burden of proof.

The argument that the right to silence is anachronistic had less force in Northern Ireland than in England and Wales given the emergency powers. So greater emphasis has been given to the argument that the right to silence protects the guilty. But even here it is questionable whether the measures were really necessary, because of the extensive measures already available for the control of terrorism so it was difficult for the guilty to evade justice. The balance between the state and suspect was already heavily weighted against the accused, by means of the emergency powers, the use of delegated legislation and the denial of jury trials in certain cases. Although in recent years there has been an increased commitment to narrowing the gap between the ordinary law and emergency law, and it is hoped that this will narrow further with the peace process, the emergency legislation has nonetheless remained in place. The arguments for retention of the right to silence therefore apply even more strongly in the Northern Ireland context. These issues will be considered before examining the impact of the Criminal Evidence Order.

The use of emergency powers

Although the emergency legislation was originally intended as a temporary measure, this legislation is now assuming the mark of permanence. In contrast in the Republic of Ireland the Irish Government announced the ending of the state of emergency in the Republic in October 1994. The powers under the Northern Ireland (Emergency Provisions) Act 1987[44] are confined to Northern Ireland while the powers under the Prevention of Terrorism (Temporary Provisions) Act 1989 apply to England and Wales as well as Northern Ireland.[45] Both Acts are reviewed annually. The PTA was first enacted in 1974 and has subsequently been renewed annually and reenacted with certain amendments. The most important provisions remain in force, namely the power to make exclusion orders, the powers of arrest, and the provisions dealing with proscribed organisations. The Prevention of Terrorism Act gives extended powers of detention under the Act compared to the powers to detain under PACE. While PACE provides for a maximum period of detention of 96 hours, under the PTA 1989 a person may be detained for questioning for up to 7 days and clearly the PTA rather than PACE, is likely to be used when dealing with terrorist suspects. Although the initial period of detention is limited to 2 days, the police may apply to the Secretary of State for an extension of up to a maximum of 5 days. Hall[46] refers to the fact that when the Colville Inquiry examined reasons for the extension of detention, it included the checking of fingerprints, forensic tests, interrogation and translation. He points out that while Colville thinks these reasons are good grounds to justify extended detention, these activities could be seen as constituting ordinary police work and are not peculiar to terrorist cases and could be completed after charging the suspect. Given this, the extended powers of detention might be construed as designed to weaken the resolve to remain silent.

Suspects arrested under the EPA in Northern Ireland may be denied access to a solicitor for 96 hours and solicitors are not permitted to be present during interviews. People may be arrested early in the morning, held for long periods without access to a solicitor, be subject to a number of interviews and deprived of sleep and exercise. Conditions in the Castlereagh Holding Centre have also been criticised by the Independent Commissioner for the Holding Centres, Louis Blom-Cooper.[47] As well as being subjected to long periods of detention, suspects at Castlereagh are usually held in solitary confinement, denied access to reading materials and to radio and television and do not have enough facilities for exercise. The detainee's solicitor and spouse may not be informed of his arrest for 48 hours and he may be interrogated during the night until midnight. There is minimal supervision of interviews. Without a solicitor present and in the absence of recording, the suspect is in a vulnerable position and trials may be extended by lengthy arguments over the admissibility of any confession evidence and allegations of ill-treatment. The conditions at Castlereagh have been criticised by international human rights bodies, including the United Nations Human Rights Committee,[48] which recommended that Castlereagh be closed as a matter of urgency, the tape recording of all interviews, including those concerning terrorist-related activities, and the provision for counsel to be present during interviews.[49] Criticism has been directed at the physical conditions, the denial of legal advisers and the failure to record interviews. The Independent Commissioner for the Holding Centres has recommended that audio and video recording of police interviews should be introduced.[50] The Government has said that it intends to introduce video recording in the future. Full recording would benefit the interviewing officer as well as the suspect.

In Northern Ireland ordinary suspects enjoy similar protections under the 1989 PACE (Northern Ireland) Order as those in England and Wales. But terrorist suspects are treated differently in the province where they may be interviewed without a solicitor present and the interview is not required to be tape-recorded. The disadvantages of Northern Ireland detainees were exacerbated by the effect of the Criminal Evidence Order. The effect of changes in the right to silence is therefore of particular concern in relation to terrorist suspects. If crucial comments are not written down adverse comment may be made on matters which the suspect has apparently failed to mention in interview. The suspect's decision on silence may be crucial to the outcome of the case. The Criminal Evidence Order does not expressly require the court to take account of the absence or presence of a lawyer in drawing an adverse inference from silence. This was established in *Quinn*[51] which is being taken to the European Court of Human Rights. However in *Murray v UK*[52] the Court took the view that the scheme in the 1988 Order was such that it was of paramount importance for the rights of the defence that an accused had access to a lawyer during police interrogation. When evidential significance is attached to silence it is crucial that legal advice is available and that detainees are fully aware of the case against them. For this reason SACHR has recommended that safeguards should be implemented to accompany the Order, namely attendance of a solicitor at interviews, an immediate right of access to legal advice, independent electronic recording of all interviews and statutory guidance on when inferences may be drawn under the Order.[53] Precisely because of the unusual conditions in Northern Ireland, and the absence of strong controls on the over-zealous use of powers to detain and search, human rights protection is even more important. The rights and freedoms guaranteed by the European Convention on Human Rights do not provide a sufficient basis for protection because the procedures are cumbersome, and because of the use which has been made in the past of the derogation provision in Article 15(1) of the Convention which allows states to derogate 'in time of war or other public emergency threatening the life of the nation.' The power to arrest under the 1974 Prevention of Terrorism Act allowed the police to arrest, without a warrant, a person whom the officer has reasonable grounds for suspecting to have any connection with terrorism which, until 1984, was limited to terrorism in connection with Northern Ireland. It was subsequently extended to international terrorism. The suspect did not need to be suspected of a specific offence and could be held for 7 days without charge.[54]

It was affirmed by the European Court of Human Rights in *Brogan, Coyle, McFadden and Tracey v UK*[55] that detention for such long periods did contravene Article 5(3) of the European Convention on Human Rights which provides that:

> Everyone arrested or detained in accordance with the provisions of paragraph 1(c) of this Article shall be brought promptly before a judge or other officer authorised by law to exercise judicial power and shall be entitled to trial within a reasonable time or to release pending trial. Release may be conditioned by guarantees to appear for trial.

However, the United Kingdom chose to derogate and during the Parliamentary debates on the 1989 Act the Government announced its intention to continue its derogation under Article 15 until it could devise a suitable means of complying with the Court's decision. It has continued its derogation from the ECHR and the ICCPR despite the peace process. The basis of the derogation is to be challenged. *Brogan* was one case in a line of findings against the United Kingdom in relation to its treatment of prisoners undergoing interrogation in the province. This willingness to derogate has further undermined confidence that human rights will be respected in Northern Ireland, although it should be noted that some reforms have been implemented, most notably, the ending of internment. Since *Brogan* the use of extended interrogations has declined and suspects have been held for shorter periods under the PTA in the 1990s. Hopefully the period of detention will be reduced as the peace process continues. The PTA could also be amended to reduce the maximum power of detention. Recently lawyers have been initiating judicial review proceedings where access to a lawyer has been denied for suspects interrogated under the EPA and PTA, with the result that access to lawyers is being granted more readily by the police. In *Ireland v UK*[56] the Court found that the techniques of interrogation used on detainees in Northern Ireland did constitute inhuman and degrading treatment, under Article 3 of the Convention, from which no derogation is possible under Article 15(2). The killing of three terrorist suspects, Daniel McCann, Sean Savage and Mairead Farrell, in Gibralter by SAS officers, was also found by the Court to breach Article 2, the right to life, of the European Convention.[57] No weapons were found on them or in their car, but a car rented by them and found in Spain contained Semtex and detonators. The soldiers' automatic recourse to lethal force, the authorities decision not to prevent them entering Gibralter and the failure to allow for the possibility that their intelligence was wrong, were criticised by the court.

The European Court of Human Rights considered the status of the right to silence provisions in the Criminal Evidence Order in *Murray v UK*,[58] and found that in Murray's case the drawing of inferences from his refusal to account for his presence could not be regarded as unfair or unreasonable in the circumstances, but that his right to a fair trial guaranteed by Article 6 of the European Convention was breached by the denial of access to a lawyer during the first 48 hours of his detention. The United Nations Human Rights Committee has been very critical of the infringement of civil liberties resulting from the use of emergency laws and detention centres and the failure to comply with the International Covenant on Civil and Political Rights.[59]

The use of the PTA was also challenged in *Brannigan and McBride v UK*.[60] Here the applicants had been detained for over four days under the PTA without being brought before a judge. Although this practice had been declared unlawful by the European Court of Human Rights in *Brogan*, the UK government derogated under Article 15 for PTA detainees. The applicants challenged the lawfulness of the derogation. The Commission declared the case admissible although it accepted the government's arguments on the merits, and referred the case to the court. The Government argued that extended detention was essential to combat terrorism and to disclose relevant material would compromise and endanger informers, and that the independence of the judiciary would be undermined if detention powers were conferred on them. The defence argued that the extended powers of detention were open to abuse and that the judiciary were able to deal with other matters, such as search warrants and false imprisonment, without undermining their independence. The majority of the court held that that the derogation from Article 5(3) regarding prevention in excess of 4 days was lawful. The terrorist activity in Northern Ireland did constitute an emergency threatening the life of the nation. The court held that the problem of terrorist violence in Northern Ireland and the UK was sufficiently serious to justify the use of emergency measures under the PTA, including extended detention, which *prima facie* breached Article 5, so the derogation by means of Article 15 could be used.[61]

But as most confessions are likely to be made within the first 48 hours of detention, it is questionable whether the extended powers are needed and whether they are likely to produce reliable evidence. Under the EPA a maximum of 72 hours was deemed to be adequate.

The 1974 PTA prohibited public expressions of financial and other forms of support for proscribed organisations. This was aimed initially at the IRA, but later broadened to include the Irish National Liberation Army, following the murder of Airey Neave. In the 1976 Act, it was made an offence to contribute to or solicit contributions towards acts of terrorism in Northern Ireland, or to withhold information pertaining to acts of terrorism.

There are also extensive powers to exclude British citizens from England and Wales under the PTA. The Secretary of State was given the power in the 1974

Act to make an exclusion order against a person 'as appears to him expedient to prevent acts of terrorism'. These powers to make exclusion orders were retained in the 1989 PTA despite extensive criticism and the recommendation of Viscount Colville that they should be abolished. In the 1974 Act the exclusion orders were indefinite, in the 1976 Act they were limited to three years, but further orders can be made. This constitutes a form of internal exile and conflicts with the right to freedom of movement within one's own country, guaranteed under Protocol 4 to the European Convention on Human Rights, which provides that 'Everyone lawfully within the territory of a State shall, within that territory, have the right to liberty of movement and freedom to choose his residence.' This has prevented the United Kingdom from ratifying this Protocol. It adversely affects individuals with families in England and discriminates against Irish people.

In *R v Secretary of State for the Home Department ex parte Gallagher*,[62] the Court of Appeal affirmed that the Home Secretary is not required to give reasons when making an exclusion order under the PTA 1989 because s 4 gives him the widest possible discretion where matters of national security are in issue. In *R v Secretary of State for the Home Department ex parte Adams*[63] the Divisional Court said that the decision to impose an exclusion order under the PTA is usually incapable of judicial review because the Home Secretary is not required to give reasons.

However, following the ceasefire declared by the IRA in 1994 and in the context of the peace process, exclusion orders were revoked on Sinn Fein President Gerry Adams and Martin McGuiness in October 1994. By June 1995 20 orders had been revoked on persons wishing to travel to Great Britain from Northern Ireland as well as orders excluding Irish citizens from entering the UK, leaving 38 exclusion orders in force by 19 May 1995.

The 1976 Act made it an offence to refuse to disclose information about a future act of terrorism or about people involved in such acts, effectively weakening the right to silence. Large numbers of people have been detained under the PTA in relation to Northern Irish terrorism although the majority have not been charged with any offence. The Act has been used to search and question at ports and airports. It has been argued that the widespread use of these powers under the Act has meant that the whole Irish community has effectively been placed under suspicion. A campaign has been launched to repeal the PTA and to monitor its effects while in force. In 1995 the Secretary of State announced that an independent review of the anti-terrorism laws will be undertaken by Lord Lloyd to consider whether permanent counter-terrorist legislation is necessary in the context of the peace process and to receive submissions from interested parties, but the Government is not obliged to accept its recommendations. He also announced the intention to introduce electronic recording of interviews in holding centres and improvements in compassionate parole for convicted prisoners. Since 1995 the political climate has changed with the ending of the ceasefire by the IRA in February 1996 and the hardening of attitudes towards republicanism.

Attention should also be given to those jurisdictions, including the Republic of Ireland, which have faced similar problems, yet have sought to maintain human rights protection.[64] If it is deemed necessary to retain strong powers to deal with terrorist activity, these could be included within the Prevention of Terrorism Act, applicable to Great Britain as a whole, rather than confined to Northern Ireland.

The changes to the right to silence in Northern Ireland were therefore used to bolster what were already extensive concessions to the police and military in the apprehension, detention and interrogation of suspects under the Prevention of Terrorism Acts and Emergency Provisions Acts. The Criminal Evidence Order was enacted at a time of increasing concern over these powers. The armoury of state powers was also subsequently intensified further by a package of measures to combat terrorist activity, including broadcasting restrictions, the latter lasting until 1994. Furthermore, the major reviews of these provisions, such as the Diplock, Gardiner and Baker Reports, as Hogan and Walker[65] point out, have largely been conducted on the tacit assumption of the necessity for emergency provisions. The question which needs to be addressed is whether special legislation is necessary, or whether terrorist crimes can be controlled and punished by means of the ordinary criminal law. If we look back at the history of criminal activity undertaken by the members of paramilitary groups, the crimes could have been dealt with under the ordinary criminal law and detected using ordinary police work. Given that very few people have been convicted under the PTA its usefulness is highly questionable. The actual number of incidents of terrorism is too low to justify a separate criminal justice system. Using the ordinary criminal law also strengthens the rule of law when it is perceived that all suspects are treated alike regardless of their political or religious views. Strong judicial control of the powers of the police and the security forces enhances the legitimacy of the criminal justice system, but in Northern Ireland judicial control has been seen as too weak. It has been argued[66] that if the PTA is to be retained in the new political climate, then it would be better to draft a permanent code to deal with terrorism rather than relying on panic measures, one that respects human rights and provides accountability, but the danger is that any extraordinary laws tend over time to permeate ordinary laws.[67] The powers to stop and search under emergency legislation were increased in 1996. As MI5 becomes involved in counter-terrorism it is feared that accountability and control may diminish.

The Criminal Evidence Order is unlikely to be repealed given that similar provisions have been applied to the rest of the UK by the CJPOA. However, it could be argued that such a step should be incorporated into the reforms as part of the peace process and democratisation of Northern Ireland. The report of the Haldane Society[68] was very critical of the use of emergency powers, the Criminal Evidence Order, the treatment of detainees in interrogation, the strong reliance on uncorroborated confessions and the use of unreliable evidence and argued for an immediate restoration of the right to silence.

Non-jury trials

The position of the suspect has also been undermined by the loss of the right to trial by jury since 1973 in relation to certain 'scheduled offences', including murder, offences against the person and firearms offences and membership of a proscribed organisation as stipulated in a Schedule attached to the Northern Ireland (Emergency Provisions) Act. These provisions were originally set out in the 1973 Northern Ireland (Emergency Provisions) Act, subsequently revised, and are now contained in s 10(1) of the 1991 Act which provides that 'A trial on indictment of a scheduled offence shall be conducted by the court without a jury.' The Northern Ireland (Emergency Provisions) Act 1987 did not broaden the scope for jury trial. These courts have survived the peace process. There are also differences in the level of remission of sentences between scheduled and non-scheduled offences. The Diplock Commission[69] recommended removal of the right to a jury trial in 1973 and the courts were created following the Northern Ireland (Emergency Provisions) Act 1973 and the offences to which it applied, were set out in the schedule to the Act. This mode of trial has been retained as the Act has been renewed, but the Attorney-General's powers to certify cases out of the non-jury system, including kidnapping and certain firearms offences, have been extended to give effect to the recommendations of the Baker Report.[70] Some offences may be de-scheduled permitting jury trial in certain circumstances.[71] In Diplock trials the judge is required to given written report of the reasons for a conviction and there is an automatic right of appeal. This has influenced the approach of the European Court of Human Rights to cases from Northern Ireland, such as *Murray v UK*,[72] where the court emphasised the distinction between jury and non-jury trials. Approximately one third of Crown Court cases in Northern Ireland are 'scheduled' cases.

The use of non-jury trials has been strongly criticised, especially in the context of the emergency legislation, human rights violations and the loss of the right to silence, raising the issue of whether the right to a fair trial is possible in Northern Ireland. The justification for the introduction of this mode of trial was concern over intimidation of jurors and perverse verdicts particularly by loyalist juries, that is, verdicts which rest on bias against the defendant or sympathy with him. These fears have been seen as exaggerated by Greer and White who describe the evidence of intimidation as 'sketchy'[73] and that of perverse acquittals as weak and inconclusive. In neither case is the evidence sufficiently compelling to warrant removal of the jury. The 'intimidation' argument, advanced both inside and outside Parliament, relied on anecdotal evidence and many of the incidents cited related to witness intimidation rather than juror intimidation; no clear proof of reprisals resulting from jury service was established. Demands to be released from jury service often resulted from work demands. But if evidence of anxiety on the part of jurors were adduced, these fears could be assuaged by providing greater anonymity, concealing the identity of jurors, improving their protection by screening them from the public gallery and similar measures. Very little empirical work on the workings of the Northern Irish jury system has been conducted, but at the time there were higher acquittal rates for Protestants than Catholics, which aroused fears of sectarian verdicts and perverse acquittals. But these fears could have been addressed by less drastic means, including improving the randomness of juries.

Jackson and Doran[74] compared Diplock and jury trials in Northern Ireland, and discovered the following differences:

> (T)he substitution of the judge for the jury was found to effect a change in the nature of the arguments that were run, particularly by the defence against the prosecution case. Counsel reported, and it was observed, that they were able to run "sympathy points" much more easily in jury trials. Within more relaxed standards of relevance they were able to build up a more rounded picture of a defendant or a witness, which then enabled them to appeal to the merits of the case. In Diplock trials by contrast, the scope of the context was much more restricted and there could be little consideration of the merits of conviction other than on the basis of the legal standards to be applied by the defendant... Certain judges admitted that they felt compelled to allow "sympathy" points to be put before a jury because of the danger of being seen to be consistently interrupting counsel all the time in front of a jury. In professional trials where the jury is absent it is much easier for judges to curb counsel's questioning.[75]

Judges have more influence on the proceedings than passive juries. Judges are also more likely to adopt an interventionist or inquisitorial stance when sitting without a jury. Jackson and Doran therefore conclude that the 'presence of the jury helps to make the adversary trial a genuinely participative proceeding between the parties in contest. A criminal trial which retains the trappings of the adversarial system without any recognition given to the absence of the jury is a much less participative proceeding.'[76] The removal of the jury 'has profound procedural implications for the entire tradition of the adversary trial.'[77] Their findings are based on a study of 43 Diplock and jury trials in Belfast Crown Court from 1989-1991. They interviewed counsel and judges working in the Diplock courts and studied trial transcripts to ascertain the nature of the judicial role and factors affecting decision-making. They found considerable variation in approaches towards judicial questioning, although judges were very wary of appearing partisan and thought it 'inappropriate to deviate from the umpireal role required in adversarial proceedings.'[78] They found that the accused did experience 'an adversarial deficit'[79] because the trial tended to focus more intensely on the weight of the evidence and the determination of legal guilt while the jury, as representatives of the community, 'can afford to take a wider view of both the merits of the proceedings and the merits of convicting the defendant as charged.'[80] Furthermore, judges are more likely than juries to become aware of inadmissible evidence.

Since 1973 the jury system has been improved and made more representative by the Juries (Northern Ireland) Order 1974 which was modelled on the 1974 Juries Act. Prior to the enactment of the Order, juries were dominated by Protestants, males and the middle-class, because of the qualifications for jury service. But the over-representation of Protestants was reduced through the 1974 reforms which removed the property qualification for jury service. Abolishing the right to jury trial in relation to scheduled offences was therefore disproportionate to the scale of the problem as it would have been possible to introduce measures to strengthen the jury system rather than abolishing it. At the very least it would be possible to commence on the assumption that all trials are jury trials and to permit a non-jury trial only when the threat of intimidation has been established in that particular case, rather than routinely using Diplock courts for scheduled offences. So far there has been no commitment to abolish Diplock trials as part of the reforms accompanying the peace process.

Defenders of the Diplock courts might point to the fact that the conviction rate in the Diplock courts in the 1970s increased while the acquittal rates in conventional jury trials in the province increased.[81] However, this might be attributed to a range of factors including the case-hardening of the judiciary and differences in the use of evidential rules. The majority of convictions in scheduled offences have relied on confession evidence alone. Few confessions are excluded by the Diplock courts and there is a lower threshold for the admission of confession evidence in Diplock trials. Greer argues that the Diplock Commission's proposals generated a 'confession-based prosecution process centred around non-jury, single judge courts and serviced by extended police and army powers to stop and question, search and seize and arrest and detain.'[82] Furthermore, a single judge obviously cannot be as representative as a mixture of jurors. The 1987 Emergency Provisions Act extended the grounds on which an admission could be excluded to include the threat of violence.[83]

Problems may also arise in relation to the admissibility of evidence which would be met by the *voir dire* in the jury trial. Provision is made for a new trial in such cases but is not often used. Reasons must be given for a conviction and there is an automatic right of appeal against conviction and sentence, but a low success rate. What the shift towards non-jury trials means, in effect, is a move towards an inquisitorial trial but without corresponding changes in the procedural rules.

In the jury debate, like the right to silence debate, a moral panic has flared up regarding a perceived problem which is not based on the actual scale of the problem. In each case, the panic has been followed by a draconian measure which extends far beyond the original class of suspects it was designed to deal with. But it is debateable whether special institutional arrangements and emergency provisions are necessary or whether armed robbers, for example, could be apprehended and adequately punished under the existing criminal law, even if the robbery is undertaken for purposes such as fund-raising for a terrorist group. A large proportion of non-jury trials have been conducted where the accused has no connection with terrorist activities. The Haldane Society's report on criminal justice under the emergency powers notes that 40% of the cases heard in the Diplock Courts had no connection with para-military activity.[84] In any event the ordinary criminal law may be sufficient to deal with offenders even where there is a terrorist connection. It is difficult to see how the argument that a non-jury trial is essential in a particular case could be tested. But it would seem that in practice the Diplock courts are being over-used where a normal trial would be sufficient. The use of Diplock courts may also provide a model for further erosion of jury trials in England and Wales as increasing dissatisfaction is voiced with using juries in complex trials.

The use of supergrasses

Non-jury trials raise particular problems in relying on accomplice evidence especially supergrasses, where assessing the informer's credibility is a key jury function. If we compare English juries to the Diplock courts we find that conviction rates differ on this issue: juries in England are unwilling to convict on the basis of the uncorroborated evidence of an accomplice but in Northern Ireland Diplock judges did initially show a willingness to do so, although relatively few convictions based on supergrass evidence stood up on appeal. In some cases the informers retracted their evidence before trial. It was also noticeable that the convictions on the uncorroborated evidence of supergrasses primarily involved evidence of republican supergrasses, thereby generating claims of sectarian justice.

A distinctive feature of the Northern Irish criminal justice system in the early eighties was the use of supergrasses. Supergrasses were informers who were usually associated with organised crime and so were able to implicate large numbers of people.[85] Greer[86] reviews the supergrass evidence which was used in the early 1980s. The use of supergrass evidence has declined since 1984 but although now 'dead and buried, ... its ghost still haunts the Diplock process'[87] and there are periodic rumours that supergrasses have been recruited or are being used. No supergrass trials were conducted in the period from 1986 to 1993 in Northern Ireland. Supergrass evidence had been used in England in the 1970s in investigations into London gangs of bank robbers, but juries in England were reluctant to convict defendants on the uncorroborated and unsupported evidence of a supergrass and judges, while anxious to avoid wrongful acquittals of the guilty, had expressed reservations about such convictions. The courts resolved this tension by displaying a willingness to convict on the evidence of a supergrass if it was corroborated.

In the period surveyed by Gifford's[88] study of accomplice evidence, he found no instance of a conviction in England on the basis of uncorroborated evidence of a supergrass. Yet in Northern Ireland a quite different picture emerged. In the ten supergrass cases, 54% of the defendants convicted were convicted on the basis of uncorroborated evidence. However the conviction rate fell from 1983 to 1986 and many of the appeals against conviction on supergrass evidence succeeded. The convictions that were sustained were those based principally on confession evidence.

Corroboration is used here in the *Baskerville* sense of corroboration, namely that:

> evidence in corroboration must be independent testimony which affects the accused by connecting or tending to connect him with the crime. In other words, it must be evidence which implicates him, that is, which confirms in some material particular not only the evidence that the crime has been committed but that the prisoner committed it.[89]

Prior to the CJPOA, a corroboration warning was mandatory in relation to accomplice evidence but is now discretionary in England and Wales. However the use of corroboration warnings has not yet been abolished in Northern Ireland. The rationale of the accomplice warning established in *Davies*[90] is the potential unreliability of accomplice evidence. By definition an accomplice, involved in the offence, is of bad character and there is also the danger of fabrication due to self-interest. The fact that he can display considerable knowledge of the alleged offence may also mislead the jury. The accomplice warning pointed to the dangers of convicting on the uncorroborated evidence of an accomplice, but did not require corroboration as a precondition of conviction, because some accomplices may be trust-worthy.

These problems are intensified in Northern Ireland where the offences are usually serious offences and there is a network of organised political and military activity. An accomplice warning would therefore be especially important in relation to supergrasses with a strong involvement in previous crimes and a clear motive to avoid a further custodial sentence. While the warning is designed to be given to the jury, in a non-jury trial on indictment, the judge will warn himself, but the fusion of the functions of judge and jury may render this warning less effective. In fact during the early supergrass period, the Diplock judges did show a greater willingness than juries to convict on the uncorroborated evidence of an accomplice. Given the particular problems of non-jury trials, it would be preferable to impose a statutory requirement for corroboration where the jury is absent. But this is very unlikely to be introduced, given the current move away from corroboration.

The use of supergrasses is also questionable because there is no evidence that their use has led to any reduction in political violence, any more than the other measures discussed above, including the loss of the right to silence. If the effect of these measures is to make para-military groups more secretive by developing organisational structures which protect individuals from observation by other members of the group, it will become harder for the police to investigate or infiltrate them. Furthermore, the use of such a controversial means of securing convictions undermines the legitimacy of the criminal justice system. Supergrasses were used initially successfully to secure convictions despite their low credibility.[91] But the use of supergrasses declined as it became harder to sustain convictions on the uncorroborated evidence of an accomplice where errors were found, for example, in the *Steenson* case.[92] Greer[93] distinguishes two phases in the use of supergrasses, the first embracing the Bennett, Black and McGrady trials, in the autumn and winter of 1983, where there was a very high conviction rate and which included convictions on uncorroborated evidence, and the second phase, including the Quigley and Gilmour cases, where the conviction rate fell. He attributes this decline to a shift in judicial attitudes as judges became much more critical of this form of evidence. This might be interpreted as a shift away from crime control towards the reassertion of respect for due process. Convictions relying on supergrass evidence were quashed in *Graham*[94] and it was made clear by the Northern Ireland Court of Appeal that for supergrass evidence to justify a conviction in the Diplock courts, it had to be of a very high standard. The Northern Ireland Court of Appeal also held in *Crumley*[95] that before supergrass evidence could provide the basis for a conviction, the court must be satisfied regarding the supergrass's rehabilitation and credibility. The courts are now unlikely to convict on supergrass evidence in Northern Ireland without strong independent evidence.

Greer[96] argues that when internment ended in 1975 the police were under greater pressure to extract confessions, but complaints about the treatment of detainees led to stronger controls on interrogation making it harder to obtain confessions. Consequently, the police turned to informers as a means of extracting confessions. The use of informers provided a substitute for internment as lengthy periods were spent on remand on charges arising out of supergrass evidence. He identifies three factors which accompanied the use of such evidence: the development of intelligence systems so that potential informers could be identified, the failure of existing methods to deal with the perceived problem and the crises of loyalty of members of paramilitary organisations exploited by the police.

There is a danger that the Criminal Evidence Order may be used to corroborate accomplice evidence or to facilitate the reintroduction of supergrasses. Advising a client to remain silent in the past would have been sound advice to defeat allegations made by an accomplice, but would now be more perilous. If the peace process does not succeed there is always the possibility that the supergrass system will be resurrected.

In *Graham*[97] the trial judge saw Bennett's evidence as strengthened by the failure to testify of the defendants. This was criticised by the Court of Appeal, but now of course silence can corroborate other evidence against the accused. The effect of the Criminal Evidence Order may be to encourage the use of supergrass evidence if that evidence could be corroborated by the defendant's silence. Greer argues that allowing silence in interrogation and at trial to constitute corroboration of other evidence, may facilitate the resurgence of supergrass trials in which supergrass evidence could be corroborated by the silence of the defendant. However he notes that in practice since the Order was passed silence has so far not been used to supplement accomplice, supergrass or informer evidence. It would also be difficult, he argues, for the court to treat the accused's silence as clear and compelling corroboration because of the alternative explanations for silence in the Northern Ireland context, principally the desire to avoid being seen as an informer.

The impact of the Criminal Evidence Order

What have been the effects of abolition of the right to silence in Northern Ireland? It is difficult to obtain information on the number of suspects exercising their right to silence before and after the Order in Northern Ireland on which to base a meaningful comparison. Although the Secretary of State for Northern Ireland did give the figure of over half detained on serious crimes, which he obtained from the RUC, during the debate on the Order, no figures were ever published to substantiate that claim.[98] In the past most defendants in jury trials have testified.

However, the impact of the Criminal Evidence Order was researched by Justice and the Committee on the Administration of Justice and their research suggests that the Order has not strengthened the fight against crime. The project examined three areas, changes in rates of charge and conviction, the experience of legal advisers and the way the judiciary interpreted the provisions, using official statistics and interviews and analysis of judicial decisions in the Diplock courts.[99] The Report questions the effectiveness of the Order in combatting crime. In fact clear up and conviction rates in Northern Ireland have fallen since the Order was passed. Although the number of recorded crimes has increased since 1988, the percentage of criminals caught and convicted has fallen. Between 1988 and 1992 official statistics show that the clear-up rates fell by 11% and the conviction rate for scheduled and unscheduled offences fell, respectively, by 3% and 4%. The percentage of guilty pleas declined in that period. The argument that the Order would assist in catching hardened criminals with previous convictions was not supported as there was little change in the percentage of males convicted with previous criminal convictions. The value of the Order in achieving its stated aims is therefore questionable.

Initially Diplock judges were cautious in using the provisions of the Order to draw adverse inferences from silence and unwilling to use the Order provisions to shore up a weak prosecution case. As Jackson[100] notes, initially judges showed 'a marked reluctance to draw inferences from an accused's refusal to testify'. One of the problems is that the Order gives little guidance on what kinds of inferences may be drawn and gives wide discretion to the court. Ruddell[101] surveyed reported and unreported decisions in the period between June 1989 and February 1991 and could find no case which had been decided principally on the basis of a failure to testify or a failure to give an account at the time of arrest. In *Smyth*,[102] for example, Kelly LJ stated that the provisions of the Criminal Evidence Order should be used only when the prosecution had a strong case but which fell just short of beyond reasonable doubt, 'where the weight of the prosecution evidence just rests on the brink of the necessary standard of proof.' However in a later case, *McLernon*,[103] he said that his comments in *Smyth* were not intended to limit the scope of the Order. In *Smyth* he acknowledged that the courts have 'long recognised that there may be reasons innocent as well as sinister for the refusal of an accused to give evidence.'[104]

However, in the cases cited by Ruddell, it was emphasised that it is open to the court to draw an adverse inference even if it is not deemed appropriate in the instant case. In *Fegan* the fact that the accused failed to testify was used to found an adverse inference against him when viewed in relation to videotape evidence of the incident and Fegan was convicted of highjacking and false imprisonment.[105]

Subsequently the judges' attitude has changed and the courts have made more extensive use of the provisions. A significant turning point was the case of *McLernon*[106] in 1990. Here the defendant did not account to the police for his presence in a house containing firearms and did not testify. In both cases adverse inferences were drawn. Article 3, concerning the failure to mention a fact when charged, the equivalent of s 34 has been used even if the defendant does not give evidence or call witnesses. In *McLernon* the accused did not speak during interrogation but after six days he made a written statement. The trial judge rejected the written statement, saying it was false, and drew adverse inferences from his initial refusal to give an account of his presence at a house where firearms had been found. The Northern Ireland Court of Appeal said that at trial:

> the accused can "rely on a fact in his defence" within the meaning of Article 3 even though neither he nor a witness called on his behalf has given evidence of that fact. One way in which this could happen (and there may be others which may fall to be considered in other cases) would be where

defence Counsel suggested a fact, which assisted the accused, to a prosecution witness in the course of cross-examination and the witness accepted it. In that instance we consider that the fact would be one "relied on in his defence in those proceedings", even if no evidence was called on behalf of the accused.[107]

The Court of Appeal also concluded that the trial judge can draw an inference against the accused under Article 3 in determining an application on whether there is a case to answer, but it could not be the only evidence in support of a prima facie case. The inference from silence can be used to bolster weak prosecution evidence to raise it to a prima facie case and silence can then be used at the end of the trial to infer guilt.

But in *Devine*[108] the Court said that simply probing the prosecution case would be insufficient to bring Article 3 into operation:

> it cannot be said (here) that the accused "relied on a fact in his defence" within the meaning of Article 3(1)(A) because all the defence counsel did was to probe the prosecution case, without suggesting a fact which the accused relied on to a prosecution witness. In our opinion there is a contrast between Article 3 on the one hand and Articles 5 and 6 on the other. In the circumstances set out in Articles 5 and 6 the failure to account for certain matters when requested to do so by a constable may permit the Court to draw an adverse inference against the accused. But for an adverse inference to be drawn under Article 3 there must be more than a failure to mention a fact when questioned by a constable, there must be reliance on that fact in the defence of the accused at the Trial. And we consider that there was no such reliance in this case. Therefore we consider that the learned Trial Judge was not entitled to draw an adverse inference against the appellant under Article 3.[109]

In 1993 the Northern Irish Court of Appeal also upheld the view of the trial judge in *Quinn*[110] that the absence or denial of legal advice does not prevent the drawing of adverse inference under Article 3. Quinn had been questioned under the EPA which does give a right to legal advice as well as powers to delay it in certain circumstances and he had been interviewed without his solicitor present. The Lord Chief Justice Sir Brian Hutton said in *Quinn* that:

> I consider it to be clear that Parliament did not intend that the change in the law brought about by Article 3 which permits and contemplates the drawing of a common sense inference in

an appropriate case should be stultified by the existence of the right to legal advice given by section 15 of the 1987 Northern Ireland (Emergency Provisions) Act.[111]

A challenge to this is being mounted in the European Court of Human Rights. This issue was also considered by the European Court of Human Rights in the case of *Murray v UK*[112] where the Court stressed that the right to legal advice was crucial for fairness to be satisfied in such a scheme. Similarly, the CJPOA does not treat legal advice as a justification of silence and the absence of legal advice does not prevent an adverse inference being drawn against the accused, although it may be a factor to consider, among others, in determining the reasonableness of the accused's refusal to speak.

In *Kinsella*[113] the accused had been advised by his solicitor not to speak to the police but McDermott LJ said that an experienced solicitor would have made clear that while the defendant could remain silent, he would run the risk of adverse inferences if he failed to answer relevant questions. Given that the quality of legal advice may be variable the outcome of the trial may be affected by one's luck in choosing a solicitor.[114]

Article 4 was used in *McLernon*[115] where Kelly LJ said that Article 4 may be construed 'in the widest terms. It imposes no limitations as to when it may be invoked or what result could follow if it is invoked'. He stressed that no limits were intended by his earlier comments in *Smyth*:

> Once the court has complied with the preliminaries in Article 4(2) and called upon the Accused to give evidence and a refusal is made, the Court has then a complete discretion as to whether inferences should be drawn or not. In these circumstances it is a matter for the Court in any criminal case (1) to decide whether to draw inferences or not; (2) if it decides to draw inferences what their nature, extent and degree of adversity, if any, may be. It would be improper and indeed quite unwise for any court to set out the bounds of either steps (1) or (2). Their application will depend on factors peculiar to the individual case.[116]

The argument that Article 4 should be used only when the prosecution case is on the brink of proof beyond reasonable doubt was rejected. Instead it was accepted that: 'In certain cases a refusal to give evidence under the Article may well in itself, but nothing more, increase the weight of a prima facie case to the weight of proof beyond reasonable doubt.'[117]

In *Murray v DPP*[118] the Northern Ireland Court of Appeal held that Article 4 permitted the judge to draw adverse inferences from the defendant's failure to testify using a common sense approach. This was upheld by the House of Lords which held that where the prosecution had established a prima facie case against a defendant who refused to give evidence, the court could draw such inferences from the refusal as might properly be drawn in the circumstances of the particular case, including an inference that the defendant was guilty of the offence with which he was charged. In Murray's case the judge had been entitled to infer that there was no innocent explanation and that he was guilty. Reference was made to the CLRC's Report to resolve any uncertainties regarding the nature of the inferences to be drawn.[119]

Article 4 had been intended to change the law and practice regarding the inferences which could be drawn from a failure to testify. The defendant Kevin Murray was charged with attempted murder and possession of a firearm with intent to endanger life. He would not speak after being arrested but when his home was searched, he did speak briefly to the police and told them where he had been at the time of the shooting being investigated and why his clothes had certain marks on them, but remained silent during interrogation and did not testify at trial. The Northern Ireland Court of Appeal held that Article 4 permitted the trial judge to draw adverse inferences from Murray's failure to give evidence:

> The refusal of the accused to give evidence on his own behalf does not in itself indicate guilt. Under Article 4 it would be improper for the court to draw the bare inference that *because* the accused refused to give evidence in his own defence he was *therefore* guilty. But where common sense permits it, it is proper in an appropriate case for the court to draw the inference from the refusal of the accused to give evidence that there is no reasonable possibility of an innocent explanation to rebut the prima facie case established by the evidence adduced by the Crown, and for the drawing of this inference to lead on to the conclusion, after all the evidence has been considered, that the accused is guilty.[120]

Inferences cannot be drawn until the prosecution has established that there is a case to answer.

This approach was affirmed by the House of Lords[121] which said that in using Article 4, where the defendant does not testify, the prosecution must establish a prima facie case which calls for an explanation by the accused and the court may as a matter of common sense draw the proper inference that the accused is guilty if he fails to give an explanation which he should be in a position to give and that there is such an explanation. A prima facie case here meant a case which is strong enough to go to a jury, a case consisting of direct evidence which, if believed and combined with legitimate inferences based upon it, could lead a properly directed jury to be satisfied beyond reasonable doubt that each of the essential elements of the offence is proved. So the refusal to testify does not of itself indicate guilt and it would be improper to draw an adverse inference just because the defendant does not testify. But in an appropriate case, it would be proper to infer that there is no reasonable possibility of an innocent explanation. Lord Mustill stressed that 'the fact-finder is entitled as a matter of common sense to draw his own conclusions if a defendant who is faced with evidence which does call for an answer fails to come forward and provide it.'[122] However, he did state that that even where the prosecution has established a prima facie case:

> it is not in every situation that an adverse inference can be drawn from silence, the more so because in all but the simplest case the permissible inferences may have to be considered separately in relation to each individual issue. Everything depends on the nature of the issue, the weight of the evidence adduced by the prosecution upon it... and the extent to which the defendant should in the nature of things be able to give his own account of the particular matter in question. It is impossible to generalise, for dependent upon circumstances the failure of the defendant to give evidence may found no inference at all, or one which is for all practical purposes fatal.[123]

Lord Slynn approved Lord Diplock's common sense approach in *Haw Tua Tau v PP*:[124] 'what inferences are proper to be drawn from an accused's refusal to give evidence depend upon the circumstances of the particular case, and is a question to be decided by applying ordinary common sense.'[125] The inferences drawn under Article 4 therefore go to guilt and to credibility. The Northern Ireland Court of Appeal has also said that the court must be satisfied regarding the fitness of the witness to testify before using Article 4.[126]

The common sense approach was also used in *Martin* where the court said that whether inferences are drawn under Article 4 depends upon the circumstances of the particular case and is an issue to be decided by applying ordinary common sense.[127] This case also illustrates the particular problems in interpreting silence in Northern Ireland where there may be a well-established tradition of nonco-operation with the RUC. The case involved Danny Morrison[128] who, when interviewed in Castlereagh, refused to explain his presence at a house where a man was being held against his will and was about to be shot when the RUC rescued him. The reason for his silence, Morrison argued at trial, was that as a Sinn Fein officer he could not speak to the RUC and as publicity officer, he had written pamphlets on police misconduct at Castlereagh and had advised others to remain silent. At trial he admitted being at the house where the man was being held, but said that he did not know the man was being held against his will and had gone to the house to organise a press conference to discuss the man's statement that he had been forced to inform by the RUC. The Lord Chief Justice refused to accept the explanation that he had not answered police questions on principle, and said that on the simple principle of common sense he was entitled to draw adverse inferences from his failure to explain his presence at the house and his silence during interrogation. Reference was made to the CLRC Report on which Article 4 was based.

It has also been successfully argued in a number of trials involving multiple defendants in the province, that article 4 should not be invoked where reluctance to testify may be a result of fear or unwillingness to inculpate a co-defendant.

But as Treacy[129] notes, in the different context of jury trials in England and Wales, the issue will arise of whether a judge *must* caution the jury that there are reasons for silence other than guilt and if so what terms he should use. In effect this means that the problems arising from the 1898 Criminal Evidence Act will not disappear and the wording of the judicial direction is crucial.[130]

The Order was also considered by the European Court of Human Rights in the case of *Murray v UK*.[131] John Murray was charged with conspiracy to murder and aiding and abetting the false imprisonment of an informer and with membership of the IRA. He was cautioned under the Order that adverse inferences might be drawn if he refused to answer questions prior to trial. He was arrested in a house in which a Provisional IRA informer had been held captive. His access to a solicitor was delayed for 48 hours, despite an express wish for access to a lawyer. He was interviewed at Castlereagh 12 times in two days during which he remained silent; he saw a lawyer for the first time before the final two interviews but the solicitor was not permitted to attend the interview. The solicitor advised Murray to remain silent and he was silent during police questioning and at trial. Murray was convicted by a Diplock court for aiding and abetting the false imprisonment of the informer and the trial judge drew strong inferences from his silence in interrogation and at trial and this was upheld by the Court of Appeal.

The issue addressed by the European Court was whether John Murray's denial of his right to silence under the Criminal Evidence Order and the delaying of access to legal advice breached Article 6 of the European Convention of Human Rights, the right to a fair trial and the presumption of innocence.

The comments of the Commission in its report and the Court in its judgment are significant because the case has implications for the interpretation of sections 35 and 37 of the Criminal Justice and Public Order Act. In the particular facts of this case, the Commission decided that Murray had not been denied his right to silence because he did remain silent and did not give evidence against himself but the denial of access to legal advice breached Article 6.

The Commission took account of the fact that the adverse inference was drawn by a judge rather than a jury and a Diplock judge is required to give a reasoned judgement which includes the basis on which he decides to draw adverse inferences and the weight which he gives them. The exercise of his discretion may then be examined on appeal.

The absence of the jury was also stressed by Mr Bratza in his dissenting opinion: a judge is better equipped by his training to draw only the inferences which are justified by the defendant's silence and he gives a reasoned judgement which sets out the grounds on which he decided to draw inferences and the weight given to them and which can be reviewed by the Appeal Court. But these safeguards are missing in a jury trial and the risk of unfairness increased, however carefully the judicial direction to the jury is formulated.

Although the Commission did not find a violation of Article 6 in respect of the right to silence, they stressed that if inferences may be drawn from silence it is crucial that access to legal advice be granted as early as possible, for the decision whether or not to speak may affect what happens at trial. The Commission attached importance to the fact that Murray's access to legal advice was restricted. Prior to *Murray* in cases such as *Quinn*[132] in Northern Ireland the court had drawn adverse inferences even if access to a lawyer was denied. But in *Murray v UK* the Commission and the Court took the view that given that adverse inferences could be drawn under the 1988 Order from the suspect's failure to answer questions by the police or to account for certain facts at the pre-trial stage, then it is essential for the suspect to receive legal advice at an early stage.

The Commission found that in Murray's case his rights of defence 'were adversely affected by the restrictions on his access to a solicitor, and that these restrictions were not in conformity with his right to a fair hearing under Article 6, para.1 and his right to legal assistance under Article 6, para 3(C) of the Convention.'[133]

As the Commission's finding was upheld by the European Court of Human Rights, it would seem that inferences should not be drawn in respect of the pre-trial position where the accused had not had access to a solicitor who was present during the interview.[134] If inferences are drawn or the jury is invited to do so, despite the absence of legal advice, then it would appear to constitute a breach of Article 6 of the European Convention on Human Rights. Murray's right to silence and privilege against self-incrimination were not violated in his case, the Commission found, because he did not speak and did not offer any evidence to incriminate himself, but it accepted that the threat of adverse inferences constituted an indirect pressure to give evidence. However, the majority of the Commission found that the trial had been fair. Fairness depends on an assessment of the circumstances of the case as a whole and the 1988 Order was described as 'a formalised system which aims at allowing common sense implications to play an open role in the assessment of evidence.'[135]

A similar approach was taken by the European Court of Human Rights.[136] In its judgement delivered in 1996 the majority of the Court held that there had been a violation of Article 6(1) of the Convention with regard to the defendant's lack of access to a lawyer for the first 48 hours of his detention. But the Court held that there had been no breach of Article 6 in relation to drawing adverse inferences from silence. The Court did hold that while not specifically mentioned in Article 6 the right to remain silent and the privilege against self-incrimination were generally recognised international standards which lay at the heart of the notion of a fair procedure under the Convention. The Court stressed that it would be incompatible with these immunities to base a conviction solely on the accused's silence or a refusal to answer questions or to testify. But at the same time these immunities did not prevent the accused's silence, in situations which clearly called for an explanation from him, be taken into account in assessing the persuasiveness of the evidence adduced by the prosecution. The right to silence was not absolute. Whether the drawing of adverse inferences from silence infringed Article 6 was a matter to be determined in the light of all the circumstances of the case, having particular regard to the situations where inferences might be drawn, the weight attached to them by the national courts in their assessment of the evidence and the degree of compulsion inherent in the situation.

In Murray's case, he had in fact been able to remain silent in interrogation and at trial despite the warnings given and was a non-compellable witness. Moreover as the national court had already stressed in its decisions,[137] silence in itself could not be seen as an indication of guilt. While there was a certain level of indirect compulsion in the warnings he received, he could not be compelled to speak or to testify. The Court emphasised that the proceedings took place in a Diplock court conducted by an experienced judge and subject to the safeguards under the Order, namely that warnings had to be given before adverse inferences could be drawn and that the prosecution had to establish a prima facie case against the accused.[138]

The question in each case was whether the evidence adduced by the prosecution was sufficiently strong to require an answer. The trial judge could not conclude that a defendant was guilty merely because he chose to remain silent. It was only if the evidence against the accused called for an explanation which he should be in a position to give, that a failure to give any explanation may, as a matter of common sense, allow the drawing of an inference that there is no explanation and that the accused is guilty.[139] But if the prosecution case had so little evidential value that it called for no answer, a failure to provide one could not justify an inference of guilt. Like the House of Lords, the European Court of Human Rights stressed a common sense approach to the drawing of inferences under the Order. Moreover the trial judge retained a discretion not to use the silence provisions against the accused, for example if he did not understand the warning. But in Murray's case, taking account of the weight of the evidence against the accused, the drawing of inferences from his failure to account for his presence was a matter of common sense and could not be regarded as unfair or unreasonable in the circumstances. The Order allowed commonsense implications to play an open role in the assessment of evidence. The Court rejected the claim that drawing inferences had the effect of shifting the burden of proof or denying the presumption of innocence.[140]

But as the attitude of the accused during interrogation had significant consequences, the assistance of a laywer at the earlier stages was demanded by Article 6, although the right might be restricted for good cause. The question was whether the restriction deprived the accused of a fair hearing. Given the choices faced in interrogation under the Order, fairness demanded the assistance of a lawyer at the initial stages of interrogation and delaying access for 48 hours, for whatever reason, was incompatible with the rights of the accused under the Convention. So the majority of the court held that the accused's denial of access to legal advice was a breach of Article 6. The effect of the Court's judgment is likely to lead to a new requirement that access be granted to legal advice during interrogation under the EPA in Northern Ireland. It also has implications for access to legal advice in England and Wales.

This common sense approach also was followed in *Murray v DPP* and *McLernon*.[141] In *Murray*[142] the House of Lords held that as Article 4 closely followed the wording recommended in the CLRC report, it was clear that Parliament intended to remedy the defect which prevented judges from allowing juries to draw common sense inferences from the failure to testify. But common sense runs a risk of introducing unfairness if insufficient weight is given to procedural protection of the defendant, particularly access to legal advice, an issue emphasised by the European Court of Human Rights.[143] Moreover, the common sense inference of guilt may be problematic given the possibility of alternative explanations of silence. While the existence of alternatives has been acknowledged by the courts, the fear is that in a particular case the court or jury may not be aware of the alternative accounts. This also raises the issue of the degree of certainty regarding the reasons for the accused's silence. As Jackson[144] notes this has strong implications for the burden and standard of proof. While not formally shifting the burden of proof, the Order does make it easier for the prosecution to discharge its burden if it is entitled to infer that the reason no explanation is given is because there is no innocent explanation, the point made in *Murray v DPP*. If the jury cannot be sure of the reason for silence, then the best approach would be to draw an inference only when it is already satisfied by the other evidence of guilt beyond reasonable doubt. But in this case then the silence provision becomes redundant. If the jury is convinced of guilt on lesser proof than proof beyond reasonable doubt, then silence is used to supply evidence to bring it up to the required standard of proof and this is problematic because of the questionable evidential status of silence.

As Barra McGrory argues, opening the door to common sense is problematic because:

> ... what may seem common sense to a trial judge is not
> necessarily common sense to someone from a working-class
> background living in a community with a history of mutual
> distrust and dislike of members of the Security Forces and
> members of that community.[145]

The major problem for the courts and legal advisers is the absence of statutory guidance in the 1988 Order on the circumstances in which it is reasonable to draw inferences from silence and what inferences are proper, allowing courts a considerable degree of discretion. The only limit in the Order is that the accused may not be convicted solely on an inference drawn from his silence. When similar changes were considered for England and Wales the Home Office Working Group[146] had proposed statutory guidelines on the factors to consider in deciding whether to draw inferences. Following the common sense approach, formulated in *McLernon*,[147] it seems likely that judges and juries will tend to infer guilt, effectively undermining the presumption of innocence. Under the Criminal Evidence Order and CJPOA pre-trial behaviour during interrogation becomes the central focus of the trial and may be crucial in the determination of guilt.

Furthermore, the individuals most likely to be persuaded to speak by the Criminal Evidence Order may not be sophisticated terrorists or racketeers familiar with interrogation procedures who may wish to speak to establish an alibi, but rather those ignorant of criminal procedure, the ill-educated and ill-informed. The effect of the Order also has particular significance in view of specific features of the Northern Irish dialect and speech patterns in which a question may be answered by rephrasing the question, although tape recording would assist to some extent, in accurately recording the nuances of speech.

Many of the arguments in favour of retention in England and Wales apply *a fortiori* to Northern Ireland in view of the failure to safeguard human rights in the province. Given the complexity of the issues in Northern Ireland originating in long-standing social, economic and political problems, there are limits to what the law can achieve. Repressive measures may fuel further violence. In the past the use of internment increased support for the IRA rather than quenching it. Despite the use of a range of repressive measures over the past twenty years, political violence was not eliminated. The protection of human rights must be a central consideration to ensure respect for human dignity and also to retain legitimacy.

The issue of legitimacy is especially significant in a political context where the army is involved in the policing of a civilian population and where the Catholic minority is under-represented in the police force, partly because the police force is seen as a unionist force. Ninety-three percent of the RUC are Protestant and although efforts are being made to recruit more Catholics only 27 were recruited in 1995. Although within the security forces emphasis is given to the RUC for the primary policing role, with the army being assigned specific tasks, such as border patrols, the accountability of the police and the army to the local community needs to be increased, especially in view of the number of civilian deaths, including children, at the hands of the security forces using rubber and plastic baton rounds, which are still being used. There has been particular concern over the claims of security force collusion in some loyalist killings of civilians, such as Pat Finucane, and the low rate of conviction and prosecution following the use of lethal force.[148] The police complaints procedures and the inquest system have been criticised. Complaints of police misbehaviour are referred to an Independent Commission for Police Complaints and investigated by serving police officers. The Secretary of State has said that the RUC will continue to be responsible for policing Northern Ireland.[149]

Against a background of continuing concern over the abuse of lethal force and the accusations of a shoot to kill policy on the part of the security forces, including Bloody Sunday and the Gibraltar Killings, the abolition of the right to silence has been construed as a further attack on the rights of the individual.

These new pressures to speak during interrogation resulting from the Order mean that the suspect is in effect being persuaded to disclose his defence before trial, before he has heard the full case against him. It poses particular dangers for vulnerable defendants who prefer to remain silent because of fear of reprisals, or of being seen as an informer, or to protect their families. Communities with a history of conflict and distrust of and hostility to the police may well be unwilling to speak during interrogation, despite penalties attached to silence, for reasons other than guilt. In the Justice/CAJ study[150] solicitors reported that some clients would deny anything the police put them because of the fear that any information given, even if unrelated to the offence, would be used by the police for other reasons. The particular problems faced by defendants and witnesses in the context of the Northern Ireland conflict are likely to be exacerbated by the penalties attached to silence. It also opens up the possibility of police or accomplice evidence being shaped to fit that defence and erodes a fundamental right of crucial importance in the context of policing by both the security forces and the civilian police force.

The Order strikes at the heart of the adversarial relationship between the state and the accused, by focusing on the defence's refusal rather than the strength of the prosecution's case and undermines the presumption of innocence. At trial the failure to testify may be used to draw an inference of guilt even where the defendant has spoken to the police. The effect of recent judicial decisions is to shift the burden of proof. Inferences from silence may be used to support the case against the accused at each stage of the process and a conviction can be based on a weak case supported by silence.

The process of giving advice, as in England and Wales, has become more cumbersome and bureaucratic. The role of professional advisers is crucial as they have to consider carefully the situation and advise their clients accordingly and to be particularly cautious in advising silence and to be clear on their reasons for doing so and to record these reasons. The Justice/CAJ[151] study of the operation of the new Order in Northern Ireland showed that solicitors found their position very difficult. It was hard to advise clients without full knowledge of the case against them during the early stage of detention. If they do advise silence they risk adverse inferences being drawn and if they advise clients to speak they are removing their clients' right of silence. If lawyers advise silence they may be called to give evidence which undermines their professional position and lawyer-client privilege. At the trial stage, counsel felt pressured to advise clients to testify even if they were likely to make poor witnesses and respondents thought that the trial process had been changed by the Order. Even if the accused does not testify Article 3 may be used if questions posed by defence counsel in cross-examination of prosecution witnesses raise an innocent explanation.[152] Because of the problems of predicting the interpretation by the judge in a Diplock court, it makes it difficult for lawyers to present the case for the defence or to advise their clients. If the accused does not testify at trial, Article 4 may be used to draw adverse inferences even if the accused made an earlier statement to the police, and despite the possibility of innocent reasons for failing to testify, such as implicating others, the fear of reprisals, the genuine fear of appearing in court and of being cross-examined. In the Justice/CAJ study, lawyers felt that the usual inference in such cases was one of guilt. If he does testify, having failed to answer some or all questions during interrogation, he is unlikely to be believed.

There have been some improvements following the ceasefire as the broadcasting ban was lifted in September 1994, closure orders on border roads have been lifted and many roads reopened, some exclusion orders have been revoked and army patrols have been reduced. The number of troops used in Northern Ireland fell from between August 1994 and February 1996 by about 1,500 but has now returned to pre-ceasefire levels.[153] Tape and video recording of interviews has been strongly recommended by the Independent Commissioner for the Holding Centres[154] and it is hoped that recording in some form will be introduced. The new Criminal Cases Review Commission, whose powers are set out in the Criminal Appeal Act 1995, will cover Northern Ireland as well as England and Wales.

All political parties in Northern Ireland agree on the urgent need for a Bill of Rights, improvements in the criminal justice system and the extension of prisoners' rights. It has been argued by Winter[155] that violations of human rights, contrary to international human rights treaty obligations, are crucial to the conflict. As she argues, these rights violations lie at the root of the Northern Ireland conflict and have deepened it. So a Bill of Rights is essential to a settlement in Northern Ireland although it will not solve all problems. With the resumption of violence since the ceasefire ended in February 1996, the prospect of peace has diminished. Winter argues that the failure to implement reforms and to improve the protection of human rights has damaged the peace process. She cites the retention of emergency laws, the failure to release prisoners and the failure to deal with the use of lethal force.

Notes

1.   (18.1.94) No. 18731/91; [1996] Times, 9 February, Case no 41/1994/488/570.
2.   Schedule 10, para. 61(2).
3.   [1995] Practice Note (Crown Court: Evidence: Advice to Defendant) Times 12 April; [1995] 1 WLR 657; [1995] 2 All ER 499.
4.   Corroboration warnings were abolished in England and Wales by the CJPOA but have not yet been abolished in Northern Ireland.
5.   Articles 2 and 4 came into effect on 21 November 1988, Articles 3, 5 and 6 came into effect on 14 December 1988.
6.   Criminal Law Revision Committee [1972] *Eleventh Report, Evidence (General)* London, HMSO, Cmnd 4991.
7.   J. Jackson [1989] 'Recent developments in criminal evidence', NILQ 105.
8.   J. Winter (1995), 'Human Rights and the Peace Process in Northern Ireland', International Journal of Discrimination and the Law, 1: 1, 63-76.
9.   J. Jackson, *op.cit.*; see also J. Jackson [1994] 'The Right of silence: judicial responses to Parliamentary Encroachment', MLR, 57:2, 270.
10.   J. Jackson (December, 1992) 'The dangers of discretion', Legal Action 8.
11.   *R v McLernon*, Belfast Crown Court, December 20, 1990; C.A., April 1, 1992; [1990] 10 NIJB 91, [1992] 3 NIJB 41.
12.   Report of the Working Group on the Right of Silence (1989) Home Office, C Division, London.
13.   Practice Note [1995] 2 All ER 499.
14.   J. Jackson [1989] 'Recent developments in criminal evidence', NILQ 105.
15.   See Code of Practice C, PACE (Northern Ireland) Order 1989.
16.   *R v Martin*, Belfast Crown Court, May 8, 1991, C.A. July 1992; [1992] 5 NIJB 40.
17.   Guidance to the Chief Constable on the Criminal Evidence (Northern Ireland) Order 1988, p 2.
18.   Fourteenth Report of the Standing Advisory Commission on Human Rights for the Period 1 November 1987 - 31 March 1989, London, HMSO.
19.   The Standing Advisory Commission recommended instead a two-stage caution, beginning with a caution based on the old caution used under

the Judges' Rules, to be followed by a caution reflecting the provisions of the Order after the suspect has been charged and has had access to legal advice.

20.   JUSTICE/Committee on the Administration of Justice (1994) *The Right of Silence Debate: The Northern Ireland Experience*, London.

21.   I. Clare and G. Gudjonsson (1993) *Devising and Piloting an experimental version of the Notice to Detained Persons*, RCCJ Research Study no. 7, London, HMSO.

22.   Before the CJPOA there was a further difference between Northern Ireland and England and Wales regarding the extraction of bodily samples. A mouth swab, which would formerly have constituted an intimate sample in England, was treated as a non-intimate sample in Northern Ireland, which meant that it could be obtained by force and without the suspect's consent if necessary. This anomaly has now been removed by s 54 of the CJPOA which reclassifies samples taken by mouth as non-intimate samples. See chapter 8 below.

23.   PACE Code C 10.4 (1995), HMSO; see chapter 1 above.

24.   B. Hadfield (1990) 'Direct Rule, Delegated Legislation and the Role of Parliament', in J. Hayes and P. O'Higgins (eds.) *Lessons from Northern Ireland*, Belfast, SLS Publications.

25.   SACHR, *op.cit.*

26.   The question has also been raised of whether the use of the Order in Council procedure was ultra virus the powers within the Northern Irish Constitution Act 1773. This would hinge on whether the measure was primarily aimed at terrorists or seen as a matter of general criminal law.

27.   See SACHR, *op.cit.*

28.   The RUC Chief Constable's Annual Report (1987) p xiv.

29.   Reported in Guardian, 21 October 1988; see also AnPhoblacht/Republican News.

30.   T. Gifford (1984) *Supergrasses, the use of accomplice evidence in Northern Ireland*, London, The Cobden Trust.

31.   See J. Jackson (1989) *op.cit.*

32.   Report of the Commission to consider legal procedures to deal with terrorist activities in Northern Ireland [1972] HMSO, Cmnd 5185.

33.   *Ibid*, para. 1.

34.   (1975) Report of a Committee to consider, in the context of civil liberties and human rights, measures to deal with terrorism in Northern Ireland, London, HMSO, Cmnd 5847.

35.   Viscount Colville of Culross QC (1987) Review of the Operation of the Prevention of Terrorism (Temporary Provisions) Act 1984, HMSO, Cmnd 264.

36.   *Ibid*, para. 15.1.4.

37.   Criminal Justice Act 1984, ss 18, 19.

38.   H.C.Off. Report (8 November 1988) Vol. 140 Cols 183-4.
39.   *Ibid*, Vol. 140 Col. 187.
40.   See C. Scorer *et. al.* (1985) *The New Prevention of Terrorism Act - the case for repeal*, London, NCCL. In support of this point reference is made to the Shackleton Report (1978) Review of the Operation of the Prevention of Terrorism (Temporary Provisions) Act, 1974 and 1976, London, HMSO, Cmnd 7324; see also A. Jennings (ed.) *Justice Under Fire* (1990) London, Pluto Press.
41.   See Lord Diplock in *CCSU v Minister for the Civil Service* [1985] AC 374; *R v Secretary of State for the Home Department, ex p Benwell* [1985] 2 QB 554; *Wheeler v Leicester City Council* [1985] AC 1054.
42.   S. Livingstone (1989) 'Policing, Criminal Justice and the Law in Northern Ireland', Conference Paper, King's College, London.
43.   Answer to PQ 3.3.1995, cited in J. Winter (26 June 1995) Human Rights and the Peace Process, Briefing, British Irish Rights Watch.
44.   The Northern Ireland (Emergency Provisions) Act 1987, which amends the 1978 Emergency Provisions Act, reflects the recommendations of the 1984 Baker Report (Review of the Operation of the Northern Ireland (Emergency Provisions) Act 1978, London, HMSO, Cmnd 9222. The new legislation amends the powers of arrest and search, imposing a requirement of reasonable suspicion rather than suspicion. Additional powers were created to combat the use of private security businesses by para-military groups. Provisions regarding proscribed organisations were rationalised.
45.   See B. Dickson (1989) 'The Prevention of Terrorism Act 1989', *NILQ* 40, 250. The 1989 Act contained minor modifications concerning financial assistance to terrorists, the power to investigate terrorist activities, reviews of detention and remission of sentences.
46.   P. Hall (1988) 'The Prevention of Terrorism Acts', in A. Jennings (ed) *Justice Under Fire, The Abuse of Civil Liberties in Northern Ireland*, London, Pluto.
47.   L. Blom-Cooper (1993) Report of the Independent Commissioner for the Holding Centres in Northern Ireland, London, HMSO.
48.   CCPR/C/79/ Add 55, see J. Winter (1995) *op.cit.*
49.   SACHR, Eighteenth Report, 1992-3, London, HMSO.
50.   L. Blom-Cooper (1993) *op.cit.*
51.   *R v Quinn*, C.A. September 17, 1993.
52.   [1996] Times, 9 February.
53.   SACHR (1995) Submission to the United Nations Human Rights Committee.
54.   See J. Winter (1995), *op.cit.*
55.   *Brogan, Coyle, McFadden and Tracey v UK* 11209/84, 11266/84, 11386/85, 9 EHRR 378; 29 Nov. 1988 Series A 154B.

56.   *Ireland v UK* 5310/71 ECHR, Series A, No.25. See also *Fox, Campbell and Hartley v UK*, ECHR May 1989.

57.   [1995] Times 9 October.

58.   [1996] Times, 9 February.

59.   CCPR/C/79/ Add.55

60.   (3.12.91) No. 14544/89.

61.   [1993] Times, 27 May; (26.5.93.) Series A Vol 258-B. 34.

62.   [1994] Independent, 28 February.

63.   [1994] Times, 10 August.

64.   G. Hogan and C. Walker (1989) *Political Violence and the Law in Ireland*, Manchester University Press.

65.   *Ibid.*

66.   C. Walker, C. Gearty et al (1996) *A Hostage to Fortune: Do we need permanent counter-terrorism laws?*, British Irish Rights Watch.

67.   *Ibid.*

68.   Haldane Society (1992) *Upholding the Law? Northern Ireland: Criminal Justice under the Emergency Powers in the 1990s*, London.

69.   Report of the Commission to consider legal procedures to deal with terrorist activities in Northern Ireland (1972) Cmnd 5185, London, HMSO (Diplock Report).

70.   Review of the Operation of the Northern Ireland (Emergency Provisions) Act 1978, (1984) HMSO Cmnd 9222, London, HMSO (Baker Report).

71.   See Schedule 4, Note 1.

72.   [1996] Times, 9 February.

73.   S. Greer and A. White (1986) *Abolishing the Diplock Courts*, The Cobden Trust.

74.   J. Jackson (1995) 'The Value of Jury Trial' in E. Attwooll and D. Goldberg (eds.) *Criminal Justice*, Franz Steiner Stuttgart, pp 79-94.

75.   *Ibid*, pp 87-8.

76.   *Ibid*, p 93.

77.   *Ibid*, p 93.

78.   J.Jackson and S. Doran, (1995) *Judge without Jury: Diplock Trials in the Adversary System*, Oxford University Press, p 389.

79.   *Ibid*, p 294.

80.   *Ibid*, pp 293-4.

81.   D.P.J.Walsh (1983) *The Use and Abuse of Emergency Legislation in Northern Ireland*, London, The Cobden Press.

82.   S. Greer [1987] The Rise and Fall of the Northern Ireland Supergrass System, Crim LR 663.

83.   See s 5A of the Emergency Provisions Act 1987, which substitutes a new s 8 to the Emergency Provisions Act 1978.

84.   See Haldane Report (1992).

85.	The motivation of supergrasses is usually seen as self-interest but McGrady claimed that he volunteered the information to the police following a religious conversion.

86.	S. Greer (1995) *Supergrasses: A Study in Anti-Terrorist Law Enforcement in Northern Ireland*, Oxford, Clarendon Press.

87.	*Ibid*, p vii.

88.	T. Gifford (1984) *Supergrasses, The Use of Accomplice Evidence in Northern Ireland*, London, The Cobden Trust.

89.	*R v Baskerville* [1916] 2 KB 658.

90.	*Davies v DPP* [1954] AC 378.

91.	Bennett, for example, committed perjury during the trial. See *R v Graham* [1983] 7 NIJB 23.

92.	*R v Steenson* [1986] 17 NIJB 36.

93.	S. Greer [1986] Supergrasses and the Legal System in Britain and Northern Ireland, LQR 198; [1987] 'The Rise and Fall of the Northern Ireland Supergrass System', Crim LR 663.

94.	[1984] 18 NIJB 23.

95.	[1986] 14 NIJB.

96.	S.Greer [1987] *op. cit.*

97.	[1984] 18 NIJB 23.

98.	Hansard 8.11.88 col. 189.

99.	Justice/CAJ (1994) *op.cit.*

100.	J. Jackson (1990) 'Recent developments in Northern Ireland' in S. Greer and R. Morgan, *The Right to Silence Debate*, Bristol Centre for Criminal Justice, p 44. He could find only one case during that period where the failure to testify was used to ground an adverse inference against the accused, *R v Gamble and others* [27 October, 1989] unreported judgment of Carswell J.

101.	G.Ruddell (1990) 'A Summary of Recent Judicial Decisions in Northern Ireland', in Greer and Morgan, *op.cit.*, p 53.

102.	*R v Smyth*, Belfast Crown Court, 20 October 1989.

103.	*R v McLernon*, Belfast Crown Court, December 20, 1990; C.A., April 1, 1992; [1992] 3 NIJB 41.

104.	*R v Smyth*, Belfast Crown Court, 20 October 1989.

105.	*R v Neeson, Hill, McIlhone, McKee and Fegan* [2 February 1990] unreported judgment of McCollum J, cited in Ruddell, *op.cit.* See also *R v McGrath* [16 February 1990] BNIL 42.

106.	*R v McLernon*, Belfast Crown Court, December 20, 1990; C.A., April 1, 1992; [1992] 3 NIJB 41.

107.	*Ibid.*

108.	*R v Devine*, C. A. 13 May 1992.

109.	*Ibid.*

110.	*R v Quinn*, C.A. 17 September, 1993.

111. *Ibid.*
112. [1996] Times, 9 February.
113. [December 1993] Belfast Crown Court.
114. See chapter 4 above.
115. *R v McLernon*, Belfast Crown Court, December 20, 1990; C.A., April 1, 1992; [1992] 3 NIJB 41.
116. *Ibid.*
117. *Ibid.*
118. [1994] 1 WLR 1.
119. Criminal Law Revision Committee (1972) *Eleventh Report: Evidence (General)*, London, HMSO, Cmnd 4991.
120. (1993) 97 Cr App Rep 151.
121. [1994] 1 WLR 1.
122. at p 5.
123. at p 5.
124. [1982] AC 136.
125. [1994] 1 WLR 1 at 11.
126. See *Harkin and Gordon*, CA January 16, 1995.
127. *R v Martin*, Belfast Crown Court, May 8 1991, C.A. July 1992, [1992] 5 NIJB 40.
128. *Ibid*; see also J. Barra McGrory, 'The Solicitor's Advice to the Accused in the light of the Criminal Justice and Public Order Act 1994', London, 1994, seminar paper, chambers of Mr. Rock Tansley QC.
129. S. Treacy, 'The Right of Silence and the Courts, including the European Convention on Human Rights', London, 1994, seminar paper, chambers of Mr. Rock Tansley QC.
130. See *R v Cowan, R v Gayle, R v Ricciardi* [1995] 4 All ER 939.
131. 27.6.94 No. 187831/91.
132. *R v Quinn*, C.A. September 17, 1993.
133. para. 73.
134. See Treacy, *op.cit.*
135. 27.6.94 No. 187831/91.
136. [1996] Times, 9 February.
137. See *Murray v DPP* [1994] 1 WLR 1.
138. [1996] Times, 9 February.
139. *Murray v DPP* [1994] 1 WLR 1.
140. [1996] Times, 9 February.
141. *Murray v DPP* [1994] 1 WLR 1; *R v McLernon*, Belfast Crown Court, December 20, 1990; C.A., April 1, 1992; [1992] NIJB 41.
142. *Murray v DPP* [1994] 1 WLR 1.
143. *Murray v DPP* [1994] 1 WLR 1
144. J. Jackson [1995] 'Interpreting the Silence Provisions: The Northern Ireland Cases', Crim LR, 587.

145.   J. Barra McGrory (1994) *op.cit.*

146.   Report of the Working Group on the Right to Silence (1989) Home Office, C Division, London.

147.   *R v McLernon*, Belfast Crown Court, December 20, 1990; C.A., April 1, 1992; [1992] 3 NIJB 41.

148.   There were 348 civilians killed by British Forces in period 1969-1993, and 6 convictions, cited in J. Winter (1996) 'Why the Northern Ireland Peace Process has Failed: The Human Rights Perspective', International Journal of Discrimination and the Law, Vol 2, no. 1, pp 39-51.

149.   Speech, Northern Ireland Police Federation, June 1995.

150.   JUSTICE/CAJ (1994) *op.cit.*

151.   *Ibid.*

152.   *R v Devine*, C. A. May 13, 1992.

153.   See J. Winter (1996) *op. cit.*

154.   See L. Blom-Cooper (1993) *op.cit.*

155.   J. Winter (1995) *op.cit.*; (1996) *op.cit.*

4 The right to silence in modern conditions: the impact of PACE

Critics of the right to silence have argued that the right to silence is anachronistic, by comparing the civilised treatment of the suspect today to the methods used in the seventeenth century by the interrogators of the iniquitous Star Chamber and the High Commission. The bulwark of this argument, in recent debates, has been the specific protections embodied in PACE which are portrayed as tilting the balance in favour of the suspect.

The 'Star Chamber' argument

Defenders of the right to silence have often pointed to the excessive zeal and inhuman methods used by the Star Chamber and High Commission and have argued that it is better to prohibit compulsory questioning than to expose the accused to the risk of such practices. Bentham however, challenged the rejection of compulsory questioning based on its association with these institutions. He considered the issue in his *Rationale of Judicial Evidence*[1] where he was principally concerned with the examination of the accused at trial. The 'Star Chamber' argument takes the form: 'Whatever Titius did was wrong; but this is among the things that Titius did; therefore this is wrong.'[2] But it would be absurd to say that because the Star Chamber sat in a room with the stars in the roof, engaged in terrible actions, that judges should not sit in a room with stars in the roof, or that because the judges in the High Commission court behaved badly, therefore judges should not be appointed by a Commission. Rather than condemning all the procedures of such courts we should be clear where their defects lie, in the end or the means used to achieve them, and to distinguish desirable and undesirable features. What was wrong was that the Star Chamber

105

sought to strengthen the power of the monarch and to weaken Parliament and that the High Commission used its power to coerce men's conscience on matters of religion, rather than the fact that they engaged in questioning and interrogation. Simply putting a question to the accused cannot be equated with, or associated with, an act of torture. Bentham therefore rejects the association of questioning the accused with the 'thumbscrew' as unjustified and illogical:

> No practice could come in worst company, than the practice of putting adverse questions to a party, to a defendant, and in a criminal, a capital case, did in that instance. If however, the practice be itself subservient to the ends of justice, the having been resorted to in company with others of an opposite tendency is a circumstance which, how natural a cause soever for reprobation, can never be a just one.[3]

The right to silence has been seen as anachronistic because in the past such measures were vital to protect the accused from the excesses of torture and inquisition but with modern procedural protections the significance of the right has declined. The Criminal Law Revision Committee, for example, placed great stress on the fact that by the 1970s the balance had swung so far in favour of the defendant that the measures which may have been justified in the past, had now become a hindrance to justice and 'there has been a great deal of feeling in the Committee that the law of evidence should now be less tender to criminals generally.'[4] Similar fears were expressed by the Home Office Working Group in its report[5] and in debates on the CJPOA. Some Chief Constables have also been highly critical of the law of evidence in general and the right to silence, in particular, in impeding police work.

Nonetheless, the continuing need for the privilege has been stressed by defenders of the right to silence who see the threat of inhuman methods, including, but by no means confined to, torture, as an important justification for the right. Although the use of torture in the modern court may be seen as inconceivable, the use of coercive techniques remains. There are numerous ways of pressuring suspects, including inducements, bullying, harrassment and trickery. While falling short of torture, such methods still undermine the dignity of the accused and the legitimacy of the criminal justice system. The privilege against self-incrimination expresses a civilised society's aversion to the coercive methods of persuading an individual to speak against his own interest and may therefore still have a role to play in curbing the over-zealous interrogator. This was stressed in the landmark judgement in *Miranda v Arizona*[6] where the United States Supreme Court responded vigorously to the abuse of police powers. The continuity between past and present abuses is also reflected in the numerous references in American case law, to the historical background to the privilege, demonstrating the continuing awareness of the need for protection within modern liberal democracies as well as under more repressive regimes. The right to silence affirms the existence of a boundary beyond which the state's scrutiny of thoughts and beliefs is prohibited, although efforts are made periodically to move that line, for example, by the construction of inchoate offences such as conspiracy.

If an essential purpose of the right to silence is to compensate for the inequality of resources between prosecution and defence, then it could be argued that the prosecution's resources today are much greater than in the seventeenth century, with the development of a highly organised and professional police force with sophisticated communications and forensic techniques. Scientific advances and the development of computerised intelligence networks have also strengthened the hand of the state against the individual, leading to massive differences between the state and citizen in terms of levels of organisation and resources, including access to sophisticated technology, comprehensive databases and surveillance facilities. Without these facilities, the citizen is much more vulnerable. The private life of the citizen has been subject to intense examination by authoritarian structures creating a 'carceral society'[7] in which more and more areas of life are subjected to scrutiny. Without the restraint of the right to silence, this process would accelerate with the suspect's thoughts, beliefs and ideas, being subject to examination. Although one might argue that forensic science can also benefit the defence, it is only quite recently that the defence has had access to forensic services and even then cost constraints and problems in obtaining legal aid may limit their use. While the zealous investigations of the Star Chamber were primarily directed at members of the aristocracy and higher social classes, most suspects today are from the working class and in a weaker position. Yet the fear of 'abuse' of the right to silence by working class suspects has stimulated demands for its abolition in the twentieth century, even though in practice the majority of suspects have waived their right to silence. The unequal relationship between state and citizen may also be viewed in the wider context of the absence of substantial human rights protection in the United Kingdom, of the use of derogations under Article 15 of the European Convention on Human Rights.[8]

Wigmore[9] has characterised the relationship between the state and the individual as a contest but one which should be governed by fairness, which means that the state should take the weight of the burden and should not obtain the evidence necessary to establish a *prima facie* case from the accused. It should not interfere with the individual by compulsory disclosures without sufficient evidence. For Wigmore the proper rules of battle between the government and individual mean that he should not be recruited by his opponent to defeat himself. Wigmore's reference to battles and wars stands in sharp contrast to the English debate on the right to silence where the assumption of abolitionists seems to be that all parties are, or should be, united in the common cause of crime control.

But is the imbalance between the state and the suspect rectifiable at the trial stage, in a public setting with immediate access to counsel and where the full prosecution case against him has been made out in his presence? For Bentham[10] the publicity of the trial afforded sufficient protection to the defendant. The abolitionist might argue that the right to silence is even more anachronistic here than at the pre-trial stage. But, the position of the defendant is still weaker than that of the prosecutor. The atmosphere of the court has the effect of intimidating the defendant and leading to the status degradation of the accused, so that the defendant is still in a vulnerable position, especially if he is from a lower social class[11] or is vulnerable for other reasons. Even when defending a middle-class client, counsel may decide to advise his client not to testify for tactical reasons as, for example, in the Bodkin Adams case, where the accused was extremely loquacious and it was clear that he would make an unsatisfactory witness.[12] The advice to remain silent at trial was not given lightly but solely because it was anticipated that the negative inferences drawn from silence would be less harmful than the effects of testifying.

The impact of the Police and Criminal Evidence Act 1984

The argument that the right to silence is anachronistic has received a new lease of life with the enactment of the Police and Criminal Evidence Act in 1984, which some have seen as rendering the right to silence superfluous. The balance of power between prosecution and defendant has shifted in favour of the defendant, it is argued, so the right to silence may be safely jettisoned. This argument focuses primarily on the pre-trial stage. The safeguards afforded to the accused during interrogation, by the PACE Codes of Practice, are often used to underpin the claim that the right to silence is expendable. They were issued under s 66 of the Police and Criminal Evidence Act 1984, which came into force on 31st December 1985 and subsequently have been amended. The Codes cover the detention, treatment and questioning of suspects by police officers and include access to legal advice, time limits and conditions in which individuals may be questioned. Special provision is made for vulnerable groups such as people with learning disabilities and juveniles.[13] Under the Judges' Rules insufficient consideration was given to these suspects,[14] but PACE has improved the position of juveniles and suspects with learning disabilities.[15]

Breaches of the Codes may be taken into account if the court thinks that they are relevant to any question arising in the proceedings.[16] Evidence obtained where breaches of the Codes of Practice have occurred may be excluded under the court's exclusionary discretion under s 78(1) of PACE:

> In any proceedings the court may refuse to allow evidence on which the prosecution proposes to rely to be given if it appears to the court that, having regard to all the circumstances, including the circumstances in which the evidence was obtained, the admission of the evidence would have such an

adverse effect on the fairness of the proceedings that the court ought not to admit it.

This could be seen as broader than the common law discretion to exclude and it encompasses a wider range of behaviour than that envisaged by s 76.[17] Section 78 has been used robustly by the Court in a number of cases.[18] Provisions relating to the exclusion and admissibility of confessions obtained in circumstances of oppressive, inhuman or degrading treatment, or in circumstances which are likely to render them unreliable, may be found in s 76 of PACE. But the court's common law discretion to exclude evidence is preserved in s 82(3) of PACE:

> Nothing in this Part of the Act shall prejudice any power of a court to exclude evidence (whether by preventing questions from being put or otherwise) at its discretion.

This section is designed to exclude confessions obtained by unfair or improper methods which would otherwise be admissible.

A further significant step towards controlling police behaviour during interrogation was provided by the tape recording of interviews. Tape recording was used initially on an experimental basis in selected stations, and was extended to all police stations on January 1, 1992. A Code of Practice issued in pursuance of the duty placed on the Home Secretary under s 60(1)(b) of PACE sets out the procedures for tape recording interviews with suspects. The master tape is to be sealed in the presence of the suspect.[19] Tape recording is to be used when interviewing a person cautioned of an indictable offence, including an offence triable either way, or where further questioning takes place following charging a suspect or informing him that he may be prosecuted, or where in such circumstances, the suspect is confronted with a written statement made by another person or the contents of an interview with another person.[20] If the machine is switched off, then he should be cautioned again before resuming the interview.[21]

Willis[22] found only one challenge by the defence to the police evidence, during the two-year period of the trials, which examined 6 districts involving 20,000 suspects and 45,000 tapes. The use of tape recording also led to more charges, more information about other offences and more confessions. It has encouraged greater spontaneity in interviews and enables juries to hear the precise questions, answers and silences. If adverse inferences are to be drawn from a defendant's silence during interrogation, then clearly a reliable account of what occurs in interrogation is essential. The use of tapes, it is argued, approximates the private context of the police station more closely to the public setting of the trial. The CLRC, while acknowledging the concern of some of its members over the dangers of police brutality and oppression during interrogation owing to the presence of a 'small number of black sheep',[23] expressed confidence in the use of tapes to prevent the fabrication of confessions, combined with exclusionary rules to exclude confessions improperly obtained. The Royal Commission on Criminal Justice saw the answer to police malpractice as improved police disciplinary procedures, better training and dealing firmly and quickly with perpetrators and better supervision of police work.[24] The Commission thought that the safeguards in PACE against false confessions were basically sound, but not foolproof, as the Cardiff Three case occurred after the Act and Codes were in force.

The PACE provisions and Codes according to Williamson and Moston[25] have led to a strengthened spirit of professionalism in the conduct of interrogation which means that interviewing techniques are less confrontational. They point to various factors which may further this sense of professionalism, including the development of skills training and ethical awareness, stricter supervision and increased resources.[26]

For abolitionists PACE has removed the need for the right to silence as suspects are now sufficiently well protected and have improved access to legal advice and legal aid. It is also argued that the duty solicitor scheme, now in operation, offers further protection of the suspect and reduces the risk of police impropriety. Others have suggested building on the safeguards in PACE and boosting other disciplinary measures, to compensate for the loss of the right to silence.[27]

The question of whether the Police and Criminal Evidence Act has tilted the relationship between the state and the individual, in favour of either the accused or the prosecution, is crucial to the debate on the right to silence. Critics of the right to silence see the impact of PACE benefitting the accused in terms of access to legal advice and verification of interviews, diminishing or removing the need for the right to silence during police interrogation. But defenders of the right to silence argue against this, that the Act rests on the right to silence and without it, the PACE provisions will be less effective. Furthermore, the safeguards in the Act and the Codes may be insufficient to protect the suspect. McConville, Sanders and Leng[28] argue that the effect of police strategies and tactics is to maintain the position prior to PACE. So formal rights and protections may be evaded by informal rules and practices. This is significant when we consider that some of the problems in the miscarriages of justice began very early on in the criminal justice process: suspects had been arrested and detained on weak grounds but still were convicted. The enactment of PACE was intended to strengthen public confidence in the police, which crime surveys showed was very low,[29] as well as offering substantial protection to the suspect. However, the increasing evidence of police malpractice as a factor in miscarriages of justice has undermined the confidence which might have accrued from PACE. Some of the worst instances have occurred where PACE has been in place, or because the suspects were interrogated under the Prevention of Terrorism Act, rather than under PACE. PACE cannot protect those highly suggestible suspects who run the risk of making false confessions.[30]

These arguments will be evaluated with reference to empirical research on the impact of the Act as well as the courts' treatment of breaches of the Act and Codes. Factors to be considered here include the access to legal advice, the recording of interviews, informal interviews, the courts' use of its exclusionary discretion to deal with breaches of the PACE Codes and the police complaints system.

Access to legal advice

While PACE does mean that there is greater access to legal advice than previously, the number of suspects receiving advice is still very low, although it has increased since 1991. The majority of suspects are subject to the additional powers endowed on the police by PACE without the benefit of legal advice. The Codes of Practice were revised in 1991 and 1995. The 1991 revisions included amendments to the Code of Questioning, including changes relating to the notification of the right to legal advice and procedures for verifying interview records. Under the revised Code suspects are required to be told that the legal advice to which they are entitled is free of charge, as suspects otherwise may be deterred from exercising their right if they are worried about the cost. The suspect is advised that his right to a solicitor is a continuing one so that if he does not exercise it at the point when he is informed of it, he may do so at any time while in custody. The notification of the right to a solicitor should ideally be given at the earliest possible opportunity and immediately before commencement of the interview and a prominent notice should also be displayed pointing to this right. If a solicitor has already been called for him by a third party he should be told and asked whether he wishes to speak to him.

While these changes are desirable, enforcement is difficult to guarantee and they do not remove the need for the right to silence. The right should not depend on the presence of a solicitor as one purpose of seeking legal advice might be precisely to ascertain whether or not to exercise the right.

When PACE was being enacted, there was an opportunity to consider the virtues of changes to the right, especially in the light of the research of the Royal Commission on Criminal Procedure, but the Commission made it very clear that it did not favour any changes in the right to silence at the pre-trial or trial stage. The protection of the citizen was an essential principle of the Commission's report, which emphasised the vulnerability of the suspect during interrogation:

> He is unlikely to be properly aware of the legal intricacies of
> the situation, to understand, for example, the legal concept of
> intent or the application of the laws of evidence in his case, or

the full implications or the desirability of exercising his right to silence.[31]

The Commission therefore was concerned to enhance access to legal advice and to develop strategies to discourage improper police practices. It approached the problem by seeking to strike the right balance between police powers and individual rights, given that police powers are so much greater than those of individual citizens. But this balancing approach may be problematic as rights cannot simply be put into the equation in this way, but demand a special protected status. Yet so soon after the passing of PACE, its provisions were used as a springboard from which to launch an attack on the right to silence.

Although in recent years there has been improved access to legal advice with the development of the duty solicitor scheme and increased legal aid, interrogation at the police station which may produce fear and disorientation. There has also been criticism of the quality of legal advice at the police station which has been given by untrained and unqualified representatives. The Royal Commission on Criminal Justice stressed the need to improve the quality of legal advice and favoured a review of training methods.[32]

Empirical studies have confirmed the gulf between the formal 'right' of speedy access to a solicitor and reality. Before the PACE Codes were revised only 20% of suspects received legal advice during interrogation. What the research both before and after the enactment of PACE has shown, is that, for a variety of reasons, most suspects undergoing interrogation do not have a solicitor present. There may be variations between police stations and there is nothing in the PACE Codes to guarantee uniformity in the implementation of rights.

Maguire[33] conducted a preliminary study of detention and questioning immediately after PACE came into force. He found that only a small proportion of suspects asked for a solicitor or actually saw one. Although he thought that informing suspects of the right to legal advice had improved substantially, he was sceptical whether the majority of detained suspects would ask for a solicitor even if legal advice were easily available. He also found that juveniles spent longer in detention than adults, because of the time spent in waiting for an 'appropriate adult' to arrive.

Sanders'[34] study of 10 police stations found that police techniques tended to discourage access to a solicitor, by suggesting that waiting for a solicitor would mean more time spent at the police station. Often the advice received from legal advisers was of poor quality: over half of the cases in his study involved non-qualified representatives. In one quarter of cases advice was given over the telephone; telephone advice was more likely to be given by duty solicitors than the clients' own solicitors, but the latter were more likely to use representatives to attend rather than attending themselves.[35] Baldwin found that in two-thirds of the cases in his sample the legal adviser did not speak during the interview.[36] He described how the police take charge of the interview which is on their territory, treating lawyers with suspicion and tolerating them only if they were passive: 'Advising clients not to answer questions or intervening at interviews are not seen by the police as reasonable forms of behaviour. It is only if they toe the line that lawyers are regarded as acceptable participants at police interviews.'[37]

McConville and Hodgson[38] conducted fieldwork over a period of 3 years from 1988-1991, studying the practices of 22 firms of defence solicitors from all over England. They attended the police station, examined files, sat in on interrogations and meetings with counsel and conducted formal and informal interviews. They considered all stages including police station advice and trial. In addition to the main sample of 22 firms, they also undertook research for the Royal Commission on Criminal Justice, examining a further 26 firms intensively over a three-week period in 1992.[39]

On the basis of their research, they were very critical of the poor quality of advice as some solicitors' representatives lacked the required legal knowledge, some left before the interview or gave advice only by telephone. There was a heavy reliance on non-qualified representatives. Seventy-five percent of the firms they studied over the three-year period used non-qualified advisers, many of whom were former police officers and the level of training was inadequate. Interrogations were strongly controlled by the police with the adviser remaining passive.[40] In their study for the Royal Commission 47% of firms employed former police officers for police station advice work which meant that the advisers tended to identify with the police rather than the suspect.[41] In the light of their findings, McConville and Hodgson strongly recommend retention and strengthening of the right to silence.

They found many examples of incompetent representation, particularly at the police station, failures to object to police bullying in interviews, pressuring clients to plead guilty and the use of unsupervised and unqualified staff to advise clients. They focused on the criminal defence culture which emphasises the efficient processing of guilty pleas. Advisers rarely advised suspects to remain silent. In some cases silence was advised because the adviser was uncertain regarding the law, or criminal procedure or because insufficient information had been given by the police.[42]

The passivity of some defence lawyers was criticised by the Court of Appeal in *Glaves*.[43] The Court said that the solicitor should interfere if police questioning went too far. There is no point in a solicitor's representative just going along and simply taking notes. In *Miller*[44] Lord Taylor emphasised that the solicitor advising his client in interview should act courageously and criticised Miller's solicitor for sitting passively through an interview which was being improperly conducted. Defence lawyers have been criticised in several of the miscarriage of justice cases which arose both before and after PACE.[45] Because the Court of Appeal has also in some cases[46] treated the presence of a lawyer as sufficient to counterbalance minor breaches of the code, it is all the more important that the lawyer is active when actually in attendance, especially if he is representing vulnerable individuals. If he does not intervene at the time a breach occurs then he is less likely to succeed later in excluding evidence obtained as a result of the breach. He should challenge improper questioning, or any threatening behaviour or breaches of the codes and be prepared to interrupt questioning to advise his client.

Since the revision of the PACE Codes in 1991 which enhanced the information given to suspects regarding their right to legal advice, there does appear to have been an increase in the number of suspects requesting legal advice from 24% to 32% according to Brown, Ellis and Larcombe.[47] This probably reflects the fact that it is now made clear the legal advice is free. However, it still means that a substantial number of suspects do not avail themselves of this right. They found that the rates varied considerably between police stations. In some stations telephone advice was the norm, attendance at the police station being the exception, and suspects who used the telephone to seek advice did so with no privacy and with some difficulty, in noisy conditions. Even where advisers did attend the police station they were not necessarily present during interviews. There were frequent failures by custody officers to give information on the right to legal advice in accordance with the revised codes, for example that the advice was free and independent. These deficiences are attributed to the fact that familiar tasks become routinised rather than a deliberate design to deny suspects their rights. They did find a decline in the frequency with which suspects were questioned outside the police station and improvements in the appropriate adult provision. However, the decision on seeking advice was delayed for juveniles while waiting for appropriate adults to arrive.

Nonetheless there has been some progress. When the CJPOA was enacted it was predicted that it would necessitate an increase in the demand for lawyers at the police station and for advisers to be present during interviews. The early indications are that this has occurred. 660,000 suspects received legal advice under the duty solicitor scheme in 1995.[48] Seventy-seven percent of the advice given was given at the police station and the remainder by telephone. Efforts have been made to improve the training and monitoring of legal advisers at the police station by the new system of accreditation. However, many suspects when cautioned under the 1995 PACE Codes, and warned of the adverse effects of his silence, may well be reaching a decision on whether or not to speak alone, in isolation and possibly ignorant of the real meaning of his rights or the caution. The decision may have far-reaching effects on the outcome of the case even though it may be taken before he is fully aware of the case against him. Even if a solicitor is present, it will often be difficult to determine the best course of action and as we have noted, the quality of advice may be unsatisfactory.

A new training kit has been designed for the Law Society and a new accreditation scheme for unqualified legal advisers, imposing strict tests and procedures, has been introduced. Since February 1 1995 the Legal Aid Board will not pay for advice given by police station advisers who have not been accredited under the new scheme. Training involves submitting a satisfactory portfolio and passing a written examination on criminal law and procedure and demonstrating skills in dealing with a range of different situations which may arise in the context of giving advice.

A skills book 'Becoming Skilled' was published by the Law Society, as part of the effort to improve the quality of advice. But Bridges and Hodgson[49] are critical of this guidance given on the exercise of the right to silence because, they argue, it anticipates that the changes in the CJPOA would make little difference to the advice given. It suggests advising silence where police questioning is inappropriate or when the adviser is unsure of the relevant law. The amount of information and guidance for unqualified advisers and use of psychological language may be confusing and over-estimates the amount of time advisers are able to spend giving advice or in discussion with custody officers.

Fenwick[50] argues that the role of the adviser in the police station will be changed as a result of the changes in the CJPOA. The adviser is unlikely to advise silence in future in many circumstances in which it might have been advised before the Act. However, there will still be contexts in which silence in response to a particular question might be advised despite the risk of adverse comment in court, where the disadvantages of speaking outweigh the risk of remaining silent, for example if the suspect is confused or distressed. Also silence might be advised on matters which fall outside the situations covered by sectionss 34, 36 and 37. Although she prefers the term curtailment to abolition because the common law right to silence will survive where it is not expressly limited by the Act, nonetheless the impact of the Act is to increase substantially the pressure on the accused to speak. The position still remains after the CJPOA that access to a solicitor cannot be delayed on the ground that the solicitor might counsel silence.[51] If the solicitor advises a client not to answer a particular question, this would not constitute obstructing the interview.[52]

From the police standpoint, because silence now has evidential significance the police will need to plan interviews more thoroughly and to be very specific regarding the content of the questions, so that it is quite clear which questions the suspect is refusing to answer, and to ask questions as neutrally as possible, so the suspect cannot say that the hostile manner in which the question was asked was the reason for refusing to answer. Conducting the interview in strict accordance with the Codes and in a proper manner will mean that all responses to the questions can be put in evidence.

The recording of interviews

The introduction of tape recording has been a key argument in the case against the right to silence. The Royal Commission on Criminal Justice noted the benefits of tape recording but stressed that:

Tape recording of interviews by itself is not a sufficient safeguard for those in police custody. It needs to be supplemented by the provision of adequate legal advice, protection against oppressive treatment both before and after the interview, and medical treatment or independent assistance from an appropriate adult where called for. The role of the custody officer is the key to most of this, but custody officers cannot by themselves guarantee it. Suitably competent legal advisers, appropriate adults, police surgeons, and interpreters must be available.[53]

In any case, the requirement to record the interview is waived in certain circumstances. Tape recording is not compulsory in interviews of people arrested under the Prevention of Terrorism Act or suspected of offences under the Official Secrets Act.[54] If, during the course of an interview with a suspect, it becomes clear that he may have been involved in terrorist offences or offences under the Official Secrets Act, then at that point the machine should be switched off.[55] However in practice in England and Wales interviews with terrorist suspects are tape recorded but not in Northern Ireland.[56] Further exceptions include where it is not 'reasonably practicable to do so because of the failure of the equipment or the non-availability of a suitable interview room or recorder.'[57] Strategic editing of tape recordings also becomes more feasible with technical advances. There may also be legitimate breaks in recording for technical reasons or because of interruptions. It is precisely the threats or inducements, which recording is designed to deter, which are least likely to be recorded. The Code does issue instructions on changing tapes and dealing with breaks during interviews, for example, recording the reason for the break.

Transcripts, rather than the original recordings, may be used at trial which may well distort the questions and responses, by obliterating variations in the tone or speed of the interview and transcripts may be edited. Peirce[58] points out that the use of tape recording means that interviews proceed at a much faster pace which increases pressure on defendants.

Although the failure to record, which is not justified by the Code, may be the subject of comment in court, incriminating statements would not automatically be excluded, although it is open to the Court to exclude such statements under s 78 on grounds of fairness, or under its general exclusionary discretion retained in s 82. But is unlikely that a statement would be seen as inherently unfair or that its prejudicial value would be seen as outweighed by its probative value simply because it is unrecorded.[59]

While tape recording may contribute to a reduction of abuse and of allegations of abuse, it may only displace the problems of pressure outside the police interview. In *Maguire*[60] it was held that the PACE Codes did not prohibit the police from asking questions at the scene of the crime and that the resulting admissions were admissible even though they were made by a juvenile without an appropriate adult present. Many cases of police misbehaviour after PACE have been revealed. In *Paris, Abdullah and Miller*[61] hectoring and bullying occurred despite the fact that the interview was being recorded. Although this meant that the Court of Appeal was able to hear what went on, the fact of recording apparently did not deter improper questioning.

The value of tape recording as a shield for suspects against fabricated admissions therefore should not be over-estimated. Questioning may still take place prior to interrogation at the police station, generating arguments over what was said or why the suspect made certain statements. The extension of tape recordings to cover questioning outside the police station has been resisted on grounds of costs and practicability, but these arguments are less compelling technological advances now that allow for increasing portability and reduced costs. The fact that tape recording occurs during interrogation does not mean that interviewing will cease before arrival at the police station. Now that silence has increased evidential significance there will be more arguments about the questions which elicited silence and the fabrication of questions.

Tape recording does not remove the need for the right to silence. When PACE was enacted it was intended that tape recording should be used alongside the right to silence rather than instead of it. The Royal Commission on Criminal Procedure expected tape recording to be used in conjunction with, rather than as a means of replacing the right to silence.

Willis[62] found that in two of the field trial areas in her study there was a significant increase in the number of confessions obtained for taped cases and in the amount of information obtained about other offences. The number of suspects charged in two areas also increased after the introduction of tape recording and there were fewer challenges to police evidence. This suggests that police efficiency in processing suspects has increased rather than declined in recent years, in terms of the quantity and quality of information obtained. This raises the question of whether a further increase in the armoury of the prosecution, namely abolishing the right to silence, was necessary.

Ideally to capture the demeanour and tone of interviews accurately video recordings would be preferable to either tapes or transcripts. The use of video recording in police stations was supported by Baldwin's research.[63] He studied 400 videotaped interviews in 4 police stations between October 1989 and November 1990. He concluded that provided nothing improper happens off camera, false allegations of corruption are discouraged by video recording. Video recording can benefit the police as well as suspects. Abuse is more likely to be revealed and it provides the best way for third parties to determine subsequently whether interviews have been conducted fairly. Although he found some minor problems with the new method, not least the problem of mechanical failures, he felt that they could be overcome. The best pictures were provided where the suspect alone was filmed and the interviewer excluded; if the whole scene was filmed, it was harder to capture changes of expression. He also compared video and audio recording. Although in about 80% of the interviews he considered, audio recording was adequate to record the interview in the remaining 20% of cases video recording was useful, and in some cases crucial, in giving the court a full picture of the defendant's responses and in allowing it the opportunity to assess the propriety of the interview procedures.

McConville[64] considers whether using video recording would provide greater protection to suspects and officers and end disputes over the admissibility of interrogation evidence. Based on an experimental study of the use of video recordings over a five-week period in 1991, his research considered the behaviour of officers on and off camera. Video recording is widely seen as better than audio recording because the demeanour of the suspect may be observed and this increases confidence in the reliability of statements made during interrogation. But the video and custody record do not make clear what occurred prior to interrogation. Offical interrogation records do not not necessarily provide a reliable account of police interrogation practices. As he says: 'The value of the video recording as an "accurate and objective record" is sustainable only on the basis that it produces as nearly faithfully as possible what is recorded. The judgment is not sustainable if what is recorded has been affected by exchanges which preceded it. Positive judgements about the reliability of video recordings are usually based on the premise that no such unseen pre-interrrogation exchanges have occurred.'[65] As greater control is exercised over the conduct of the formal interview and better methods of recording are introduced, however, this may increase the pressure on the police to conduct informal interviews.

If the official recording is preceded by unethical or improper treatment of suspects this will not be clear in the recording and the fact that video recordings are so persuasive makes them dangerous for suspects. Precisely because members of the jury see the video tape they may be inclined to take it at face value and place too much weight on the demeanour of the suspect. He is also critical of the claim that the police are opening up their internal methods and procedures to outsiders. McConville argues that the system of supervision and accountability has not penetrated police working practices and relationships. While video recording is now covered by the revised PACE Codes, there still remains the problem of interviews which are not recorded but which may influence or exert pressure on the accused.

This was recognised by the Runciman Commission who stressed that advanced electronic recording will not solve all the problems of safeguarding the suspect.[66] The Commission expressed some reservations over the use of video recordings. While it may be advantageous to see the demeanour of the suspect, in some cases the suspect could be prejudiced if symptoms of anxiety or nervousness in interrogation are misread as signs of guilt. The Commission proposed further research on the use of video recording. It was more positive about the use of video recording in custody suites and proposed video recording of the custody office and the passage to the cells,[67] and of suspects being asked their reasons for waiving their right to see a solicitor. It also recommended giving suspects the chance to comment on any alleged untaped admissions during the tape recorded interview. The Commission also saw video taping of interrogations as providing a useful aid to police training.

The Home Office[68] has examined the costs of using video recording more widely and suggested confining it initially to more serious cases, but leaving it to the discretion to officers. If the suspect objects to being video recorded this would be respected. The Association of Chief Police Officers[69] has also supported video recording of interviews.

Informal interviews

The PACE Codes were intended to reduce the number of informal interviews. Once the decision has been made to arrest a suspect, interviews outside the police station are prohibited. An interview is defined in the 1995 PACE Code as 'the questioning of a person regarding his involvement or suspected involvement in a criminal offence or offences which, by virtue of paragraph 10.1 of Code C, is required to be carried out under caution.'[70] A single question and answer can constitute an interview if the question relates directly to the crime for which the suspect is arrested.[71] However, various exceptions are permitted in paragraph 11.1 which states that following a decision to arrest a suspect, he must not be interviewed about the relevant offence except at a police station unless the delay would lead to interference with evidence or harm to others, alert others suspected of having committed an offence or hinder the recovery of stolen property. So there are still circumstances in which interviews may be conducted outside the police station.

Wolchover and Heaton-Armstrong[72] argue that since PACE came into force the use of informal interviews has increased considerably. The research undertaken by Moston and Stephenson[73] for the Royal Commission on Criminal Justice of three police forces found that the arresting officers at the police stations being studied acknowledged that they had interviewed suspects before arriving at the police station in 8% of the cases in the sample, while 31% of the 641 suspects said they had been questioned before their arrival at the police station. These interviews were conducted mostly in the police car or at the crime scene and in a large number of these cases suspects made admissions. In many cases no records were kept and where they were kept, were inadequate.[74]

Moston and Stephenson recommend the use of portable tape recorders to ensure that informal interviews are properly recorded although, as they point out, there is the danger that their use will serve to legitimise these interviews. Brown, Ellis and Larcombe[75] found that questioning outside the police station occurred in 10%

of the cases they studied. It is outside the formal interview that the individual may be most vulnerable to false confessions, because of the absence of a solicitor. So an automatic exclusion of comments outside the formal interview might be preferable.

The Runciman Commission[76] recommended that when a confession has allegedly been made outside the police station the suspect should be invited to comment on it at the beginning of the interview at the police station and after he has consulted his solicitor,[77] and this is incorporated in Code E 4.3B. The new verification requirement in the revised Codes requires the police to show the suspect written records of comments made outside the context of an interview which might be relevant to the offence, even if those comments were unsolicited. Following the CJPOA the PACE Codes were amended so that at the beginning of the interview, when the accused is informed of his rights:

> The police officer shall then put to the suspect any significant statement or silence (i.e. failure or refusal to answer a question or to answer it satisfactorily) which occurred before the start of the tape-recorded interview, and shall ask him whether he confirms or denies that earlier statement or silence or whether he wishes to add anything. A 'significant' statement or silence means one which appears capable of being used in evidence against the suspect, in particular a direct admission of guilt, or failure or refusal to answer a question or to answer it satisfactorily, which might give rise to an inference under Part III of the Criminal Justice and Public Order Act 1994.[78]

This revision also reflects the approach of the Court of Appeal in *Matthews*[79] where the court held that if the police had discussed the alleged offence with the suspect this would constitute an interview, regardless of who had begun the discussion and the suspect should be shown a copy of notes taken by the officer. The Royal Commission also suggested that the police could carry portable tape recorders to record comments made by suspects before arrival.

There is no specific exclusionary rule to clearly exclude questions and silences prior to taping. It is a matter for the court's discretion whether to exclude informal interviews and one cannot always predict whether such interviews will be excluded.

Breaches of the Codes: the use of the courts' exclusionary discretion

Breaches of the PACE Codes need to be serious and substantial for evidence obtained therein to be excluded under s 78.[80] The court can take into account the revised codes in considering breaches of the earlier codes even though they were not in force when an offence was committed.[81] Minor breaches are unlikely to lead to the exclusion of evidence, particularly if a lawyer is present or the defendant is familiar with interrogation procedures.[82] Even if evidence is obtained in the absence of a solicitor it may still be admitted. In *Alladice*,[83] for example, although the police had breached s 58, the evidence obtained in the absence of a solicitor was still admitted by the trial judge. This was upheld by the Court of Appeal. But even if the solicitor had been present at Alladice's interview, said the Lord Chief Justice, his advice:

> would have added nothing to the knowledge of his rights which the appellant already had. The police, as the judge found, had acted with propriety at the interviews and therefore the solicitor's presence would not have improved the appellant's case in that respect.[84]

The denial of the right to see a solicitor would not *per se* guarantee exclusion as an extra dimension is needed, such as bad faith, and the extent to which the fairness of the trial is affected. Although the request to see a solicitor had been refused in *Alladice*, the confession was admitted. The Court of Appeal also took the opportunity to stress the need for 'proper comment' where a detainee was silent and said that the effect of s 58 meant that the balance of fairness between prosecution and defence could not be maintained without such comment. Here the dilution of the right to silence seems to be viewed as a *quid pro quo* for the enforcement of rights under s 58.[85] In *Anderson*[86] the Court of Appeal expressed reluctance to interfere with the discretion of a trial judge who admitted a confession despite a breach of s 58, because even if a solicitor had been present and had advised silence, it was unlikely the accused would have followed such advice. But in *Joseph*[87] the Court of Appeal allowed Joseph's appeal against conviction on the basis of an alleged admission made during an interview at his parent's house, because he had not been told he was under arrest, or that he could get legal advice and no contemporaneous note had been made, breaching paragraphs 10.2 and 10.5 of Code C. Evidence will not be excluded just because the suspect has been wrongfully denied legal advice or to 'punish the police'.[88]

The court's commitment to enforcing the right to legal advice has wavered. For example, in *Samuel*[89] it was argued that the suspect would not have spoken had he received legal advice. Samuel had been arrested on suspicion of robbery and burglary. He requested access to a solicitor, but the police refused because they thought other suspects would be alerted. Under s 58(8) of PACE access may be delayed, for a limited period, if exercise of the right to legal advice would result in interference with evidence, harm to others, or alert others involved in the offence. To deny the accused access to a particular solicitor, the officer must have reasonable grounds to believe that it is very probable that the solicitor will, if permitted to consult with his client, interfere with the course of justice, commit a criminal offence or inadvertently do something which would have this effect. The Court of Appeal in *Samuel* stressed that this is likely to occur only in very rare cases and there needed to be a very high probability that the solicitor would alert other suspects either deliberately or inadvertently and it would not be easy for the police to establish this. The court also said that if the motive for delaying access in Samuel's case, was that the solicitor was likely to advise his client to remain silent, this was not a sufficient justification to deny access. Annex B to the Code of Practice, to which the court referred, states that 'access to a solicitor may not be delayed on the grounds that he might advise the person not to answer any questions...'.[90] The court exercised its exclusionary discretion under s 78 because Samuel 'was denied improperly one of the most important and fundamental rights of the citizen'.[91] It was clear that the solicitor, if present, would have advised his client to remain silent and Samuel would not have confessed. The court said that access to a solicitor was a 'fundamental right' of the accused and it would not be sufficient to deny access just because to do so might lead to other suspects being alerted. The court is likely to consider the vulnerability of the accused, whether he is experienced and whether he is likely to have spoken and whether the police have acted in good or bad faith. However, in *Walsh*[92] the Court of Appeal said that significant and substantial breaches would not be negated by the good faith of the police.

When PACE was enacted it was widely expected that s 78 would have little impact and that the discretion would be rarely exercised in favour of the defendant. The decision in *Samuel* and similar cases[93] rebutted this expectation, but precisely because exclusion here is discretionary, this trend is reversible and the outcome will be uncertain in any particular case. The breach of s 58 was seen as insufficient to justify exclusion in *Alladice*.[94] But in *Chung*[95] the appellant was questioned before being allowed access to a solicitor, his admission was not recorded immediately and when a note was made of it, it was not shown to him and the solicitor was not advised of the existence of the note. His confession was deemed unreliable under s 76(2)(b) and also inadmissible under s 78, following *Absolam*[96] where the Court of Appeal said that an interview should be interpreted to mean all questioning designed to elicit an admission on which criminal proceedings could be founded.

In *Dunn*[97] the defendant denied making a confession, which was allegedly made after a formal interview, during the signing of the interview notes. The conversation in which the confession was made was not recorded contemporaneously and no record of it was shown to Dunn. Yet the Court of Appeal held the evidence to be admissible, notwithstanding these breaches, because a solicitor's clerk had been present. It was deemed that her presence would discourage the police from fabricating evidence and she would be able to protect Dunn's interests. In *Dunford*[98] the appellant was unlawfully denied access to a solicitor but the Court of Appeal said that his initial refusal to answer police questions and his previous criminal experience meant that it was unlikely that receiving the advice of a solicitor would have added anything to his knowledge of his rights.

Exclusions under s 78 thus have developed in an ad hoc way. While the Court of Appeal has resisted being tied by specific principles, the reliability, protective, disciplinary and legitimacy principles may be found in particular cases.[99] The predominant criterion for exclusion has been significant and substantial breaches of PACE and the accompanying Codes, including access to legal advice,[100] failure to caution,[101] failure to follow proper identification procedures,[102] failure to observe requirements for interviewing suspects,[103] including the provision of an appropriate adult[104] and evidence obtained by police deception.[105] But we can also find cases in which evidence has been admitted despite such breaches.[106] The Court of Appeal has resisted the formulation of clear guidelines, preferring to consider each case on its own facts. But if the breach is significant and substantial, and affects the proceedings unfairly it should be excluded. In *Mason*[107] and *Delaney*[108] the Court of Appeal stressed that its exclusionary decision should not be exercised just to discipline the police.

Sanders has argued that 'there therefore appears to be no more substance to the "right" to advice now than there was prior to PACE'.[109] Denial of access may mean that the suspect's detention is unnecessarily prolonged, exposing him to energetic questioning and to the risk of making a false confession. The cases of Evans, Confait and the Guildford Four are timely reminders of the serious consequences following from statements made in the absence of legal advice.[110] Without the right to silence, the right to see a solicitor may be even harder to enforce. It would have been very difficult for Samuel[111] to argue for the exclusion of the evidence under s 78 if he had not been able to invoke the right to silence.

Fenwick[112] argues that the disciplinary effect of s 78 in relation to access to legal advice may be weakened further by the CJPOA. The use of discretion under s 78 to exclude admissions made in the absence of legal advice, for example, before being cautioned, may be less readily exercised. However, a defendant denied legal advice might argue that silence should not be admitted in evidence because he would not have been silent had he received proper legal advice on the effects of silence. It is not yet clear how the weakening of the right to silence will affect the courts' attitude to breaches of s 58. It will be harder to infer that the solicitor would have advised silence if he were present. But the presence of a solicitor during interrogation may be seen as a precondition of drawing adverse inferences following the decision of the European Court of Human Rights in *Murray v UK* and in *Argent* the Court of Appeal saw it as one factor to take account of in considering whether the accused could reasonably have been expected to mention a fact he later relies on.[113]

The Law Society has said that there are still situations in which advising silence would be appropriate. But given the risk of adverse inferences lawyers will be less likely to advise silence. If the accused does confess in the absence of a solicitor he may well argue that his solicitor would have advised silence if he had been present, so it will be interesting to see how the courts deal with the problem. The Law Society Advice issued in 1994 before the bill had been enacted said that it would make little practical difference: if the lawyer thinks there is insufficient evidence to convict he should still counsel silence.[114] Circumstances in which silence would be recommended include if the client is distressed or confused at the time of the interview, or is suggestible, or under pressure from the police. If the client is advised to remain silent, he may still be advised to make a statement giving his account. The solicitor should make a note of his advice and reasons for it in writing and on the police tape. At trial the defence can argue that silence was exercised on the basis of the legal advice and that the jury should not draw an adverse inference, as the defendant simply followed the solicitor's advice. It will then be up to the jury whether it sees this as persuasive. The judge could direct the jury that because the silence was chosen on legal advice adverse inferences should not be drawn from it, but it seems unlikely that this will happen in most cases without an additional factor.

If we consider the vulnerability of the suspect during questioning, the importance of access to legal advice and of the right to silence is clear. If the individual is in alien surroundings and subject to interrogation by experienced interrogators, then there is a tremendous pressure on him to speak.[115] There may be problems in maintaining full cover for duty solicitor schemes in some areas. Even if the solicitor is present, he may not receive full details of the case against the suspect, so it may well be that the suspect would wish to remain silent, in the presence of his solicitor, until he knows more of the case against him. Yet under the CJPOA, the suspect may well be prejudiced by failing to mention a factor relevant to his defence at the earliest opportunity, whether or not his silence is exercised as a consequence of legal advice.

Complaints against the police

The impact of PACE on the relationship between the powers of the police and the corresponding rights of the subject and the implications for the right to silence, has been considered by Sanders[116] who argues that the rights of suspects, embodied in the Act, are unmatched by any corresponding remedies for the police misuse of their powers. The police complaints procedure is unsatisfactory because it is primarily concerned with police discipline rather than with compensating citizens.[117] Its investigations are secret and the reports on which the PCA makes decisions are prepared by the police. Without adequate remedies, he says, such rights are just 'empty rhetoric'. However, he does see the transformation of this empty rhetoric into reality as possible through remedies such as exclusionary rules. Increasing awareness of rights is also essential. The absence of remedies in the Act is also curious as the Royal Commission on Criminal Procedure advocated the provision of remedies to deal with abuses of police powers. Sanders argues that the accountability of the police to the courts, which was already weak, has been lessened by PACE and that even if PACE enhanced the rights of suspects in some contexts this cannot justify the dilution of the right to silence.[118]

The Police Complaints Authority set up by PACE has the power to direct that disciplinary charges be brought against police officers, to supervise the investigation of complaints, to recommend the investigating officer, and to impose requirements for the conduct of the investigation and to issue a statement on whether it is satisfied with the way the investigation is carried out. While an improvement on its predecessor, the police complaints board, the PCA has been criticised for the fact that the police investigate the police and for the secrecy surrounding investigations.

Objections to setting up a wholly separate independent group to investigate complaints have usually been cost-related. The PCA has criticised the high standard of proof required to mount a disciplinary charge and the cumbersome, slow procedure, and the constraints on publishing full details of an investigation.[119] Since June 1994 the complainant can use material generated by the investigation as evidence in a civil action. Most complaints relate to assaults. The PCA also investigates cases involving firearms, all deaths in custody, matters of corruption and public order incidents and misuse of the police national computer. The PCA has argued for the speeding up of the process to deal with complaints[120] and has recommended that an independent tribunal with lay members should investigate serious complaints. It also advocates a less rigid, costly, legalistic and lengthy police disciplinary process. The PCA has no power to investigate special constables or the expanding private security industry.

Complaints against the police in England and Wales increased by 11.8% in 1994. But very few complaints which are investigated lead to disciplinary action. In the period from 1985-94, figures range from 8.2% to 11.1%.[121] Disciplinary charges have been avoided by taking early retirement on medical grounds, a practice criticised by the PCA. Even where disciplinary action is taken, the CPS may not bring charges. Forty-five officers were investigated in Stoke Newington of whom only 2 were prosecuted.

The Royal Commission on Criminal Justice[122] also recommended improvements to police disciplinary arrangements, less formal disciplinary hearings and lowering the standard of proof. It also proposed that the acquittal of a police officer in a criminal court should not bar disciplinary proceedings on the same facts, and those proceedings should be able to end in a dismissal if the officer's conduct shows that he is unsuitable to remain in the police force.

For Sanders[123] the balance between the police and suspect has changed in the police's favour following PACE. What is needed to rectify this imbalance, he suggests, are punitive and compensatory remedies, to benefit the individual as well as to act as a deterrent, rather than abolition of the right to silence. Police discipline needs to be strengthened by a strong code of police conduct and proper methods of enforcement.

Because of the problems with the complaints procedure many lawyers favour taking civil actions against the Metropolitan Police using the tort of false imprisonment.[124] The use of such actions increased during the 1990s. Exemplary damages have been awarded by juries to punish the police for oppressive conduct. Because of the high levels of awards the police have begun to contest these actions rather than settling, but the financial costs to the police remain high.

Changes to the police discipline system were proposed by the Home Secretary, Kenneth Clarke, in 1993 in a consultation paper on police personnel procedures. The Police and Magistrates' Courts Act 1994 lays the foundation for a new discipline system. The revised system is based on a managerial approach. There will be two levels to deal with complaints depending on whether they are seen as cases of misconduct, or cases of unsatisfactory performance. Cases of misconduct are cases where a police officer is believed to have committed an offence or breach of the PACE Codes and by doing so has affected a member of the public. He would be required to attend a misconduct hearing which would be similar to the old disciplinary system but the standard of proof will be lower, namely that it is reasonably believed that there has been misconduct rather than beyond reasonable doubt. The officer concerned will no longer have a right to silence on disciplinary matters but will be required to give a full account of his actions if requested by a senior officer. The right to silence would remain in any criminal proceedings on the terms appropriate to any other suspect. In the past the police use of the right to silence in disciplinary procedures had been criticised. The officer will be able to appeal to a new appeal tribunal. Other cases will be dealt with by managers and treated as unsatisfactory performance. The managers will consider ways in which the officer's behaviour can be improved and the implications for future career advancement. Underpinning the changes is the desire to treat the police service like any other industry. These changes have been criticised by the PCA as the police themselves decide whether to record a complaint and if a complaint is classified as unsatisfactory performance, rather than misconduct, then the PCA would not be used to oversee the proceedings.

Conclusion

Despite the above problems, PACE has improved the position of suspects. The changes in the PACE codes in 1991 generated an increase in requests for duty solicitors, as suspects now are advised of their right to free legal advice. Changes to the duty solicitor scheme require mandatory attendance in certain circumstances, for example, where suspects allege mistreatment by the police. These improvements in PACE need to be strengthened by improved training and supervision of the police. Section 78 of PACE could be changed so that evidence obtained as a result of serious and substantial breaches of PACE is automatically excluded rather than leaving this to the Court's discretion. This would provide a further brake on unrestrained interrogation. Improvements could be made to compensate for the loss of the right to silence. In *Edwards*[125] Lord Lane said that officers who are not believed by juries can be cross-examined in subsequent hearings where similar allegations are made, under strict conditions. It will be possible to cross-examine the officer concerned about any unrelated criminal or disciplinary charges proved against him or her if they cast doubt on the officer's credibility and if that is in issue in the subsequent case. This means that disclosure of police disciplinary records will be required. The DPP subsequently has advised chief officers how to comply with this duty. A new Defendants' Information Service has also been set up to furnish lawyers with details of cases where allegations of misconduct have been made against officers leading to acquittals, complaints or damages.[126]

Concern over deaths in police custody and over a series of wrongful convictions has highlighted the vulnerability of the accused while undergoing interrogation. PACE was intended in part to eliminate and deter malpractice, to increase the accountability of the police and to redress the imbalance between the state and the citizen. As the effects of PACE have come to be felt, the police have searched for ways of recovering that lost power. In this context 'noble cause' corruption' may occur, where the police act improperly and increase pressure to obtain a conviction of the person they believe to be guilty.[127] The problems of enforcing the Codes and relying on exclusionary discretion, the continuing revelations of miscarriages of justice, the problems of vulnerability and false confessions, all indicate the continuing importance of a right to silence in safeguarding the individual. But the curtailment of the right to silence in the CJPOA has changed the relationship between prosecution and defence and undermined the principles on which PACE was constructed.

Notes

1.   J. Bentham (1843) Rationale of Judicial Evidence, *The Works of Jeremy Bentham*, Bowring edition, Edinburgh, William Tait.
2.   *Ibid*, p 455.
3.   *Ibid*, p 462.
4.   Criminal Law Revision Committee (1972) *Eleventh Report, Evidence (General)* HMSO, Cmnd 4991, para. 21.
5.   Report of the Working Group on the Right of Silence (1989) Home Office, C Division, London.
6.   384 US 436 (1966).
7.   See M. Foucault (1979) *Discipline and Punish, The Birth of the Prison*.
8.   J. Wigmore (1961) *Evidence*, 8, McNaughten rev. ed., para. 2265.

9.   See chapter 3 above.

10.   J. Bentham, *op.cit.*

11.   See H. Garfinkel (1956) 'Conditions of successful degradation ceremonies', *American Journal of Sociology*, 61, 420.

12.   See P. Devlin (1986) *Easing the Passing*, London, Bodley Head.

13.   See PACE, s 77; Code C 11.14, 11.16.

14.   See Report of an Inquiry by the Hon. Sir Henry Fisher into the circumstances leading to the trial of three persons on charges arising out of the death of Maxwell Confait and the fire at 27 Doggett Road, London S.E.6 (1977) HMSO; Report of the Royal Commission on Criminal Procedure (1981) HMSO, Cmnd 8092.

15.   See s 77 and Code C, Annex E.

16.   PACE, s 67(11).

17.   The common law discretion to exclude improperly obtained evidence had been narrowed in *R v Sang* [1980] AC 402.

18.   See for example *R v Keenan* [1989] Crim LR 720, *R v Canale* [1990] 2 All ER 187, *R v Weekes* [1993] Crim LR 211, *R v Samuel* [1988] 2 All ER 135.

19.   Code E 2B.

20.   Code E 4.11.

21.   See *R v Bryce* (1992) 95 Cr App Rep 320.

22.   C. Willis *et.al.* (1988) *The Tape Recording of Police Interviews with Suspects*, Home Office Research Study, no. 97.

23.   CLRC Report, para. 52.

24.   Report of the Royal Commission on Criminal Justice, (1993) London, HMSO, Cmnd 2263, paras. 1.22, 4.33.

25.   T. Williamson and S. Moston (1990) 'The extent of silence in police interviews', in S. Greer and R. Morgan (eds.), *The Right to Silence Debate*, Bristol Centre for Criminal Justice, pp 36-43.

26.   See Home Office Circulars 22/1992, 7/1993 and T. Williamson (1994) 'Reflections on Current Police Practice' in D. Morgan and G. Stephenson (eds.) *Suspicion and Silence, the Right to Silence in Criminal Investigations*, London, Blackstone, pp 107-16.

27.   See A. Zuckerman [1989] 'Trial by Unfair Means - the Report of the Working Group on the Right of Silence', Crim LR 855; [1994] 'Bias and suggestibility: is there an alternative to the right to silence?' in D. Morgan and G. Stephenson (eds.) *op. cit.*, pp 117-140.

28.   M. McConville, A. Sanders and R. Leng (1991) *The Case for the Prosecution*, London, Routledge.

29.   See Policy Studies Institute (1983) *Police and People In London*. One result of this problem of legitimacy is that juries may be reluctant to convict.

30.   See chapters 9 and 10 below.

31. RCCP Report, para. 4.89.
32. RCCJ Report, para. 3.63.
33. M. Maguire (1988) 'Effects of the PACE Provisions on Detention and Questioning', British Journal of Criminology, 19.
34. A. Sanders, L. Bridges, A. Mulvaney and G. Crozier (1989) *Advice and Assistance at Police Stations and the 24-hour Duty Solicitor Scheme*, London, Lord Chancellor's Department.
35. *Ibid*; see also A. Sanders [1990] 'Access to Legal Advice and Police Malpractice', Crim LR 494.
36. J. Baldwin (1992) *The Role of Legal Representatives at the Police Station*, RCCJ Research Study no. 3, London, HMSO.
37. *Ibid*, p. 52.
38. M. McConville, J. Hodgson, L. Bridges and A. Pavlovic (1994) *Standing Accused: The Organisation and Practices of Criminal Defence Lawyers in Britain*, Oxford, University Press.
39. M. McConville and J. Hodgson (1993) *Custodial Legal Advice and the Right to Silence*, RCCJ Research Study no. 16, London, HMSO.
40. M. McConville, J. Hodgson, L. Bridges and A. Pavlovic (1994).
41. M. McConville and J. Hodgson (1993).
42. *Ibid*.
43. [1993] Crim LR 685.
44. [1990] Crim LR 572.
45. See chapter 10 below.
46. See *R v Dunn* [1990] Crim LR 572.
47. D. Brown, T. Ellis and K.Larcombe (1992) *Changing the Code: Police Detention under the Revised Codes of Practice*, Home Office Research Study no. 129, London, HMSO.
48. Legal Aid Board (1995) Annual Report 1994/5, London, HMSO.
49. L. Bridges and J. Hodgson [1995] 'Improving Custodial Legal Advice', Crim LR 101.
50. H. Fenwick [1995] 'Curtailing the Right to Silence, Access to Legal Advice and Section 78', Crim LR 132.
51. Code C Annex B3.
52. Code C, 6D.
53. RCCJ Report, para. 2.4.
54. Code E 3.2.
55. Code E, Notes for Guidance 3H.
56. See chapter 3 above.
57. Code E 3.3.
58. G. Peirce (1996) *A Hostage to Fortune? Do we need permanent counter-terrorism laws?*, London, BIRW.
59. See *Dunn* [1990] Crim LR 572.
60. (1990) 90 Cr App Rep 115.

61.   (1993) 97 Cr App Rep 99.
62.   C. Willis, *op.cit.*
63.   J. Baldwin (1992) *Videotaping police interviews with suspects - an evaluation*, Police Research Series Paper 1, Police Research Group Publications, Home Office.
64.   M. McConville [1992] 'Videotaping interrogations: police behaviour on and off camera', Crim LR 532.
65.   *Ibid*, p 548.
66.   RCCJ Report, para. 3.6.
67.   *Ibid*, para. 3.7.
68.   Home Office, Circular 6/93 (1993).
69.   See C. Pollard [1996] 'Public Safety, Accountability and the Courts', Crim LR 152.
70.   Code C 11.1A (1995).
71.   *Ibid.*
72.   D. Wolchover and A. Heaton-Armstrong [1990] 'Last fence for the new PACE Codes', Counsel, 15.
73.   S. Moston and G. Stephenson (1993) *The Questioning and Interviewing of Suspects outside the Police Station*, RCCJ Research Study no. 22, London HMSO; (1994) 'Helping the Police with their Enquiries outside the Police Station', in R. Morgan and G. Stephenson, *op.cit.*, pp 51-65.
74.   *Ibid.*
75.   D. Brown, T. Ellis and K. Larcombe, *op. cit.*
76.   RCCJ Report, para.3.14.
76.   RCCJ Report, para.3.14.
78.   PACE Code C E.4.3B
79.   [1990] Crim LR 190; see also *R v Canale* [1989] Times, 8 November.
80.   See *R v Absalom* [1988] Crim LR 748 and *R v Sanusi* [1992] Crim LR 43.
81.   See *R v Ward (Wayne)* (1994) 98 Cr App Rep 337.
82.   See *R v Elson* (1994) Times 30 June, where an identification parade was not recorded and the witnesses spoke to each other.
83.   (1988) 87 Cr App Rep 380.
84.   *Ibid*, at 387.
85.   See D. Birch [1989] 'The PACE hots up', Crim LR 95.
86.   [1993] Crim LR 47.
87.   [1993] Crim LR 206.
88.   See *R v Delaney* [1988] 2 All ER 135.
89.   [1988] 2 All ER 135.
90.   Code C, Annex B 2.3.
91.   at 147.
92.   [1989] Crim LR 822.
93.   *R v Davidson* [1988] Crim LR 422; *R v McIvor* [1987] Crim LR 409.

94.   (1988) 87 Cr App Rep 380.
95.   (1991) 92 Cr App Rep 314.
96.   (1989) 88 Cr App Rep 32.
97.   (1990) 91 Cr App Rep 237.
98.   (1990) 91 Cr App Rep 150.
99.   See A.J. Ashworth [1977] 'Excluding Evidence as Protecting Rights', Crim LR 723 and I. Dennis (1989) 'Reconstructing the Law of Criminal Evidence', Current Legal Problems 21.
100. *R v Delaney* [1988] 2 All ER 135.
101. *R v Hunt* [1992] Crim LR 582.
102. *R v Payne and Quinn* [1995] Times, 15 March.
103. *R v Keenan* [1989] Crim LR 720.
104. *R v Glaves* [1993] Crim LR 685.
105. See *R v Mason* [1987] 3 All ER 481.
106. See *R v Dunford* [1991] Crim LR 370, *R v Alladice* (1988) 87 Cr App Rep 380, *R v Quinn* [1990] Crim LR 581, *R v Dunn* [1990] Crim LR 572, *R v Smurthwaite, R v Gill* (1994) 98 Cr App Rep 437.
107. [1987] 3 All ER 481.
108. (1988) 88 Cr App Rep 338.
109. A. Sanders [1988] 'Rights, Remedies and the Police and Criminal Evidence Act', Crim LR, 802 at 807.
110. See H. Fisher (1977); *R v Armstrong, Conlon, Hill and Richardson* [1989] Times, 20 October.
111. [1988] 2 All ER 135.
112. H. Fenwick [1995] 'Curtailing the Right to Silence. Access to Legal Advice and Section 78', Crim LR 132.
113. *Murray v UK* [1996] Times, 9 February; *R v Argent* [1996] Times, 19 December.
114. Law Society (October 1994) 'Changes in the Law Relating to Silence: Advice to Practicioners from the Criminal Law Committee of the Law Society', Criminal Practicioners Newsletter.
115. See the study by M. Wald *et al* of police interrogation in New Haven following the introduction of the *Miranda* guidelines, (1967) 'Interrogations in New Haven: The Impact of *Miranda*', Yale Law Journal, 76, 1519 at 1614.
116. See A. Sanders [1988] 'Rights, Remedies and the Police and Criminal Evidence Act', Crim LR, 802.
117. *Ibid*.
118. *Ibid*, at 812.
119. PCA (1995) *Police Complaints Authority - The First Ten Years*, London, HMSO.
120. PCA Report (1992) HC 611.
121. Police Complaints Authority (1995).

122.   RCCJ Report, para. 3.103.
123.   A. Sanders (1988).
124.   See G. Smith [November 1996] 'Playing politics with the law' Legal Action 8. In 1995 awards amounted to £1,560,000.
125.   [1991] 2 All ER 266.
126.   Reported in G. Smith and R. Miller (September 1995) 'Redressing the Balance', Legal Action, 10.
127.   See Sir J. Woodcock (1992) 'Trust in the Police - The Search for Truth', Address to the International Police Exhibition and Conference, 13 October, London.

5 The right to silence and the protection of the guilty

Opponents of the right to silence frequently argue that the right to silence has served the interests of the hardened professional criminal seeking to evade justice. This view of silence as a weapon of the guilty originates in Bentham's critique of silence at trial.[1] Bentham's argument reflected a general aversion to exclusionary rules which he saw as subverting the goal of rectitude of decision. Bentham's scepticism on the right to silence is echoed by modern critics who see abolition as the solution to the alleged problem of ambush defences. It was concern over ambushing which underpinned the provisions in s 34 of the Criminal Justice and Public Order Act. Bentham's argument that the right to silence benefits the guilty has been reflected in the modern critiques of the right to silence of the Criminal Law Revision Committee[2] and the Home Office Working Group,[3] the police and successive governments in the 1980s and 1990s. The Home Office Working Group accepted that the CLRC had 'identified a legitimate problem which time has not lessened' and echoed the view that 'it is wrong that offenders - usually the more intelligent and serious offenders - should be able to manipulate the criminal justice system to their own advantage, either to escape conviction entirely or to delay and obstruct the judicial process.'[4] Some critics have argued that the right to silence may pose a problem if it is fully used, because it would be impossible to convict the guilty if the police are dependent on the cooperation of suspects to obtain information but they refuse to speak. An example often cited is where a child has been murdered, both parents are suspected and it is not clear who killed the child and where they both maintain silence. However, even drawing adverse inferences from silence would not establish which of the parents committed the crime or against whom silence should count as corroborative evidence. One solution offered by the Royal Commission on Criminal Justice was to extend the idea of absolute liability for the safety of a child.[5]

The abolitionist argument found some support in the findings of Irving and McKenzie[6] who conducted research on a small sample for the Police Foundation to ascertain the effects of the PACE Codes. They found a steep rise in the number of suspects refusing to answer questions after PACE came into force and also discovered a positive correlation between the seriousness of the crime and the refusal to answer: the more serious the crime the more likely it was that the accused would not speak. But in comparing figures before and after the enactment of PACE, we need to be satisfied that we are drawing a meaningful comparison. The yardstick used prior to PACE is usually the Royal Commission on Criminal Procedure study which found that 4% of the sample exercised their right to silence.[7] But this figure was based on a substantial exercise of the right to silence. The studies undertaken for the Home Office Working Group by the Metropolitan Police in 1987 and the West Yorkshire Police in 1988,[8] included three categories: (i) those who refused to answer any questions from the beginning of the interview; (ii) those who failed to answer any questions relevant to the offence and (iii) those who failed to answer some questions relevant to the offence. The aggregate figure in the Metropolitan study was 23% and in the West Yorkshire study was 12.3%. But aggregating the figures can distort the picture, as the figures for complete silence from the beginning to the end of the interview were 6% of the sample in the London study and 2.3% of the sample in West Yorkshire. This is closer to the earlier studies. Moston, Stephenson and Williamson[9] found that 16% of suspects out of a sample of 1,067 cases exercised their right to silence but of this group, only half were completely silent and the other half did answer some questions. They also found that legal advice correlated strongly with exercise of the right. Further statistically significant correlations were found between exercise of the right to silence and previous convictions and offence severity.

The study undertaken for the Association of Chief Police Officers of 3600 suspects from 8 forces in 1993 found that 21.9% of suspects refused to answer some or all questions and 10% answered no questions at all.[10] Moreover suspects with previous convictions were more likely to exercise their right to silence.

Critics of the right to silence have identified two principal areas where the guilty may hide behind silence: ambush defences and terrorist activities. The Criminal Evidence (Northern Ireland) Order considered earlier was designed to meet the concern regarding the 'wall of silence' used by members of the Irish Republican Army and other sectarian para-military groups during interrogation in Northern Ireland. In England and Wales the CJPOA was intended to deal with the problems raised for the prosecution by so-called ambush defences.

Ambush defences

The argument for change

Ambush defences are defences 'sprung' at trial, which take the prosecution by surprise, allowing insufficient time for preparation of the prosecution's case and, it is argued, consequently lead to wrongful acquittals. These explanations could be given on arrest, during police interrogation, but by withholding them until trial, it has been argued, it becomes much harder for the prosecution to challenge them or the police to investigate them. In 1987 Douglas Hurd, the Home Secretary,[11] asked whether it was in the interests of justice that professional criminals should be able to refuse to answer questions put by the police, knowing that their refusal would not be brought to the attention of the jury or be the subject of adverse comment. The former Metropolitan Police Commissioner, Sir Peter Imbert, claimed in 1989 that 'the right to silence might have been designed by criminals for their special benefit and that of their professional advisers. It has done more to obscure the truth and facilitate crime than anything else this century.'[12] It is these types of defences which were targetted by the CJPOA. Paul Condon, the Metropolitan Police Commissioner, stated that more and more people especially persistent offenders, were exercising the right to silence. He was also highly critical of the existing rules of disclosure.[13] Similarly, Charles Pollard, Chief Constable of the Thames Valley Police has consistently criticised the criminal justice system for neglecting the needs of victims and for treating the public's need for protection as peripheral.[14] He has focused specifically on the problems with the adversarial system and the impact of exclusionary rules of evidence. Like Bentham, he sees the legal system as controlled by lawyers rather than by the interests of the public.

Greater efficiency in convicting the guilty is therefore a recurring theme in critiques of the right to silence. To tackle ambush defences, the CLRC[15] proposed that if the accused relies in his defence on a fact which he failed to mention when questioned or charged, then the court or jury should be able to draw such inferences as appear proper and treat silence as corroboration of any evidence given against the accused where the failure to mention is material and the fact relied on at the trial or committal proceedings, is one that it would have been reasonable for him to mention. Examples envisaged here are the defences of innocent association, or the belief that goods were not stolen on a charge of handling. The proposal was intended to include interrogations by the police and others who have the duty of investigating and charging offenders, for example, customs officers. The question of whether silence is capable of amounting to corroboration would be a matter for the judge and whether it is corroboration would be a matter for the jury. In the view of the Committee it was quite wrong that the jury or magistrates were unable to draw appropriate inferences from the accused's failure to mention in interrogation defences advanced at trial, because it gives an 'unnecessary advantage to the guilty'.[16]

The Committee emphasised that the public interest is served by convicting the guilty as well as protecting the innocent. Bentham's observation in his *Treatise on Judicial Evidence*[17] that the rule prohibiting defendants from testifying is one that criminals might have devised for themselves, was applied by the CLRC explicitly to ambush defences. Reference was made by the Committee to the 'changed conditions' of modern society, to the fact that there is now 'a large and increasingly sophisticated class of criminals who are not only highly skilful in organizing their crimes and in the steps they take to avoid detection but are well aware of their legal rights and use every possible means to avoid conviction if caught.'[18] Hardened criminals, the Committee argued, are able to take advantage of the right, thereby impeding proper police investigations. Although there were disagreements within the Committee regarding the extent of wrongful acquittal, the majority concluded that changes in the rules of evidence, including the removal of restrictions on admissibility, were essential to strengthen crime control. It was also argued that accomplices were receiving protection because of the right to silence. Although the Committee's recommendations were not implemented, concern over the exploitation of the right to silence by professional criminals was still being voiced in the debate in the late eighties. It was expressed by the Home Office Working Group[19] although, as noted earlier, its recommendations did not go quite as far as those of the CLRC.

The Royal Commission on Criminal Justice favoured a form of advance disclosure as the best way of dealing with ambush defences and as an alternative to abolition of the right to silence. Despite the Commission's claim that this would not infringe the presumption of innocence, the proposal was criticised for effectively undermining the right to silence and weakening the burden of proof on the prosecution.[20] What would be disclosed in advance would be the substance of the defence, or if no evidence is to be called by the accused, this should also be made clear. Adverse comment would be permitted at trial only if the defence introduced a new defence not previously disclosed. The Commission argued that this would speed up the trial process and prevent defences being sprung on the prosecution. Like other proposals relating to ambush defences, it still presupposes that there is an ambush problem which was challenged by the Royal Commission's own research studies.[21]

However, the reasoning behind the CLRC report and particularly the concern over the cynical abuse of the right to silence continued into the 1990s and provided an impetus for s 34 of the Criminal Justice and Public Order Act, although the Act did not treat silence as corroborating other evidence against the accused. But the fact that the right to silence has now been curtailed has not satisfied its critics, for attention has now shifted to other aspects of criminal procedure, particularly the exclusionary rules of the law of evidence.[22]

The view that professional criminals were 'abusing' the right to silence was repeatedly expressed by the police who argued that it was undermining their efforts to control crime. Removal of artificial restrictions on enquiry, it was claimed, would facilitate discovery of the truth. It has also been argued that the existence of the right to silence encourages police officers to subvert the formal rules of PACE, as they try to compensate for silence by illicit means.[23]

The extent of the ambushing 'problem'

The case for abolition is flawed not least because it was not proved that there was a serious ambushing problem sufficient to justify abolition, or that the police were impeded in their work. Little evidence was offered to support the assertion that the guilty were abusing the right to silence. The assertion that defendants were acquitted by juries because they hid behind the right to silence was not supported by any convincing evidence of wrongful acquittals, but rather rested on mere speculation. No evidence was offered to support the claim of an ambushing problem by the Home Office Working Group even though this was the reason why the Group was formed, or in the research studies for the Royal Commission on Criminal Justice. Moreover, the allegation that the right to silence facilitates crime deflects attention from the complexity of the wider causes of crime and the ways in which crime prevention might be improved. It fails to take account of the principal aims of the law of evidence, to provide fairness to the accused, and to determine the truth. It will be argued that the right to silence can facilitate the pursuit of the truth. But, in any case, it is difficult to see how the right to silence could facilitate crime as relatively few suspects exercise the right to silence. The exercise of the right to silence is unlikely to have an impact on the number of acquittals or to adversely affect police work.

This was recognised by the Royal Commission on Criminal Procedure[24] which stressed the importance of considering the right to silence in the light of the empirical evidence and found that most suspects did account for their conduct while undergoing police interrogation.[25] This was confirmed by subsequent studies before and after the enactment of PACE including those undertaken by Smith and Gray[26] and Mitchell[27] when there was no penalty for silence. Mitchell examined 400 cases in 1983 and found only 4.3% remained silent in interrogation. A study of contested cases in the Crown Court in London and Birmingham by Baldwin and McConville[28] in 1980 found that the number of suspects who exercised their right to silence at the police station was low: 6.5 % of the London sample and 3.8% of the Birmingham sample. Sanders, Bridges, Mulvany and Crozier[29] found that just 2.4% of suspects in a sample of 527 interrogations exercised their right to silence in police interrogation. Most of the solicitors they interviewed rarely advised silence. The Royal Commission on Criminal Justice also found that the right to silence was exercised only in a minority of cases.[30] A review of research on the use of the right to silence was carried out for the Commission by Brown[31] who points to the problems of differing definitions of the right to silence and whether samples are representative and other methodological problems. Nonetheless he estimates that between 6% and 10% of suspects outside the Metropolitan police district exercise their right to silence to some extent, that is, who refuse to answer some questions but not others and within the Metropolitan police district the proportion is estimated to be between 14% and 16%. The numbers who refused to answer any questions at all was calculated to be 5% in most provincial police areas and 9% in the Metropolitan police district.

It has been argued that there is a potential problem facing the police in that if the right were to be fully exercised, this would have a great impact on investigation.[32] Zuckerman[33] has argued that if the suspect is removed from any pressures to speak and told in the presence of his solicitor that he will not be interrogated without his consent, then he is unlikely to agree to be questioned at all. But this argument does not take sufficient account of the *informal* pressures to speak or the fears that adverse inferences might still be drawn from nonco-operation, which mean that few individuals exercise the right to silence despite the formal protection of the privilege against self-incrimination.[34] Such anxieties are therefore quixotic and offer a meagre justification for abolition.

Empirical research has failed to find a link between the exercise of the right to silence and the gravity of the offence or prior convictions. In Zander's study of cases at the Old Bailey in 1979 only 4% exercised their right to silence.[35] Furthermore 9 of the 12 suspects who remained silent were convicted. Willis[36] also found that only 3% of her sample of cases between 1984 and 1986 exercised their right to silence in interrogation. No positive correlation was found between the exercise of the right of silence and long criminal careers. Her study was based on a larger sample and encompassed a much longer period than the London and West Yorkshire studies for the Home Office Working Group, which covered only one month.

The use of the right to silence has been the exception rather than the rule. The pressure to respond when asked questions is intense because it is so deeply grounded in the rules of everyday conversational discourse. It is very exceptional to say nothing, not least because before the 1994 Act judges were permitted to comment if the accused was silent in interrogation or at trial albeit within certain boundaries, as defined by *Sullivan*,[37] *Gilbert*[38] and *Sparrow*.[39] In any case, a jury cannot be prevented from drawing the inferences it thinks proper regardless of judicial directions to the contrary. The view that the right to silence impedes the truth because it shields the professional criminal does not withstand scrutiny. As both the Royal Commission on Criminal Procedure and the Royal Commission on Criminal Justice recognised, the right is rarely exercised. When viewed in this context the zest for abolition is difficult to comprehend. The Runciman Commission could find no evidence to show that silence was used

138

disproportionately by professional criminals or that silence in interrogation increased the chances of an acquittal. The majority therefore recommended that adverse comment on silence should not be permitted, because professional criminals would simply blame their silence on legal advice. The Commission also stressed the need for independent evidence rather than relying on the accused's evidence.[40] But it rejected the introduction of a legally enforceable rule preventing the prosecution from proceeding on the basis of confession evidence alone, favouring instead the use of warnings.

The claim that there was an ambushing problem was not supported by the empirical research undertaken for the Royal Commission on Criminal Justice. Zander and Henderson in their Crown Court study found that late defences sprung on the prosecution occurred in no more than 10% of Crown court trials but they were more likely to end in convictions than acquittal.[41] The study examined 3191 cases in the Crown Court over a two-week period, involving over 3600 suspects. They did find that the incidence of the exercise of the right to silence was higher in cases tried in the Crown Court, which are usually the more serious cases and where the consequences of comment would be more graver.[42]

Leng[43] tried to quantify the use of the right to silence, to ascertain whether silence was a significant factor in the number of arrests where no further action was taken and in acquittals. He looked at 1080 cases from 1986-8 in 6 police stations. In only 4.5% of the 848 cases he studied in which interviews occurred, did suspects exercise the right to silence, about half of whom were convicted. He emphasised the importance of being clear on whether the suspect is refusing to answer all questions, or being silent selectively or simply denying the charge, or refusing to speak but later advancing an ambush defence. He argued that 'a suspect should be considered to exercise the right to silence only where he persists in refusing to answer some or all substantial questions relating to his own culpability, or where he fails to disclose a defence which he later relies on at trial and which he might reasonably have been expected to mention in the circumstances.'[44] Those who did exercise the right to silence were more likely to have a solicitor present and about one half exercising the right to silence were subsequently convicted. As he observed: 'The right of silence is rarely exercised...about half of those who exercise it are convicted. For cases which fail, there is little evidence to suggest that the prospects for conviction would be enhanced by inducing the suspect to speak or treating his silence as evidence against him.'[45] In the small percentage who did remain silent the principal motivation was not to conceal guilt:

> In 6 (12%) of the 49 cases in which the suspect was silent at some stages of the interview, the motive was to protect others. The actual proportion of cases in which the motive for silence was the protection of others may well be higher than this since

in the majority of silence cases there is no means of determining the suspects' motives.[46]

Where suspects were silent, silence had little effect on the outcome of the case and in some cases was prejudicial rather than beneficial. One half of those who were silent pleaded or were found guilty and only 10% (5 cases) of those who were acquitted had refused to speak to the police. So approximately 2% of suspects who were silent in interrogation were not convicted. Leng found that in most of the acquittals the evidence against the accused was weak. He found no evidence to support the argument that hardened criminals are using ambush defences. In Leng's study only one case out of 59 contested trials was a possible ambush. He failed to discover a correlation between ambushing and acquittal. Much more common than ambushes were defences won unexpectedly because defence lawyers had raised valid legal arguments or cases where there were challenges to prosecution evidence for which the prosecution was unprepared. He emphasised the need to distinguish true ambushes from late defences, for example, based on pure legal arguments which the suspect could not reasonably have been expected to raise at interview, or issues which are more properly addressed at trial. Defences based on interpretations of the accused's answers during interrogation or challenges to the admissibility of alleged confession evidence, argued Leng, should not be seen as ambush defences. An ambush defence is a defence raised for the first time at trial and of which the police or prosecution had no prior notice. It should not include cases where the suspect is not given enough information about the case against him to show the relevance of the facts to his defence or where he is not given an opportunity to give the factual basis of his defence during the interview, or where he is unaware of the potential for using that defence. Leng also examined cases where no further action was taken to see if silence was significant and found that the right to silence was used in only 4% of such cases. He calculates that in only about 2% of the no further action cases would compelling the suspect to speak have made a difference to the outcome. But in most cases of silence, inducing the suspect to speak would be of little benefit to the investigation. A number of factors may influence the decision to take no further action, including the fact that the police are satisfied of the suspect's innocence, or a complaint is withdrawn, or policy grounds rather than simply evidential weakness. Leng therefore argued that curtailing the right to silence is unlikely to provide the benefits claimed by abolitionists.

There are methodological problems in measuring silence: for example, whether one is comparing total or partial silences, and the question of whether the size of the sample is sufficient to be generalisable. One needs to be clear whether the silences of individuals or interrogations are being compared as the same suspect may be interviewed on a number of occasions which would give a higher figure. Conversely, where the suspect refuses to answer initially, but does so in later interviews, should this be construed as silence? Studies which define silence as refusing to answer some questions may inflate the figures for silence but the consensus seems to be that total silence is rare.

In McConville and Hodgson's research only 2.5% of suspects in their sample remained completely silent.[47] They also were unable to find a consistent relationship between offence seriousness and the decision to exercise the right to silence. In their study conducted before the CJPOA came into force, they found that despite the common belief of police officers that solicitors will encourage their clients not to answer questions, advice to remain silent is the exception rather than the norm: 'Even those solicitors who had a reputation for being "progressive", "radical" or "civil-rights oriented" had recourse to silence only in exceptional cases.'[48] Instead the advisers, who included clerks, secretaries and former police officers, mostly advised co-operation with the police, or left the decision whether or not to speak up to the client. Among the reasons for favouring co-operation were that the suspect admitted the offence or had a defence or explanation which the adviser recommended giving to the police, or because the client denied involvement, or the adviser thought the client would appear in a bad light if he remained silent; co-operation was also viewed as a means of extricating information from the police about the evidence against the client. They could find no evidence to support the claim that advisers counsel silence to obtain an acquittal. Rather they assume that most suspects will speak. When legal representatives do advise silence, McConville and Hodgson observe,[49] the principal reasons include the lack of information available to the adviser about the police case, the fear that some suspects, particularly suggestible ones, will make incriminating remarks, or because they believe the police did not have a case or one that would stand up in court. Sometimes silence was recommended as a defensive measure because the adviser was unqualified and lacked the necessary knowledge to advise the client, or because of the hostile attitude of the police to the adviser. Moreover when suspects do exercise their right to silence, this may not necessarily result from legal advice as the client may well have his own views on silence, or decide to ignore advice to co-operate. McConville and Hodgson therefore challenge the claim that an increase in legal representation would lead to an increase in the use of the right to silence, as suspects will assert their right despite legal advice or in the absence of clear advice. However, the presence of an adviser may give the suspect confidence to pursue his desire to assert his right to silence. They also emphasise that police questioning may contain irrelevant or illegitimate questions or concern the involvement of others. In those circumstances the suspects' silence, they argue, should not be seen as an exercise of the right to silence.

McConville et al argue that the assumption that the police are caught out by ambush defences 'misrepresents the reality of police interrogation',[50] for they found that it was only in exceptional cases that the police checked the accounts given by suspects:

whereas suspects are generally keen to proclaim their innocence and endeavour to furnish evidence in support of their claim, these attempts are routinely rebuffed by the police. For the interviewing officer the suspect is presumptively guilty and the purpose of the interview is to produce a confession. Lines of defence raised by the suspect are irrelevant red-herrings to be ignored or argued away...To permit material which contradicts guilt into the interview is to build weakness into the case and is the antithesis of constructing a case for the prosecution.[51]

A further question which needs to be considered in relation to ambushing is the importance of the suspect's own admission for obtaining a conviction. This may be over-estimated by critics of the right to silence. A study of police interrogation in New Haven found that in the majority of cases the police had sufficient evidence to convict a suspect without interrogation.[52] Arrests usually followed the receipt of witness statements and by the time the arrest was made, a considerable amount of evidence had been amassed. The police themselves did not find interrogation helpful and it was often undertaken on a casual and haphazard basis. The importance of confession to successful prosecution and conviction has also been challenged. The study by Williamson and Moston[53] in 1990 of over 1,000 interviews conducted by the Metropolitan Police found that silence in interrogation had no effect on whether a suspect was charged in cases where the evidence was strong or weak, but in cases where the evidence was borderline, silence made a charge more likely. Suspects who were silent were also more likely than those who spoke to plead guilty. In the Crown Court study undertaken by Zander and Henderson[54] the acquittal rate in contested cases was lower for those who exercised their right to silence than for those who answered questions. On the basis of these findings the Royal Commission recommended retaining the right to silence.[55] The majority thought that experienced professional criminals who wished to remain silent would still do so under a regime which penalised silence, and would then argue at trial that they were silent on the basis of legal advice. It is possible that some defendants who refuse to speak would be convicted, but the numbers would not be great, concluded the Commission. However, less experienced and vulnerable suspects would be exposed to risk if the right to silence were lost. Given this, it seems unlikely that increasing the pressure on suspects to speak will lead to an increase in convictions of the guilty. As most suspects in the Crown Court plead guilty, the impact of silence may be limited. A large number of those who are silent in the police station do subsequently plead guilty.

The professional criminal also is more likely to be aware of the need to have an explanation prepared in advance of any interrogation and is unlikely to be caught by the penalty of adverse inferences from silence, or any form of advance disclosure as it is still open to him to construct a false alibi. He may well blame his lawyer for the way the defence was presented or changed.

Moreover, in the majority of cases evidence can be obtained from independent sources which is highly desirable as uncorroborated confession evidence may be unsafe. This has been vividly illustrated by the history of wrongful convictions in the United Kingdom in which confession evidence was crucial.

In any case should the use of silence by the guilty be equated with abuse or exploitation of the right to silence? If a right exists, predicated on principles such as equal treatment and the presumption of innocence, then it should be available to everyone regardless of the reasons for exercising that right. The principle of equal concern and respect demands that both the guilty and innocent are afforded procedural protections. The use of the privilege by the guilty does not negate its value or constitute a reason for abandoning it. The protection of the guilty might be seen as an inevitable by-product of safeguarding the innocent. An analogy might be drawn here with the granting of bail. The fact that some suspects, who are granted bail, are ultimately convicted, would not be a ground to withhold bail in the future from them, or from others. The legitimate reasons to deny bail include substantial grounds for believing that the defendant, if released, would fail to surrender to custody, commit an offence while on bail or interfere with witnesses or obstruct the course of justice, or the court is satisfied that he should be kept in custody for his own protection. While the nature and seriousness of the offence with which he is charged and the strength of the prosecution case, are factors for the court or custody officer to consider in reaching a decision, the guilt of the accused, which has yet to be established, cannot determine the issue. Even if some suspects granted bail did abscond, this would not negate the presumption in favour of bail for suspects in general. Yet this type of reasoning seems to underpin the claim that the right to silence, because it protects the guilty, should be abolished.

Wrongful acquittals

If a correlation could be found between an increase in the use of the right to silence since PACE and an increase in acquittals in a particular sample, one still could not infer that the acquittal was wrongful or that, in those cases, adverse comment on the accused's silence by the judge or prosecution would have led to a conviction. It is difficult to see how such hypotheses could be verified. It may be hard to isolate silence as the crucial determining factor influencing the jury's verdict. Equally it does not follow that the removal of the right to silence will increase the number of cases brought to trial which are dropped because of a lack of evidence, or that adverse comment on silence will always lead to a conviction.

Wrongful acquittals may occur for a number of reasons, including the failure of the police and prosecution to marshal cogent evidence rather than a consequence of the exercise of the right to silence. The reason for many acquittals is simply that the case is not proved beyond reasonable doubt in the view of the jury. Other causes include instances where the judge himself has decided that there is insufficient evidence to convict, directing the jury accordingly. A study by the Oxford Penal Research Unit found that one-third of all acquittals in the sample studied resulted from judicial directions.[56] A more fruitful line of enquiry might be to consider the reasons for the relatively high number of judicially directed acquittals.

The number of non-jury acquittals increased in the 1980s, representing an increase in ordered acquittals and a small decrease in directed acquittals. Block, Corbett and Peay examined 100 non-jury acquittals in the Crown Court.[57] They found 71 ordered acquittals, 28 directed acquittals and 1 mixed acquittal. While less than half of the ordered acquittals were foreseeable, three quarters of directed acquittals were felt to be foreseeable. They attribute this to the fact that they were weak cases which should not have been continued, in contrast to those where the outcome reflected unexpected circumstances which could not have been foreseen, so some weak cases, they argue, could have been identified and discontinued before committal. They recommend increasing the power of the CPS to discontinue cases at any time up to the beginning of Crown Court trial. This view was also advanced by the Runciman Commission.[58] Cases may also fail because of the absence of key witnesses or for procedural defects during the investigation.[59] In any case, as the number of defendants who do not speak is so low it is questionable whether silence offers a useful explanation for acquittals.

The problem of wrongful convictions is widely seen as a more pressing and extensive problem than wrongful acquittals. A recurring feature of these miscarriages of justice has been the lack of independent evidence. Paradoxically, the police themselves have pointed to the importance of the need for independent evidence, while at the same time supporting the loss of the right to silence.

Critics of the right to silence also appear to operate with a static model of the criminal process. Depending on one's standpoint and the stage of the proceedings, whether preliminary investigation, cautioning and interrogation, trial or sentencing, the perception of the relevance of the evidence to the ultimate probandum may alter. What might appear to be a peripheral factor in this early stage, and not mentioned, could later transpire to be crucial to the defence. During the initial stage of police interrogation, the suspect may not be aware of the full extent of the case against him, the full legal consequences of silence and lack the benefit of legal advice. For this reason the Royal Commission on Criminal Procedure recommended retaining the right to silence.[60]

Innocent and guilty silences

Underlying many of the demands for change is the assumption that failure to mention a particular fact is evidence of guilt. Attention is often drawn to the common sense assumption that confronted with an accusation in everyday life, an individual would normally make an effort to explain himself. But there may be a number of reasons for failing to mention a particular fact during interrogation other than guilt. Fear, anxiety, the desire to protect someone else, embarrassment, outrage and anger may account for silence, all of which are compatible with innocence. There may be fears that statements will be misconstrued. If the suspect has previously had a poor relationship with the police, he may be particularly anxious about speaking or sceptical about being believed by the police. Dennis[61] has argued that these justifications of silence offer a weak ground for retaining the right to silence. Even if it means that an adverse inference would be dangerous in such cases, it does not follow that silence has no probative value or that it should be excluded from the jury's consideration in all cases.

But the problem here is how to reliably distinguish between them, to prevent defendants from being prejudiced. It would be difficult to formulate a reliable means of distinguishing the suspicious silence from silence in response to other factors. The population of suspects and detainees is heterogenous; it includes professional criminals, but it also encompasses vulnerable groups such as those with learning disabilities and juveniles, who are at risk of making damaging or unreliable statements.[62] The particular problems faced by these special groups was recognised by the Fisher Inquiry[63] into the Confait case. As its Report noted: 'Not all persons interrogated by the police or subjected to prosecution are mentally subnormal, near-illiterate youths, any more than they are all 'sophisticated professional criminals', consequently the rules of law and criminal procedure must accommodate both classes.'[64] Sixteen years later, following the PACE reforms, the Runciman Commission said that it was not fully satisfied with the rules and arrangements for the advice and protection of vulnerable groups during police interrogation.[65] The Commission supported a review of the role, functions and training of appropriate adults. Even if ambushing was a problem, which was highly questionable, weakening the right to silence for all suspects was not the fairest solution. By speaking, one may seriously undermine one's credibility at trial, in cases where one lies or makes omissions to cover up personal embarrassment; silence may be a rational response in certain circumstances rather than an indication of guilt. It may also, of course, be chosen on the basis of legal advice. The solicitor will assess the situation and may advise his client to remain silent, to allow time for reflection, although this may be risky. Under the CJPOA, the lawyer still may counsel that silence is the best course of action if the case against the accused is weak.

It is questionable whether ambushing was a major problem for the prosecution. Few suspects exercised the right to silence and there may be a number of reasons for failure to mention a fact during interrogation. Furthermore, the law prior to the 1994 Act was sufficient to deal with ambush defences in the sense that the boundaries of judicial comment did enable juries to take account of those individuals surprising the prosecution at trial. It was open to the judge to point out to the jury that the accused could have mentioned it earlier. It may well be that jurors did take account of the initial failure to mention a crucial fact on the issue in question in their deliberations. The Crown Court study found that the jury would have been aware of the fact that the accused had been silent in interrogation in over 80% of the cases under scrutiny.[66]

The failure to testify

The failure to testify at trial has also been seen as protecting the guilty, most notably by Bentham.[67] In his *Rationale of Judicial Evidence* he questioned whether talk of rights, such as the right to silence, was a meaningful or useful way of approaching evidential problems. Bentham saw the rule prohibiting defendants from giving evidence as serving the interests of evil-doers: 'not only are the guilty served but it is they alone that are served: they alone, and without any mixture of the innocent'.[68] In this way the truth is obscured. The only beneficiaries are criminals and their lawyers:

> In seeing the mischiefs entailed by this rule upon the community at large, we see its uses to criminals, delinquents, *mala fide* defendants, extortious and oppressive plaintiffs; in a word, to evil-doers of all sorts and sizes... Moreover, in seeing the persons to whom it is of use, the persons whose sinister interests are served by it, we see the hands and hearts that stand pledged for its support.[69]

Bentham's comments need to be seen in the context of his hostility to exclusionary rules in general which he sees as encouraging crime. At the time he was writing there were numerous limits on competence principally based on the fear of bias from interest. The rule prohibiting the defendant's testimony by 'shutting the door against an article of true and unfallacious evidence necessary to conviction, operates', said Bentham, 'as a licence for the commission of a crime.'[70] In his *Treatise on Judicial Evidence*[71] he speculated that if criminals had met to devise a rule guaranteed to protect them, this is the first rule that they would have established. For Bentham the trial is essentially a search for the truth in which all available evidence should be accessible to the tribunal provided that it is relevant. Once the prosecutor is denied access to the accused's testimony, he is forced to search for inferior forms of evidence.

In the twentieth century attention has focused on the prohibition on comment in the 1898 Criminal Evidence Act which was subjected to sustained criticism. Critics argued that there should be greater freedom for the judge and the prosecution to comment on the refusal to testify than that permitted by the 1898 Act, in order to prevent wrongful acquittals. The Criminal Law Revision Committee saw the limits on judicial comment on the accused's failure to testify as 'much too favourable to the defence.'[72]   Both judge and prosecution, argued the CLRC, should be free to comment on the refusal and the court or jury should be able to treat his refusal to testify as corroboration of the evidence against him. The prohibition on comment in s 1(b) of the Criminal Evidence Act 1898, the Committee argued, 'is wrong in principle and entirely illogical.'[73] The Home Office Working Group did not go quite so far as the CLRC in its recommendations on the nature of the inferences to be drawn from silence, but it did advocate that in the Crown Court, the prosecution should make more frequent and robust use of their existing right to comment.[74] The right not to testify was also criticised in the debate on the Criminal Justice and Public Order Act. In the original Criminal Justice Bill the accused would have been addressed directly by the judge on this issue and advised of the consequences of the failure to testify. However, following strong opposition this was amended, so that this is now a matter for the defendant's legal representative to report on.[75]

Advocates of change, such as Glanville Williams,[76] argued that juries may be reluctant to convict a defendant who does not testify. He cites the example of George Ince in the Barn Murder trial of 1973, where the jury could not agree and said that they found it very difficult to reach a decision because of 'there being no defence.' The right not to testify can prejudice the victims of crime whose interests need to be considered.[77]

These arguments are problematic. Bentham's remarks should be seen in the light of the undeveloped police force and crude systems of interrogation and crime control of the early nineteenth century. His objections have less force today, when there are numerous aids to assist in crime control unavailable in the early nineteenth century. The prosecution has increased opportunities to obtain independent evidence prior to trial.

Moroever, if the accused is silent, it is questionable whether the scope for judicial comment was too weak, as the possibility of 'strong comment' on failure to testify already existed before the 1994 Act, following the guidelines in *Sparrow*.[78] The *Bathurst* direction, as Greenawalt[79] notes, allowed an oblique intimation that the accused is acting suspiciously if he remains silent. The defendant who did not enter the witness box did so at the risk of the 'worst being thought' by the jury and for this reason counsel would advise him not to testify only in exceptional cases. Lawton LJ, who was critical of the right to silence in *Sparrow*, nonetheless acknowledged that 'In our experience of trials, juries seldom acquit persons who do not give evidence when there is a clear case for them to answer and they do not answer it'.[80]

The example of George Ince, given by Glanville Williams, may well be exceptional but given the secrecy of jury deliberations, it is difficult to speculate on what happens in the jury room. Even if an individual juror were subsequently to avow the significance of silence in securing an acquittal, this does not mean his view is shared by all members of the jury or that it was crucial to the verdict at that time. It may be that it is given significance only in retrospect.

Similar considerations apply at both the trial and pre-trial stages. The unattractive, inarticulate defendant may do himself more harm than good by speaking, or if he speaks in an unpopular dialect may prejudice the jury against him; if he is garrulous he may let his tongue run away with him. If the jury is likely to respond negatively to his appearance, or demeanour while giving evidence, he might well be advised to stay out of the witness box whether or not comment is permitted or adverse inferences may be drawn from silence. Before the CJPOA if the accused was silent at trial or during interrogation, nothing could prevent the jury from drawing adverse inferences from silence, if it so chose, notwithstanding judicial directions or rules of evidence to the contrary. As Zander notes: 'There is no way a rule of law could ever prevent a jury... or magistrates from using ordinary common sense.'[81]

If the suspect speaks in interrogation he may well be more likely to testify. The number of defendants who fail to testify is low. In the research undertaken for the Royal Commission on Criminal Justice, it was found that about one quarter of defendants in contested cases in the Crown Court did not testify.[82] The Runciman Commission argued that: 'Given the principle that the burden of proof should rest on the prosecution, it must be wrong for defendants who leave the prosecution to prove its case to be exposed to comment by either the prosecution or the judge to the effect that their failure to enter the witness box corroborates the prosecution case.'[83] The Commission thought that the existing direction was sufficient to inform the jury of the defendant's right not to testify, and that silence does not establish guilt, but it also means there is no evidence to undermine the prosecution's case.

Silence and the need for corroboration

The right to silence has been construed by some writers as particularly damaging in certain types of crimes, namely offences committed in private, such as sexual offences, where there are problems of corroboration and where admissions may be therefore be of greater significance in obtaining a conviction.

Before the Criminal Justice and Public Order Act was passed, a formal corroboration warning was required when dealing with sexual offences, warning the jury of the danger of convicting on the uncorroborated evidence of the

148

complainant. Without hearing the defendant's testimony, but taking account of the judge's warning, juries could be very reluctant to convict whereas if the accused were encouraged to speak, then curtailing the right to silence would increase the conviction of the guilty.

Glanville Williams[84] cites the case of a man charged with 'the rape of a young girl of blameless life', to whom he was a complete stranger. The defendant pleaded not guilty and although his counsel argued that she consented, this was strongly denied. The defendant did not testify and because the jury felt uneasy at not hearing his account, says Williams, acquitted him. After the trial the judge said he thought the girl was speaking the truth. There are, however, a number of problems with this argument. First, it is difficult for the reader to form a judgement on the guilt or innocence of the accused without having heard all the evidence. Second, it does not follow that the failure to testify was the reason, or the only reason the defendant was acquitted. Third, even if one were to accept that the problems of corroboration are so daunting in sexual offences that adverse inferences from silence should be permitted, it would not follow that this should be generalised to offences which do not raise such difficult problems of corroboration. In any event these problems were considered by the Law Commission.[85] In its review of corroboration the Commission criticised the rules relating to sexual offences and accomplice evidence for their complexity and inflexibility leading to bizarre results and recommended that mandatory corroboration warnings in relation to both types of evidence should be abolished. Its proposals were implemented by s 32 of the 1994 Act.

Prior to the Act, a conviction would have been possible without corroboration, but the judge was required to warn the jury of the dangers of convicting on accomplice evidence unless that evidence was corroborated. A failure to warn would mean that a conviction would be quashed on appeal. Similarly, a judge was required to warn the jury of the dangers of convicting the accused on the basis of uncorroborated evidence of the complainant of a sexual offence. Following the Act the judge still has the discretion to warn the jury of the dangers of convicting on uncorroborated evidence if he is concerned about a particular witness, but a failure to do so will not automatically lead to a conviction being quashed.

In *Makanjuola*[86] the Court of Appeal said that under s 32 it is a matter of discretion for the trial judge what, if any warning, to give in respect of such a witness. Whether or not to give a direction depends on the circumstances of the case, the issues raised and the contents and quality of the evidence of the witness. There should be an evidential basis for suggesting the witness is unreliable. It is for the judge to decide the strength and terms of the warning and it does not have to be invested with the florid regime of the old law. The Court of Appeal also said that it will be reluctant to interfere with a trial judge's exercise of his discretion unless it is unreasonable in the *Wednesbury* sense.

The Law Commission's recommendations for reform were supported by the Royal Commission on Criminal Justice. There had already been a move away from corroboration in s 34 of the Criminal Justice Act 1988 and s 52 of the Criminal Justice Act 1991 in relation to children's evidence.[87] Now most of the requirements for corroboration have been abolished.

Clearly there are particular problems with sexual offences where the act in question has taken place in private, with no witnesses, and conviction rates are very low, but the fact of silence itself may be less significant in securing a wrongful acquittal than other factors such as discussion of the complainant's sexual history, either with the defendant, or when permitted under s 2 of the Sexual Offences (Amendment) Act 1976, with other men, the judicial interpretation of which has largely favoured the defendant.[88] If a consent defence is run, the accused may well be eager to testify especially if he has a previous sexual relationship with the complainant. Given that only a small proportion of rapes are reported, abolishing the right to silence in court, or at the pre-trial stage, is unlikely to be effective in combatting this type of crime. By speaking the accused may be better able to exploit the prejudices of the jury.

A number of recommendations have been made by campaigners in England and the United States to strengthen the position of the complainant, including redefining rape as aggravated assault; relationships with other men could be rendered inadmissible in all cases. Good practice in other jurisdictions such as Canada has been highlighted by some commentators which could provide a potential model for the UK.

The prohibition on judicial comment on the accused's failure to testify in cases of child abuse where the defence challenges the child's veracity, is also criticised by Williams.[89] But ways of improving the reception and treatment of child witnesses are being explored and some changes have already been implemented. It could be argued that these initiatives may prove more effective than changing the right to silence.

The right to silence and the protection of the innocent

The corollary of the argument that the right to silence protects the guilty is that abolition of the right will not harm the innocent. The innocent have nothing to fear if the right is lost, on this argument, for if they tell the truth they are in no danger, particularly in the light of procedural safeguards. An initial explanation of apparently incriminating circumstances would not prejudice the innocent but on the contrary enable the matter to be resolved more swiftly to the accused's advantage. Given the restraints on the manufacture of confessions and restrictions on the admissibility of involuntary confessions they are, it is argued, unlikely to be led into inculpatory admissions and tape-recording provides further protection of the innocent.

A 'good cause' provision it is argued will cover any legitimate reasons for initial silence. Where the accused has 'good cause' for refusing to answer questions in interrogation or trial, it could be left open to the defence to show that no weight should be attached to the accused's silence in determining guilt or credibility because of these extenuating circumstances. Such a 'good cause' provision is included in s 35(2) of the CJPOA. In addition the court retains its general discretion to excuse silence or the accused may be excused from speaking on grounds under statute or privilege. It is also stipulated in s 35(1) that the provisions of s 35 will not be activated if it appears to the court that the defendant's age, mental or physical condition make it undesirable for him to give evidence. But these factors do not encompass all innocent silences. It is also unclear how knowledge of good cause will come to the knowledge of the court's attention in the less obvious cases.

At the pre-trial stage s 34 refers to whether the suspect could reasonably have been expected to mention the fact later relied on and reasonableness will encompass the circumstances of the offence and the particular characteristics of the suspect.[90] In determining the appropriate inference, the court or jury will take account of the characteristics of the suspect. But this still leaves the problem of 'borderline' cases, where the mental or physical condition may not be obvious, as well as the other possible reasons for silence, including protection of others or avoiding embarrassment, which may not be brought to the court's attention.

The court can use its general discretion to allow the defendant not to answer specific questions. If the accused had, for example, been found in embarrassing circumstances, the jury could be directed that drawing adverse inferences would be inappropriate. It might be argued that preventing personal embarrassment to a defendant should not be a major consideration in the debate. Witnesses could not refuse to answer questions at trial simply because they would cause embarrassment, argues Williams, so why should this indulgence be given to the accused? 'Even if a particular defendant finds himself in a bit of a pickle are we obliged to frame our law of evidence in order to protect him.'[91] Appeals to sparing the feelings of such defendants are unrealistic, he says, as they arise so rarely: 'Practically all defendants who do not give evidence are motivated by a desire to avoid conviction, not by a desire to avoid confessing peccadilloes.'[92] Similarly, Cross admitted to having a 'stony heart in all cases except that of an accused with a criminal record' and said he was 'left completely in the cold by horror stories about the innocent man advised not to give evidence because he would be such a bad witness, or the innocent husband who did not want his wife to know that he had been with his mistress at the material time'.[93] In such cases the innocent accused runs a greater risk by not answering a complainant's allegations than by exposing himself to cross-examination.

Cross[94] was unsympathetic to the person who refuses to speak because he does not wish to reveal his activities or whereabouts at a particular time, simply because of embarrassment. But there may be instances where more important

151

matters are at stake. There is no evidence that the reasons for maintaining silence are always trivial. For weaker, ill-educated, inarticulate and poorer defendants, there may well be genuine fears of making themselves understood during cross-examination and they may prefer to take the risk and remain silent even under the new regime. A nervous and unprepossessing individual, ignorant of criminal procedure and lacking interpersonal skills, intimidated by the atmosphere of the court, is likely to make an unfavourable impression on the tribunal. Here the risks of adverse inferences being drawn from silence may be outweighed by the effects of testifying. Likewise, at the pre-trial stage, remaining silent gave the weak or confused suspect in the past the opportunity to take time to reflect rationally on his situation. The majority of suspects do find being in police detention extremely threatening and while in such a fearful state, may be at risk of making false admissions. But now under the provisions of the CJPOA they will be prejudiced by remaining silent.

Some argue further that the exercise of the right to silence can actually harm the innocent, while protecting the guilty. The Criminal Law Revision Committee noted, for example, that advising the suspect of his right to silence did not assist the innocent suspect as it might discourage him from making an exculpatory statement. However advance disclosure will help the innocent by allowing for early verification of an explanation which establishes innocence. The sooner the suspect speaks the earlier the charges against him may be cleared up, with the prosecution dropping the charge once a satisfactory explanation is given. However, the fact of silence may mean the prosecution is less willing to drop a charge against the accused, entailing long periods spent on remand or at worst to a wrongful conviction.[95] The claim that the innocent are more often harmed than helped by the right to silence is advanced by Friendly[96] and by Williams, who argues that failing to answer questions 'would greatly increase the risk of being wrongfully convicted'.[97] He cites a Justice Report which referred to 'a number of cases where defendants with a valid defence had been found guilty because they had been foolishly advised not to give evidence.'[98] Furthermore the innocent also may be convicted because a guilty person stays silent, as in the Sacco and Vanzetti case[99] and other cause célèbres. Williams[100] cites examples where the defendant has been wrongfully convicted because he has been wrongly advised not to testify. But this needs to be considered in relation to the number of cases in which the defendants have been wrongfully convicted, despite giving evidence. Silence was rarely advocated by counsel even when comment was prohibited.

There are difficulties with the argument that the innocent have nothing to fear from the loss of the right to silence. There is no clear evidence that waiving the right to silence does have the effect of an early release from detention. Large numbers of people do spend considerable time on remand awaiting trial. But as very few suspects remain silent, it is hard to conclude that silence is the reason for a delay in a case coming to trial. Delays may be due to a variety of administrative problems and to over-loading of the courts. Clearly, the right of the innocent not to be wrongfully convicted should not be overshadowed by the issue of the wrongful acquittal of the guilty. What evidence is available suggests a link between waiver of the right and confession and conviction, rather than between silence and conviction.[101]

It is vulnerable suspects rather than professional criminals who are most likely to be adversely affected by losing the right to silence. The waiver of the right to silence has figured in several miscarriages of justice, including the cases of Judith Ward, Stefan Kiszko, the Bridgewater Three, the Birmingham Six and the Guildford Four. These cases illustrated the problem of false confessions and recent psychological research has enhanced our understanding of this problem.[102] Once silence is given evidential significance it becomes a weapon in the prosecution's case, then weaker defendants are at greater risk of being wrongfully convicted. For this reason groups and lawyers actively involved in the miscarriage of justice cases and campaigns have been most fearful of the loss of the right to silence.[103] The danger was also recognised by the Runciman Commission.[104]

As well as prejudicing the innocent, loss of the right to silence may also adversely affect what Greenawalt[105] has called the 'borderline innocent', that is, those people who are mixed up to some extent in a series of events which make up the crime even though they may not be guilty. If they forget to mention anything when answering police questions or what they say is misconstrued, this could have prejudicial consequences.

The fact that an innocent person might be convicted while someone else remains silent cannot justify the loss of the right to silence. If someone is wrongfully convicted, clearly this is a cause for great concern. It suggests serious problems with the conduct of the investigation which demand attention. But inquiries into wrongful convictions have shown that the suspect's own admissions may be crucial to conviction. Moreover without the right to silence it is even harder for those appellants to win their appeal. It is therefore difficult to see how the innocent can be helped by the abolition of the right to silence. Rather, pressures to speak can only further weaken their position.

Common sense and the right to silence

Underpinning many of the claims that the right to silence protects the guilty is the appeal to common sense. Common sense recognises that only the guilty would wish to hide behind the veil of silence so allowing adverse inferences, including inferences of guilt, to be drawn from silence, would bring the law closer to common sense thinking. This would relieve the jury from engaging in mental acrobatics by denying the dictates of common sense under the judge's direction. Common sense on this view is seen as superior because it accords with our intuitions: we intuitively know that the innocent will wish to speak to clear themselves, while the guilty are more likely to remain silent, the judicial direction formerly used to repress an inference of guilt from silence is counter-intuitive. To repress such inferences is contrary to common sense. This argument has a long history and was advanced by Bentham who asked, if a man, although really innocent, is unlucky enough to become the object of suspicion, 'does he fly to any of these subterfuges?'.[106] He would not do so, says Bentham, if he valued his reputation and good character.[107]

The appeal to common sense has resurfaced in modern critiques of the right to silence. Glanville Williams,[108] for example, argued that to allow no inference to be drawn from silence is 'contrary to commonsense'. It runs counter to our realisation of how we ourselves would behave if faced with a criminal charge. If we were innocent we would not normally stay silent. Rather we would make every effort to reject the accusation by trying to draw attention to any facts inconsistent with it. 'If the suspicion is a serious one', he says, 'we would be ready and anxious to answer the questions of the doubters.'[109]

Allowing adverse inferences to be drawn from silence is therefore seen as rescuing the jury from the artificial situation of trying to follow the judge's direction, while repressing 'natural' assumptions. Given that it is doubtful whether juries did succeed in banishing these assumptions on judicial direction, the changes in the CJPOA might be seen as having the merit of honesty, of recognising what actually happens behind the doors of the jury room and of making this clear to the defendant. Irving,[110] for example, argues that juries are expert at drawing inferences from silence in everyday life, they do so repeatedly, and no doubt do so even if explicitly prohibited from doing so. If tape-recordings allow the jury to see where the silences lie and their context, he says, it is still be open to the defence to explain to the jury the reasons for them, to prevent adverse inferences from being drawn.

Greenawalt[111] points to the fact that in everyday life, people expect others charged with wrong-doing to make some response if the accusation is substantial. We expect it because of the strong psychological pressures to speak and jurors may well expect it even when directed otherwise. Of course we would not sanction the use of torture to extract an answer, he says, but equally we would not deny the right to ask; if silence then ensued, we would normally see it as a sign of guilt and an individual staying quiet in such circumstances might well expect to lose his friends or employment. We would not think it morally reprehensible for a friend or employer to take action on the basis of such an inference. Similarly, Zuckerman points to the fact that if we have violated or offended a moral norm or legal rule, 'our natural moral reaction is to offer an explanation.'[112] Giving an answer is seen as the natural reaction to an accusation.[113] He acknowledges that the police, in the course of interrogation, can exploit this reaction to pressure the individual to speak against his better judgment. If we expect people to answer serious accusations in everyday life, and usually do draw unfavourable inferences from a failure to respond, then it might be argued that it is irrational to acknowledge such a right to silence in public life, when we are dealing with the relationship between the state and the individual, rather than the relationship between citizens. Although Greenawalt[114] does express reservations regarding the loss of the right to silence, he argues that the law of evidence should normally conform to common sense thinking and that where it deviates from it, this divergence should be justifiable.

But this common sense view that confronted with an accusation an individual would normally make an effort to explain himself is problematic. Like many common sense assumptions, it is untested, speculative and highly contentious. Should the judicial direction be based on common sense? Given that common sense is unreliable, impressionable and unsystematic, it provides a poor model for the law of evidence to follow. The latter, it could be argued, is or should be closer to scientific thinking in involving the assessment of evidence, conceptual analysis, abstraction and generalisation and applying legal concepts and rules to the facts of a particular case. It is because of the weaknesses of common sense thinking that a firm judicial direction is so important. Defenders of common sense might argue that this distinction between common sense and legal thought is elitist and that what is admirable about jury trials is precisely that they are composed of ordinary people using common sense and making inferences, just as they do in everyday life. But the reason why common sense is unreliable here is precisely because it may wrongly equate silence with guilt. If the common sense inference is that the innocent would obviously speak, and no account is taken of other possible factors accounting for silence, then this highlights the difficulties with this mode of thinking. There may be a number of reasons for failing to mention a particular fact during interrogation other than guilt. Fear, anxiety, confusion, the desire to protect someone else, embarrassment, outrage and anger may account for silence, all of which are compatible with innocence, so the probative value of silence in establishing guilt is low.

The problem for the jury is how to reliably distinguish the 'suspicious' from the 'innocent' silence, to prevent innocent defendants from being prejudiced. It would be difficult to formulate a reliable test for distinguishing between them. Silence may be a rational response in certain circumstances rather than an indication of guilt although this may not be obvious to the jury. It may also be chosen on the basis of legal advice as McConville and Hodgson[115] have shown. Vulnerable suspects are more likely than professional criminals to be adversely affected by losing the right to silence. Gudjonsson[116] and Kassin and Wrightsman[117] have demonstrated the significance of vulnerabilities, suggestibility and compliance in the production of false confessions. Even where suspects do not suffer from mental illness or have learning difficulties, Gudjonsson argues, they may in some situations falsely confess to very serious crimes, even with a lawyer present and where the interview is recorded.

Notwithstanding the Court of Appeal's concern over the gulf between law and common sense in *Sullivan*,[118] there was also a clear line of cases which emphasised the distinction between silence and guilt, perhaps best exemplified by the case of Dr. Bodkin Adams. When he failed to testify, the then Mr. Justice Devlin asserted that: 'It would be utterly wrong if you were to regard Dr. Adams' silence as contributing in any way towards proof of guilt.'[119]

For Glanville Williams, however, the issue is clear that an innocent person would be anxious to dispel the doubts and accusations of others. But this assumption amounts to a rejection of the presumption of innocence and a shifting of the burden of proof onto the accused.

Over the past twenty years, the law has moved closer to common sense on this issue. *Chandler*,[120] as noted earlier, limited the right to silence, by seeing the presence of a solicitor overcoming the inequalities between the parties and the same reasoning seems to underpin the provisions of the CJPOA. But everyday life is not comparable to the context of the police station and courtroom and therefore common sense assumptions which equate silence with guilt, drawn from everyday life, cannot be legitimately applied to the latter contexts. The relationship between citizens is quite distinct from the position of the accused undergoing interrogation in the police station, or subject to examination and cross-examination in the formal structure of the court-room. Private accusations cannot be compared to accusations by the police, given the inequalities between prosecution and defence. Once the accuser is the state, then questions of fundamental rights come to the forefront of the discussion.

The Home Office Working Group proposed that inferences should be permitted to be drawn from initial silence but the appropriate inference would be that the later explanation is unreliable so the inference would be limited to undermining credibility rather than indicating guilt.[121] However, it is difficult to see how the inference could be confined to credibility as the jury may well find it difficult to distinguish clearly between credibility and guilt, especially when confronted with adverse comments by the prosecuting counsel or the judge. Once the jury is sceptical regarding the credibility of the defendant, it is more likely to find him guilty. The relationship between credit and the issues in the case has been a vexed problem for the law of evidence; it has presented problems for lawyers and judges familiar with the principles of evidence so that it may be very difficult for juries to comprehend and apply. In any event sections 34-37 of the CJPOA make clear that silence is a factor to consider in determining the guilt of the accused.

The common sense approach is likely to figure in future interpretations of the provisions on silence in the CJPOA. It has been widely used in interpreting the Criminal Evidence Order in Northern Ireland, despite the particular problems of interpreting silence in the context of cultural traditions of nonco-operation in the province, discussed earlier. The European Court of Human Rights also stressed a common sense approach to drawing inferences under the Order in *Murray v UK*[122] and it was stressed by the Court of Appeal in *Argent*.[123]

The cases on the Northern Ireland Order are instructive here. In the case of *McLernon*[124] Kelly LJ stressed that it is a matter for the court to decide what inferences should be drawn and that Article 4, the equivalent of s 35, should be construed in the widest terms and no limits are imposed on what results could follow if article 4 is invoked. In *Murray v DPP*[125] the House of Lords endorsed the use of a common sense approach in drawing inferences. The CLRC's report was cited to resolve uncertainties over what inferences could be drawn. The House of Lords held that if the prosecution has established a prima facie case against a defendant who refuses to testify, the court could draw such inferences as appear proper in the circumstances including an inference of guilt.[126] The House of Lords supported the Northern Ireland Court of Appeal's view that while it would be improper to draw the inference that because he did not testify he was therefore guilty, the court could use common sense to infer from his refusal to testify that there is no reasonable possibility of an innocent explanation to rebut the prima facie case against him adduced by the Crown, and from this, to conclude that after all the evidence has been considered that the accused is guilty. So the inferences drawn under Article 4 have encompassed both guilt and credibility. The situation in Northern Ireland is more complex because silence can constitute corroboration of other evidence against the accused.

Section 38(3) of the CJPOA makes clear that the accused cannot be convicted on silence alone: there must be some evidence against him; a conviction cannot be based just on an inference from silence permitted under ss 34, 35, 36 and 37, and silence cannot be used to corroborate other evidence against the accused. But in practice it may be difficult to prevent juries from doing this. No guidance on the proper inference is given in the Act but it is left to the jury using ordinary common sense. The new Judicial Studies Board direction states that the judge should direct the jury that 'Failure to give evidence on its own cannot prove guilt but depending on the circumstances, you may hold his failure against him when deciding whether he is guilty.' While silence is a factor for the jury to consider in determining guilt, it cannot by itself determine the issue. However it may be difficult for juries to draw such fine distinctions.

Notes

1.   J. Bentham (1825) *A Treatise on Judicial Evidence*, London, ed. Dumont.
2.   Criminal Law Revision Committee (1972) *Eleventh Report, Evidence (General)*, London, HMSO, Cmnd 4991.
3.   Report of the Working Group on the Right of Silence (1989) Home Office, C Division, London, July 13.
4.   *Ibid*, para. 7.

5.   Report of the Royal Commission on Criminal Justice (1993) London, HMSO, Cmnd 2263, para. 4.25.
6.   B. Irving and I. McKenzie (1989) *Police Interrogation: The Effects of the Police and Criminal Evidence Act 1984*, London, Police Foundation.
7.   Report of the Royal Commission on Criminal Procedure (1981) London, HMSO, Cmnd 8092.
8.   See Report of the Working Group on the Right of Silence (1989), Appendix C.
9.   S. Moston, G. Stephenson and T. Williamson (1992) 'The effects of case characteristics on suspect behaviour during questioning', British Journal of Criminology, vol. 32, pp 23-30; see also (1993) 'The incidence, antecedents and consequences of the use of the right to silence during police questioning' Criminal Behaviour and Mental Health, vol. 3 pp 30-47; T. Williamson and S. Moston (1990) 'The extent of silence in police interviews', in S. Greer and R. Morgan (eds.) *The Right to Silence Debate*, Bristol Centre for Criminal Justice.
10.   ACPO (1993) *The Right of Silence, Briefing Paper*, London, ACPO.
11.   Home Secretary (July 30, 1987) Lecture, Police Foundation.
12.   Sir Peter Imbert, interview reported in The Guardian (30 November, 1989).
13.   Sir Paul Condon (1993) Conference on Report of the Royal Commission on Criminal Justice, London School of Economics.
14.   C. Pollard [1996] 'Public safety, accountability and the courts', Crim LR 152.
15.   CLRC, *op.cit.*, paras. 28, 40.
16.   *Ibid*, para. 30.
17.   J. Bentham, *op.cit.*
18.   CLRC, *op.cit.*, para. 21.
19.   Home Office Working Group, *Report*, para. 57.
20.   See M. Zander, Note of Dissent, RCCJ Report, pp 221-35.
21.   See R. Leng (1992) *The Right to Silence in Police Interrogation*, RCCJ Research Study no. 10, London, HMSO.
22.   See C. Pollard, *op. cit.*; [1994] 'A Case for Disclosure', Crim LR 42; 'Criminal Injustice', BBC, March 12 1995.
23.   See Guardian, 20 July 1992.
24.   RCCP Report.
25.   *Ibid*, para. 4.43; P. Softley (1980), *Police Interrogation: an observational study in Four Police Stations*, RCCP Research Study no.4, London, HMSO.
26.   D. J. Smith and P. Gray (1983) *Police and People in London,* Policy Studies Institute.

27.   B. Mitchell [1983] 'Confessions and police interrogation of suspects', Crim LR 596.

28.   J. Baldwin and M. McConville (1980) *Confessions in Crown Court Trials*, London, RCCP Research Study no. 5, London, HMSO; [1981] *Courts, Prosecution and Conviction*, London.

29.   A. Sanders, L. Bridges, A.Mulvaney, and G. Crozier (1989) *Advice and Assistance at Police Stations and the 24 Hour Duty Solicitor Scheme*, London, Lord Chancellor's Department, p 135.

30.   RCCJ Report, para. 4.19.

31.   D. Brown, *The Incidence of Right to Silence in Police Interviews, The Research Evidence Reviewed*, Home Office Research and Planning Unit, unpublished; see RCCJ Report, para. 4.15.

32.   See D. Galligan (1988) 'The Right to Silence Reconsidered', Current Legal Problems, 69.

33.   A. Zuckerman (1989) *The Principles of Criminal Evidence*, Oxford, Clarendon.

34.   See chapter 9 below.

35.   M. Zander [1979] 'The investigation of crime, a study of contested cases at the Old Bailey', Crim LR 203.

36.   C. Willis *et al* (1988) *The Tape Recording of Police Interviews with Suspects*, Home Office Research Study, no. 97, HMSO.

37.   (1966) 51 Cr App Rep 102.

38.   (1977) 66 Cr App Rep 237.

39.   [1973] 1 WLR 488.

40.   RCCJ Report, para. 4.22.

41.   M. Zander and P. Henderson (1993) *The Crown Court Study*, RCCJ Research Study no. 19, London HMSO.

42.   *Ibid.*

43.   R. Leng, *op. cit.*

44.   *Ibid*, p 20.

45.   *Ibid*, p 74.

46.   *Ibid*, p 20.

47.   M. McConville and J.Hodgson (1993) *Custodial Legal Advice and the Right to Silence*, RCCJ Research Study no. 16, London, HMSO.

48.   *Ibid*, p 89.

49.   *Ibid*, see also M. McConville, J. Hodgson, L. Bridges and A. Pavlovic (1994) *Standing Accused: The Organisation and Practices of Criminal Defence Lawyers in Britain*, Oxford University Press.

50.   M. McConville, A. Sanders and R. Leng (1991) *The Case for the Prosecution*, London, Routledge, p 76.

51.   *Ibid*, p 76.

52.   J. Griffiths and R. Ayres [1967] 'A Postscript to the Miranda Project: Interrogation of Draft Protestors', 77 Yale Law Journal, 305.

53. See T. Williamson and S. Moston (1990) 'The extent of silence in police interviews', in S. Greer and R. Morgan (eds.) *The Right to Silence Debate*, Bristol Centre for Criminal Justice. See also J. Baldwin and M. McConville (1980).

54. M. Zander and P.Henderson, *op. cit.*

55. See chapter 10 below.

56. S. McCabe and R. Purves (1972) *The Jury at Work*, Oxford, Blackwell, 1972.

57. B. Block, C. Corbett and J. Peay [1993] 'Ordered and Directed Acquittals in the Crown Court: A Time of Change', Crim LR 95.

58. RCCJ Report.

59. A major study of ordered and directed acquittals is now being conducted at the University of Birmingham.

60. RCCP Report.

61. I. Dennis (1989) 'Reconstructing the Law of Criminal Evidence', Current Legal Problems, 21.

62. See PACE, Code C, Annex E.

63. Report of an Inquiry by the Hon. Sir Henry Fisher into the circumstances leading to the trial of three persons on charges arising out of the death of Maxwell Confait and the fire at 27 Doggett Road, London S.E.6 (1977) London, HMSO.

64. *Ibid*, para. 1.8; see chapter 9 below.

65. See Report of the Royal Commission on Criminal Justice, para. 3.85.

66. See M. Zander and P. Henderson (1993).

67. J. Bentham (1825) *A Treatise on Judicial Evidence*, London, 338; (1843) *Rationale of Judicial Evidence, The Works of Jeremy Bentham*, Bowring edition, Edinburgh, 459.

68. J. Bentham (1843) 454.

69. *Ibid*, 449.

70. *Ibid*, p 338.

71. *Treatise on Judicial Evidence*, 241.

72. CLRC Report, para.110.

73. *Ibid*, para.110.

74. Report of the Home Office Working Group, para. 127(xix).

75. Practice Note (Crown Court: Evidence: Advice to Defendant) 1995, Times 12 April, [1995] 1 WLR 657, [1995] 2 All ER 499.

76. G. Williams [1987] 'The Tactic of Silence', NLJ 1107.

77. See D. Q. Miller 'Turning a blind eye', Counsel, May/June 1994, 18.

78. [1973] 1 WLR 488.

79. K. Greenawalt (1974) 'Perspectives on the Right to Silence' in R. Hood (ed.) *Crime, Criminology and Public Policy*, London, Heinemann, 235.

80. [1973] 1 WLR 488.

81. M. Zander (1978) 'The Right to Silence in the Police Station and the Caution' in P. Glazebrook (ed.) *Reshaping the Criminal Law*, London, Stevens, at p 355.

82. See M. Zander and P. Henderson, *op.cit.*

83. RCCJ Report, para. 4.26.

84. G. Williams, *op.cit.*

85. Law Commission (1990) *Corroboration of Evidence in Criminal Trials*, Working Paper no. 115, London, HMSO.

86. *R v Makanjuola; R v Easton* [1996] Crim LR 44.

87. See Criminal Justice Act 1988, ss 32, 33 and 34, which abolished the proviso to s 38(1) of the Children and Young Persons Act 1933, which had stipulated that the accused could not be convicted on the unsworn testimony of a child unless her evidence was corroborated.

88. J. Temkin (1993) 'Sexual History Evidence - The Ravishment of Section 2', Crim LR 3.

89. G. Williams, *op.cit.*

90. *R v Argent* [1996] Times, 19 December.

91. G. Williams, *op.cit*, 1108.

92. *Ibid.*

93. R. Cross [1973] 'The Evidence Report: Sense or Nonsense - A very Wicked Animal Defends the Eleventh Report of the Criminal Law Revision Committee', Crim LR at 336.

94. *Ibid.*

95. Sir James Miskin (8 October, 1988) Lecture, Inner Temple.

96. H. Friendly (1968) 'The Fifth Amendment Tomorrow: the case for constitutional change', University of Cincinatti Law Review, 37, 676.

97. G. Williams, *op.cit.*, 1107.

98. *Ibid.*

99. H. Ehrman (1970) *The Case That Will Not Die*, London, W.H. Allen.

100. G. Williams, *op.cit.*

101. See P. Softley (1980), R. Baldwin and M. McConville (1981); Zander (1988).

102. See G. Gudjonsson (1992) *The Psychology of Interrogations, Confessions and Testimony*, Chichester, John Wiley.

103. See, for example, P. Thornton, A. Mallalieu and A. Scrivener (1992) *Justice on Trial*, London, Civil Liberties Trust.

104. RCCJ Report, para. 4.23.

105. K. Greenawalt, *op.cit.*

106. J. Bentham, *Rationale of Judicial Evidence*, 454.

107. *Ibid.*

108. G. Williams, *op.cit.*, 1107.

109. *Ibid.*

110. B. Irving (1980) *Regulating Custodial Interviews*, Vol 1, London, Police Foundation.

111. K. Greenawalt, *op.cit.*

112. A. Zuckerman, *op.cit.*

113. A. Zuckerman (1990) 'The privilege against self-incrimination and procedural fairness', in S. Greer and R. Morgan (eds.), *The Right to Silence Debate*, Bristol Centre for Criminal Justice.

114. K. Greenawalt, *op.cit.*

115. See M. McConville and J. Hodgson, *op.cit.*

116. G. Gudjonsson, *op.cit.*

117. S.M. Kassin and L.S. Wrightsman (1985) 'Confession evidence', in S.M. Kassin and L.S. Wrightsman (eds.) *The Psychology of Evidence and Trial Procedure*, London, Sage.

118. [1966] AC 102.

119. See *R v Adams* [1957] Crim LR 365 and P. Devlin (1986) *Easing the Passing*, London, Bodley Head.

120. [1976] 1 WLR 585.

121. Report of the Home Office Working Group, para. 86.

122. [1996] Times, 9 February.

123. [1996] Times 19 December.

124. [1990] 10 NIJB 91.

125. [1994] 1 WLR 1

126. See also *R v Martin*, Belfast Crown Court, May 8, 1991; [1992] 5 NIJB 40.

6 Justifications of the right to silence: rights versus utility

Arguments for and against the right to silence may be distinguished in terms of a contrast between rights and utilitarian-based arguments. On the one hand defenders see the right to silence as a fundamental human right which is recognised as such in many jurisdictions, and is enshrined in the Fifth Amendment in the United States. On this view it is inherently wrong to expect a man to accuse himself and unfair in principle to allow adverse inferences. On the other hand, critics of the right to silence are sceptical of rights-based arguments. Bentham questioned not only whether the right to silence was a fundamental right but also whether rights talk *per se* is a meaningful or helpful way of approaching evidential issues.[1] The Criminal Law Revision Committee rejected the view that requiring a man to accuse himself is inherently unfair and could find no principled objection to allowing an adverse inference to be drawn.[2] Zuckerman[3] has attributed the lukewarm support for the privilege by the courts not just to the awareness of the practical problems facing criminal investigators but the fact that the justifications of the privilege itself are relatively weak. The debates of the 1980s and 1990s focused on technical problems which arise when permitting adverse inferences from silence rather than matters of principle. This was exemplified by the approach of the Home Office Working Group[4] and the Royal Commission on Criminal Justice.[5] The Runciman Commission emphasised cost-effectiveness rather than human rights issues.[6] Human rights issues were given less prominence than efficiency and value for money considerations although they do acknowledge matters of principle, including the presumption of innocence and the provision of safeguards for suspects. The Commission emphasised the need to strike a balance between the interests of justice and the individual's right to fair and reasonable treatment to restore public confidence in the criminal justice system. The earlier Philips Commission on Criminal Procedure[7] tried to balance rights and crime control. The tendency has been for rights issues to be eclipsed by the focus on practical issues. Abolitionists have often been criticised for the lack of evidence to support their claims. However, a substantial number of empirical studies were undertaken for the Royal Commission on Criminal Justice, but the evidence pertaining to the right to silence, as we have seen, supported the retentionist case rather than the abolitionist case.[8]

But both practical and rights issues need to be addressed. While abolitionists have treated rights in a cavalier way, defenders of the right to silence have tended to place less importance on public interest and policy issues because of the belief that rights should prevail even when their protection undermines the public interest. These arguments and the problems they raise will now be considered.

Costs and benefits of the right to silence

Instead of appealing to human rights in assessing the value of such a 'right', Bentham favours an assessment of the utility of the privilege by examining its consequences and a number of desirable consequences resulting from the loss of the right to silence have been predicted.

Bentham addressed this issue by pointing to the advantages to the defendant and to society, of obliging him to testify at trial which, he argues, clearly outweigh the costs. 'Tenderness' to the accused, by releasing him from an obligation to give evidence, is misguided, he argues, because by denying this source of evidence to the court, more violent methods than mere interrogation may be used, such as 'stealing into his house at the dead of night to seize evidence by force'.[9] The publicity of the trial protects the accused against the exercise of arbitrary power. Society benefits if the accused is encouraged to speak because he is clearly an indispensable source of information regarding his own activities. Although Bentham's argument is less persuasive now in the light of search and seizure protection, the calculation of costs and benefits is still important to modern debates on the right to silence. From this standpoint, the loss of the right to silence might be seen as the 'lesser of two evils' if the alternative methods of evidence-collection were to include the use of informers, or extensive surveillance or eye-witness identification evidence, which may be more threatening to civil liberties and more unreliable than the suspect's own testimony. The experience of supergrass trials in Northern Ireland might be cited in support of this argument.[10] Bentham's critique was mounted at a time when there were a number of bars to the competence of witnesses in criminal and civil proceedings, most of which have now been eroded. The Evidence Act 1843 abolished the principal bar on those with an interest in the outcome of the proceedings.[11]

Modern critics of the right to silence also defend themselves against the charge of 'laziness' in relying on the accused's evidence rather than other sources of evidence, by arguing that they simply wish to use the best, that is, the most reliable, form of evidence which, in many cases, is the evidence of the accused himself. This point was made by Bentham who saw the 'most satisfactory species of evidence'[12] as that given by the accused. Once the prosecutor is denied access to this he is forced to search for inferior forms of evidence.

If adverse inferences are permitted from silence, pressure on the individual to speak will be increased and it may be argued that this will save costs by encouraging admissions and guilty pleas, resulting in shorter sentences and relieving pressure on prisons, although of course this might be offset by the overall increase in convictions of the guilty; the number of non-jury trials would probably increase adding to the savings to the public purse. However, it is difficult to isolate the causal specificity of the construction of silence in determining a guilty verdict.

Costs could also increase if there are more arguments at trial and appeals over confession evidence, over the meaning of the caution and whether it was fully grasped by the accused, whether it would have been reasonable to mention a fact in interrogation or whether there is a legitimate reason for silence in court. Arguments can be expected on the role of legal advice in determining the suspect's decision whether or not to speak. The Lord Chancellor's Department anticipated an increase in demands for legal aid following from changes to the right to silence in the CJPOA and there was a 21% increase in requests for legal advice in the police station after the CJPOA came into force.[13] In Northern Ireland clear-up and conviction rates fell between 1988, when the Order curtailing the right to silence was passed, and 1992.[14]

Nonetheless, it might be argued that if adverse inferences lead only to a small number of additional convictions of the guilty, this is important to the victims and to the morale of law-enforcers. The most important benefit is the contribution of the accused's testimony to the determination of the truth. The loss of dignity and potential embarrassment to the individual resulting from increased pressure to speak may seem minimal compared to the benefits of convicting a greater number of guilty defendants. If one could be confident of convicting the guilty, then controlling crime, providing a deterrent to criminals and offering greater protection to the innocent public from criminals, could offset the very small numbers of the innocent adversely affected by the loss of the right.

If the alleged benefits of improved crime control and enhanced rectitude, followed from abolition of the right to silence, the aggregate benefits would still be relatively low as the number exercising the right to silence has been so small. As most defendants testify, the effect of abolition on the crime rates is unlikely to be dramatic.

Bentham acknowledged that punishing the innocent is a greater evil than acquitting the guilty. The judge should proceed on the presumption of innocence and 'in doubtful cases, to consider the error which acquits as more justifiable, or less injurious to the good of society, than the error which condemns.'[15] The benefits accruing to the public interest would need to be substantial to justify the loss of the right to silence on utilitarian grounds. So far these benefits have not been established. Even if vigorous interrogation in the context of the threat of adverse inferences being drawn from silence, enhances the supply of reliable information, the price paid for this would be the loss of dignity and substantive rights. Furthermore the public interest argument assumes the right to silence favours the guilty. But this is not proven. In what types of crime is the individual likely to be the most reliable source of evidence? The 'offence' of heresy springs to mind here because independent evidence of the individual's thoughts and beliefs is unattainable. But it is in this private realm of conscience that there is least justification for state intervention and scrutiny. If we consider the period immediately preceding the development of the privilege against self-incrimination in English law, when religious and political beliefs were subject to judicial interrogation, the privilege was crucial to the freedom of thought and the protection of the accused against unwarranted incursions into the realm of private thoughts and beliefs. In the twentieth century, the use of compulsory questioning and 'show trials' has found most support in totalitarian regimes. But beliefs become dangerous only if translated into participation in criminal acts and there are already extensive powers available to modern states to control such acts.

Rectitude of decision

Underpinning Bentham's critique of the privilege against self-incrimination was his commitment to the goal of rectitude of decision-making, which he sees as undermined by the existence of the privilege. The rational determination of guilt and innocence is, for Bentham, the central goal of the judicial process. It is his pursuit of this goal that has led many[16] to see him as the leading figure in the rationalist tradition in the law of evidence. The goal of rectitude supersedes the concern with procedural fairness to the defendant and, for Bentham, would justify the loss of the privilege. The jury needs as much information as possible if it is to conduct a rational examination of the case and any barriers to examination in open court must be removed. The rules of adjective law, like those of substantive law, should be judged by the principle of utility. Once relevant and reliable evidence is withheld from the jury, its task is made considerably harder. Bentham was therefore critical of the justification of silence in terms of fairness to the accused, which he describes as 'the foxhunter's reason':

> The fox is to have a fair chance for his life: he must have (so close is the analogy) what is called *law* - leave to run a certain length of way for the express purpose of giving him a chance to escape. While under pursuit, he must not be shot.[17]

166

Fairness, Bentham argues, might be appropriate in a sporting context and practical, for certain means of killing might lead to extinction and the loss of the game as well as the prey, but it is far less appropriate to the judicial process, where it is necessary to hear from all the parties in order to arrive at the truth. The safest evidence, in Bentham's view, is from the accused himself, because, he says, he is the very last person to 'willingly speak falsely to his own prejudice.'[18] His evidence is the most trustworthy and should not be withheld from the jury.

Bentham's argument that silence inhibits the rational determination of guilt should be seen as part of his general attack on exclusionary and technical rules which obfuscate the truth. Instead he favours admitting as much evidence as possible: 'Let in the light of evidence. The end it leads to is the direct end of justice, rectitude of decision.'[19] Ideally, Bentham favours a system of free proof which he sees as the best environment or means of pursuing the truth. Constraints on that system which rest on reasons external to the process of proof, such as tenderness to the accused, should not be permitted. The argument that we should refrain from questioning, because it is 'hard' on a man to incriminate himself, is dismissed by Bentham as an 'old woman's reason'.[20] We might equally say that it is hard on an individual to be punished, but we would not advocate refraining from the use of punishment for this reason. Neither should we hold back from questioning the accused. Nonetheless, he recognises that limits on admissibility are necessary, namely the constraining principles of relevance and materiality, which are internal to the process of proof. Relevant evidence should be excluded only when 'the letting in of such light is attended with preponderant collateral inconvenience, in the shape of vexation, expense and delay'[21] and where no harm would result from its exclusion. Apart from these exceptions, exclusion should be avoided because it is 'contrary to reason'.[22] This mode of thinking is reflected in the United States' Federal Rules of Evidence and in England, in PACE, as well as the general common law principles of relevance in both jurisdictions.[23] The meaning of 'relevant' has been defined as follows:

> any two facts to which it is applied are so related to each other
> that according to the common course of events one either taken
> by itself or in connection with other facts proves or renders
> probable the past, present, or future existence or non-existence
> of the other.[24]

Under the Federal Rules, relevant evidence is to be admitted unless prohibited by statute or constitution. Relevant evidence also may be excluded if 'its probative value is substantially outweighed by the danger of unfair prejudice, confusion of the issues, or misleading the jury, or by considerations of undue delay, waste of time, or needless presentation of cumulative evidence.'[25] From this standpoint, the vexation, expense and delay would need to outweigh the failure of justice which might follow from its exclusion. The Royal Commission on Criminal Justice[26] strongly recommended the adoption of Federal Rule 403 in England to enhance the powers of judges to exclude evidence.

Evidence is the 'basis of justice', Bentham argues: 'to exclude evidence is to exclude justice.'[27] Exclusionary rules serve the interests of crime and criminals and the interests of lawyers, whom he calls derisively 'Judge and Co.' They help to strengthen the belief of evil-doers that 'no cause whatsoever, no cause, however bad, ought to be given up as desperate'[28] thereby providing more fee income for lawyers. Lawyers who defend the defendant's right not to testify, he argues, display a taste for bad evidence.

For Bentham, the discovery of the truth is the prime purpose of the trial, and when considered against this goal, appeals to human rights are unpersuasive. The rational determination of guilt and innocence is the central goal of the judicial process and supersedes procedural fairness to the defendant. The network of exclusionary rules, including the privilege against self-incrimination, all inhibit the realisation of this objective. Although when Bentham was writing the number of exclusionary rules was greater than now, the privilege against self-incrimination was one of the few which survived to the twentieth century as the 1898 Criminal Evidence Act rendered the defendant a competent but not compellable witness. While the Criminal Justice and Public Order Act permits adverse inferences from silence in court and thereby increases the pressure to speak, the defendant still cannot be *forced* to speak. However, clearly he is much more likely to speak given the risk of adverse inferences being drawn from his silence.

The claim that abolition of the right to silence favours the pursuit of the truth has been strongly challenged by retentionists on the grounds of futility and unreliability. The appeal to rectitude has also been subject to criticism.

Futility and unreliability

A major objection to Bentham's argument is that if the suspect speaks only under pressure, his testimony may be unreliable. Although Bentham sees the accused's testimony as the most satisfactory species of evidence, if the prosecutor is forced to search for independent evidence, this may strengthen the quality of the evidence.

The superiority of the accused's evidence is by no means guaranteed, for confusion or distress at the fact of being interrogated, by the police, or in court, or the individual's general mental state may taint that evidence. The assumption that encouraging the suspect to speak, by permitting adverse inferences from silence, would yield useful information is therefore challenged by defenders of the right to silence on the ground that increased pressure on the suspect would in fact produce only unreliable evidence. This 'futility argument' claims that any attempt to encourage the individual to speak against his or her interests will lead to perjury. The privilege against self-incrimination constitutes the recognition of the limits of governmental power, as Wigmore[29] points out, for if it is impossible to guarantee that the accused will speak the truth, given his desire for self-preservation, it is pointless to force the suspect to speak.

The development of the privilege in the United States, through interpretations of the Fifth Amendment, has been fashioned, as we have seen, by the dangers of perjury in forced testimony: confronted with the cruel trilemma of choosing self-incrimination, contempt or perjury, the accused may well prefer to lie. Wigmore argues that the right to remain silent takes us nearer the truth by rescuing the individual from this cruel trilemma. Conversely, relying on the individual undermines the search for independent evidence and runs the risk of perjury. The right to silence may be seen as embodying the law's acknowledgement that it cannot command the impossible, a view advanced by Lilburn in the seventeenth century. Although Wigmore finds this a less compelling argument in modern societies, it could be argued that he underestimates its significance, for example, in relation to Northern Ireland where the sanctions introduced by the Criminal Evidence Order have not demolished the IRA's wall of silence. As we saw earlier, defendants have been convicted of serious offences, in cases such as *Murray*,[30] where the crucial factor has been the evidential significance attached to silence. Even if terrorist suspects are persuaded to speak, the information received may be false: 'the rack and the thumbscrew...and other less awful, though not necessarily less potent, means of applying pressure to an accused person to speak do not necessarily produce speech or the truth.'[31] The professional criminal, operating in such a regime would be well prepared with an appropriate account of his actions. On the Benthamite view, however, the truth or falsity would be a matter for the tribunal to decide so that the evidence should still be available to them.

Although the rationalist model sees the individual's account as the most useful source of evidence, one of the original objections to enforced testimony was precisely that pressures to speak could lead to perjury and thus to the frustration of the search for the truth. The expense, vexation and delay arising from perjured evidence was an important justification of the privilege. The recognition that involuntary testimony could lead ultimately to the wrong decision, complemented the view that it was morally wrong to force the witness to lie on oath, committing a crime against God, as well as against society. Wigmore[32] says that perjury is now so prevalent it is doubtful whether the average witness is awed by the prospect of eternal damnation. But perjury prosecutions in England are very rare and irrespective of the belief in divine retribution, the existence of a right to silence with a free choice to waive the right, is arguably more likely to produce reliable testimony than testimonial compulsion. However, Zuckerman is unconvinced by the appeal to false testimony as a justification of the privilege. One might seek to deal with the dilemma of speaking the truth and being convicted or perjuring oneself to avoid punishment, he suggests, by abolishing charges of perjury in relation to the accused's own testimony.[33] He argues that untruthful or evasive testimony can itself be a useful contribution to the ascertainment of guilt. But the difficulty with this view is that while evasiveness may be readily identified by the jury, untruthfulness may be harder to discern. In any case, evasion and lies may not establish guilt but undermine credibility and may result from causes which are quite irrelevant to the determination of the truth of the particular issue.

The appeal to the pursuit of the truth may be made by both sides of the right to silence debate: some argue that the right to silence obscures the search for the truth, but others argue that the right to silence facilitates that goal, by reducing the risk of false confessions.[34]

The current rules on the admissibility of confessions, which focus on oppression and unreliability in s 76 of PACE, reflect the courts' and Parliament's recognition of the vulnerability of the accused in police detention and the need for statements to be reliable. Moreover, following several miscarriages of justice, and the consequent loss of jury confidence in confession evidence, the need for increased use of forensic evidence is being recognised by the police. Greater use is now being made of DNA profiling, for example, in cases of burglary as well as offences against the person. This trend is likely to continue with the increased police powers to obtain samples in the CJPOA and the establishment of a DNA database of those persons convicted of a criminal offence.[35]

Rectitude and realism

It is questionable whether rectitude of decision, is or should be, the prime goal of the judicial process. If other goals may be identified, which conflict with that objective, should the goal of rectitude necessarily prevail? Constraints on the pursuit of this objective are already accepted as legitimate. Torture is prohibited, reflecting the moral imperative that it is better for the guilty to be acquitted than to establish guilt by unjust means which violate human rights and dignity. The law governing the use of confessions is designed to discourage inhuman and degrading treatment, even when such treatment produces reliable evidence. Rectitude has to be placed in the context of these other values. Even without the survival of the privilege, the modern criminal justice system does not conform to Bentham's ideal of an 'open' trial operating within a system of free proof, as in practice numerous cases are disposed of before the trial stage, by means of cautions and decisions not to prosecute. If pre-trial negotiations result in a guilty plea, then the courts' concern is confined to sentencing rather than rectitude. These form the majority of cases processed by the criminal justice system. In magistrates' courts the rate of guilty pleas is over 90% and in the Crown Courts 70%, although there are regional variations.

The rationalist model sees the tribunal arriving at the right answer by considering all the evidence, governed by the notion of verisimilitude, that is, that there is one single truth to be determined at trial, by a thorough and progressive examination of the evidence. This has been challenged by rival models which see the trial as a plurality of competing truth-claims. McConville argues that 'the trial is not a search for the "truth". It is an arena in which different versions of reality compete. Legal truth is not a discoverable entity existing outside the trial process'. Instead it is the outcome of the trial process itself and 'established by the winner'.[36] Jackson and Doran argue that the view that the truth emerges at the end of the trial, when both sides have given a full presentation of their arguments, is distorting.[37] It presupposes a basic distinction between the evidence and those inferences and judgements which are drawn from that evidence. 'But this distinction', they claim, 'does not make much sense in terms of modern psychology. Perception is no longer considered a passive process of encoding external stimuli. Instead, we construct truth as we go along; we do not discover a reality that is in some way fixed or permanent.'[38]   A similar point is made by Ashworth:

> central concepts such as 'the facts', 'innocence', and 'guilt' are sometimes not objective phenomena (as often assumed), but rather compromises or value-judgements emanating from the practices and pressures of the process.[39]

The notion of a fixed truth to be revealed by the trial process is therefore problematic. There are parallels here with the search for truth maximisation which dominated logical empiricist and logical positivist approaches to the understanding of scientific inquiry during the first half of the twentieth century, and which has been subject to extensive criticism. The realist tradition accepts that there is a real external world and that scientific research and investigation enable us to acquire more accurate knowledge about that world and that there is a correspondence between beliefs about the external world and objective facts. However, as Kuhn[40] and Feyerabend[41] have shown, science is marked by disputes in which there may be no agreement on what would count as conclusive evidence for or against hypotheses. Each competing theoretical framework provides its own criteria for truth and testability. They therefore reject the view that science progresses towards 'the truth'.

As Gross[42] argues, realism is problematic because it is difficult to identify a reality independent of our perception of it or to see key scientific terms referring to real objects. Even if we acknowledge the existence of mind-independent entities, there is still the problem that they 'cannot be independently characterised'[43] and are accessible only through language. Gross sees the notion of 'brute facts' as an oxymoron, for 'Facts are by nature linguistic - no language, no facts.'[44] Gross offers an alternative, which he describes as rhetorical epistemology, in place of the realist view of science. The adherence to realism in the scientific community, he argues, is essentially motivational, a means of making scientific life meaningful. Without the belief in realism science would lapse into senseless empiricism: 'When scientific truth is seen as a consensus concerning the coherence of a range of utterances, rather than the fit between the facts and reality, conceptual change need no longer be justified on the basis of its closer approximation to that reality.'[45] Because truths conflict, truth cannot be the final arbiter in choosing between statements. If realism is problematic in science, in dealing with problems such as the structure and nature of the material world, then it is inevitably harder to apply it to the context of the criminal trial.

One might argue, however, that there are important differences between scientific endeavour and the criminal trial. In the criminal trial the theory of truth may be less important than the test of truth. The realist notion of truth may be most applicable to the *actus reus* of the offence, the external elements, but harder to apply to the *mens rea*. Where the mental element is concerned it is difficult to establish an objective and clear-cut test, comparable to the replicatory tests used in the experimental sciences to test hypotheses. It might be argued that scientists may see themselves as engaging in a cooperative enterprise to search for the truth while the criminal trial is essentially adversarial. But the cooperative model is difficult to reconcile with the intense competition and priority disputes of the scientific community[46] although there may be cooperation within paradigms and schools. In the criminal trial, the belief in truth is an article of faith and a way of legitimising the trial, but closer scrutiny reveals rival perceptions of the rules of evidence. *A fortiori* in the criminal process where the credibility of witnesses and the reliability of identification evidence may be crucial, the notions of truth and verisimilitude are even more problematic.

While verisimilitude might be seen as the manifest goal of the trial, it competes with and may be overshadowed by other latent processes, including the status degradation of the defendant, dramaturgical processes and the goal of crime control as well as due process, which may conflict with each other as well as with the pursuit of the truth. Emotions, feelings and prejudices may also cloud the pursuit of the truth and contribute to the final determination. It is questionable whether juries do in practice reach verdicts through a rational appraisal of the evidence rather than under the influence of emotions and prejudices in some cases. The rules of evidence partly reflect the recognition that juries may be tempted to over-estimate the probative value of some forms of evidence to the prejudice of the accused, or ignore evidence favourable to the defence because of the 'yuk' factor, for example, because of the bad character of the accused.

This is not to reject the rationalist model as an ideal but to recognise these rival processes. Those who criticise the intrusion of prejudices and discriminatory attitudes into decision-making, presuppose the goal of rectitude as a yardstick against which the existing state of affairs may be judged. Anxiety over miscarriages of justice has reflected concern at the failure to find the truth, as well as fears regarding oppressive police tactics. Apart from the human rights implications and the blighting and shortening of individuals' lives, these miscarriages represent the failure to discover the truth. The wrong people have been convicted and the guilty have not been punished.

The development of exclusionary rules relating to confession evidence also reflects the recognition that testimony produced under pressure, whether through fear of sanctions or hope of benefits, may produce unreliable testimony. This recognition developed in the context of concern with the practices of the Star Chamber and the High Commission. Apart from the inherent undesirability of exerting pressure on individuals and the need to deter oppression, the view developed at common law that reliability is likely to be undermined by such pressure. Confession evidence in English law has been accepted as sufficient to obtain a conviction without corroborative evidence, provided that the confession is made voluntarily. This was affirmed in *Ibrahim* by Lord Sumner:

> It has long been established...that no statement by an accused is admissible in evidence against him unless it is shown by the prosecution to have been a voluntary statement, in the sense that it has not been obtained from him either by fear or prejudice or hope of advantage exercised or held out by a person in authority.[47]

Although this approach reflected, in part, concern regarding the reliability of evidence obtained in those circumstances, the courts in practice tended to focus on whether an inducement or threat persuaded the suspect to confess, rather than whether the confession was in fact unreliable. Section 76(2)(b) of PACE refers explicitly to reliability rather than voluntariness although it does not define reliability: the confession is inadmissible 'if it is made in consequence of anything said or done which was likely in the circumstances existing at the time to render unreliable any confession which might be made by him in consequence thereof.' There may be problems in determining causation and it is unclear whether the test of reliability is subjective or objective. The reference to 'anything' suggests that the potential scope is broader than inducements, threats or impropriety. At common law the notion of inducement meant that a statement could be excluded even if it did not affect reliability, provided that it had been induced, but s 76(2)(b) directly focuses on the question of reliability. Oppression is also covered in s 76(2)(a) and is defined in s 76(8) as including torture, inhuman or degrading treatment, which is based on Article 3 of the European Convention on Human Rights, and the use or threat of violence. 'Oppression' suggests some impropriety, said the Court of Appeal in *Fulling*.[48] In *R v Bailey and Smith*,[49] the Court of Appeal held that an incriminating conversation between co-defendants in the cells talking voluntarily to each other recorded by the police was rightly admitted. There was nothing to suggest that it was unreliable or obtained oppressively.

The law governing confession evidence thus reflects a number of principles which move beyond the goal of rectitude, including the disciplinary principle, which seeks to deter police misbehaviour by excluding evidence resulting from impropriety or where the police act in bad faith. Ashworth has also referred to a move towards the protective principle in the law of confessions which recognises a right 'not to be subjected to certain forms of inducement and oppression', and aims to protect suspects 'from the disadvantage which might result if evidence obtained through a violation of those rights were admitted at his trial.'[50] On this principle the court performs a remedial role in enforcing and raising standards for the treatment and questioning of suspects and compensating those suspects whose treatment falls below that level, although exclusion may also discourage the police from subverting the rules to obtain an admission. On the protective principle the key issue is whether the defendant was adversely affected by police misbehaviour rather than whether or not it was intended, which would be relevant to the disciplinary principle. Section 78 takes account of the effect of admitting evidence on the fairness of the proceedings and s 82(3) makes clear that the preceding sections do not undermine the court's power to exclude evidence at its discretion.

Special reference is made to the particular problems of confessions by mentally handicapped persons in s 77 of PACE and in Code C to the special treatment during interrogation of the suspect who is mentally handicapped, mentally disordered or mentally incapable of understanding the significance of questions put to him.[51] The definition of mental disorder used is that given in s 1(2) of the 1983 Mental Health Act as 'mental illness, arrested or incomplete development of mind, psychopathic disorder and any other disorder or disability of mind.'

Section 77 provides that if the case against the accused who is mentally handicapped relies entirely, or for the most part, on confession evidence and if the confession is made in the absence of an appropriate adult, then the judge should warn the jury of the special need for caution before convicting in reliance on it. This recognises the importance of protecting disadvantaged groups as well as the quest for reliability but does not resolve the problem.

Dennis[52] treats truth-finding as a means by which the ultimate goal of the legitimacy of the verdict is achieved. Rectitude is thus relegated to a significant but nonetheless merely instrumental position. The notion of the legitimacy of the verdict incorporates both the factual dimension of the accuracy of the verdict and a moral dimension, namely the integrity of the judgement. The moral authority of the verdict would be undermined if it were to be achieved by the violation of fundamental values of the criminal law, such as the right of all citizens to equal respect and dignity, recognition of autonomy and freedom of individuals and the punishment of those who deserve to be punished. On this view, the laws of criminal evidence can be seen as reflecting and expressing those values. While a factually inaccurate judgement should always result in an acquittal and can never possess legitimacy, the moral authority of the verdict is not reducible to the factual judgement. Use of improper tactics, for example, at any stage of the process, including the pre-trial stage, would violate it even if those tactics had generated a factually accurate result. On this approach, relevant evidence would be excluded if there is a risk of unreliability, but reliable evidence should also be excluded if it undermines the moral authority of the verdict. It is essential for the criminal law to be effective that the verdict is seen as having moral authority. Rectitude is part of the integrity of the judgement. Dennis stresses that we are dealing here with values which are internal to the process of proof rather than external to it. The merit of this approach is that it can provide a rational foundation for exclusionary discretion. The approach of the courts to s 78 of PACE and to the construction of fairness can be interpreted in terms of this theory. The wider scope of s 78 enables the court to go beyond the protective, disciplinary and reliability principles toward this principle of the moral integrity of the verdict. Section 78 embraces the whole process of criminal investigation, including the pre-trial stage, to exclude evidence which would otherwise be reliable.[53] It may include cases of bad faith on the part of the police as well as cases where the police, while acting within their powers, exploit a particular situation in an unfair way.[54]

While the courts have been prepared to use s 78 robustly to exclude evidence, their approach has varied. In *Alladice*[55] there was a breach of s 58 but the conviction was still upheld. In *Christou*[56] the appellants were caught handling stolen goods by a police undercover operation, and their conviction was upheld. Lord Lane stressed that here the discussion took place in a jeweller's shop, rather than in detention. But in *Bryce*,[57] a case which also involved an undercover police operation, the conviction was quashed; here the focus was on what happened during the interview. In *R v Smurthwaite, R v Gill*,[58] the Court of Appeal said that s 78 gives the court discretion to exclude evidence but the use of an agent provocateur or entrapment does not *per se* require exclusion. In *R v Lin, Hung and Tsui*[59] the Court of Appeal held that a defendant who had made incriminating statements to an undercover officer was not automatically entitled to have the record of the statements excluded under s 78, unless he had been forced to incriminate himself by threats, inducements or violence.

Dennis[60] sees the two issues arising from the use of confession evidence as authenticity and legitimacy: was the confession made at all and made as described? If it was authentic, were the means used to procure it acceptable? He concludes that a corroboration warning is the best way of addressing the problem of false confessions as well as the development of techniques such as the ESDA test and stylometry, that is, using statistical analysis to identify ways in which the speech and writing of one person differs from another, and statement reality analysis, which examines how the recall of real events differs from fictitious recall. The problem in many criminal investigations is that the inquiry is confined to a particular track so that other relevant evidence and suspects are excluded.

He is critical of the principal justifications of the privilege, namely that it embodies the presumption of innocence and reflects the procedural right to a fair hearing, a view expressed in the jurisprudence of the European Court of Human Rights.[61] However, he also finds the view that the right to silence protects criminals unconvincing. In practice the privilege may not assist the weak and vulnerable because it is so often waived. While it may offer greater protection to hardened criminals, again the number of suspects exercising the right to silence is small even without the risk of adverse inferences from silence. He argues that the privilege against self-incrimination is 'best accounted for not as an instrumental protection, nor as a human right, but as a feature of the criminal justice system which is required as a functional necessity in certain contexts.'[62] The context in which Dennis sees the privilege as most appropriate is during custodial interrogation where there is a risk of the state exploiting its strength to place the individual in a vulnerable position:

> The vulnerability consists of a risk either that the investigative powers may be used to obtain evidence which is factually unreliable or that they may be misused to compel the production of incriminating evidence by means inconsistent with the fundamental values of the common law. If either of these risks materialises the legitimacy of the criminal verdict may be compromised.[63]

In the context of interrogation there is the possibility of suspects being pressured to make incriminating statements and a well documented danger of unreliable statements being produced, when the individual is subject to pressure[64] and the risk that fundamental values of the criminal law may be infringed, including respect for privacy, human autonomy and dignity, the presumption of innocence and principles of natural justice. In contrast:

> Judicial questioning of a suspect under conditions of natural justice, for example, does not in modern times present the same kind of risk of abuse of power or of unreliability. In this or a related context the claim that compulsory incrimination is unfair should therefore be given less weight when considering the extent to which the pursuit of factual accuracy of criminal adjudication should be compromised.[65]

While Dennis rightly emphasises the risks in the pre-trial context, he sees the inequalities between prosecution and defence at trial as less significant and he does not accept that the drawing of inferences from silence at the trial stage *per*

176

se undermines the fundamental presumption of innocence or shifts the burden of proof.

The debate on the right to silence may be seen as part of a wider debate on whether the quest for the truth is facilitated or obscured by the rules of evidence. Exclusionary rules may be framed to pursue the goal of rectitude but also to protect the accused, where the prejudicial effect of evidence exceeds its probative value, and to encourage good practice in policing and interrogation. The elevation of rectitude to the paramount purpose of the criminal trial by Bentham is therefore problematic. But even if one were to accept rectitude as the ultimate goal, is it necessarily undermined by the right to silence? The right to silence can be seen as consistent with the goal of rectitude. It is because information extracted involuntarily is so unreliable that a number of exclusionary rules have developed. Exclusionary rules may reflect the disciplinary principle and may be intended to discourage improper police practices, by excluding improperly obtained evidence, even when its reliability is not in question. But the central aim is to exclude admissions and testimony which are potentially unreliable. The reliability principle sees truth-finding as the prime goal of the criminal trial so the exclusion of evidence is justified only if it is unreliable. It is in the light of both these goals that the right to silence, like the law on the admissibility of confessions, may be understood.

Problems with the quality of interrogation and investigation have been identified by a number of commentators. Baldwin[66] refers to the poor quality of recordings of interviews and the passivity of legal representatives. Baldwin also found that many officers began an interview assuming guilt and expecting a confession, so that the suspect's explanation was dismissed at the beginning, regardless of how he responded. He also refers to the lack of supervision of investigations. Too much responsibility is placed on officers of lower rank and as far as the supervision of investigations is concerned, he argues, existing procedures 'contain the potential for laxity, if not abuse.'[67]

A particular line of investigation may be pursued to the exclusion of other possible leads, with implications for the pursuit of the truth. As McConville[68] observes, pressure on police resources may result in poor investigative work, failure to review the investigation at an early stage, which in turn may lead to delays in the collection of evidence and its possible loss. Once time has elapsed it becomes harder to trace witnesses and to obtain medical evidence. The failure to obtain forensic evidence was crucial in some of the miscarriage of justice cases.

In *The Case for the Prosecution*, McConville *et al*[69] argue that criminal cases are constructed by the police according to their own view of who is guilty. Instead of going out and searching for the facts of the case, they focus on a narrow section of the population, as defined by class, race and gender, they then place those suspects in the hostile environment of the police station, and having reached a prior decision on their guilt, proceed to confirm their hypothesis by interrogation designed to obtain a confession. A case is not an objective set of facts, which are either right or wrong, but is constructed out of incidents which may be ambiguous and on the basis of beliefs and goals of the officers involved, which shape the way in which the evidence is constructed:

> Police practice is not, therefore, designed to ensure that the maximum possible reliance for evidential purposes can be placed upon suspects' statements in all cases where they are made, but instead to ensure that statements of confession are made in the maximum number of cases. Through experience, the police have learned that statements are more likely to be made when the suspect is psychologically most vulnerable, a state best achieved by compulsory confinement, isolation and manipulation of self-esteem. It is to these features that they direct their attention rather than to questions of the reliability of statements... Contrary to the rhetoric of law, which depicts the police as neutral investigators earnestly seeking 'the truth' in an impartial setting, the first concern of the police is to place the suspect into an environment which is hostile for the suspect and favourable to the police themselves. In this way, the police lay the foundations for the construction of a case *against* the suspect rather than for an impartial inquiry.[70]

When the suspect is brought into custody, facts may be selected or exaggerated to justify or extend detention. Because the police are in a strong position to control the interrogating environment, cases may be manipulated to obtain what they see as the crucial confession evidence.

While the paperwork and supervision of PACE was intended to prevent such tactics, it may be used to legitimate them while concealing the true nature of that process. The police construction of the case then colours the CPS review of the case in considering the evidential sufficiency for a prosecution. As McConville *et al* argue:

> The CPS, far from being an independent agency, is a police-dependent body, confining review to evidence-sufficiency questions, eschewing public interest criteria, utilizing the contradictory and malleable nature of the principles in the codes to further narrowly conceived objectives...[71]

The decision whether or not to proceed will be based on this previously constructed case rather than on an objective set of facts. Despite the formal changes of PACE, police culture has adapted to use the formal procedures to preserve that culture.

Maguire and Norris also argue that police investigation methods are open to abuse and that the police are under too much pressure to obtain results.[72] Problems identified in their research for the Royal Commission on Criminal Justice were the lack of supervision in the CID, the use of conversations outside the police station and the routine breach of rules because the police are convinced they have the right suspect. One officer described how he regularly took the 'scenic route' back to the police station in order to question suspects, although he was aware that he was breaching the PACE Code and would deny it if challenged. He would do this only with colleagues he could trust or when he was alone. What is required, Maguire and Norris argue, is 'a change in managerial culture so that as much emphasis is placed upon ensuring procedural and legal compliance as upon securing results.'[73]

An examination of cause célèbres, where individuals have been wrongfully convicted on the basis of uncorroborated confession evidence, shows the dangers of relying on the individual's speech as the prime source of evidence. In the Confait[74] case the preoccupation of the prosecution with the admissions of the defendants meant that far less attention was paid to the relevant medical and forensic evidence determining the time of death or the starting of the fire. Such objective evidence was sometimes ignored, on other occasions underplayed, in the effort to focus the jury's attention on those admissions, even though it would have been crucial in assessing the probative value of alibi evidence. During investigation and at trial, attention was focused primarily on the statements of three suspects, Salih, Leighton and Lattimore and other potential suspects such as Winston Goode, who later committed suicide, were given only a cursory examination. With limited resources, the police will inevitably want to narrow the scope of their inquiries and loss of the right to silence will exacerbate this tendency of criminal investigations to run in a single groove once underway. This problem was highlighted by the Runciman Commission who stressed the need for thoroughness in investigations: 'the police should see it as their duty when conducting investigations to gather and consider all the relevant evidence, including any which may exonerate the suspect',[75] rather than rushing too quickly to the conclusion that they have arrested the offender. The new disclosure regime set up by the Criminal Procedure and Investigations Act 1996 is intended in part to address this problem.

The right of silence is therefore compatible with the pursuit of the truth. A rule of procedure or law which demands independent evidence and which encourages the prosecution to go farther than the suspect's admissions, must be crucial in facilitating the goal of rectitude. Far from undermining the objective of rectitude, the right to silence may be instrumental in achieving it, in forcing the police to search more widely for probative evidence. To some extent this is already happening as investigations are making more use of independent evidence, possibly because of the problems of obtaining convictions on the basis of confession evidence, following the recent miscarriages of justice. If this were reinforced by a formal rule requiring corroboration of confession evidence, it would further strengthen this process.[76]

The protection of rights can thus favour the pursuit of the truth. For if the individual is relied on as the source of the prosecution's case against him, this can only weaken the effectiveness of the prosecution in obtaining evidence and it may encourage improper police practices.

What is most worrying in criminal investigations is precisely this danger of investigation being confined to a particular track so that other relevant evidence and suspects are excluded. The Royal Commission on Criminal Procedure saw police questioning as the key component of criminal investigation. However, advances in forensic science and techniques such as DNA profiling may mean that the interrogation of the suspect assumes less importance than when Bentham was writing, or when the Royal Commission was reviewing criminal procedure.

The burden of proof

Underpinning the right to silence debate is the question of the burden of proof. Although the effect on the burden of proof is one of the most troublesome aspects of abolition, it has been argued by some commentators that the burden of proof will not be affected if adverse inferences are permitted from silence. Galligan, for example, denies that the burden of proof is reversed as 'the prosecution would still have to prove its case, the only argument being about which bits of evidence it may use',[77] although he acknowledges that the relationship between state and suspect will be altered. This issue is also addressed by Williams who argues that discussion of the right to silence has been wrongly confused with the issue of the burden of proof. 'It is illogical', he claims, 'to argue that reasonable changes in the law of evidence to help the prosecution to *discharge* their burden of proof *shift* the burden of proof.'[78]

Similarly, Dennis argues that 'the legal burden of proof is not reversed by the restriction of the right to silence.'[79] The accused must still be given the benefit of any reasonable doubt on the part of the tribunal once it has considered all the evidence. As noted earlier, Dennis finds the curtailment of the right to silence in interrogation as unacceptable because of the danger of unreliability and the failure of police interrogation to conform with the principles of natural justice. But to resist the loss of the right to silence by appealing to the presumption of innocence, he argues, is misguided, for it 'seems to imply a claim that it is necessarily improper to draw any inferences from a person's failure to explain away incriminating evidence. This is contrary both to common sense and to existing law. Common sense argues that if other evidence yields a prima facie inference of guilt a failure to provide an innocent explanation suggests that one does not exist.'[80]

The problems with a common sense approach have already been considered, but does the claim that the burden of proof remains on the prosecution have validity? First, even if the legal burden is not shifted formally on to the accused, the loss of the right to silence is of tremendous symbolic significance. Lord Sankey's comments in *Woolmington v DPP*[81] that the 'golden thread running through the web of English law' was that the burden lay exclusively on the prosecution to prove the accused's guilt: 'the principle that the prosecution must prove the guilt of the prisoner is part of the common law of England and no attempt to whittle it down can be entertained.'[82] The burden of proof has been a key argument for defenders of the right to silence as it constitutes the symbolic and practical expression of the principle of the presumption of innocence.

But even if the burden of proof is not shifted by statute, if adverse inferences are drawn from the accused's silence, pressure will be exerted on the defendant to cooperate with the police. Although formally the burden lies on the prosecution, in practice the suspect becomes the first port of call for evidence to incriminate him. When silence is given evidential significance the suspect is under increased pressure to speak to the police. He is effectively being asked to establish his own innocence, rather than leaving it to the prosecution to establish his guilt. Moreover, the burden weighs much more heavily on him in view of the vast inequality of resources between the suspect and the prosecution. By remaining silent, he runs the risk of adverse inferences being drawn and of strengthening the prosecution's case against him. This was recognised by the Royal Commission on Criminal Procedure, who saw a conflict between allowing adverse inferences from pre-trial silence and the incidence of proof at the trial stage: 'There is an inconsistency of principle in requiring the onus of proof at trial to be upon the prosecution and to be discharged without any assistance from the accused and yet in enabling the prosecution to use the accused's silence in the face of police questioning under caution as part of their case against him at trial.'[83] The Philips Commission rejected any modification of the right to silence at either stage for this reason.

The majority of the Royal Commission on Criminal Justice, while stating its commitment to retention of the right to silence, because of its concern that the risk of false confessions would increase with additional pressure on suspects, nonetheless advocated a form of advance defence disclosure.[84] After the prosecution case had been fully disclosed to defendants, they would be required to give an answer or to run the risk of adverse comment at trial by the judge on new defences offered or a change to the original defence. The majority of the Commission advocated a new pre-trial procedure to define the issues in the case before the jury is empanelled.[85] The defendant would still be entitled to remain silent at trial. But it is difficult to amend the pre-trial procedure without implications for the accused's decision to testify at trial. Changes to the right to silence at the investigation stage make it easier to accept erosion of the right to silence at the trial stage. In the end, the CJPOA[86] removed the right to silence at both stages, interrogation and trial, effectively shifting the burden of proof on to the defence.

Dennis[87] has argued that appeals to the presumption of innocence by defenders of the right to silence lack plausibility, for while the presumption of innocence identifies the bearer of the burden of proof, it says nothing regarding the methods by which that burden is discharged. But they cannot be separated as easily as Dennis suggests. The principle that the prosecution should carry the burden of proof surely entails that it should establish guilt by its own efforts. He sees the assumption that the defendant should never supply evidence of his own guilt as absurd and unrealistic and points to examples such as blood testing and fingerprinting as confirmation that this assumption is not held. But his argument does not take account of the fact that efforts have been made to exclude such evidence, and have sometimes succeeded, on the ground that the accused should not be coerced to supply bodily samples where the resulting evidence would connect him with the crime.[88]

The privilege is built into the edifice of the adversarial system. When the right to silence is lost and the defendant encouraged to answer at risk of adverse inferences, this shifts the trial process from an adversarial to an inquisitorial one. A case might be made for the merits of an inquisitorial system. But if permission to draw adverse inferences from silence is simply grafted on to the existing adversarial system, we are left with the worst aspects of each system. In *R v Cowan, Gayle and Ricciardi*[89] the Court of Appeal, in interpreting s 35 of the CJPOA, emphasised that the burden of proof still remained on the prosecution throughout and silence in court cannot be the only basis of a conviction and this had to be emphasised in the judge's direction to the jury. But once comment is permitted on silence, whether in police interrogation or at trial, then the whole focus of the trial shifts onto the defence and assessment of its arguments, rather than on the prosecution's case against the accused so it is hard to sustain the view that the burden of proof is not affected. The defendant becomes the focus of attention and his account, or failure to supply an explanation of his conduct, rather than the strength of the prosecution's case, dominates the trial.

The implications for the burden of proof and for civil liberties have been emphasised by retentionists. McConville,[90] for example, argues that drawing adverse inferences from silence, constitutes a substantial change to the burden of proof as the burden is shared between prosecution and defence. It also means that the suspect is required to reveal his defence at a very early stage or run the risk of adverse inferences being drawn from his silence. If this silence is used later to corroborate evidence against him, then the *prima facie* case, 'the lowest threshold of evidence' is in effect, says McConville, elevated into the highest form, proven beyond reasonable doubt.[91] This use of silence was supported by the Northern Ireland Court of Appeal in the case of *McLernon*.[92]

Drawing adverse inferences from silence will have most effect where there is relatively little evidence against the accused; by definition, inferences are most likely to made where strong forensic evidence or other evidence is lacking. In view of these implications for the burden and standard of proof, many critics of the right to silence who would countenance the drawing of adverse inferences at trial when the full panoply of the prosecution evidence has been presented in the defendant's presence with counsel to represent him, baulk at the prospect of such inferences being permitted from such an early stage of proceedings. Yet under the CJPOA adverse inferences may also be drawn from silence at the pre-trial stage if the suspect fails to mention a fact which he later relies on in his defence.

Zuckerman also considers the question of the standard of proof. He notes that 'it is difficult to see how the abolition of the privilege would lead to a reduction in the standard of proof. It is already the case that in many trials the prosecution is able to rely on some statements made by the accused but it is not suggested that in these trials guilt is proved by a lower standard than in cases where the accused has insisted on his privilege.'[93] Even if the privilege is lost in criminal cases, one may still place a burden on the prosecution to establish a prima facie case before exposing the individual to questioning. In civil proceedings there is a duty of mutual disclosure yet this is not seen as undermining the adversarial nature of the proceedings. But Zuckerman's argument here is unpersuasive as the situation where two individual parties face each other is hardly comparable to the relationship between prosecution and defence which is characterised by inequalities of power and resources. If full mutual disclosure existed in criminal proceedings, the prosecution's resources would ensure that it was in a much stronger position to use any information obtained by that means.

In preparing the groundwork for the PACE changes, the Philips Commission[94] following an extensive examination of the available evidence, made it clear that the burden on the prosecution should not be weakened and this argument is supported by recent studies of the operation and impact of PACE and the continuing failure to afford legal advice to all suspects during interrogation.[95]

The lazy prosecutor

Once the burden of proof is effectively shifted by abolishing or diluting the right to silence, then the incentive to the prosecution to search for independent evidence is weakened considerably. This was stressed in *Miranda v Arizona*[96] where the need for the prosecution to obtain evidence, by its independent labours rather than by the cruel, simple expedient of compelling it from the suspect's own mouth, was emphasised. By relying on the suspect to furnish the case against himself, other independent evidence may be ignored and remain undiscovered.

This contention, known as the 'lazy prosecutor' argument, is closely allied to the burden of proof argument, and it is here that the protection of rights can be seen most clearly to favour utility. For if the individual is relied on as the source of the prosecution's case against him, this can only weaken the effectiveness of the prosecution in obtaining evidence and it may encourage improper police practices. When Sir James Stephen was drafting the Indian Code of Criminal Procedure,[97] he asked the police why they sometimes used force. He was told: 'There is a great deal of laziness in it. It is far pleasanter to sit comfortably in the shade rubbing red pepper in a poor devil's eyes than to go about in the sun hunting up evidence.' Before the right to silence was modified, the law encouraged the search for independent evidence but when the suspect is seen as the prime source of evidence, this is more likely to encourage 'lazy prosecutors' than a system which requires independent evidence. If confusion or distress during police interrogation, or cross-examination in court, affects the individual's mental state, then his testimony may be unreliable. But a requirement to procure independent evidence may enhance the value of prosecution evidence. In this way utilitarian considerations may be invoked in favour of the right to silence. Although critics of the right to silence usually appeal to utility, defenders tend to argue from a rights-based perspective. But as well as offering a defence framed in terms of rights, defenders do need to consider consequentialist arguments in a political climate where the commitment to rights is weak.

If police powers are much greater than those of the private citizen, safeguards against abuse are essential. The Philips Commission stressed the crucial importance of regulating police conduct as part of the maintenance of the balance between the two parties and placed great emphasis on the importance of the right to silence. But holding the threat of adverse inferences above the suspect's head, like the sword of Damocles, amounts to an inducement to talk and means the incentive for the prosecution to search for independent evidence is weakened. Instead the prosecution might content itself with eliciting the defendant's testimony at trial, abating its search for independent evidence and trying to prove its case through the accused.

What is needed is the restoration of the right to silence and the introduction of a corroboration requirement where the right is waived and a confession put in evidence. A corroboration requirement is essential because of the dangers of relying on confession evidence alone. It would encourage the search for independent evidence.

The rhetoric of rights: nonsense upon stilts

Bentham's critique of the rule excluding self-incriminating evidence may be seen as part of his general and vitriolic attack on non-legal rights, expressed principally in *Anarchical Fallacies* where he dismisses 'rights talk' as empty and harmful 'nonsense upon stilts' and even 'mischievous nonsense'.[98] Talk of fundamental rights is vacuous nonsense, he says, because it lacks a rational foundation, appealing to emotions rather than logic, it is 'on stilts' in the sense that it exaggerates its own self-importance and is removed from everyday life, and it is mischievous nonsense for although empty rhetoric, it may nonetheless inspire discontent and disorder: 'Out of one foolish word may start a thousand daggers'.[99] While the object of Bentham's attack in *Anarchical Fallacies* is the *Declaration of Rights* published by the French National Assembly, in the *Rationale of Judicial Evidence* he focuses specifically on the rule excluding self-incriminating evidence. He refers to the way in which the propriety of the rule is assumed as 'a proposition too plainly to be true to admit of dispute'.[100] For Bentham the rule is grounded in the 'affections' rather than the understanding, in rhetoric rather than logic.[101] It is also presented, he says, as receiving universal support. Yet no evidence, he argues, is forthcoming to support such a proposition, perhaps because there can be no rational basis to such a rule. It is just empty harmful nonsense in so far as it excludes useful evidence that should be available to the tribunal.

Dismissing rights as nonsense and empty rhetoric, he assesses the utility of the privilege against self-incrimination, applying consequentialist arguments and claims that no evidence can be advanced in support of the privilege. The rejection of rights in favour of utilitarian considerations, such as the public interest in apprehending the guilty and crime control, found in Bentham's discussions of the privilege,[102] is reflected in modern discussions of this question. The CLRC's report gave priority to the public interest in crime control and could find no rational foundation for the privilege. The extent to which rights arguments have receded into the background of contemporary debates is also exemplified by the report of the Home Office Working Group which focused on pragmatic matters rather than rights and formulated proposals based on utilitarian considerations.[103] But although rights arguments have been overshadowed by vociferous claims of public interest, they have not been totally eclipsed and still haunt modern discussions. Although the Criminal Law Revision Committee based its report on questions of utility, it still recorded disagreements on the issue of right to silence, when preparing its report, implicitly acknowledging that fundamental moral and political questions are embodied in the right. The Philips Commission[104] did acknowledge the importance of taking account of citizens' rights and sought to strike a balance between those rights and the public interest in crime control, but rights cannot be placed in the balance in this way without the risk of erosion. Respondents to the Home Office Working Group's Consultation Paper also reaffirmed the importance of rights-based arguments.[105] The Runciman Commission, however, gave more weight to arguments of efficiency and economy than to rights-protection.[106] Although the search for truth, defined as the conviction of the guilty and acquittal of the innocent, was the central goal of the criminal justice system, the efficient use of resources in pursuing this goal was a key consideration. But adopting a utilitarian approach, the Commission still arrived at the conclusion that the benefits of abolition would be outweighed by the costs. Rights-based arguments have also underpinned the challenges to

185

restrictions on the right to silence in the European Court of Human Rights, for example, in the cases of *Murray* and *Saunders*.[107]

While rights may be given a substantive content in modern liberal democratic societies, there is one sense in which Bentham's accusation of the emptiness of rights does have some validity. If a formal right is rarely exercised in practice, it might well be seen as vacuous. For a variety of reasons, including psychological and social pressures built in to the nature of interrogation, as well as ignorance or incomplete comprehension of the nature of the right which may not be overcome by the caution, the right to silence has mostly been waived in practice.[108] Differential use of the waiver may be linked to variables such as class and educational achievement with middle-class suspects possessing greater knowledge of civil rights and greater confidence in asserting those rights. The formal equality of procedural and substantive rights may conceal fundamental inequalities at the heart of society which may inhibit the use of those rights.

Indeed a sceptic might argue that as the middle-class suspect arguably has a greater choice than his working-class counterpart over whether or not to exercise or waive his right to silence, abolition of the right to silence will contribute to greater equality, by sanctioning and acknowledging the existing pressures to speak. But should the issue be resolved in this way? If there is a differential use of the right to silence between classes, it would be better to combat this by strengthening awareness of rights during police interrogation. The mere existence of a right, without a full understanding of its implications and scope by the right-holder, is of limited value. It means that weaker groups will be effectively denied these rights. Given that these inequalities may persist through the various stages of the criminal justice process, an extensive programme of education is needed to remove these inequalities. Furthermore, once the right to silence is fully realised through maximisation of awareness, the weakest groups may receive the greatest protection from it. Box[109] has likened the processes of prosecution and conviction to a series of interconnected rooms: at every stage there is someone to open the door for the wealthy middle-class suspect, while the poorer working class, or underprivileged suspect, continues inexorably to the point of conviction. Similarly McBarnet has demonstrated the contrast between the formal rhetoric of the criminal justice system with its operation in practice, in her study of the process of conviction.[110]

Taking rights seriously

Bentham is too dismissive in sweeping rights issues out of the picture and in construing rights only in a deontological form. Rights do not rest on irrational emotions or on appeals to religious sanctions. Rather they can have a rational and non-metaphysical foundation, in the procedural protections of liberal democratic societies. Contemporary rights theorists such as Dworkin[111] offer rigorous analyses rather than the empty rhetoric portrayed in Bentham's caricature of rights arguments. It is therefore necessary to distinguish deontological conceptions of rights from the issues of procedural and substantive fairness, grounded in a particular historical and empirical context, namely the relationship between the individual and the modern state, which is marked by disparities and inequalities of power and where the the individual is the weaker party. For Dworkin, rights emerge out of the organisation of liberal democratic societies rather than being derived from a metaphysical standpoint. The idea of individual rights, he postulates, 'does not presuppose any ghostly forms'.[112] Individual rights are trumps which prevail over practical and majoritarian considerations. The most fundamental right from which other rights and liberties are derived, is the right to equal concern and respect.

The right to silence and the presumption of innocence may be construed in terms of this claim to equal respect of all citizens, so the loss of the privilege and the encouragement of inculpatory admissions and confessions would contradict these underlying moral principles. When these rights conflict with practical needs, says Dworkin, these conflicts 'are not occasions for fair compromise, but rather, if the principle must be dishonoured, for shame and regret.'[113] Moral rights, argues Dworkin, cannot be avoided in considering issues of due process:

> The difficult clauses of the Bill of Rights, like the due process and equal protection clauses, must be understood as appealing to moral concepts rather than laying down particular conceptions; therefore a court that undertakes the burden of applying these clauses fully as law must be an activist court, in the sense that it must be prepared to frame and answer questions of political morality.[114]

Bentham's view of moral rights as 'nonsense on stilts', Dworkin argues, has never been part of our orthodox political theory.[115] Constitutional rights are fundamental moral rights in a 'strong sense' and should not be undermined simply on the basis of the benefit to the majority. The rights to human dignity and equal respect, which Dworkin sees as fundamental, are especially relevant to the right to silence. By relieving the accused from pressure one accords the suspect a level of human dignity which would otherwise be missing from interrogation and trial. Even if one could establish an increase in convictions of the guilty by curtailing the right to silence, this would not justify the loss of human dignity of the accused and his guilt or innocence is irrelevant here. To curtail such rights as the privilege against self-incrimination, he says, we would need a reason consistent with the original rationale for the right in question and marginal benefits to others would be insufficient. The state should therefore look elsewhere for the means of protecting the public interest. This view is reflected in the approach of the United States Supreme Court in *Miranda v Arizona*:

affirming the privilege (against self-incrimination) is the respect
a government - state or federal - must accord to the dignity and
integrity of its citizens.[116]

In *Law's Empire*[117] Dworkin develops a normative and empirical theory of
adjudication in which judicial decisions do and should affirm existing political
rights. Decisions in hard cases, where there is more than one view of what the
law is, may be construed as interpreting new problems in the light of existing
principles rather than in terms of what is best for the future on policy grounds.
The court in deciding which view to take, will ask which view will respect the
virtue of integrity. Integrity is used by Dworkin to explain legal reasoning, but
may also be seen more broadly, as expressing moral and political principles held
by the community. Political life is construed as a moral sphere in which all are
equally positioned in relation to the essential moral principles valued by the
community. Integrity is satisfied when a community's legal system is coherent
in the sense of achieving consistency on matters of principle. It demands that the
same principles apply equally to all members and to all areas of community life
and constitutes a constraint on majoritarianism. In dealing with difficult cases, the
court will seek the principles which are expressed across different areas of the
legal system and which are embedded in the past. The explanation which
provides the best fit to those principles will be sought. Dworkin uses the analogy
of the chain novel in which a series of authors write consecutive chapters of a
novel, but aim to give the impression that the novel is written by one author. As
well as striving for the appearance of unity, the writer must consider the question
of literary merit. Similarly in adjudication, argues Dworkin, the courts do and
should see themselves engaged in this type of enterprise. When reviewing the
past, they should ask themselves which interpretation would best reflect these
moral principles embedded in the past and in the life of the community. Political
morality is internal to the question of what the law actually is, so the judge is not
just explaining past decisions but justifying them.

In *Life's Dominion* integrity in law is defined as consisting of the following
dimensions:

> First, it insists that judicial decision be a matter of principle,
> not compromise or strategy or political
> accommodation...Second... integrity holds vertically: a judge
> who claims that a particular liberty is fundamental must show
> that his claim is consistent with principles embedded in
> Supreme Court precedent and with the main structures of our
> constitutional arrangement. Third, integrity holds horizontally:
> a judge who adopts a principle in one case must give full
> weight to it in other cases he decides or endorses, even in
> apparently unrelated fields of law.[118]

Integrity, he says, demands 'that the principles necessary to support an authoritative set of judicial decisions must be accepted in other contexts as well.'[119] The purpose of integrity is to preclude political compromises but to take account of fundamental principles, such as the principles of autonomy and moral independence. This means that the court must be prepared to engage in answering questions of political morality, for example, in considering the extension of a right to privacy to homosexuals.[120] Measures may be judged and choices made according to the extent to which they violate fundamental rights and principles. On the Dworkinian view, these moral questions cannot be avoided by appeals to the original intent of the framers of the constitution.

The idea of 'balancing' rights against utility is problematic for Dworkin, because rights, by their very nature, cannot be 'weighed' against practical public benefits, but are designed to protect individuals from the pressure of majoritarian demands. But this balancing approach has been a feature of the English debate on the right to silence where the rights most often invoked by retentionists are the rights of privacy, the presumption of innocence and the *Woolmington*[121] rule, that the prosecution must prove the guilt of the prisoner. These rights have deep roots reaching back to the English revolution. They should ideally be entrenched if this were possible under existing constitutional law, but at the very least deserve full consideration when contemplating change. Although fundamental rights were underplayed by the CLRC, they were given greater emphasis by the Philips Commission.[122] Acknowledging the importance of safeguarding fundamental rights, the Commission saw its task as trying to 'strike a balance' between civil rights and police powers rather than according a protected status to rights. The danger is that once rights are put into the equation, they can easily be overwhelmed by the weight of utilitarian considerations. In the recent debate, rights issues appear to have been overlooked altogether by critics of the right to silence, who simply invoke the public interest unsupported by persuasive evidence that the public interest will be best served by abolition. The 'public interest', on closer examination, embraces a number of distinct interests: the interests of citizens who may be suspected of offences and subject to interrogation, the interests of the police in investigating crime, and the public's interest in securing protection from criminals.

Although Bentham did offer reasons and arguments to support his critique of the privilege, in modern debates the right to silence has been condemned without a full consideration of the evidence or the underlying principles. For example, the provisions relating to the right to silence in Northern Ireland were rushed through Parliament by means of an Order in Council. The Home Office Consultation Paper on changes for England and Wales was given a very limited circulation. A short time was allowed for responses and comments were invited only on the feasibility of implementation rather than the desirability of change, although more time was allowed for debates on the Criminal Justice and Public Order Bill.

The emphasis on a rights-based approach would also be consistent with the protection of rights guaranteed by the European Convention on Human Rights and the International Covenant on Civil and Political Rights. Cases on the right to silence are now being brought to the European Court and in considering these claims, empirical evidence on the practical problems of policing and the reality of the waiver of the right to silence, may result in less weight being given to the protection of the public, crime prevention and public order by the Court. There is also scope for the greater development of the protective principle.[123] In *Funke v France*[124] the European Court of Human Rights said the right to silence was embodied in the right to a fair hearing under Article 6(1) of the Convention and this right was violated by the applicant's conviction for refusing to disclose bank statements and other documents to French customs officials. His right to remain silent and not to contribute to incriminating himself was infringed by the fact that Customs officers initiated criminal proceedings against him to force him to co-operate in a prosecution against him by producing the relevant documents. The right to inspect documents in the French Customs Code could not trump the privilege against self-incrimination. The use of Article 6 to protect the privilege is also significant because there is no provision in Article 6 to limit the right in the public interest, for example to prevent disorder or crime, or in the interests of public safety.

A similar approach was followed by the European Court of Human Rights in the case of *Saunders v UK*[125] where the Court held that the applicant had been deprived of the right to a fair hearing guaranteed by Article 6(1) when the prosecution used statements at his trial which he had given earlier to DTI Inspectors under legal compulsion. The public interest in combating fraud could not justify the use of answers compulsorily obtained in a non-judicial investigation to incriminate him at his trial.

In *Murray v UK*[126] the European Court of Human Rights said that the right to remain silent, under police questioning, and the privilege against self-incrimination, were generally recognised international standards which lay at the heart of the notion of a fair procedure guaranteed by the Convention. If states permit adverse inferences to be drawn from silence, then it is crucial that the suspect has access to legal advice in deciding whether or not to remain silent. Article 6 was breached by denying Murray access to a lawyer for the first 48 hours of his detention. However, the Court did not accept the claim that drawing inferences under the Order shifted the burden of proof.

The right to silence is also protected by the International Covenant on Civil and Political Rights. Under Article 14(3)(g) the individual may not be compelled to testify against himself or to confess guilt. As there is no compulsion to speak under the CJPOA, there is no obvious breach of Article 14(3), but it could be argued that without a lawyer present, the subsequent trial is unfair and Article 14(1), the right to a fair and public hearing, has been breached. There may also be arguments in the European Court of Human Rights about compulsion given the pressures on suspects in both the Criminal Justice Act 1987 and the CJPOA. Under Article 14(2) of the ICCPR everyone charged with a criminal offence shall have the right to be presumed innocent until proved guilty according to law. This raises problems regarding the erosion of the *Woolmington* principle discussed below.[127]

The United Nations Human Rights Committee in its report published in July 1995 identified at least 11 areas where human rights were in danger in the UK.[128] It referred to the abolition of the right to silence as a particularly serious problem, violating Article 14 of the Covenant. It warned of the danger that vulnerable suspects would be intimidated and that the provisions may violate the UK's international treaty obligations. The Committee stated that the UK's legal system does not ensure that an effective remedy is provided for all violations of the rights protected by the ICCPR. It criticised the absence of a Bill of Rights, the failure of the UK to incorporate the Covenant into domestic law or to adopt the first Optional Protocol which permits individuals to petition the Committee.[129]

The right to privacy

A further rights-based justification of the right to silence has been offered by Galligan.[130] He poses the question of whether there is a right to silence during police questioning, even when it means losing probative evidence and makes the police's task more difficult. If we answer in the affirmative, we need to be clear what we are protecting, which justifies outweighing these other goals. For Galligan, the answer lies in the right to privacy which he sees as important, because it guards personal autonomy and personal identity. If an individual's thoughts and desires could be known by others, his personality would be destroyed. Liberty, autonomy, privacy and respect offer an alternative to the Benthamite stress on rectitude of decision-making and crime control, argues Galligan, for rectitude may be subordinated to the values of fairness. The right to silence may mean excluding evidence obtained in violation of the right even if that evidence is reliable. He endorses Dworkin's view that if a society takes a right seriously, it cannot be curtailed whenever it is convenient to do so in order to gain other benefits. If the right has a value independent of rectitude, says Galligan, when conflicts occur, 'marginal benefits in terms of rectitude should not be sacrificed in favour of the right'.[131]

He posits the idea of privacy as an expanding circle with the individual personality at the centre: the further an issue is from the centre, the less weight it has against competing factors, such as the public interest in crime control, the closer to the centre the greater the weight. On this model we can consider if encroachments on privacy are justified. If a suspect is asked to explain his actions, motives and thoughts, this moves closer to the centre so the right to privacy may outweigh crime control. If the police could plug the suspect into a machine recording every thought, this would strike at the heart of privacy, yet this is, in principle, the same as requiring him to disclose information. The police have no justifiable claim to direct access to that information, he says, because they are strangers to him and there is no special relationship. This is especially true where the aim of interrogation is to obtain evidence to use against him.

The appeal to privacy is especially pertinent when we consider the suspect who may wish to remain silent to avoid embarrassment to himself or his family, or to avoid giving details of his private life, particularly where he does not see these details as relevant to the offence being investigated. But Galligan concludes by saying that the right to silence cannot be made absolute and intrusions may be justifiable in the case of serious crimes. The extent of the right, he argues, depends on the balance between the right and the countervailing values in each case, although it is better to draw a clear generalised line. Although Galligan begins from a Dworkinian view by according rights primacy over other interests, he concedes that these rival considerations might ultimately lead us to sacrifice that right at the altar of these competing claims. The danger of such concessions is that one enters on a slippery slope in which a constitutional right is reduced to just one factor to take into account when making calculations and the door is opened to further changes, for example, at the trial stage itself. The initial attack on ambush defences which generated the Criminal Justice and Public Order Act thus resulted in changes to the right to silence at the trial stage.

Notes

1.   J. Bentham (1843) 'Anarchical Fallacies'; 'Rationale of Judicial Evidence', *The Works of Jeremy Bentham*, Bowring edition, Edinburgh, William Tait.
2.   Criminal Law Revision Committee (1972) Eleventh Report, Evidence (General), London, HMSO, Cmnd 4991.
3.   A. Zuckerman (1989) *The Principles of Criminal Evidence*, Oxford, Clarendon.
4.   Report of the Working Group on the Right to Silence (July 13, 1989) Home Office, C Division.
5.   Report of the Royal Commission on Criminal Justice (1993) London, HMSO, Cmnd 2263.
6.   *Ibid*, p i.
7.   Report of the Royal Commission on Criminal Procedure (1981) London, HMSO, Cmnd 8092.
8.   See R. Leng (1993) *The right to silence in police interrogation: a study of some of the issues underlying the debate*, RCCJ Research Study no.10, London, HMSO.

9. J. Bentham, *Rationale of Judicial Evidence*, 452.

10. See T. Gifford (1984) *Supergrasses, The Use of Accomplice Evidence in Northern Ireland*, London, The Cobden Trust; S. Greer, (1995) *Supergrasses: A Study in Anti-Terrorist Law Enforcement in Northern Ireland*, Oxford, Clarendon Press.

11. See also Evidence Act 1851, Evidence Amendment Act 1853, Evidence Further Amendment Act 1869, Criminal Evidence Act 1898.

12. J. Bentham, *Rationale of Judicial Evidence*, p 451.

13. See JUSTICE/CAJ (1994) *The Right of Silence Debate: the Northern Ireland Experience*, London.

14. See Lord Chancellor's Department (1995) *Legal Aid: Targetting Need: the future of publicly funded help in solving legal problems and disputes in England and Wales*, Cmnd 2854, HMSO, para. 4.44; Legal Aid Board (1995) Annual Report 1994-5, London, HMSO.

15. J. Bentham (1825) *A Treatise on Judicial Evidence*, ed. E. Dumont, London, pp 2-3.

16. For example, W. Twining (1985) *Theories of Evidence: Bentham and Wigmore*, London, Weidenfeld and Nicolson.

17. J. Bentham, *Rationale of Judicial Evidence*, p 454.

18. *Ibid*, p 452.

19. *Ibid*, p 37.

20. *Ibid.*

21. *Ibid*, pp 336-7.

22. *Ibid*, p 339.

23. See Federal Rules of Evidence, rules 401, 402 and 403. Rule 402 states that all relevant evidence is admissible, except as otherwise provided by the Constitution of the United States, by Act of Congress, by these rules, or by other rules prescribed by the Supreme Court pursuant to statutory authority. Evidence which is not relevant is not admissible.

24. Sir James Stephen (1948) *Digest of the Law of Evidence*, London, Macmillan, article 1.

25. Federal Rule 403.

26. RCCJ Report, para. 8.13.

27. J. Bentham, *Rationale of Judicial Evidence*, p 451.

28. *Ibid*, p 451.

29. J. Wigmore (1961) *Evidence*, 8, McNaughten rev. ed., para. 2265.

30. See *Murray v UK* (1996) Times, 9 February, *Murray v DPP* [1994] 1 WLR 1; see also *R v Martin* [1991] Belfast Crown Court, May 8; [1992] NIJB, 5, 1; see chapter 3 above.

31. Report of the Royal Commission on Criminal Procedure (1981) London, HMSO, Cmnd 8092, para. 4.36.

32. J. Wigmore, *op.cit.*

33. A. Zuckerman, *op.cit.*

34. See chapter 10 below for a discussion of the problem of false confessions and their role in miscarriages of justice.

35. Section 57 of the Criminal Justice and Public Order Act 1994 which amends s 64 of PACE, and PACE Code D, 5.8A (1995). However, DNA profiling raises its own methodological problems, see S. Easton (1991) 'Bodily samples and the privilege against self-incrimination', Crim LR 18, (1991) 'The evidential and methodological problems of genetic fingerprinting', Explorations in Knowledge, Vol. XVIII, No.1, 39 and chapter 8 below.

36. M. McConville (1987) 'Silence in court', NLJ, 1169.

37. J. Jackson and S.Doran (1990) Judicial Fact-Finding in the Diplock Court in Northern Ireland, University of Manchester, Faculty of Law, Working Paper No. 2.

38. *Ibid*, 15.

39. A.J. Ashworth (1994) *The Criminal Process*, Oxford University Press, pp 287-8.

40. T.S. Kuhn (1970) *The Structure of Scientific Revolutions*, Chicago University Press.

41. P.K. Feyerabend (1975) *Against Method*, London, New Left Books, (1979) *Science in a Free Society*, London, New Left Books.

42. A.C. Gross (1990) *The Rhetoric of Science*, Harvard University Press.

43. *Ibid*, p 198.

44. *Ibid*, p 203.

45. *Ibid*, p 204.

46. See R. Merton (1973) *The Sociology of Science*, Chicago University Press; D. Lamb and S. Easton (1984) *Multiple Discovery*, Avebury.

47. [1914] AC 599 at 609.

48. [1987] 1 QB 426; see also *R v Prager* [1972] 1 WLR 260 for the construction of oppression prior to PACE.

49. [1993] Times, 22 March.

50. A.J. Ashworth [1977] 'Excluding Evidence as Protecting Rights', Crim LR 723. See *DPP v Ping Lin* [1975] 3 All ER 175.

51. Paras. 1.4, 1G (1995).

52. I. Dennis (1989) 'Reconstructing the Law of Criminal Evidence', Current Legal Problems, 21.

53. See *R v Mason* [1987] 3 All ER 481.

54. See *R v O'Connor* [1987] Crim LR 260.

55. (1988) 87 Cr App Rep 380.

56. [1992] QB 979.

57. [1992] 4 All ER 567.

58. [1993] Times, 5 October. 59, [1995] Crim LR 817.

60. I. Dennis (Summer, 1993) 'Miscarriages of justice and the law of confessions: evidentiary issues and solutions', Public Law, 291.

61.   I. Dennis (1995) 'Instrumental protection, human right or functional necessity?: reassessing the privilege against self-incrimination', Camb LJ, 342; see *Murray v UK* [1996] Times, 9 February, *Funke v France* [25 February 1993] Series A No 256-A.

62.   I. Dennis (1995) at p 344.

63.   *Ibid* at p 374.

64.   See chapter 10 below.

65.   I. Dennis (1995) p 376.

66.   J. Baldwin (1992) *Preparing the Record of Taped Interview*, RCCJ Research Study no. 2, London HMSO; (1992) *The Role of Legal Representatives at the Police Station*, RCCJ Research Study no.3, London, HMSO; (1992) J. Baldwin and T. Moloney (1992) *Supervision of Police Investigations in Serious Criminal Cases*, RCCJ Research Study no. 4.

67.   J. Baldwin and T. Moloney (1992) p 78.

68.   M. McConville (1993) *Corroboration and Confessions: The Impact of a Rule requiring that no Conviction can be Sustained on the Basis of Confession Evidence Alone*, RCCJ Research Study no. 13, London, HMSO.

69.   M. McConville, A.Sanders and R. Leng (1991) *The Case for the Prosecution*, London, Routledge.

70.   *Ibid*, pp 54-5.

71.   *Ibid*, p 147.

72.   M. Maguire and C. Norris (1993) *The Conduct and Supervision of Criminal Investigations*, RCCJ Research Study no. 5, London, HMSO.

73.   *Ibid*, p 46.

74.   See Report of an Inquiry by the Hon. Sir Henry Fisher into the circumstances leading to the trial of three persons on charges arising out of the death of Maxwell Confait and the fire at 27 Doggett Road London SE6, London HMSO.

75.   RCCJ Report, paras. 2.5, 27.

76.   M. McConville (1993) *Corroboration and Confessions: The Impact of a Rule requiring that no Conviction can be Sustained on the Basis of Confession Evidence Alone*, RCCJ Research Study no. 13, London, HMSO; see chapter 10 below.

77.   D. Galligan (1988) 'The Right to Silence Reconsidered', Current Legal Problems, 69 at p 87.

78.   G. Williams (1987) 'The Tactic of Silence', NLJ, 1107.

79.   I. Dennis (1995) pp 355-6.

80.   *Ibid*, p 356.

81.   [1935] AC 462.

82.   *Ibid*, at pp 481-2. Inroads have been made into the Woolmington principle, see A. Ashworth and M. Blake [1996] 'The Presumption of

Innocence in English Criminal Law', Crim LR 306 and chapter 9 below.

83.   RCCP Report (1981) para. 66.
84.   RCCJ Report, para. 6.59.
85.   *Ibid*, para. 7.4.
86.   CJPOA, ss 34, 35.
87.   I. Dennis (1989).
88.   See chapter 8 below.
89.   [1995] 4 All ER 939.
90.   M. McConville (1987).
91.   *Ibid.*
92.   [1992] NIJB 41.
93.   A. Zuckerman, *op. cit.*, p 319.
94.   RCCP Report (1981).
95.   See chapter 4 above.
96.   384 US 324 (1968).
97.   Sir James Stephen (1883) *A History of the Criminal Law of England*, London, Macmillan, p 441.
98.   J. Bentham (1987) 'Anarchical Fallacies', in J. Waldron (ed.) *Nonsense upon Stilts*, London, Methuen, pp 46-76.
99.   *Ibid*, p 49.
100. J. Bentham, *Rationale of Judicial Evidence*, p 451.
101. *Ibid*, p 455.
102. CLRC, *op.cit.*
103. Report of the Working Group on the Right to Silence (1989).
104. RCCP Report (1981).
105. See, for example, Legal Action Group (November, 1988) Response of the Legal Action Group to the Home Office Working Group on the Right to Silence Consultation Paper, London.
106. RCCJ Report (1993).
107. See *Murray v UK* [1996] Times, 9 February and chapter 3 above; *Saunders v UK*, [1996] Times, 18 December.
108. R. Leng, *op.cit.* and D. Brown [1993] *The Incidence of Right to Silence in Police Interviews: The Research Evidence Reviewed*, Home Office Research and Planning Unit, unpublished and chapter 5 below.
109. S. Box (1971) *Deviance, Reality and Society*, Holt, Rinehart and Winston.
110. D. McBarnet (1981) *Conviction*, London, Macmillan.
111. R. Dworkin (1977) *Taking Rights Seriously*, London, Duckworth.
112. *Ibid*, p xi.
113. *Ibid*, p 13.
114. *Ibid*, p 147.
115. *Ibid*, p 184.

116.   384 US 436 (1966).
117.   R. Dworkin (1986) *Law's Empire*, Harvard University Press.
118.   R. Dworkin (1993) *Life's Dominion*, London, Harper Collins, p 146.
119.   *Ibid*, p 158.
120.   R. Dworkin (November 8, 1984) 'Reagan's Justice', New York Review of Books; see also R. Dworkin (1996) *Freedom's Law*, Oxford University Press.
121.   [1935] AC 462.
122.   RCCP Report (1981).
123.   See A.J. Ashworth (1987), (1994).
124.   *Funke v France*, [25 Feb 1993] Series A No. 256-A.
125.   [1996] Times 18 December, see chapter 9 below.
126.   [1996] Times, 9 February.
127.   See *R v Hunt* [1987] 1 All ER 1, Ashworth and Blake [1996] and chapter 9 below.
128.   UNHRC [1995] CCPR/C/79/Add.55.
129.   Other areas criticised by the Committee included extended powers of detention, the use of emergency legislation in Northern Ireland, the strip-searching of prisoners, the treatment of immigrants and asylum-seekers.
130.   D. Galligan (1988) 'The Right to Silence Reconsidered', Current Legal Problems, 69.
131.   *Ibid*, p 73.

7 The privilege against self-incrimination in the United States

The right to silence debate in the United Kingdom has been paralleled in the United States where we find a similar defence and erosion of the right to silence in the case law. Judicial attitudes towards the defendant in criminal cases have hardened in the United States. This has reflected, to some extent, the changing composition of the Supreme Court as well as increasing concern over the drug problem and persistent offenders and the political advantages of a strong position on law and order to both major parties.

The American debate on the right to silence has centred on interpretation of the Fifth Amendment of the Constitution, which states that 'no person...shall be compelled in any criminal case to be a witness against himself', in contrast to the English debate, which has focused on the specific proposals and reports of the CLRC, Royal Commission and Home Office Working Group and the Runciman Report. However, the right to silence is more firmly established in the United States than in England and Wales, having a constitutional foundation in the Fifth Amendment. Because the right to silence in the United States is grounded in this constitutional framework and protected by entrenched constitutional limitations, efforts to weaken the right have met with less success than here. Although the Supreme Court is so constrained, nonetheless there is considerable scope for argument over the correct interpretation of the Amendment. Problems of interpretation have arisen over the underlying rationale of the privilege, whether its prime rationale is privacy, in protecting a sphere in which the state cannot intrude, or autonomy, embodying the recognition of human dignity, which is balanced against the state's interest in crime control and law enforcement. Disputes have also arisen over the scope of the privilege, for example, whether it embraces the refusal to supply incriminating bodily samples.

Amar and Lettow are critical of the Court's failure to define the scope of the privilege in a logical and sensible way.[1] While finding problems with the principal rationales of the privilege they argue that focusing on reliability provides the best rationale for making sense of the self-incrimination clause and defining its scope.   Stuntz has argued that the privilege is best understood in terms of solving the problem of excusable self-protective perjury.[2] It reflects the recognition that if pressured to confess, the accused will be tempted to perjure himself and that while lying would be wrong, it would be understandable in those circumstances.

A critical point in the history of the privilege in relation to pre-trial procedures was the landmark case of *Miranda v Arizona*.[3] It needs to be considered against the background of increasing concern over unacceptable police tactics, the bullying of suspects and their isolation for long periods.[4] In *Escobedo v Illinois*,[5] the Sixth Amendment right of the defendant in criminal proceedings to counsel had been extended to cover individuals who had not yet been formally indicted, but nonetheless were the prime suspects on whom police investigations were focused. Consequently incriminating statements made by Escobedo, when denied access to his lawyer, were excluded. In *Miranda* the police had failed to inform Ernesto Miranda of his right to see a lawyer. The Supreme Court, in *Miranda*, therefore laid down new guidelines for the police, to provide a procedural protection against improper police practices of federal and state law enforcers. Prior to any questioning in custody, the suspect now had to be warned by the police of his right to silence, his right to a lawyer at the police station as well as at trial. The police had to tell him that he could stop the interrogation at any point and have access to a lawyer on demand. This was reinforced by an exclusionary rule: confessions would not be admitted unless the prosecution could show that these procedural safeguards had been observed and that the defendant had waived these rights in full knowledge and voluntarily. The aim of the *Miranda* guidelines was to prevent the mental and physical abuse of suspects at the police station and to prevent the accused from being tricked into making admissions. *Miranda* can thus be seen as a reaffirmation of the importance of the right to silence and the right to make an informed choice whether or not to exercise that right. It also expresses the Supreme Court's recognition of the importance of judicial integrity and impartiality in ensuring that abuses by the police receive as much recognition as the wrongdoing of the citizen. The court argued that:

> The privilege against self-incrimination, which has had a long
> and expansive historical development, is the essential mainstay
> of our adversary system and guarantees to the individual "the
> right to remain silent unless he chooses to speak in the
> unfettered exercise of his own free will", during a period of

custodial interrogation as well as in the courts or during the course of other official investigations.[6]

Chief Justice Warren stressed that 'procedural safeguards must be employed to protect the privilege'[7] and proposed the following procedures:

> He must be warned prior to any questioning that he has the right to remain silent, that anything he says can be used against him in a court of law, that he has the right to the presence of an attorney, and that if he cannot afford an attorney one will be appointed for him prior to any questioning if he so desires. Opportunity to exercise these rights must be afforded to him throughout the interrogation. After such warnings have been given, and such opportunity afforded him, the individual may knowingly and intelligently waive these rights and agree to answer questions or make a statement. But unless and until such warnings and waiver are demonstrated by the prosecution at trial, no evidence obtained as a result of interrogation can be used against him.[8]

Although difficulties have arisen in practice in defining the limits of both custody and interrogation for the purposes of determining at what point the warning should be given, clearly the decision in *Miranda* was intended to combat the use of tricks to inveigle the suspect to surrender his right to silence as well as police bullying. In other words, the suspect should make a free, rational and informed choice and the decision to waive the right to silence should be made knowingly and intelligently and constitute the unfettered exercise of free will. This means that the suspect should be relieved from pressures to speak, whether in the hope of positive advantage or fear of detriment. 'Knowledge' presupposes awareness of the right and 'intelligent' suggests a rational decision. The determination of a knowing and intelligent waiver may be problematic and the courts have been willing to imply a waiver in borderline cases.[9] Prima facie the *Miranda* provisions go further than the English protections under PACE, in informing the accused that the interrogation may be stopped at any time, in giving access to counsel without exceptions, and in the automatic exclusion of admissions obtained in violation of the requirements in contrast to the English courts' *discretion* to exclude admissions obtained in breach of the PACE Codes.

Following *Miranda*, the suspect being held in custody could not be questioned in the absence of his lawyer, unless he had been warned of his right to silence and his right to counsel and had waived these rights. Initially the American courts interpreted *Miranda* robustly, even to the point of absurdity in the eyes of some commentators. Some critics were concerned about the implications for the effectiveness of the police in fighting crime and claimed that the guilty would be able to hide behind these protections. The appeal to common sense also underlay criticisms of the subsequent cases which applied the reasoning in *Miranda*. In *Orozco v Texas*,[10] for example, it was held that the *Miranda* requirements applied when the questioning had taken place outside the police station. A murder suspect was questioned in the early hours of the morning in his boarding house bedroom, regarding a murder in a restaurant the previous evening. He admitted going to the restaurant and owning a gun, which he said was in a washing machine at the back of the house. The gun was found and it was proved that it was the gun which fired the shot which killed the victim. Orozco was convicted but because the questioning had not been preceded by a *Miranda* warning, notwithstanding the fact that it took place at the lodging-house rather than in the isolation of the police station, his conviction was reversed.

The decision in *Orozco* was criticised by Cross[11] for making the law 'look an ass'. Chief Justice Warren had referred in *Miranda* to the need for procedural protection arising at the point when the individual is 'taken into custody or otherwise deprived of his freedom by the authorities in any significant way and is subjected to questioning'[12] and this statement would seem to leave open whether it applies to situations where the individual has not been arrested, but makes a statement voluntarily to the police, or is subject to questioning outside the police station as in *Orozco*. For even outside the police station, the individual could perceive himself as deprived of his freedom if surrounded by the police and if he thought that resistance or flight could be construed against him.

Even if one were to accept the argument that the Supreme Court over- extended *Miranda* in *Orozco* this does not mean that the *Miranda* decision and the consequent guidelines were unsatisfactory. In any event the initial zeal of the court has now been moderated. Inroads into *Miranda* have been made in the last twenty years, reflecting the changing composition of the Supreme Court and changes in the political climate during the Reagan-Bush administrations. Subsequent cases exhibited a retreat from the early robust applications of *Miranda*, by failing to exclude automatically evidence obtained in violation of the *Miranda* requirements, in certain circumstances and adopting a narrow technical approach to the requirements, instead of giving effect to the spirit of the decision. In this respect the American approach has moved closer to the narrower discretionary approach found in England.

In *Harris v New York*[13] it was held that where a confession had been obtained without a *Miranda* warning, the accused could be cross-examined on it in order to undermine his testimony and credibility at trial. The case concerned the sale of drugs on two separate occasions to an undercover police officer. Harris denied that he had made the first sale and while acknowledging the second sale, denied that the substance sold was heroin. Incriminating statements had been made to the police, before he had received his *Miranda* warning. These conflicted with his testimony in court, and when they were put to him, the court held that he could be cross-examined on them. The trial judge had stressed that *Miranda* should not be used as a licence to commit perjury, safe in the knowledge that one would not be embarrassed by being faced with one's previous inconsistent statements at trial. His decision was upheld by the Supreme Court.

For Cross[14] the decision illustrated the irrationality of the prevailing law on the right to silence. Although criticised for undermining the rationale of *Miranda*, which was to discourage police impropriety, *Harris* was one of the first cases to show a retreat from the early vigorous interpretation of *Miranda*. Subsequently in *New York v Quarles*[15] a suspect was pursued and detained by the police in a supermarket. Believing that he had been carrying a gun, the police questioned him before giving a *Miranda* warning in order to find the loaded gun. He directed them to some boxes where the gun was found. He was then arrested and informed of his rights and charged with possessing the gun. At first instance, the judge excluded his statement locating the gun and the discovery of the gun, because he had not received the warning. The Supreme Court argued that in view of the immediate danger to the public, the possibility of a passer-by finding the gun and harming himself or others, the *Miranda* warning need not be given, and the statements of the accused, although not prefaced by the warning, were admissible. The court balanced the objective danger to the public against the preventive goal of *Miranda* in protecting Fifth Amendment rights although, as was argued earlier, it is questionable whether rights can be weighed against the public interest in this way. The decision made clear that the *Miranda* warning could now be omitted in emergencies. Yet it would have been open to the court, as Mirfield[16] observes, to protect public safety without encroaching on the Fifth Amendment rights, by permitting the police to question in emergencies, to obtain the necessary information speedily without giving the warning, while excluding the statements at trial. Similarly in *Oregon v Elstad*[17] the Supreme Court refused to evidence obtained in the context of a *Miranda* violation.

Stuntz[18] has argued that although the deterrent aim of *Miranda* to prevent police brutality, is still being pursued, the second dimension of preventing police deception, has been eroded: 'both in search and seizure law and in the police interrogation context, the Supreme Court has significantly changed the way in which it views defendants' constitutional rights.'[19] He cites the decisions in *Rhode Island v Innis*[20] and *Moran v Burbine*[21] to support this claim. In *Rhode Island v Innis* the defendant, on his way to the police station, made clear that he did not wish to speak before seeing a lawyer. On the journey the police officers discussed amongst themselves the possibility of a child finding the missing murder weapon, a shotgun, or shells, of tragic consequences as there were several children in the area, including disabled children. Following this discussion, the defendant volunteered to show them where the weapon was located and took them to the place where it had been concealed. The Supreme Court held that the weapon and the accompanying statements were admissible because the conversation with the police officers did not amount to an interrogation for the purpose of the *Miranda* rules, as the comments were not intended to produce such a reaction: 'Interrogation' on the other hand, meant expressly posing questions and actions or words of the police which they would know are reasonably likely to produce that reaction and in this case the police could not have known that their comments would have that effect.[22] This reasoning is unpersuasive, however, as most people are likely to be affected by an appeal to the safety of children and to exclude such tactics from interrogation is to draw the boundaries too narrowly, but the court nonetheless held that the accused's statements and the finding of the gun, were not subject to the *Miranda* constraints.[23]

In *Moran v Burbine*[24] when Burbine was being held by the police a lawyer obtained for him by his sister telephoned the police station, explaining who he was and asking if his client would be further questioned that day. The lawyer was informed that Burbine would not be questioned, yet later that night Burbine was interrogated without being informed that he now had a lawyer, or that he had rung the station. After receiving his *Miranda* warnings, he confessed and the court held that the police were under no obligation to disclose that information, even though it might have affected his decision to talk. Provided that he understood his right to silence, his waiver of that right was valid.

What these decisions show, argues Stuntz, is that although the tactics in *Rhode Island v Innis* and *Moran v Burbine* are precisely those which *Miranda* was designed to protect against, *Miranda* is now a shield only against police coercion but not against police deception and it can no longer be relied on to safeguard the individual's rational choice. He perceives a gulf here between the right not to be physically abused by the police, which may not be encroached upon, and the right to be told that one need not talk, which may be jettisoned when outweighed by other interests. The exclusionary rule provides absolute protection for the former right and only conditional protection for the latter right, as evidence obtained by means contrary to the spirit of *Miranda* has been admitted. Stuntz sees deception and advantage-taking as lying at the heart of criminal investigation, although they are banished from the process of gathering evidence in civil cases by the legal ethics doctrine.[25] In the United States the courts have supported the use of deception by officers to gain evidence during interrogation.[26] The Supreme Court has narrowed the boundaries of custodial interrogation and has introduced various exceptions, where breaches of the guidelines will not entail exclusion of incriminating statements or conduct. The current political climate of anxiety over law and order, including the 'toughness' of the Clinton Administration on crime and punishment, is one in which a narrower approach may flourish.

Amar and Lettow also point to the failure of *Miranda* to establish standards of propriety in the police station: 'Despite *Miranda*'s promise to open up the black box of the police station, it did not require that lawyers, magistrates or even tape or video recorders be present in interrogation rooms. In the absence of these monitors, detectives and police have often engaged in ingenious but troubling, forms of interrogation.'[27] They cite a recent study of the Baltimore homicide detective unit which identified a number of techniques including physically intimidating techniques bordering on violence, such as swearing, and kicking chairs, interrogating suspects late at night, lying about the evidence against the suspect, and the skilful use of photocopier machines in conducting lie detector tests.[28] They argue that the difficulties in construing the self-incrimination clause and the problems in using the suspect as a testimonial source in pre-trial proceedings, have sometimes driven interrogation underground, into unregulated police interrogation rooms, surprise searches, wiretapping, and intrusions of privacy. They therefore strongly favour the use of depositions and pre-trial judicial examination to prevent police abuse, modelled on that used in civil litigation. The process of interrogation would be judicially supervised and failure to answer punishable by contempt proceedings or the drawing of adverse inferences.

The right to silence at trial is still intact and no adverse comment may be made on the accused's decision not to testify. This was affirmed in *Griffin v California*[29] where the Supreme Court ruled that comment by both prosecution and judge was prohibited by the constitution. Griffin, who had been charged with murder, did not testify. The prosecution had commented on this and the trial jury had directed the jury that it could interpret his failure to account for incriminating evidence as affirming the truth of that evidence. The Supreme Court held that the state law which authorised such comments was unconstitutional. No adverse inferences may be drawn from the defendant's failure to testify at trial. Allowing such inferences said the Court would in effect mean punishing the defendant's silence and would violate the self-incrimination clause.[30] The accused should not have to choose between giving evidence or having his silence used against him. The constitutional framework of the suspect's rights in the Fifth Amendment gives a strong foundation to the right and makes it difficult to attack. However in *US v Robinson*[31] comment by the prosecution was permitted, but this was in the context of a claim that the defendant had not been given the chance to answer the case against him.

We can therefore find variations historically and cross-culturally in the treatment of the evidential significance of silence and the commitment to the privilege against self-incrimination. While deception has been tolerated in the United States, nonetheless we still find a strong commitment to the privilege against self-incrimination which contrasts with the sustained attack on the right to silence in England, despite common concerns with crime control.

Notes

1. A.R. Amar and R.B. Lettow (March, 1995) 'Fifth Amendment First Principles: The Self-Incrimination Clause', Michigan Law Rev, Vol 93, No. 5, pp 857-928 at 858.

2. Stuntz argues that excuse can also explain the line between criminal and civil penalties in Fifth Amendment law, namely the fact that some penalties are more likely to tempt citizens to lie than others. See W.J. Stuntz (1988) 'Self-Incrimination and Excuse', Columbia Law Review, 88, 1227.

3. *Miranda v Arizona*, 384 US 436 (1966).

4. *Davis v North Carolina*, 384 US 737 (1966).

5. *Escobedo v Illinois*, 378 US (1963).

6. *Miranda v Arizona*, 384 US 436 (1966).

7. at 478.

8. at 478-9.

9. It was held in *Colorado v Springs*, 107 S Ct 851 that a waiver in relation to particular offences can be construed as a general waiver so that the police may then question the suspect in relation to more serious offences; in *Michigan v Mosley*, 423 US 96 (1975) an initial refusal to be questioned was deemed not to prohibit further subsequent questioning and that in the second interrogation the subject's response could be construed as a waiver.

10. *Orozco v Texas*, 324 US 24 (1969).

11. R. Cross [1973] 'The Evidence Report: Sense or Nonsense - A Very Wicked Animal Defends the Eleventh Report of the Criminal Law Revision Committee', Crim LR 329 at p 330.

12. *Miranda v Arizona*, 384 US at 478 (1966).

13. *Harris v New York*, 401 US 222 (1971).

14. R. Cross, *op.cit.*

15. *New York v Quarles*, 467 US 649 (1984).

16. P. Mirfield (1985) *Confessions*, London, Sweet and Maxwell.

17. 470 US 298 (1985).

18. W.J. Stuntz [1989] 'The American Exclusionary Rule and Defendants' Changing Rights', Crim LR 117. See also R. Dworkin (November 8, 1984) 'Reagan's Justice', New York Review of Books and *Freedom's Law* (1996) Oxford University Press, for a discussion of the changing composition of the Court and the implications for the circumscription of constitutional rights.

19. *Ibid*, p 122.

20. *Rhode Island v Innis*, 446 US 291 (1980).

21. *Moran v Burbine*, 475 US 412 (1986).

22. The issue of interrogation had been avoided in *Brewer v Williams* 30 US 387 (1977), although it raised similar issues. The Supreme Court held that the suspect's incriminating statements were inadmissible but because of the denial of his right to counsel under the Sixth Amendment, rather than under Fifth Amendment privilege, and followed the decision in *Massiah v US* 377 US 201 (1963) rather than *Miranda*, even though here the statement which elicited the information, the 'Christian burial speech' had been made directly to the accused. The police officer had referred to the fact that the victim would not receive a Christian burial if her body was not discovered soon, as snow was falling, following which the accused showed the police where the body could be found.

23. If an item of real evidence obtained by violating the *Miranda* requirements would have been discovered in any event, it may be admitted in evidence. See *Warden v Williams*, 467 US (1984).

24. *Moran v Burbine*, 475 US 412 (1986)

25. W.J. Stuntz (1995) 'Lawyers, Deception, and Evidence Gathering', 79 Va L Rev 1903 at 1905.

26. See R.A. Leo (1992) 'From coercion to deception: the changing nature of police interrogation in America', Crime, Law and Social Change, Vol 18 pp 35-9.

27. Amar and Lettow, *op.cit.* p 873.

28. D. Simon, (1991) *Homicide: a year on the killing streets.*

29. *Griffin v California* 380 US 606 (1965).

30. *Ibid*, at 614-5.

31. 485 US 25 (1988). Moreover, at the sentencing stage the Federal Sentencing Guidelines do allow lower sentences for defendants who admit their criminal conduct.

8 Bodily samples and the privilege against self-incrimination

The precise scope of the privilege against self-incrimination has been an important issue in English and American jurisprudence. A boundary to the right to silence has been drawn in both England and the United States, by excluding the refusal to supply bodily samples from the privilege against self-incrimination. But is the refusal to supply a sample fundamentally different to refusal to speak? Are there good grounds for confining the privilege against self-incrimination to speech and not extending it to samples? Can the refusal to supply bodily samples to the police be seen as an exercise of the right to silence? There are difficulties with the exclusion of the refusal to supply samples from the privilege and with the underlying distinction between silence and samples, which have increased with the discovery of DNA fingerprinting, which will be examined.

The scope of the privilege

The United States

Although in both England and the United States efforts to include bodily samples within the scope of the privilege against self-incrimination have been been firmly resisted, nonetheless we can still find ambiguities and tensions in the courts' treatment of this question. In *Schmerber v California*[1] the issue of whether the extraction of blood and admission of the test results infringe the privilege was addressed. It was held that the privilege does not extend to the extraction and use of samples in evidence. A blood sample had been taken from the applicant without his consent when he was arrested on a drink-driving charge and being treated in hospital following a road accident. He was subsequently

207

convicted of driving under the influence of alcohol and argued that taking the blood and admitting the evidence which showed intoxication, violated his privilege against self-incrimination under the Fifth Amendment. His argument was rejected by the Supreme Court which held, *inter alia*, that the privilege could not be used in such a case because 'the privilege protects an accused only from being compelled to testify against himself, or otherwise provide the State with evidence of a testimonial or communicative nature,... the withdrawal of blood and use of the analysis in question in this case did not involve compulsion to those ends.'[2] The privilege therefore did not apply to the use of the blood test in Schmerber's case. Justice Holmes' assertion in *Holt v United States*[3] that the 'prohibition of compelling a man in a criminal court to be a witness against himself is a prohibition of the use of physical or moral compulsion to extort communications from him, not an exclusion of his body as evidence when it may be material'[4] was approved. In *Holt* the court had considered the admissibility of a statement that the accused before trial had tried on a shirt which fitted him and was self-incriminating. Counsel had argued that he did so under protest and that forcing him to try on the shirt was a violation of the privilege. But the court dismissed this argument as an 'extravagant extension of the Fifth Amendment' and Justice Holmes asserted that counsel's objection 'would forbid a jury to look at a prisoner and compare his features with a photograph in proof.'[5]

Considering the question in relation to the supply of a blood sample, the Supreme Court in *Schmerber v California* defined the privilege to refer to both testimony and communications, whatever form they take, including the production of papers by the accused, following *Boyd v United States*.[6] In *Boyd* the Supreme Court held that compelling production of an individual's papers to be used against himself was equivalent to forcing him to be a witness against himself. But photographs, fingerprints, writing, speaking or assuming a stance for identification purposes have been excluded from the protection of the privilege. The court in *Schmerber* struck a middle path between confining the privilege to testimony and extending it to physical evidence. As Justice Brennan argued 'The distinction which has emerged...is that the privilege is a bar against compelling "communications" or "testimony", but that compulsion which makes a suspect or accused the source of "real or physical evidence" does not violate it.'[7] He acknowledged that there were difficulties in applying the distinction to certain situations, such as lie-detector tests. However, in Schmerber's case, there was no question of enforced communication or compulsory testimony and he had not been required to be a witness against himself. While the blood test evidence was incriminatory and obtained by compulsion, as it did not relate to testimony or to any communicative act, it was admissible.

But in a dissenting judgement Justice Black could find no grounds for excluding the protection of the Fifth Amendment from the case of compulsory blood testing, as this activity, he argued, does have a testimonial and communicative nature. The whole point of the test is to obtain the testimony of the person who analyses the blood who then communicates to the court that the accused was intoxicated. The terms 'testimonial' and 'communication' lack clarity and precision and there are few precedents on which the court can rely in limiting the scope of privilege by the use of these words. Referring to *Boyd*, Justice Black commented that 'It is a strange hierarchy of values that allows the State to extract a human being's blood to convict him of a crime because of the blood's content but proscribes compelled production of his lifeless papers'.[8] Although the blood test analysis is not oral testimony, it still serves to communicate to the jury the defendant's guilt. It constitutes the equivalent of testimony taken from him, is seen as such by the jury and forms the basis of the jury's verdict. He criticised the majority judgement for its narrow and literal interpretation of privilege, which he saw as a move away from the liberal construction in *Boyd*.[9] Since *Schmerber*, the Supreme Court has rejected *Boyd* in *Fisher v United States*[10] and in *United States v Doe*[11] where the Court held that the state may seize documents in certain circumstances and the privilege is confined to the testimonial aspects of production rather than to the document itself. While the distinction between 'dead' papers and bodily fluids has been resolved, the problem of the distinction between speech and samples remains.

The question of whether admitting a refusal to submit to a blood-alcohol test in evidence against the accused, constituted a violation of the Fifth Amendment was reserved in *Schmerber*, but was subsequently addressed in *South Dakota v Neville*.[12] The South Dakota Supreme Court[13] had affirmed the suppression of the refusal on the ground that a state statute, permitting the introduction of the evidence, violated the privilege against self-incrimination. This judgment in turn was reversed by the United States Supreme Court. It referred to the absence of compulsion as Neville had a choice whether or not to take the test even though his refusal incurred the penalty of revocation of his driving licence, and concluded that using a refusal to take the test in evidence did not constitute a violation of the Fifth Amendment. The majority of courts have construed the refusal to submit as a physical act rather than as communication.[14]

However, there is a line of older cases where the courts have accepted that using the defendant's body as physical evidence was effectively forcing him to be a witness against himself. Some states have refused to allow suspects to be compelled to be tested for sexually transmitted diseases[15] or to be examined for evidence of childbirth.[16] The extraction and use of bodily samples raises issues of privacy which go to the heart of the Fifth Amendment. Since *Schmerber* the Supreme Court has stressed the need to admit reliable physical evidence. In *Warden v Hayden*[17] the Court allowed the admission in evidence of the clothing of the defendant found in his washing machine on the ground that clothing did not constitute testimonial or communicative evidence. Compulsion was permitted by the Court to obtain voice prints[18] and examples of handwriting.[19]

The split judgement in *Schmerber*[20] and the arguments in *Neville*[21] reflect the indeterminacy of the distinction between speech and bodily samples. What we find in the American courts' jurisprudence before *Schmerber* are a number of cases in which the privilege has been successfully invoked but neutralised by the doctrine of waiver; the privilege being deemed to be waived, either because the witness had entered the witness box or has consented to the test. A number of states have enacted 'implied consent' statutes, where the driver suspected of driving while intoxicated is deemed to have consented to the test. While refusal may be permitted to avoid a violent confrontation, nevertheless refusal is discouraged through penalties such as revocation of the driving licence for a fixed period and the admission of the refusal in evidence against the accused.

Because of the problems that have arisen since *Schmerber* Amar and Lettow[22] have argued that a case could be made for using the Fourth Amendment to protect against unreasonable searches and seizures of persons. The criterion of reasonableness would allow the court to balance the state and individual interests and to take account of the gravity of the offence, the invasiveness of the physical examination or test and the importance of the evidence to the prosecution's case.[23]

The problem of the relationship between speech and bodily samples has a long ancestry, arising in relation to the use of blood samples for intoxication tests and of the body as a means of identification, imprinting of footprints in tracks, assuming a particular stance in court and displaying tattoos. This question was considered by Wigmore who argued that an approximation of imprinting, tattoos, and blood samples to speech was absurd:

> If an accused person were to refuse to be removed from the jail to the courtroom for trial, claiming that he was privileged not to expose his features to the witnesses for identification, it is not difficult to conceive the judicial reception which would be given to such a claim. And yet no less a claim is the logical consequence of the argument that has been frequently offered and occasionally sanctioned in applying the privilege to proof of the bodily features of the accused.[24]

Wigmore challenged the extension of the scope of the privilege by arguing that the privilege against self-incrimination was designed to prevent testimonial compulsion, rather than compulsion as such:

> Unless some attempt is made to secure a communication - written, oral or otherwise - upon which reliance is to be placed as involving his consciousness of the facts and the operations of his mind in expressing it, the demand made upon him is not a testimonial one.[25]

If the court is not drawing on the accused's testimony, the privilege cannot and should not be invoked. To equate bodily action with testimonial utterances, argued Wigmore, was contrary to good sense. Of course the accused may be ruffled by having to take off his shirt, for example, but in such cases, he said, 'the public interest in obtaining the evidence is usually sufficient to outweigh by a clear margin the private interests sacrificed in the process.'[26] He cites the case of *Block v People* where it was averred that 'The purpose of the amendment against self-incrimination is to prevent a man from being compelled to utter words that will incriminate him, and not to obliterate all evidence of physical facts showing who and in what condition he is.'[27]

Wigmore resisted a broader interpretation of the privilege, making clear that it referred only to testimonial compulsion and did not extend to tests of intoxication. Objections to the invasion of the body in blood-testing cases rest on quite distinct arguments, including violations of due process and the right to be free from unreasonable searches or seizures and problems of illegally obtained evidence. Similarly the 'consent' requirements in PACE which permit taking intimate samples only with the accused's consent are designed to prevent allegations of assault rather than to acknowledge the privilege.[28] In cases of conventional fingerprinting, or making tracks or revealing distinguishing features, such as tattoos, what is significant, said Wigmore, is that in none of the cases is one asking the accused to disclose his knowledge. Moreover, it would be possible to obtain the evidence without the co-operation of the accused, provided that one had access to his passive body. Consequently for Wigmore, these cases lay outside the scope of the Fifth Amendment privilege.

Wigmore also identified a class of cases where the suspect was asked to pronounce words, to spell a particular word or submit to a medical examination to determine his sanity, or to make a particular stance in court.[29] Here co-operation of the accused is required but knowledge is not being extracted. Wigmore again stressed the importance of testimonial compulsion and the reliance on the accused's own knowledge as essential components to justify invoking the protection of the privilege and argued that such cases should also be excluded from the scope of the privilege.

The final category, distinguished by Wigmore, includes the use of truth serums and lie detectors, which he placed on the borderline of the privilege. Although normally they would be used only with consent, one could drug the defendant to weaken his will to resist disclosure, or bombard him with highly charged words to see if he responds. Wigmore acknowledged that this class of situations was 'logically close' to the situation where the accused was confronted with an accusation which he does not deny, or with something which causes him to blush, cry or faint in spite of himself which would be barred by the privilege. The use of a lie detector is both logically and intuitively close to cases where the suspect is forced to make an incriminating communication of knowledge, where the accused is protected by the privilege. There may be difficulties at the boundary where 'not only is the person's affirmative participation essential (at least in the form of physical responses) but his knowledge, despite his will to the contrary, is extracted.'[30]

The fact that Wigmore sees these situations as lying on a continuum, rather than as a sharp dichotomy, shows that it may be difficult to draw rigid distinctions here. Moreover, the relative positions of the items of evidence may change with technological and scientific progress. Future technological advances may make possible the extraction of bodily samples without the co-operation of the accused.

The difficulty of defining the scope of the privilege against self-incrimination has meant that bodily identifications and examinations have occasionally been excluded as privileged. For example, in the *State v Newcomb*[31] a compulsory examination of the defendant to obtain evidence to support an accusation of rape was held to violate the privilege. In *Cooper v State*[32] the refusal of the defendant to make tracks to compare with those found at the scene of the crime was held to be inadmissible as it fell within the privilege, although at trial it was proper to ask the defendant the number of toes he has on one foot. While the body has mostly been construed as an item of real, physical evidence, just like a knife or murder weapon, in some cases of self-identification the privilege has been successfully invoked. In *Allen v State* although the accused had testified, it was held improper to compel him to try on a hat in cross-examination: 'If the accused, especially if in open court and on the witness stand, is made to do so by performing an act or experimentation which might aid in connecting him with the crime and establishing his guilt, it is inadmissible.'[33] Here the forging of a link between the accused and the crime by his own act was seen as significant. But where the privilege has been acknowledged its impact has usually been softened by the doctrine of waiver, privilege being deemed to be waived by the decision to testify or by the fact that the evidence has been provided voluntarily rather than obtained by compulsion. If the accused has entered the witness box, he is deemed to have waived his privilege and can be asked to stand in a certain way. For example, in *Neely v United States*[34] a defendant who voluntarily testified and denied that he had been shot in the arm, was required in cross-examination to remove his coat to show his arm on the ground that he had waived his privilege. Evidence of a voluntary visit to the doctor for an examination for symptoms of gonorrhoea was held not to violate the privilege in *Garcia v State*.[35] In *Alldredge v State*,[36] comment on the defendant's refusal to submit was held not to violate the privilege against self-incrimination because of the absence of the element of testimonial compulsion. Waiver has also been used to admit evidence in intoximeter cases. In *Spitler v State*[37] it was held that a motorist who voluntarily submitted to an intoximeter test had waived his constitutional protection against self-incrimination. But once waiver is relied on, the original protection of the privilege is being acknowledged. The testing of bodily fluids for intoxication is usually regulated by statute, but the effect of a refusal to take the test has varied according to the jurisdiction,[38] with some states permitting comment on refusals, others expressly forbidding it or remaining silent. The issue of privilege may also be side-stepped by admitting testimony concerning bodily identifications because it comes from a third party, for example, the testimony of prison officers regarding their observation of scars on the accused, so the accused is not being asked to incriminate himself. These strategies and variations reflect the difficulties the courts have faced in formulating a workable distinction between the body and its secretions as an object of evidence and communication.

England and Wales

In England and Wales the extraction and use of bodily samples as items of evidence which may be used against the accused, is governed by the Police and Criminal Evidence Act 1984 as amended by the Criminal Justice and Public Order Act 1994, following the the recommendations of the Royal Commission on Criminal Justice.[39]

In PACE a distinction is drawn between intimate and non-intimate bodily samples. Intimate samples are obtained by the physical examination of body orifices. In *Hughes*[40] the Court of Appeal held that an intimate body search as defined by PACE requires a physical intrusion into a body orifice and a physical examination rather than a merely visual examination. It would not include what happened in *Hughes*, namely an attempt to make the suspect spit out a plastic bag containing drugs by holding his jaws open and his nostrils shut. Section 59(1) of the CJPOA defines an intimate search as a physical examination of a person's body orifices other than his mouth, because saliva and mouth swabs are now defined as non-intimate samples. Intimate samples may be obtained only under specific circumstances set out in s 55 and s 62 of PACE and require the authorisation of a superintendent and the suspect's consent. Force cannot be used. In PACE as originally enacted the refusal to provide an intimate sample could have been taken as corroboration of other evidence against the accused but this provision was repealed by schedule 11 of the CJPOA. However, in practice the jury may well see the refusal as corroborating other evidence against the accused and the corroboration provision remains in Northern Ireland. Section 62 of PACE provides that the court or jury, in determining whether the defendant is guilty of the offence charged, may draw such inferences as appear proper. The suspect must be warned that if he refuses 'without good cause' to provide an intimate sample, his refusal may harm his case if it comes to trial'.[41] 'Good cause' would include the accused's mental or physical condition. He must also be reminded of his right to free legal advice.

Under the original provisions of PACE, before taking a sample the officer had to have reasonable grounds for suspecting the involvement of the suspect in a serious arrestable offence and to believe that the sample will confirm or disprove his involvement. The reference to a 'serious arrestable offence' has now been replaced by a 'recordable offence' in determining the criterion for authorising both intimate and non-intimate samples, thereby increasing the range of offences for which the taking of samples may be authorised.[42]

Non-intimate samples may be taken with consent by any police officer without authorisation once the suspect has been charged with a recordable offence. If consent is refused, then the sample may still be taken and reasonable force used provided it is authorised by a superintendent with reasonable grounds for suspecting that the person is involved in a recordable offence and the officer has reasonable grounds for believing that the sample will prove or disprove that person's involvement in the offence.[43] This is intended to limit mere fishing expeditions. Non-intimate samples are itemised in s 65 of PACE to include samples of hair, other than pubic hair, samples taken from under nails, swabs from any part of the body including the mouth but not from any other body orifice, saliva, and a footprint or similar impression of any part of a person's body other than his hand.[44] Samples of hair may now be taken by cutting or plucking.[45] This is intended to overcome the problems in *Cooke*.[46] The inclusion of the mouth has been criticised on human rights grounds, as force might be necessary to overcome non co-operation. If DNA can be extracted from hair without consent, the need for the provision is questionable as there will be few cases where hair is not available.

The consent requirement reflects an individual's right not to be assaulted. The PACE provisions crystallise the decision in *Smith*,[47] where the Court of Appeal firmly declined to extend the right to silence to bodily samples and affirmed that the right to co-operate with the police by supplying specimens is not comparable to a refusal to speak. The Court of Appeal refused to accept the analogy between refusing to supply samples and the right to silence claimed by the defence. Dismissing Smith's appeal, the Court of Appeal said that the context of his refusal to supply a sample and the presence of a solicitor meant that his refusal was evidence that the jury could consider in assessing Smith's involvement in the crime. Although it might have been better if reference had been made by the trial judge to Smith's right to refuse, failure to warn that the refusal may have resulted from fear or panic did not constitute a misdirection. The Court of Appeal was reticent regarding the basis of this right to refuse, or its reasons for distinguishing speech from samples. The argument of Lawton LJ in *Chandler*[48] that failure to answer an accusation might provide some evidence in support of it, depending on the circumstances,[49] was approved in *Smith*, but the reasoning in *Chandler* could have been used to develop the similarity between speech and samples. The Court of Appeal could have focused on the presence of the solicitor, a feature of both cases, to approximate Smith's situation to the common law limitation[50] of the right to silence where silence is open to adverse inferences because a 'denial' is expected and where the parties are on even terms, applied in *Horne*,[51] instead of rejecting the analogy of silence.

The 1994 Act also widens the contexts in which an intimate sample may be taken.[52] An intimate sample may be taken from a person who is not in police detention if two or more non-intimate samples have been taken in the course of investigation which proved insufficient, if authorised by an officer of at least the rank of superintendent and with the suspect's consent.

Section 56 of the CJPOA inserts a new s 63A into PACE and provides that persons may be required to attend the police station specifically to provide bodily samples in certain circumstances, for example, where a sample was previously given but was not suitable for analysis, or the person has been convicted of a recordable offence and has not previously provided a sample. Section 64 of PACE still remains in force so samples which have been taken from individuals subsequently cleared of the offence with which they are charged must be destroyed. If a person is entitled to have a sample destroyed, then information based on it cannot be used in evidence against him, or for the purpose of any investigation of an offence.[53] Because PACE was enacted prior to the discovery of DNA it did not refer to the treatment of information derived from samples so the appropriate action for dealing with that information was unclear and is clarified by the CJPOA.

Section 57(3) of CJPOA adds a new s 64(3)(b) to PACE. It states that where a sample is required to be destroyed under s 64, the information derived from the sample of the person entitled to its destruction shall not be used in evidence against the person so entitled or for the purpose of investigation of an offence. However the implication is that the information may be retained for statistical purposes.

The CJPOA allows for speculative searches by adding 63A to PACE: fingerprints or samples, or the information derived from samples, taken under powers conferred by PACE, from a person who has been arrested on suspicion of being involved in a recordable offence, may be checked against other fingerprints or samples, or the information derived from other samples contained in records held by the police, or held in connection with, or as a result of, the investigation of an offence. Before the sample is taken at the police station he should be warned by the officer that it may be the subject of a speculative search.[54] A sample can be taken from one investigation and checked against a sample from other investigations regarding different offences. The same applies to non-intimate samples. In *Kelt*[55] the Court of Appeal had ruled that a DNA sample lawfully obtained from a suspect in one investigation may be compared with blood found at the scene of another crime. But the DNA samples taken for the purposes of one criminal investigation may not be used in another investigation if the accused is assured that the sample will be destroyed if he is acquitted of the crime and the sample is mistakenly retained and used in a trial relating to a separate and earlier incident. The appellant had been convicted of armed robbery partly through blood found at the scene of the robbery which was linked to him through a sample taken during an earlier murder enquiry. In

215

Nathaniel[56] the accused provided a sample for a profile when charged with rape for which he was acquitted. The information should have been destroyed but was inadvertently retained on the computer index. When charged later with another rape the police found a match between the information on file and semen on the victim. Here a DNA profile from a blood sample was unlawfully retained and the accused gave blood on the assumption that it would be destroyed. The Court of Appeal held that the evidence should have been excluded. To use the evidence in a later trial had an adverse effect on the fairness of the trial.

The new provisions came into force in April 1995. So the effect of the CJPOA, particularly the broadening of the offences for which a sample may be taken, is to increase the power of the police to obtain bodily samples. Samples of saliva taken from the mouth are now classified as non-intimate samples and may be taken by force under the conditions set out in s 63 of PACE. With the establishment of a national DNA database in 1995, it is possible to conduct speculative searches by checking against the database.

The guidelines concerning the National DNA database are set out in a Circular issued by the Home Office.[57] DNA samples may be taken from every suspect arrested, suspected, cautioned or convicted of recordable offences and profiles will be taken from crime stains. The information can be used to check whether a suspect is involved in other unsolved crimes recorded on the database. The database consists of two parts, the DNA database which will store the data taken from DNA profiles and will be where the searches are carried out, and profiling services which take individual samples and analyse them to produce the DNA profiles. Initially the custodian will be the Forensic Science Service. Profiling may be carried out by the Forensic Science Service or by other organisations which will be chosen by individual police forces, provided that they are of sufficient quality and compatible with the national database and use quality assurance procedures.

Material for DNA profiling may include samples for elimination purposes, from victims and witnesses. Profiles taken from samples for elimination purposes will not be used in speculative searches and will not be placed on the DNA intelligence database. Under the new PACE provisions, samples may be taken for all recordable offences. However, chief officers have agreed that in the first instance, the police will obtain samples from offenders involved in offences against the person, sexual offences and burglaries. The operation of the database will be governed by the Data Protection Act. Individuals whose profiles appear on the database will have the right to a copy of any personal data relating to them. Samples will be taken usually by mouth swabs or by plucking hairs.

The mind-body problem

There is arguably no fundamental difference between relying on words from the individual or on the composition of his blood. Whether torture is used to extract a confession, or gentle persuasion used to obtain a sample, in both cases the individual is the source of incriminating evidence. The distinction between testimony and the communication of knowledge, on the one hand, and the inert body on the other hand, reflects the mind-body dualism of Cartesian thought[58] and its difficulties. The mind-body debate has progressed since the seventeenth century and it is now recognised that rigid dualism distorts our understanding of the question since the relation between them is not as clear-cut as was depicted by the traditional model. Even materialists now recognise a complex range of interactions between the mind and body.[59] The traditional Cartesian model distinguished between mental and physical functions according to which only processes intentionally activated by the former have communicative meanings. Studies of abnormal mental states such as schizophrenia and neurologically impaired states, such as Parkinsonism and epilepsy,[60] have revealed the inadequacies of this model. Dreaming and the experience of pain have posed problems for dualism. Given that the mental properties of persons have a behavioural and experiental dimension, the view that the mind may be equated with the spiritual, or the body with the material, has been widely criticised.[61] But it is not just philosophers who recognise this. Ordinary language and discourse reveal the artificiality of the traditional model. It is generally accepted that non-verbal gestures, whether voluntary, subconscious or involuntary, may communicate information, even where the individual does not 'intend' that behaviour. The importance of 'body language' is stressed in training programmes for business and personnel managers and interviewers as a means of recognising desirable and undesirable character traits in other people. In everyday life people constantly look for visual clues and make judgements according to demeanour, or the shape or position of the body, and often treat them as better guides to mental attitudes than the spoken word. If judgements are made in this context on the basis of what these signs convey, the restriction of the imparting of knowledge to testimony, found in Wigmore's analysis and in the case law, is too narrow.

Instead of a sharp distinction between oral testimony and the physical functions, between cognitive mind and inert mechanism, in which meanings cannot be ascribed to the latter, and in which the mind is construed as the 'ghost in the machine', the traditional model needs to be replaced with a continuum or differential scale as follows:

A --- B --- C --- D --- E --- F

At one end of the scale, A, would be placed oral communication, including accounts of one's presence in a particular place, admissions, and statements of intentions but also exculpatory or neutral statements. At B would lie body language intended to communicate, such as the miming of a knife slitting the throat, intended as a threat. At C would be placed non-verbal communications lacking the dimension of intentionality, for example, demonstrating timidity or fear or a sense of inferiority. Here the subject might intend the opposite message and there may be cases at the borderline where it would be difficult to establish whether or not the effect is intentional. At D, one could locate external bodily signs such as tattoos, scars or other distinguishing features. Here one might also include physical signs yielding evidence of life-style such as the hands of pianists, the muscles of athletes, the effects of occupational diseases and wounds in cases of personal injury. At E one could place bodily fluids; one might distinguish between the voluntary supply of an intimate sample and the use of samples given involuntarily or unknowingly, such as a hair found on a coat. At the extreme end of the scale, one might site the extraction of DNA from a corpse.

Furthermore, in other areas of the law of evidence the mind-body distinction is transcended. In the common law rule against hearsay a statement for the purposes of the hearsay rule may include oral or written statements or signs, symbols or gestures or silence. In *Rice*,[62] for example, the issue was raised of whether a used airline ticket was admissible as evidence that someone holding the name on the ticket had actually been aboard that particular flight. Propositions about the actor's state of mind have been inferred from silence and non-verbal communication as well as the making of a statement. Assertions implicit in non-verbal conduct have also been recognised in England and the United States for the purposes of the hearsay rule. If it is accepted that communication and knowledge can be imparted by non-testimonial means in certain contexts, then its exclusion from the privilege would seem arbitrary. What counts as a statement for hearsay purposes has been construed broadly, although this broad construction of a statement to include nonverbal conduct has been criticised by Guest[63] for adding to the difficulties of applying the hearsay rule. The Law Commission[64] has also criticised the hearsay rule for its complexity and uncertainty and recommended reform.

Moreover, rights issues also arise in relation to the taking of samples just as they do to speech. In New Zealand, in *R v Martin*[65] the refusal to give a blood sample for DNA profiling was held to be a basic human right and no adverse inferences could be drawn from that refusal. Although the status of samples was not an issue in *Saunders v UK*, the European Court of Human Rights noted that the right not to incriminate oneself under Article 6 did not extend to the use in criminal proceedings of material which might be obtained from the accused under legal compulsion but which had an existence independent of the accused's will, such as breath, blood and urine samples and bodily tissue for the purpose of

DNA testing.[66] But obtaining a sample by force, it could be argued, breaches Article 3 of the European Convention of Human Rights because it is degrading: no one shall be subjected to torture or inhuman or degrading treatment or punishment. This Article allows no exceptions but clearly it depends on the method used to obtain a sample. The taking and storing of samples might also be seen as breaching Article 8(1): everyone has the right to respect for his private and family life, his home and correspondence. However, Article 8(2) does allow for interference with the right if it is necessary for the prevention of disorder or crime. But questions of proportionality arise here, for if the sample is taken or retained for a relatively minor offence the invasion of privacy may not be seen as justified.

One difference between speech and samples, it might be argued, is that the futility argument does not apply to samples. Formal or informal pressure exerted on the suspect cannot guarantee that he will tell the truth, whereas DNA testing is in no way dependent on the volition of the accused. One could remove the DNA evidence from a passive body, even from an exhumed corpse. The suspect cannot intentionally produce a false negative. The most he can do to conceal his link to the crime is to use a substitute, as Pitchfork, the man ultimately convicted of the Leicester murders, did, or to receive a bone marrow transplant.[67] The second option would necessitate massive collaboration with medical personnel who might be suspicious to say the least. Without such a transplant he cannot alter his DNA. Even if the suspect is initially nervous, this would not undermine the integrity of the sample whereas confusion in the face of police questioning may taint the subsequent investigation. Nonetheless, the evidence may still be marred by handling at the profiling stage due to poor quality control.

However, the other justifications of the privilege, including the right to privacy and autonomy and the presumption of innocence, apply to speech and samples. Given the difficulty of drawing a sharp distinction between speech and bodily samples, it is artificial to separate the extraction and use of the sample from the self-incrimination of the accused. This is illustrated forcefully by the Criminal Evidence (Northern Ireland) Order 1988.[68] If forensic evidence establishes the presence of the accused in a particular place or traces of a particular substance on his person, and his silence may corroborate other evidence against him, then the issues of speech and samples are part of the same process. Forensic techniques, such as DNA fingerprinting, may be used to mount a case against the accused, which is then bolstered by the corroborating provision in the Criminal Evidence Order.

If the accused does refuse to supply a sample, it means that the attention of the jury is focused on the defence rather than on the nature and strength of the prosecution's case just as it is when the suspect is silent. A reliance on DNA evidence may also discourage the search for other evidence, so that the investigation may stop at the stage of DNA testing when there is a need for additional independent evidence. The distinction between speech and samples drawn by Wigmore, and expressed in contemporary statutes and decisions raises a number of problems. While the distinction might be justified on grounds of policy or expediency, nonetheless it is artificial and problematic, because both samples and speech are subject to similar considerations and arguments, and because the law already construes actions as a form of speech in certain cases.

Genetic fingerprinting and the privilege against self-incrimination

The discovery of genetic fingerprinting[69] with its high specificity and extraordinary probative properties highlights the question of the scope of the privilege against self-incrimination. On Wigmore's classification, for example, genetic fingerprinting would appear to fall well outside the scope of the privilege for even if an element of co-operation is required in the case of a blood or semen sample, identity rather than knowledge is in issue. If one defends the distinction between speech and samples, by comparing the inherent unreliability of speech and the danger of false admissions with the objective truth of DNA fingerprinting evidence, this might appear to rescue the distinction. Stuntz,[70] for example, sees excuse as a more persuasive explanation of Fifth Amendment jurisprudence than either autonomy or privacy. If the aim of the privilege against self-incrimination is to prevent self-protective perjury and if it is difficult to falsify nontestimonial evidence, such as handwriting and voice exemplars, there is no reason to grant immunity for nonco-operation in such cases. Stuntz does not consider DNA profiling but his argument would carry more weight if it were applied to a technique which was accepted as having unquestionable reliability. If account is taken of current concern regarding profiling procedures, this distinction between the two types of evidence, testimonial and nontestimonial, is harder to maintain. DNA sampling does not necessarily provide more objective data than speech, as both are subject to distortion in certain circumstances and to problems of interpretation.

Initially DNA profiling found no problems in gaining acceptance in the United States of America although there were variations between states. The majority of states were then using the *Frye* test, derived from the case of *United States v Frye*[71] in determining whether evidence based on new scientific discoveries is admissible in court proceedings. The court at a pre-trial hearing would consider whether the scientific principle or discovery, from which the expert testimony is deduced, has received 'general acceptance in the particular field in which it belongs'. This entails identifying the appropriate field and then determining the degree of acceptance. DNA profiling has satisfied this test and even after the problems raised in *Castro*[72] it has been admitted. However, in *Daubert v Merrell Dow Pharmaceuticals Inc.*[73] the Supreme Court held that in federal courts, the *Frye* test has been superseded by the Federal Rules of Evidence. General acceptance of the principles underlying scientific evidence is no longer a necessary precondition to the admissibility of scientific evidence under the Federal Rules; the requirements, instead, are relevance and reliability. In the UK there is no test comparable to the *Frye* test, but the court will consider the relevance and reliability of such evidence and at the new preparatory hearings permitted for complex cases under the Criminal Procedure and Investigations Act 1996, the judge may rule on any question as to the admissibility of evidence.

DNA evidence has been challenged in the American Courts since *Castro* in 1989 and has also been subject to criticism in the United Kingdom.[74] While the theoretical foundations of DNA fingerprinting are accepted by the scientific community, problems may arise during the process of profiling which affect its probative value. Just as the way the interview is conducted may taint the evidence arising from it, so careless procedures and lack of regulation at the profiling stage may raise doubts about the reliability of the results as illustrated by *Castro*,[75] the first case to successfully challenge DNA evidence, where questions arose over the way band sizes were calculated and the numbers of bands. Here a pre-trial hearing was conducted to consider the admissibility of DNA evidence, at the time a new technique. The court in *Castro* used the *Frye* test. While Sheindlin J. in *Castro* accepted that DNA fingerprinting can be reliable evidence, he saw the procedures followed by the testing laboratory as inadequate: 'the testing laboratory failed in its responsibility to perform the accepted techniques and experiments in several major respects.'[76] Evidence showing that the blood of the victim matched blood found on the defendant's watch was excluded. Criticising the laboratory for its unscientific methods and methodologies, he recommended guidelines for future pre-trial hearing procedures and stressed the need for greater accessibility to the types of testing used and for quality assurance procedures. Where testing is conducted by private laboratories, companies may be reluctant to reveal methods of testing which they see as trade secrets or proprietary information, although the Federal Bureau of Investigation has also been criticised for secrecy regarding the methods it uses to compile its prints.

The genetic principles underpinning DNA analysis have been accepted by the scientific community but there may be disagreements on the guidelines used for interpreting test results. The forensic context in which DNA profiling may be used presents particular problems where there may be deterioration of the samples from the crime scene or the sample may be too small to retest. However, with the development of PCR, a technique for amplifying DNA, this problem is being resolved. What was unusual in *Castro*, as Sufian[77] notes, was that the defence and prosecution expert witnesses met to discuss the scientific evidence in the case and issued a statement about its inadequacy and the process for its assessment. Although the judge would not admit this statement in evidence at the pre-trial hearing he did allow the defence to call the prosecution expert witnesses to testify as to the contents of the statement. At that time it was difficult for the defence to obtain access to enough information on the new techniques from independent experts.[78]

In *Castro* the defence argued that the forensic application of DNA profiling demanded agreement by the scientific community on the appropriate standards for calculating probabilities and for declaring a match. If different laboratories use different methods for calculating these probabilities and each has its own database of frequencies of bands in particular groups, then it is essential to ensure reliability and standardisation and agreement on the appropriate statistical tests to be used. The United States Office of Technology Assessment has considered various standards for forensic uses of DNA profiling including monitoring, voluntary and mandatory regulation. Similar problems have been found in Britain, although there are fewer laboratories in the UK, with laboratories operating their own internal quality assurance procedures. The BSI standard used does not include interpretation of data. Guidelines are being developed for interpretation of the results and legislation has been proposed to establish standards for forensic testing. In *Schwartz*,[79] the Minnesota Supreme Court ruled that DNA fingerprinting evidence could not be admitted unless proper controls and standards are used and unless the testing data and results are made available to the defence.

Problems have also been encountered with 'band-shifting', a shift in the mobility of the DNA fragments through the agarose gel during analysis which leads to problems of interpretation and concern over the procedures used to arrive at a match.[80] Bandshifting occurs when samples pass through the gel at different speeds and the bands appear at different levels on the autoradiograph, while giving similar patterns. This discrepancy in the number of bands may be interpreted as resulting from problems in the process of profiling rather than from a genetic cause. But it means that there is an element of subjectivity, interpretation and argument, although efforts are being made to deal with these problems.[81]

There are also statistical problems in calculating the odds of a chance occurrence of band-matching. Bands may be concentrated in small sub-populations. Further research is needed on the frequency of bands within populations with a high degree of inbreeding, to enable calculations of the statistical significance of a particular match to be modified accordingly.[82] The statistical probability of a random match has to be calculated, using assessments of the frequency of DNA bands in specific populations. Research has been undertaken to establish the frequencies of patterns in subpopulations, but it is still based on small samples, so there is a problem of identifying the number of potential suspects with matching allele configurations. There are problems in calculating the probability of a match occurring by chance. Calculations of match probabilities depend on the basic data on populations and sub-populations. But it is the calculation of the match probability, using what has become known as the 'product rule' which was questioned in *Deen*[83] in England and in a number of cases in the United States beginning with *Castro*. These problems also may be illustrated by a German case where the German Federal Court decided that a conviction could not be based on DNA evidence alone without supporting evidence.[84] The DNA fingerprints from the accused matched those found on the victim. They were compared with a random sample of 'possible assailants' to calculate the probability that another man in the same area had the same profile. But the court questioned whether the random sample was appropriate. In the instant case the suspect was from Kosovo in Serbia whose population's genetic material could differ from Hanoverians. The suspect's genes might be common in Kosovo but unusual in Hanover so he would be disadvantaged by the profiling results.

Van Kampen and Nijboer argue that DNA profiling 'may produce very accurate results... but the reliability of the ultimate result depends on the technique used to construct DNA profiles as well as how the comparison is actually made.'[85] Once DNA evidence is used, other evidence may be ignored or downplayed. Little attention may be paid to other evidence presented at the trial or to problems with DNA fingerprinting itself. Moreover, DNA evidence is not conclusive evidence in relation to all elements of a crime. DNA evidence establishes identity but not guilt so it is dangerous to convict primarily on DNA evidence. If other evidence against the accused is weak, we need to treat it more cautiously. In the United States some states have excluded DNA evidence because the jury will attach too much probative force to it. The use of compulsion to obtain samples in the Netherlands has been criticised for violating the privilege against self-incrimination as well as the right to privacy and the right to physical integrity, protected by the Dutch Constitution and the European Convention on Human Rights, although these rights may be infringed to prevent disorder and crime. The powers of the prosecution and defence are unequal and the defendant's rights to counter DNA evidence are limited, in part because it is assumed that DNA evidence is infallible, whereas its reliability has been questioned. Human errors may occur in the interpretation of results and particularly in comparing samples. These problems of interpretation raise questions regarding the weight of the evidence, as well as its admissibility in common law jurisdictions, comparable to those which arise when dealing with speech.

In the UK there has been far less controversy over the validity of DNA evidence, but forensic evidence has been viewed with suspicion as forensic evidence was misused and misinterpreted in some of the miscarriages of justice and there is unequal access to scientific evidence. Human error may arise in the labelling, recording and storing of samples, giving false positives. This has been an issue in some American cases. Sending samples to different laboratories may assist in checking this but it is expensive and time consuming for the defence.[86] Quality assurance procedures in laboratories are crucial to maintaining confidence in the reliability of this evidence. There has been criticism of the DNA database of the Metropolitan Police Forensic Science Laboratory.[87] Errors were made in the preparation and processing of profiles onto the computer and some results were entered twice.

In *Gordon*[88] the Court of Appeal ordered a retrial because of uncertainty over the presentation of the DNA evidence and the probability statistics. Here a prosecution expert witness on DNA was criticised for his methodology. The court allowed another expert to be called and the prosecution witness to be reheard. The second expert was critical of the other expert's measurements, including the lack of precision and of the statistical inferences which he drew from them. The Court of Appeal said that any scientific analysis would produce some variation between samples from an identical source, so some allowance should be made for an acceptable range of variation in assessing whether there was a match. However, it allowed a retrial because the criticism could have engendered doubts on the part of the jury. At the same time the Court of Appeal stressed that the general value and the validity of DNA profiling was not in question.

Even if the DNA evidence is properly obtained using tried and tested scientific procedures, problems will occur in interpreting the evidence. In *Deen*[89] the appellant had been convicted of three rapes on the basis of DNA evidence. The Court of Appeal allowed the appellant's appeal and ordered a retrial because the trial judge had misinterpreted the significance of expert evidence on DNA profile matching and had misdirected the jury accordingly. The prosecution's experts said there were 10 matching bands. The defence expert said that there was a mismatch because there was a band on the defendant's profile but not on that from the swab. The jury might have thought that 9 out of 10 matches was sufficient. The trial judge did not state that if there was only one discrepant band which was not sufficiently explained, then a match would not be established. The judge had not drawn the attention of the jury to the non-matching band. The case was heard in 1990 and a similar mistake is unlikely to be made today, because now most laboratories use single locus probes which are more reliable, rather than the multilocus probes used in *Deen*. Although the court was critical of the use of DNA evidence in *Deen* it nonetheless acknowledged its value.

However, the court also said that the prosecution expert had fallen into the 'prosecutor's fallacy;' which misrepresents the probative value of DNA evidence, usually in favour of the prosecution. The fallacy may be committed by expert witnesses or by the judge or prosecuting counsel in summing up. It may be committed inadvertently through sloppy language or because the issues are not properly understood. Even if correctly directed the jury may make the same error. Balding and Donnelly[90] explain the fallacy by distinguishing two questions which may be raised in relation to DNA evidence:

1.   What is the probability that the defendant's DNA profile will match the profile from the crime sample, given that he is innocent?

2.   What is the probability that the defendant is innocent, given that the
        DNA profile matches the profile from the crime sample?

It is the second question which is most relevant to the court, but the fallacy is
committed by giving the answer to the first question as the answer to the second
question. The 'prosecutor's fallacy' therefore refers to the wrongful equation of
the odds against an innocent person having that DNA profile with the odds
against the accused with that profile being innocent. Moreover, the authority of
the expert witness means that his answer is likely to persuade the jury, especially
as DNA evidence is seen as highly reliable. For the expert to give an opinion
regarding common origin also usurps the role of the jury. Because of the danger
of the prosecutor's fallacy, it has been argued that it would be better if experts
did not give opinions on whether or not two DNA samples have a common
origin. As Balding and Donnelly argue: 'Inferences as to common origin remain
within the domain of the jury although the scientist may well be in a position to
provide relevant information.'[91]

So there is concern over the regulation of forensic evidence and access to that
evidence by the defence, the lack of independent scrutiny of those procedures, the
adequacy of quality assurance procedures and the absence of a consensus within
the scientific community on the best ways of dealing with bandshifting, all of
which indicate that caution is needed in evaluating results. Now that the
contribution of DNA profiling to rectitude of outcome is being disputed, the use
of samples becomes a more controversial question and moves closer to the status
of admissions, thereby rendering the distinction between speech and samples less
tenable.

Problems also arise in relation to the validity of the inferences which may be
drawn from nonco-operation in supplying samples and verbal information.
Frequent reference is made in the debate on the right of silence to the 'common
sense' expectation that people confronted with an accusation would normally
answer. Only the guilty with something to conceal are likely to refuse to
co-operate. The common sense inference may be more compelling in the context
of DNA profiling precisely because it is perceived as having greater potential
than mere speech to conclusively exculpate the suspect. The fact that DNA
fingerprinting would be seen as harder to fabricate, as more objective than a
verbal statement, may mean it is more difficult for the individual to refuse and
for his refusal to be seen as legitimate. But there may be genuine reasons for a
refusal to supply a sample and a refusal to speak, so that in each case drawing
an adverse inference may not be justified. To construe such a refusal as
corroborative may be misleading and dangerous. Fear, anxiety, embarrassment,
and anger, rather than guilt, may account for nonco-operation in supplying a
sample just as they may account for silence. The suspect might be apprehensive
regarding how the test is conducted and more importantly, how accurate it is,
especially if he does not understand what the test involves, or lacks confidence

in the testing procedures. He may also be unsure of the arrangements for storage of the test results. It is conceivable that an innocent person might refuse a sample for any of these reasons rather than for Machiavellian motives. Even if informed of the grounds for seeking the sample, and the type of offence in relation to which it is being sought and with a solicitor present, he will not know the full details of the case against him. Formal and informal pressures may be exerted on the individual to co-operate. In voluntary screenings, there is considerable pressure from the community to come forward, just as there are psychological pressures to speak during interrogation, both of which may be hard to resist. In civil proceedings where the court orders a party to submit to a DNA test to establish paternity, the court can draw any inference from such refusal as seems proper in the circumstances under s 23 of the Family Law Reform Act 1987.[92]

Questions of privacy also arise in relation to samples as well as in relation to speech. The issue of privacy in the case of samples occurs not only at the point of taking of the sample, but also in relation to control of the sample and subsequent storage of the genetic information. Band patterns constitute private and personal data. To coerce or cajole an individual into providing a sample could be seen as inherently degrading and undignified rather than simply a matter of assault. The process of taking the sample could be seen as a greater invasion of privacy than the asking of questions. Even if the accuracy of DNA fingerprinting could be guaranteed, rectitude of outcome still needs to be considered against other goals of the criminal justice process, such as respect for individual privacy and fairness to the accused.

The provision of genetic information gives the state intimate knowledge of personal relationships, such as paternity, which may be irrelevant to the case, just as a verbal account given by the suspect may reveal details which are embarrassing to him and which he sees as irrelevant to the investigation, so that he may prefer to remain silent. Many feel uneasy about the establishment of a national databank. The Women's Institute in the United Kingdom has proposed routine data-banking of DNA profiles at birth. In the United States some states, including California, have passed legislation authorising the establishment of DNA databanks. Advertising campaigns have also been mounted by private companies to urge parents to store samples of their children's DNA in databanks, to ensure a means of identification if their children are abducted. DNA sampling has been used successfully to trace the missing children of the 'disappeared' in Argentina.

Problems with forensic evidence

If a technique like DNA testing is to be used in determining guilt then it is essential that the defence have access to forensic laboratories and experts to deal with such evidence. The jury is likely to find DNA evidence extremely persuasive where experts present it as cut and dried and it is unlikely that methodological problems will be routinely considered once its use becomes established and commonplace.

The defence need proper access to resources to challenge scientific evidence, given the huge inequality of resources between defence and prosecution. Nondisclosure of crucial forensic evidence was an important factor in several of the miscarriage of justices revealed in the late 1980s and 1990s, including the cases of the Birmingham Six, the Maguires and Judith Ward.[93] Scientific evidence may not be disclosed or the evidence itself may not be fully understood or analysed when it is adduced. In the *Ward* case the Court of Appeal said that senior government forensic scientists 'knowingly placed a false and distorted scientific picture before the jury.'[94] Sir John May's report also was critical of the government scientists in the *Maguire* case. He said that if the jury had seen the contents of the notebooks he had sight of, the scientists' evidence would have been viewed very differently. In that case traces on the defendants' hands were wrongly interpreted as explosives.[95] In the Birmingham Six case, the work of the scientist Dr. Frank Skuse was censured. The scientific tests used to establish traces of nitro-glycerine were not as precise as the jury had been led to believe. Although these cases did not involve the use of DNA evidence, problems may arise in the course of DNA profiling. At the same time forensic evidence may be of value to the defence. Because of the defence's need to challenge and test scientific evidence, the state's failure to make proper provision for defence access has been strongly criticised.

The problems in the above cases included the failure of the police and prosecution to reveal information on forensic investigations being conducted. The defence lacked the necessary resources to challenge prosecution evidence, lawyers did not possess the expertise and training in scientific techniques to understand or assess the significance of forensic evidence. The defence do not receive detailed information on the tests being undertaken. Yet differing interpretations of those tests may be crucial to the outcome of the case. The Home Affairs Committee reviewed the Forensic Science Service in 1988-89 and witnesses criticised the quality of the services available to the defence outside the Forensic Science Service and the underfunding of university departments. An independent body with proper funding is needed to establish and maintain standards for forensic laboratories.

In 1991 the Forensic Science Service became an independent agency. So now the official laboratories may be more interested in securing defence work, but because it has been seen by defence lawyers as very close to the prosecution, they may prefer to use alternatives. Most of the public laboratories will undertake defence work provided that they are not analysing samples for the prosecution in that case. Alternatively the defence may use commercial laboratories. But defence work is unpopular because of the delays in payment by the Legal Aid Board.

The Runciman Commission[96] considered forensic evidence because of its importance in the earlier miscarriages of justice and found there had been considerable improvement in the way it was obtained and presented since the 1970s. It reviewed the organisation of the Forensic Science Service and other service providers. It welcomed the fact that the courts are now more willing to hear expert evidence from psychologists and psychiatrists since the *Silcott* case. However, the Commission pointed to a number of problems: for example, the Crown Court Study found that the Crown Court Rules on Advance Disclosure of Expert Evidence were often flouted by the defence.[97] At trial prosecuting counsel were often poorly prepared on scientific evidence and many defence lawyers lacked the understanding of scientific evidence needed to assess that evidence. The Commission emphasised the importance of presenting scientific issues clearly to juries: 'Serious miscarriages of justice may occur if juries are too ready to believe expert evidence or because it is poorly presented in court.'[98]

The Royal Commission rejected the analogy between speech and samples and argued that 'It seems to us that to require a suspect to supply samples is quite different from providing that inferences may be invited from a refusal to answer questions.'[99] It cited the fact that scientific evidence may prove a person's guilt or innocence. It also favoured allowing the plucking of hair and taking mouth swabs without consent and broadening the category of serious arrestable offences for the purpose of taking samples. The records of those arrested but not convicted would be kept, albeit anonymously, to provide data on DNA bands. It advocated reclassifying saliva as a non-intimate sample to avoid the need for consent. The category of intimate samples, it recommended, should be widened to include dental impressions and this recommendation was given effect by s 58 of the CJPOA which amends PACE.

Legislation allowing for the storage of DNA samples both to identify offenders and to provide a database was proposed by the Commission. The establishment of a Forensic Science Advisory Council, which would issue a Code of Practice for forensic scientists and monitor laboratories to ensure the maintenance of high standards and to promote the development of high quality work in universities and public and private laboratories, also was recommended.[100] The Commission favoured increased access of the defence to forensic scientists and automatic access to legal aid to cover this. Better defence access to public laboratories, it argued, is essential but the defence should be free to choose between public and private sector laboratories. The defence should have access to the original notes on experiments if it is concerned about the viability and reliability of the tests being undertaken. Prior to trial both defence and prosecution, it said, should discuss what expert evidence will be used, in all cases where scientific evidence will be led by either side. If there are any disputes, the defence should give advance notice of the grounds of dispute and state whether they will be calling their own experts. If both sides are calling expert witnesses, the experts should meet to draw up a report on the scientific facts and the interpretation by both sides of those facts. This document should then be available to the court as an account of what has been agreed and what is in dispute. If there is substantial disagreement, then a preparatory hearing should be arranged. In cases involving scientific evidence both sides should expect a preparatory hearing to occur unless they are both in a position to certify that it is not needed.[101] At trial the evidence should be presented to the jury as clearly as possible. Zander and Henderson in their study of the Crown Court found that it was very unusual for the two sides to discuss the scientific evidence prior to trial.[102]

Research conducted by Roberts and Willmore for the Royal Commission on Criminal Justice found problems with the Forensic Science Service, specifically the tendency for scientists to adopt an adversarial approach, offering very selective reports and not including discussions of possible objections to their findings.[103] They also found that the arrangements for finding defence experts were haphazard and that there were problems in obtaining authorisation from the Legal Aid Board to obtain the use of experts.

One of the problems in England has been the failure of the defence to challenge scientific evidence. Roberts and Willmore found that valuable opportunities to challenge evidence were lost, particularly in relation to medical evidence. While legal aid may cover part of the cost, arrangements for obtaining authorisation were difficult and time-consuming. They argue that the complexity of scientific evidence and problems of evaluation show the need to regard it with great caution. Defence lawyers often lack the expertise to use or question evidence.

Steventon's study of DNA evidence for the Royal Commission looked at the problems facing solicitors acting for the defence in DNA cases.[104] She found problems in finding suitable experts and in one case in her sample, an application for legal aid for DNA profiling was refused. She found that expert witnesses were rarely called in by the defence, even though two-thirds of the defence lawyers in her sample contested DNA evidence. Walker and Stockdale[105] identify aspects of forensic evidence which have been significant in recent miscarriages of justice: when the police or prosecution collect evidence, this may lead to omissions or accidental contamination of which they are unaware. There have been problems regarding the competence and quality of forensic scientists, misunderstandings over the way forensic evidence and scientific experimentation translates into legal proof and inadequate funding for the defence. Little support is given to research in forensic science. Where forensic evidence is put before the Court it may be difficult for the court to fully grasp its significance. They point to the fact that the Second May Report was critical of the Court of Appeal's failure to understand that challenging the specificity of forensic tests for nitgro-glycerine in the *Maguire* case also undermined the prosecution's case.[106]

The Royal Commission's recommendation for improved defence access to forensic services has been widely supported. However some of the Commission's other proposals have been criticised by civil libertarians, particularly the DNA database, the element of compulsion involved, the level of force which may be used in obtaining saliva samples, and the broadening of offences for which samples may be taken. The Commission's proposals, critics argue, do not go far enough in addressing the problems faced by the defence.

While the Forensic Science Service has been improved, with new monitoring procedures introduced, there are still insufficient controls outside the Service. Anyone can set themselves up and advertise as a forensic expert and a better system of accreditation is needed by an appropriate professional body.

If we compare the defence and prosecution positions, the police and prosecution have access to the Forensic Scientific Service, based in six regional laboratories and in the Metropolitan police laboratory in London, with huge budgets. In addition the police have their internal forensic scientists specialising in various forms of evidence, such as ballistics and graphology, and access to the DNA databank. The prosecution, unlike the defence, has access to the Ministry of Defence explosives experts and laboratory.

As Grosskurth[107] notes, there are few independent private laboratories which specialise in defence work although the defence has access to experts working in hospitals and universities but they may lack the resources to undertake substantial amounts of consultancy work. Their laboratories, equipment and libraries may not match those of the prosecution laboratories and delays in legal aid payments may not encourage people to enter such work. There are also problems in regulating the laboratories or individuals used by the defence.

Legal aid is usually granted to the defence for expert advice but may be refused and payments may be slow, or the legal aid service may refuse to meet the entire cost. It is also questionable whether legal aid officials have the competence to decide whether a particular expert should be consulted. They need to process applications and payments more quickly and the courts need to be willing to grant delays to allow access to expert witnesses. The defence need access to a high quality independent forensic laboratory, perhaps based at a university department specialising in this field, receiving public funding as well as legal aid for individual cases.

DNA fingerprinting is a double-edged weapon, of value to the defence to acquit as well as to the prosecution to convict. Indeed this may well apply to all forms of scientific evidence. In April 1995 the Court of Appeal quashed the conviction of Kevin Callan who taught himself neuropathology using books obtained through the prison library to disprove the medical evidence given at his trial in 1992. A recent study by the Department of Justice found that at least 28 prisoners convicted for sexual assault had been released after DNA tests proved their innocence.[108] The tests had not been available at the time of their trial.

In the *McLeod*[109] case, the first suspect who matched the victim's description of her attacker, was excluded through DNA profiling, while McLeod, who did not match her description, was initially identified as the assailant by DNA testing. Genetic fingerprinting might be used to expose the falsity of confessions as in the murder of two girls in Leicester in 1987, the first case to make use of genetic fingerprinting, where an individual who had confessed to one of the murders was eliminated from the investigation through DNA testing.

But the scope of DNA evidence for the defence is likely to be more limited. If the use of genetic fingerprinting is set in the context of the general inequality between the prosecution and defence, the prosecution has greater resources, including access to forensic services. It also has first use of the critical sample found at the scene of the crime. The size of the sample may be small, leading to delays while it is amplified. Even if access is granted there may problems of comparability in testing and variations in results, if the sample is tested on two different occasions and probability calculated against different databases. What is needed is the opportunity for the defence to undertake a review not just of the testing of the sample itself, but of the methodologies employed and the data pool against which the probability of a random match is calculated.

Notes

1.   384 US 757 (1965).
2.   Mr. Justice Brennan at 761.
3.   218 US 245 (1910).
4.   at 252-3
5.   at 252-3
6.   116 US 616 (1886).
7.   384 US 757 (1965) at 764.
8.   at 775.
9.   116 US 616 (1886).
10.   425 US 391 (1976).
11.   465 US 605 (1984).
12.   459 US 533 (1983).
13.   312 NW 2d 723 (SD 1981).
14.   See *People v Sudduth* 65 Cal 2d 543.
15.   See *State v Newcomb* 220 Mo 54 (1909), 119 SW 405 (Mo 1909).
16.   See *People v McCoy* 45 How Pr 16 NY Sup Ct (1873).
17.   387 US 294 (1967).
18.   See *United States v Dionisio* 410 US 1 (1973).
19.   See *Gilbert v California* 388 US 263 (1967).
20.   384 US 757 (1965).
21.   459 US 533 (1983).
22.   A.R. Amar and R.B. Lettow (March, 1995) 'Fifth Amendment First Principles: The Self-Incrimination Clause', Michigan Law Review 93, 857.
23.   See *Rochin v California* 342 US 165 (1952).
24.   J. Wigmore (1961) *Evidence* 8, McNaughton rev. ed. para. 2265.

25. *Ibid*, para. 2265.
26. *Ibid*, para. 2265.
27. *Block v People*, 125 Colo 36, 44, 240 P 2d 512 (1952); 343 US 978 (1958).
28. S 62(10).
29. J. Wigmore, *op.cit.*, para. 2265.
30. *Ibid*, 2265.
31. 220 Mo 54 (1909), 119 SW 405 (Mo 1909).
32. 86 Ala 610, 6 So 110 (1889).
33. 183 Md 601, 611, 39 A 2d 820 (1944).
34. 2 F 2d 849 (4th Cir 1924).
35. 274 Pac 166 (1929).
36. Ind 156, NE 2d 591 (1943).
37. 221 Ind 107, 46 NE 2d 591 (1943).
38. See Wigmore, *op.cit.* para. 2265, n.6.
39. See Report of the Royal Commission on Criminal Justice (1993) London, HMSO, Cmnd 2263, para. 9.40.
40. [1993] Times, 12 November.
41. Code D 5.2.
42. See s 54(3)(b) CJPOA.
43. See s 63 of PACE.
44. Footprint impressions were added by s 58 of the CJPOA.
45. S 63(A)(2).
46. In *Cooke (Stephen)* [1995] Times, 10 August, [1995] Crim LR 497, the accused consented to the plucking of his hair when the police proposed to take the sample by force and three officers entered his cell wearing riot helmets.
47. [1985] Crim LR 590.
48. [1976] 1 WLR 585
49. at 589.
50. See *R v Christie* [1914] AC 545; *Parkes v R* (1977) 64 Cr App Rep 25.
51. [1990] Crim LR 188.
52. See s 54(2) CJPOA and s 62 PACE.
53. See s 57(3) of CJPOA which adds a new s 64(3)(b) to PACE.
54. See Schedule 10, CJPOA.
55. [1993] Times, 15 December; [1994] 2 All ER 780; [1994] 1 WLR 765.
56. (1995) 159 JP 419; [1995] Times, 6 April.
57. Home Office Circular No. 16/95.
58. R. Descartes (1911) *Meditations* and *Passions of the Soul* in *The Philosophical Works of Descartes*, translated by E.S.Haldane and G.R.T. Ross, Cambridge.
59. P.M. Churchland (1979) *Scientific Realism and the Plasticity of Mind*, Cambridge; (1983) *Matter and Consciousness: A Contemporary*

Introduction to the Philosophy of Mind, Chicago; S.Shoemaker (1981) 'Some varieties of functionalism', Philosophical Topics, 12, 93-120.

60. O. Sacks (1982) *Awakenings*, Picador; A. Clare (1976) *Psychiatry in Dissent*, London, Tavistock.

61. G. Ryle (1966) *The Concept of Mind*, London, Penguin; L. Wittgenstein (1958) *Philosophical Investigations*, Oxford, Basil Blackwell; P. Strawson (1969) *Individuals*, London, Methuen.

62. [1963] 1 QB 857.

63. S. Guest [1985] 'The Scope of the Hearsay Rule', Law Quarterly Review, 10, 385.

64. Law Commission (1995) Evidence in Criminal Proceedings: Hearsay and Related Topics, Consultation Paper no 138, London, HMSO; see also Crim LR [January, 1996].

65. [1992] 1 NZLR 313.

66. [1996] Times, 18 December.

67. For discussion of the Pitchfork case, see J. Wambaugh (1989) *The Blooding*, London, Bantam.

68. Articles 5 and 6.

69. DNA profiling was discovered by Alec Jeffreys at the University of Leicester in 1984; A.J.Jeffreys, V. Wilson and S.L.Thein [1985], 'Hypervariable "mini-satellite" regions in human DNA', Nature, 314, 66; [1985] 'Individual specific "fingerprints" of human DNA', Nature, 616, 76.

70. W. Stuntz [1988] 'Self-incrimination and Excuse', Columbia Law Review, 88, 1227.

71. 293 F 1013 [DC Cir 1923]. The *Frye* test was a more stringent test than the Federal Rule test and the ordinary relevancy test. See also *State v Williams* 388 2d 500 (Me 1978).

72. *People v Castro*, 545 NYS 2d 985 (Sup Ct Bronx County, 1989); see also *McLeod* which is discussed in C. Norman (1989) 'Maine case deals blow to DNA Fingerprinting', Science, at pp 1156-8.

73. 113 S Ct 2786 (1993).

74. See *R v Deen* [1994] The Times, 10 January; *R v Gordon* [1994] The Times 27 May; [1995] Crim LR 413.

75. 545 NYS 2d 985 (Sup Ct Bronx County, 1989).

76. at p 996.

77. J. Sufian [February, 1991] 'DNA in the Courtroom' Legal Action, 7; (1991) 'Forensic use of DNA tests' 303 BMJ 4.

78. See also *United States v Two Bulls* 925 F.2d 1127 (1991), Court of Appeals. This case also raises questions about the databases of subpopulations, as it considers the use of a Native American database.

79. 447 NW 422 Minn (1989).

80. See *McLeod*, discussed in C. Norman, *op.cit.*, where the prosecution withdrew the case because of these problems.

81. See *R v Deen* [1994] The Times, 10 January.

82. See C. Joyce [July 21, 1990] 'High Profile: DNA in Court Again', New Scientist; M. Redmayne [1995] 'Doubts and Burdens: DNA Evidence, Probability and the Courts', Crim LR 464.

83. [1994] Times, 10 January.

84. Reported in New Scientist, 19 September 1992.

85. P. van Kampen and H. Nijboer 'DNA fingerprinting in the Dutch Code of Criminal Procedure' (November, 1994) Expert Evidence, Vol 3 No 2 pp 70-74, at p 72. They point out that in the Netherlands a defendant who refuses consent can be compelled to provide cell material which can be blood, hairs or mouth secretions. The defendant can himself request a test. A sample has to be taken by a doctor and enough has to be provided to allow for two later tests. The cellular material is later destroyed but profiles are stored on the database. For the defendant to be compelled to provide a sample, the charges have to be serious and the order should be necessary in the 'pursuit of truth'.

86. See S.J. Young [1991] 'DNA evidence - beyond reasonable doubt?' Crim LR 264.

87. See report in Legal Action (November 1995) 28.

88. [1994] Times May 27, [1995] Crim LR 413.

89. [1994] Times 10 January.

90. See D. J. Balding and P. Donnelly [1994] 'The Prosecutor's Fallacy and DNA Evidence', Crim LR, 711.

91. *Ibid*, p 721.

92. Before the CJPOA the court could treat the refusal to consent to the taking of an intimate sample as capable of amounting to corroboration of any evidence against the accused under s 62(10) of PACE. This how now been repealed in England and Wales but not in Northern Ireland.

93. See chapter 10 below.

94. *R v Ward* [1993] 2 All ER 577.

95. Inquiry into the Circumstances surrounding the convictions arising out of the bomb attacks in Guildford and Woolwich in 1974, Interim Report on the Maguire Case HC 556 of 1989-90 (1990) para. 14.5.

96. RCCJ Report, para. 9.2.

97. *Ibid*, para. 9.58.

98. *Ibid*, para. 9.70.

99. *Ibid*, para. 2.27.

100. *Ibid*, para. 9.33.

101. *Ibid*, para. 9.68.

102. M. Zander and P. Henderson (1993) *The Crown Court Study*, RCCJ Research Study no. 19, London, HMSO.

103. P. Roberts and C. Willmore (1993) *The Role of Forensic Science Evidence in Criminal Proceedings*, RCCJ Research Study no. 11, London, HMSO.

104. B. Steventon (1993) *The Ability to Challenge DNA Evidence*, RCCJ Research Study no. 9, London, HMSO.

105. C. Walker and R. Stockdale (1995) 'Forensic evidence and terrorist trials in the United Kingdom', Cambridge Law Journal, pp 69-99.

106. Inquiry into the Circumstances surrounding the convictions arising out of the bomb attacks in Guildford and Woolwich in 1974, Second Report HC 296 of 1992-93 (1993).

107. A. Grosskurth (May, 1992) 'With science on their side', Legal Action 7.

108. Reported in New Scientist, 22 June 1996.

109. See C. Norman, *op.cit.*

9 Infringing and waiving the right to silence

To some extent the debate between rights-based arguments and utilitarian arguments has been chimerical, for in practice the right to silence has been limited by statutory and common law exceptions to the right and by pressures on defendants to waive their right. It is important to take account of the ways in which existing precedents and procedures limit the right to silence, as well as the informal pressures to speak during interrogation. Each of these will be considered.

Statutory and common law infringements

Prior to the enactment of the 1994 Criminal Justice and Public Order Act judicial decisions indicated a readiness to curtail the right to silence in the United Kingdom. Similarly, as we saw earlier, in the United States, the scope of the *Miranda* rules was limited.[1] In England and Wales, the effect of cases such as *Chandler*[2] was to weaken the right further. Moreover a number of statutes and common law decisions had already limited the right to silence. These statutes provided a useful model for further curtailments of the right to silence.

The *Woolmington* principle, that is, the principle that the prosecution must prove the guilt of the accused, had already been modified by certain exceptions.[3] At common law where the defendant wishes to plead insanity in a criminal case, the legal burden of proof falls on him, although this defence is rarely used.

Further inroads into the *Woolmington* principle were made by means of express and implied statutory exceptions. An example of an express statutory exception, which expressly places the legal burden of proof on the defendant, would be s 1(1) of the Prevention of Crime Act 1953 which states that it is a criminal offence for a person to carry an offensive weapon in a public place, without lawful authority or reasonable excuse, the proof whereof shall lie on him to show lawful authority or reasonable excuse. A more extensive limitation is afforded by s 101 of the Magistrates' Courts Act 1980 which provides that:

> where the defendant... relies for his defence on any exception, exemption, proviso, excuse or qualification, whether or not it accompanies the description of the offence or matter of complaint in the enactment creating the offence or on which the complaint is founded, the burden of proving the exception, exemption, proviso, excuse or qualification shall be on him...

This was extended to indictable offences in *Edwards*[4] and was subsequently approved in *Hunt*.[5] In *Hunt* the House of Lords stated that Parliament could place the burden of proof on the accused by implication, that is, when the statute does not expressly provide for this. Where a statute, properly construed, creates such an implied exception, the burden of proof falls on the defendant and consequently the pressure to speak is strong, for without the accused's account the defence cannot be proved. Parliament can thus exclude the operation of the *Woolmington* rule both expressly and by implication, in relation to summary and indictable offences.

Arguments offered for statutory exceptions include the ease with which the accused can provide the evidence, his special knowledge of the issue in question and the burdens which would otherwise be imposed on the prosecution. This was stressed by the Court of Appeal in *R v Alath Construction Ltd; R v Brightman*.[6] With the extensive computerisation of records, and easy access to them by the police and prosecution, these arguments are less persuasive. Even if it were necessary to place a burden on the defendant, an evidential rather than a legal burden would be sufficient. As Stein[7] argues, *Hunt* also fails to distinguish between justifications and excuses in the criminal law and while the shifting of the burden might be appropriate in relation to excuses, individualised defences which focus on the particular circumstances of the accused, it should not extend to justifications which negative *mens rea* and directly address the question of the accused's blameworthiness. While a case might be made for placing the burden of proving an excuse on the accused, justifications should be treated differently, but *Hunt* fails to distinguish sufficiently between them.

Ashworth and Blake[8] examined all offences recorded in the 1995 edition of *Archbold* as triable in the Crown Court, including statutory and common law offences, to consider the number of exceptions to the *Woolmington* principle, to discover what proportion impose the burden of proof on the defendant and what proportion are strict liability offences. They found that 40% of offences triable in the Crown Court depart from the presumption of innocence. They considered 540 indictable offences, mostly statutory ones and found 219 offences where there were legal burdens or presumptions working against the accused. Their findings relate to the legal burden and do not include offences where the defendant bears an evidential burden. Forty-five percent of offences tried in the Crown Court impose strict liability in relation to at least one element of the offence. They criticise the casual manner in which the legislature depart from the presumption of innocence whether explicitly or by implication. They argue that 'many of those who prepare, draft and enact criminal legislation for England and Wales either fail to recognise these violations of the presumption of innocence, or disagree with the presumption of innocence or its application in this sphere, or fail to appreciate what can be achieved by placing only an evidential burden (rather than the legal burden) on defendants in respect of defences.'[9] What is required, they argue, is a parliamentary mechanism to make sure that the legal burden of proof is placed on the prosecution for all definitional and defence elements of all statutory offences: 'This would prevent the routine and probably unthinking imposition of burdens of proof on defendants and would focus argument on whether there are compelling reasons for making any particular exception.'[10]

A number of statutes impose obligations to answer questions to investigating bodies, for example, the Drug Trafficking Offences Act 1986 imposes a compulsion to answer questions put by Customs and Excise officers. The Companies Act 1985 which requires individuals to answer questions asked by DTI Inspectors, and the Criminal Justice Act 1987, imposes an obligation to answer questions from the Serious Fraud Office. Similar provisions in the Financial Services Act 1986 require individuals to respond to questions from the Securities Investment Board and these responses can subsequently be used in proceedings against the maker of the statement. The state's justification for these encroachments on the right to silence in relation to financial affairs has been the high standard of probity required of persons involved in managing the affairs of public companies. Raphael[11] has argued that if we take account of the powers of bodies to require witnesses to attend inquiries and give evidence, in relation to economic crime, we find that the right to silence had already been substantially eroded in a gradual piecemeal way. Yet this received relatively little attention, perhaps because it concerns matters such as insolvency, bankruptcy and liquidations. The evidence received in DTI inquiries may be used against those interviewed in any subsequent criminal proceedings, for example, relating to insider trading. A witness who fails to co-operate with the inquiry could be charged with contempt and imprisoned. Once the inquiry is concluded then the evidence can be used in subsequent criminal proceedings.[12] The House of Lords has affirmed that self-incriminating answers which are obtained under the Insolvency Act 1986, may be admitted against the defendant in criminal proceedings.[13]

A serious fraud may be investigated by the Serious Fraud Office as well as the DTI. Under s 2 of the Criminal Justice Act 1987, a suspect can be summoned to the Serious Fraud Office and compelled to answer questions if he is suspected of possessing information relevant to an investigation into serious fraud. If he does not answer questions he can be imprisoned for contempt. Although the information obtained cannot be used against him in subsequent criminal proceedings, it may be used to initiate proceedings against others, or to rebut statements made by the witness in court if the evidence adduced at trial is inconsistent with what is said in the s 2 interview. These statements may be obtained even when criminal proceedings have already begun according to the House of Lords in *R v Director of SFO ex parte Smith*.[14] Here their Lordships upheld the right of the SFO to compel suspects to answer questions. Given the particular problems of investigating complex fraud Parliament had decided that fewer rights for suspects in such cases could be justified. Moreover, a person questioned under s 2 receives advance notice, unlike the ordinary suspect, and is advised to have a lawyer present. Their Lordships affirmed that suspects may be questioned after being charged. Although there is a strong presumption against interpreting a statute as denying the right to silence to the accused, the House of Lords held that it was the plain intention of the 1987 Criminal Justice Act that the powers of the Director of the Serious Fraud Office did not come to an end when the person was charged; he could be compelled to answer questions and a caution would not be appropriate.

A notice served by the SFO under s 2 requires those being investigated to answer questions or to produce documents. Smith had been charged under the Companies Act with intent to defraud creditors. The SFO advised him he was being investigated and served a s 2 notice asking him to attend for interview and the documents the interview would cover. He applied for judicial review to quash the notice on the ground that the Criminal Justice Act 1987 did not authorise the Director of the SFO to serve a notice on a person who had already been charged with a criminal offence. It was also argued in the alternative, that even if the notice can be served, he must be cautioned that he is not obliged to speak. The House of Lords said that it would be illogical to empower the SFO to ask questions without any ability to compel answers, and this applied whether or not he had been charged.[15]

The Royal Commission on Criminal Justice supported the retention of powers of Serious Fraud Office investigators to require answers to questions under s 2 of the 1987 Criminal Justice Act[16] and advocated more detailed advance disclosure by the defence in serious fraud cases.[17] It was, however, critical of the cumbersome procedures demanded by the 1987 Act.

But it seems that the privilege against self-incrimination has been lost by those accused of corporate fraud and this view has been taken by the European Court of Human Rights in *Saunders v UK*.[18] In the *Saunders* case,[19] the defendants were convicted of criminal offences of theft, false accounting and offences against the Companies Act 1985, in connection with of the takeover of Distillers PLC by Guinness. The issue raised at trial and considered by the European Court of Human Rights was whether evidence obtained in interviews by Department of

Transport and Industry inspectors, with powers under ss 432(2) and 436(3) of the Companies Act 1985, to compel him to answer under threat of a fine or imprisonment for contempt of court, could be used in subsequent criminal proceedings. Saunders argued that the use of the interview evidence against him at trial undermined his right to a fair hearing. The prosecution read out to the jury over a three-day period transcripts of earlier interviews with the inspectors. He argued that these powers were oppressive and prevented him from properly conducting his defence. He also argued that the police had delayed the commencement of the police investigation to enable the statements to be obtained for intended later use in criminal proceedings.

The Court of Appeal decided that DTI inspectors were allowed to continue their inquiries into a company's affairs under ss 432 and 442 of the Companies Act 1995 when it is clear that criminal offences have been committed provided that their interviews are conducted independently of the prosecuting authorities and in a fair and unobjectionable way. Sections 451A and 449 of the Companies Act allow the Secretary of State to disclose any information obtained under those procedures to the DPP with a view to criminal proceedings. The appellants argued that the interviews by DTI inspectors, conducted under the Companies Act, in which they were deprived of the protection of the privilege against self-incrimination, should have been excluded at their trial under s 78 of PACE. Lord Taylor found that Parliament had intended to override the privilege in the Companies Act and that the admissibility of answers obtained by that means could not be regarded as unfair *per se* under s 78 simply because of the inherent features of the statutory regime under which they were obtained, or because Parliament ought not to have countenanced the possibility of self-incrimination. In considering whether the application of the statutory regime created unfairness, the judge could bear in mind that the accused was obliged to answer the inspector's questions on pain of sanctions. The powers in the Companies Act are more punitive than those under s 2(8) of the 1987 Criminal Justice Act and those under s 34 of the CJPOA because the defendant can be imprisoned for contempt if he does not cooperate.

The case was considered by the European Court of Human Rights. Under Article 6(1) of the European Convention everyone is entitled to a fair and public hearing within a reasonable time by an independent and impartial tribunal established by law. In *Saunders v UK*,[20] the majority of the Court held Article 6(1) which applied to all types of criminal investigations, including company frauds, had been breached. The applicant did not receive a fair trial. The Court also stressed the close link between the privilege against self-incrimination and the presumption of innocence in Article 6(2): 'Everyone charged with a criminal offence shall be presumed innocent until proved guilty according to law.' In 1984 the Commission had said that 'It cannot be compatible with the spirit of the Convention that varying degrees of fairness apply to different categories of accused in criminal trials. The right to silence, to the extent that it may be contained in the guarantees of Article 6, must apply as equally to alleged company fraudsters as to those accused of other types of fraud, rape, murder or terrorist offences...there can be no legitimate aim in depriving someone of the guarantees necessary in securing a fair trial.'[21]

The European Court of Human Rights in *Saunders* developed its approach in *Funke*[22] and affirmed the importance of the privilege, despite the public interest in prosecuting fraudsters. In *Funke* the European Court held that Article 6 included the right of any person charged with a criminal offence to remain silent and not to contribute to his own incrimination. In *Saunders* the Court said that the public interest in preventing fraud could not be used to justify the use of answers obtained by legal compulsion in a non-judicial investigation to incriminate Saunders at his trial and that his right had been infringed by reading out the transcripts to the jury.[23] The Court stressed that the right not to incriminate oneself is a generally recognised international standard. It lies at the heart of the notion of a fair procedure under Article 6 of the European Convention. The right is primarily concerned with respecting the will of the accused to remain silent. In determining whether Saunders' right had been infringed, the Court considered the use made by the prosecution at trial of the statements he had been compelled to give to the inspectors. The prosecution had used those statements in an incriminating way to establish his involvement in an unlawful share support operation. It was irrelevant that the statements might not have been self-incriminating because even neutral evidence might be used in a way which supported the prosecution's case.

There is also the danger that bodies with the power to deny the privilege against self-incrimination, such as the DTI and Customs and Excise, may pool information. If the police are investigating insider dealing, for example, and expect the suspect to exercise his right to silence when cautioned, they could contact the DTI to ask the Department to question him and obtain the information they need, thereby negating his right to silence. Raphael[24] points to the use of 'Hansard interviews' by the Inland Revenue, in which individuals who co-operate with an inquiry into their tax affairs would not normally be prosecuted. Similarly, under s 30 of the Finance Act 1985, a deal may be struck with VAT inspectors. If one is honest and pays back the necessary tax and a penalty, the individual usually will not be prosecuted. But a prosecution may follow, if it is discovered that the suspect has lied. His voluntary disclosures made in those interviews can then be used in evidence against him.

A number of statutes expressly stipulate a duty of advance disclosure in criminal cases, limiting the right to silence at the pre-trial stage and thereby making it harder to resist testifying at trial. Prior to the Criminal Justice Act 1967, the issue of ambush defences arose principally in relation to tactical alibi defences, at trial on indictment. Section 11 of the Criminal Justice Act 1967 aimed to prevent defendants producing surprise alibis during the trial by requiring advance notice of intention to adduce evidence in support of an alibi.[25] A further obligation to disclose part of the defence case was imposed by s 81 of PACE in 1984, which requires advance disclosure of expert evidence.

The principle of advance disclosure was further extended by the Criminal Justice Act 1987. Sections 9 and 10 enable the judge to order the prosecution to supply a statement of its case and the defence to give to the court and prosecution, a written statement giving the general nature of the defence and the essential matters on which it takes issue. The judge, or the prosecution, with the leave of the judge, may make 'appropriate' comments on a departure from the defence and on the failure to disclose and the jury is able to draw 'such inference as is proper' from that departure or failure. The section does not stipulate that failure to disclose is corroboration. These provisions for advance disclosure amounted to a significant contraction of the right to silence. Although the above infringements of the right to silence were criticised for discriminating against white collar criminals, the effect of the CJPOA has been to redress this inequality by removing the right to silence for all suspects. The provisions have been used as a foundation for advance disclosure for all criminal investigations in the Criminal Procedure and Investigations Act 1996.

The success of the 1987 Act in dealing with fraudsters also has been questioned. In his study for the Royal Commission, Levi[26] found that the defence lawyers he interviewed did not think pre-trial reviews had a significant effect as it was rarely the same judge presiding at trial and at the pre-trial review. The review judge may not wish to get involved in complex argument at that stage and the counsel at each stage may also be different. Instead of cutting costs and delays, the effect may be to add to court time and expense. Moreover the fear that s 2 statements may be used against them may actually deter suspects from testifying at trial. The use of preparatory hearings in fraud cases was seen by the Royal Commission as a useful model for pre-trial reviews.

The Roskill Committee[27] recommended specialist tribunals, others favour regulation by key bodies in the financial services sector. But if these cases are removed from the ordinary criminal justice system this would undermine its legitimacy, if it is perceived that white collar criminals receive special treatment. What is needed, as Grosskurth[28] argues, is better regulatory policing of the financial services sector. In 1995 the Attorney-General announced that the SFO's workload would be increased to deal with more financial crime.

In the above examples the right to silence has been contravened by established law and procedure rather than by the violation or subversion of procedures through improper police tactics. But police tactics and strategies also need to be considered when examining the suspect's decision whether or not to speak.

The lack of effective deterrents to improper interrogation

Methodological and evidential problems are faced in establishing and corroborating deliberate violations of the PACE Codes of Practice. The suspect is normally isolated during interviewing, and interrogation is subject to limited public scrutiny. If an observer or researcher is present, this may itself affect the conduct of the interview. The Fisher Report[29] found that many police officers were ignorant of the rules governing police practice at that time. The effect of PACE was to codify and formalise the rules governing interrogation and intensive training was given to the police to increase awareness of the rules and the need to observe them.

It is questionable, as we have seen, whether PACE does provide adequate protection for the defendant against improper pressures to speak during interrogation. Whilst torture, inhuman, degrading and oppressive treatment are prohibited by s 76, more subtle pressures, including trickery, falling short of oppressive behaviour, may be used or the Codes of Practice may be breached. These matters are considered by the court in deciding whether to exercise its exclusionary discretion under s 78. Here the court would consider if the breaches in question were substantial[30] and who else was present at the time.[31] When PACE came into force, the courts did show a willingness to make use of s 78 to enforce the Codes of Practice.[32] But an exclusionary discretion is arguably a weak basis for the protection of individual rights. Feldman[33] has argued that the courts have moved towards a recognition of the role of the judiciary in disciplining the police, by using s 78, and have construed fairness in terms of maintaining the balance between the public interest in pursuing the guilty and the protection of the suspect's liberties. This may lead to increased managerial pressure on interrogating officers. In addition the managerial ethos underpins the changes in police discipline in the Police and Magistrates' Courts Act 1994.[34]

Although the Court of Appeal has shown that significant breaches of the Codes will not be tolerated, automatic exclusion of evidence obtained by serious breaches of the Codes, underpinned by statute, would be preferable. Dennis[35] has questioned whether the law of evidence is the best site for such protection, or whether more effective punitive remedies could be found. While it is true that a stronger complaints procedure and effective sanctions are needed, nonetheless, evidentiary rules of admissibility can play a complementary role in affording a degree of protection, and police awareness of a vigorous use of s 78 may affect the conduct of routine interrogation. There is some evidence to suggest that the courts are retreating again from a liberal use of s 78 to exclude evidence on the ground of unfairness.[36] In *Delaney* it was made clear that 'It is no part of the duty of the court to rule a statement inadmissible simply in order to punish the police.'[37] In *Dunn*[38] the Court of Appeal upheld the admission of confession evidence despite the failure to contemporaneously record an interview. The presence of a solicitor's clerk, the court held, meant that the accused was not disadvantaged by the breach of the Code. In *Dunford*[39] an admission made in the absence of a solicitor was admitted on the ground that the solicitor's advice would not have added to the accused's understanding of his legal rights. Sanders[40] has argued that these cases illustrate the danger of using the protective principle to retain 'the rhetoric of liberalism' while displaying only a lukewarm commitment to the suspect's rights. The police have been campaigning against the existing rules of evidence and for changes to the rules of admissibility.[41]

The status of illegally obtained evidence also needs to be considered. Section 76(4) of PACE makes clear that evidence obtained through a breach of s 76 will not necessarily be excluded. There is no equivalent to the fruit of the forbidden tree principle in the United States.[42] Real evidence obtained by means of a breach may not necessarily be unreliable. It might be difficult to establish an independent connection to the defendant, but it does mean that there might be cases where it is in the interests of the police to increase pressure on the accused by unfair means. Ashworth[43] acknowledges that the protective principle would not entail the exclusion of all improperly obtained evidence and the protective principle might be outweighed by other factors.

The statutory rules regarding character evidence in s 1(f)(ii) of the Criminal Evidence Act 1898 may also impede a challenge by the defendant with previous convictions to police witnesses, as imputations against prosecution witnesses enable the defendant's own character to be put in evidence. Given that the most important prosecution witnesses are often the police, the chances of improper interrogations being carefully scrutinised by the courts are thereby reduced. In *Selvey*[44] the court said it might have some discretion to exclude character evidence, if the accused could not establish a legitimate defence without casting imputations on the prosecution witnesses' character, although it declined to do so in that case. In *Bishop*[45] describing a person as a homosexual was seen as constituting an imputation on his character. Guidelines for the exercise of the discretion were given by the Court of Appeal in *Britzman*[46] and *Burke*.[47]

Given that the majority of defendants plead guilty, the nature of the interrogation may not come under scrutiny. It may be worth taking the risk of exerting pressure to obtain an admission, as police misbehaviour may not come to light, if the court proceeds directly to the disposal stage. The exclusionary rule would be ineffectual if the suspect is not ultimately prosecuted, and misbehaviour may pass unchecked. Even if he is prosecuted, he may plead guilty or he may not raise the issue of treatment by the police, because of the penalty under s 1(f)(ii). This means that police conduct will be exceptionally, rather than routinely, subject to searching scrutiny.

The Court of Appeal considered the meaning of oppression in construing s 76(2)(a) in *Fulling*.[48] Here a suspect claimed that she confessed only after the police had told her that her boyfriend was having an affair with the woman being held in the adjacent cell. She said that she confessed in the hope of being released earlier and to thereby escape the distress of being so close to the woman in question. It was argued, on her behalf, that oppression meant conduct aimed at causing her will to crumble, rather than necessarily involving impropriety. The Appeal Court upheld the trial judge's decision that if the police had made such a revelation, which they denied, this would not be sufficient to count as oppression. Oppression must be given its ordinary meaning of harsh, burdensome, or acting in a wrongful manner. The trial judge had correctly admitted the confession and had rightly construed oppression as requiring impropriety. In *Emmerson*,[49] the Court of Appeal followed *Fulling* in giving oppression its ordinary meaning. It said that questioning which was rude and discourteous, involving bad language and a raised voice, which gave the impression of irritation and impatience did not amount to oppression.

Fulling and subsequent cases suggest that bullying, shouting, constant interruptions and falsely stating the evidence held by the police may all amount to oppression. In *Beales*[50] misstating the evidence against the accused and bullying the defendant was seen as oppressive and his confession excluded. In the Cardiff Three case[51] one of the defendants, Miller, was subjected to extensive interviewing over a period of 5 days and interviewed for a total of 13 hours in a bullying and hectoring way and this amounted to oppression. He made repeated denials, over 300 times, before making an admission. The Lord Chief Justice said that 'The officers...were not so much questioning him as shouting at him what they wanted him to say. It is hard to conceive of a more hostile or intimidatory approach by officers to a suspect.'[52]

Deception to obtain a confession did lead the Court of Appeal to quash a conviction in *Mason*[53] under s 78. But here the deception was practiced on a solicitor, an officer of the court, rather than the suspect, and interfered with his duty to advise his client. False information, namely that his client's fingerprints had been found at the scene of the crime, was given to the solicitor which led him to encourage his client to speak. The issue, then, is whether or not an exclusionary discretion is sufficient to protect suspects' rights and interests. The merit of discretion is that it affords a means of distinguishing between minor and more serious breaches. On the other hand, as policing, by its nature, entails a high level of autonomy, a discretionary rule gives the police greater latitude in working closer to the borderlines of impropriety.[54] In *Weeks*[55] the Court of Appeal said the fact that the interviewing officer threatened the suspect that if he did not tell the truth he would be kept in custody, was not sufficient to render his subsequent confession unreliable under s 76 of PACE, although the surrounding circumstances may do so.

McConville, Sanders and Leng[56] identified ways in which the police are able to bypass PACE. Their research revealed that police officers follow a set of 'working rules' which are inconsistent with the spirit and letter of PACE, including the use of racial stereotypes. Few sanctions are available, for example, when stops and searches and arrests are not based on reasonable suspicion. Relatively few people who are wrongly apprehended make an official complaint

245

and even fewer succeed with it. Once released a suspect may well not wish to proceed. The right to silence could be undermined by using use of informal interviews and tricking suspects into accepting statements. McConville, Sanders and Leng stress that the process of interrogation takes place 'in a social environment which increases the vulnerability of the suspects and maximizes the authority of the police'[57] and highlight ways in which questioning is used routinely to manipulate the suspect:

> The important point to appreciate is that 'confessions' which result from leading questions, or from the adoption of police formulated statements of admission, or from the assimilation of information contained in police questions which was unknown to the suspect prior to the interview, or as a result of broken resistance to varying degrees of compulsion are not the consequence of deviant interviewing practices but are *systemic* products of standard forms of interrogation.[58]

Waiving the right to silence

A further issue to consider is why the right to silence was so rarely exercised by suspects in practice, in the areas where the law did not curtail it.[59] As we saw earlier the exercise of the right to silence is exceptional.[60] But the fact that it is so rarely exercised makes it difficult to understand why it has been subjected to such virulent criticism. This voluntary waiver of the right to silence may be understood in terms of the structure of police interrogation and its psychological effects, as well as the nature of the criminal justice process as a whole, from apprehension to the sentencing stage. While voluntariness is a key issue for the court to consider when assessing the veracity of admissions, relatively little attention has been paid by commentators or judges to the pressures built into the process of interrogation, which undermine the free choice of whether or not to remain silent. Critics have tended to focus on abuses by the police, rather than on the routine nature of interrogation itself. The right to silence presupposes a free and autonomous individual but this sits uneasily with the reality of interrogation. Although the right to silence did have a real value beyond its symbolic significance, it is important to recognise the real pressures of routine interrogation, by surveying the empirical research in this field.

A range of tactics may be used by the police to encourage the suspect to speak which would not constitute oppression, but which are intended to deny or undermine the right to silence. On the basis of their research conducted before the CJPOA was enacted, McConville and Hodgson argue that 'It would be an understatement to say that the police do not have any respect for a suspect's right to remain silent during interrogation.'[61] In the interviews in their sample the fact that the adviser had told the police that the client intended to make no comment did not deter them from initiating an interrogation. A variety of strategies were used to encourage the suspect to speak, including asserting police authority over the legal adviser by treating him or her in an off-hand way and marginalizing the adviser by arranging the interrogation room so that the police and suspect were physically close and eye contact between adviser and client was impossible; sometimes the suspect would be told that silence did imply guilt, or guilt would be imputed from silence in the course of the interrogation. In this way, they say, 'the exercise of the right to silence is made the basis of suspicion and becomes the reason for attributing incriminating statements to the suspect.'[62]

Pressures to plead guilty

To obtain a full picture of the operation of the right to silence in practice, one needs to take account of the fact that the majority of defendants in the magistrates' courts and the Crown Court do plead guilty.[63] Although the proportion is lower in the higher courts, it is still substantial. This may be partly due to informal plea-bargaining where the prosecution and defence agree to a guilty plea on a lesser offence, but also due to the 'inducement' of a sentence discount which may be 25% or 30% of the sentence, in return for a guilty plea. This may be especially attractive to the defendant with previous convictions. Guilty pleas may also be offered by the accused in the hope that bail may be obtained more speedily. Those pleading guilty will include suspects who remain silent as well as those who speak during interrogation.

Pressure for the introduction of plea bargaining has increased in recent years.[64] A formal system of plea bargaining was supported by the Runciman Commission.[65] One of the reasons for support for plea-bargaining is concern over cracked trials, where the defendant decides to plead guilty on the eve of the trial or at the beginning of the trial, but these may be due to a number of factors incuding non-disclosure by the prosecution. Critics of plea-bargaining have pointed to the danger of making decisions regarding guilt on the papers in the case, rather than in open court, with full examination of witnesses, and to the additional pressure which is placed on defendants not to submit a defence.

The Runciman Commission recognised that some innocent suspects may plead guilty to obtain the discount.[66] Sentence discounts in return for guilty pleas were supported by the Commission albeit with some improvements, namely that the judge should state the maximum sentence if pleading guilty. The judge should answer the question 'what would be the maximum sentence if my client were to plead guilty at this stage?'.[67] The judge should, at the request of defence counsel, on instructions from the defendant, be able to indicate the highest sentence he would impose on the facts put to him. The sentence canvass would be considered by a judge in chambers with prosecution and defence counsel.

Written submissions would be made and the judge would indicate the maximum sentence if the accused pleads guilty. But the effect would still be pressure to plead guilty on defendants.

Some of the Commission's recommendations are reflected in the CJPOA. Section 48(1) of the CJPOA states that the court shall take into account 'the stage in the proceedings for the offence at which the offender indicated his intention to plead guilty, and (b) the circumstances in which this indication was given.' If the court offers a more lenient punishment it will state that it has done so.

A succession of guilty pleas enables speedy processing of offenders, but this pressure to plead guilty conflicts with the fundamental principles of the criminal justice system, namely the principles of voluntariness, individual responsibility and spontaneity, expressed in *Warickshall*[68] where it was noted that voluntary confession was seen as deserving of the highest credit because it was presumed to flow from the strongest sense of guilt. The law of evidence has stressed the importance of choice and the need to exclude inducements and threats from interrogation. Yet bargaining is built into the criminal justice system. In the Crown Court study Zander and Henderson found that the lawyers they interviewed suggested that there could be 1400 people each year who could be innocent who plead guilty to either reduce the charge or lessen the sentence.[69] However the Runciman Commission was sceptical regarding these figures as the lawyers could have misunderstood the question and in many cases there was little evidence that the people were innocent.[70]

Miscarriages of justice arising when innocent people are convicted on the basis of guilty pleas has received little attention until recently, but given that over 80% of Crown Court convictions are based on guilty pleas then there is considerable scope for such convictions. These types of miscarriages may also be the hardest to prove if the confessions appear to be made voluntarily or on the basis of legal advice.

Pressures to speak during interrogation

A number of factors may influence the suspect's decision to speak. The desire to co-operate with the police may discourage him from exercising his right to silence. The way the caution is given may also affect the decision. A research project in the United States found that if, for example, it is delivered in a bureaucratic or casual way or is rushed, the suspect will not be encouraged to take it seriously.[71] The procedures may be routinised to downplay their importance. In England the suspect is merely required to sign that he has been notified of the right to legal advice rather than giving a full declaration of waiver written by himself, in his own handwriting.

Some suspects may fail to grasp the meaning of the caution, for example, if they are poorly educated or have learning difficulties, or if they lack an understanding of what would be good reasons for staying silent. They may also be ignorant of the prejudicial effects of certain kinds of admissions, such as the culpability of secondary parties. The suspect's age, mental and physical condition and grasp of English, may all affect his understanding of the caution. Administering a caution will not necessarily impart to the accused a full awareness of the evidential significance of remaining silent. Researchers in Washington found that some respondents failed to understand the right to silence warning and 'presence of counsel' warnings.[72]

The *Miranda* warning, used in the United States, must establish the seriousness of the implications of waiving the right and, as stated in *Miranda*,[73] if an individual waives his right, he must do so knowingly and intelligently. The burden falls on the prosecution to show that the warning was given and that the right to silence has been expressly waived, orally, or by signing waiver forms. Following *Miranda*, attempts were made to extend waiver from express relinquishment of those rights to implied waiver, to be inferred from the individual's conduct or actions.[74]

What is remarkable is the widespread willingness of individuals to voluntarily relinquish their right to silence. A study of anti-war demonstrators, in an American university, found that despite the introduction of the *Miranda* guidelines, few of the middle-class suspects were aware of their rights. When first interviewed by FBI agents, they signed waiver forms, although when they later became fully aware of those rights and their implications, they regretted the waiver.[75] They described their nervousness during interrogation in the presence of an authority figure. Although they knew of the existence of the right to silence, their ignorance of the precise boundaries of the right made it difficult for the demonstrators to make an informed choice. Furthermore, because their opposition to the war rested on moral objections, a subjective need was felt to affirm the moral validity of that protest. Tension may also be defused by the act of speaking.

Similar studies in England have found that suspects do not fully understand their legal rights. Persons arrested in England are cautioned and informed by the custody officer of their legal rights, to have someone informed of the arrest, the right to obtain legal advice and the right to consult the Codes of Practice. They are also given a written leaflet, the Notice to Detained Persons, which gives information on the caution and these rights. Clare and Gudjonsson have undertaken a number of studies to examine suspects' understanding of the Notice to Detained Persons, including the original version, used from 1986 to 1991, the revised version introduced in April 1991.[76] They have also conducted experiments with a simplified version. Studies of the original notice found that about 59% of the sentences were understood by all subjects, with understanding correlating with intellectual ability.[77] One quarter of detainees with mild learning disabilities found difficulty in understanding the right to legal advice. The original leaflet was found to be too complex to achieve its purpose. Following the publication of these findings, the Home Office agreed to amend the Notice. The revised version was simpler, but the researchers found that the Notice could only be understood fully by a person with an IQ of 105 or over, which means that only 40% of the general population would be able to understand all of it.[78] They found that 52% of the subjects understood the right to remain silent as set out in the revised notice. The revised notice, while clarifying the right to legal advice, was still insufficiently clear, particularly for those who were disadvantaged. Clare and Gudjonsson also developed and tested a more simplified version for the Royal Commission on Criminal Justice which increased the numbers understanding the right to silence to 81%. They stress the need for information to be written in a simple form and for particular attention to be given to vulnerable individuals. It was also clear that few suspects in detention do actually read the notice. They also found a significant number of subjects whom they identified as having difficulties with reading or intellectual impairments, but who did not report their need for special help. They recommend that questions should be put directly to the detainee on the need for an appropriate adult. The authors propose that instead of supplying detainees with a Notice, information should be read out to the detainee by the Custody Officer and he should be given a card citing the most important rights.[79]

Suspects are better informed of their rights since the revised codes were introduced in 1991 but they still may not receive full information.[80] The information may be rushed or unclear or may give the impression that waiting for a solicitor to arrive may delay and extend detention. Baldwin's study of interrogations in the West Midlands, West Mercia and Metropolitan Police District found that 'in over a tenth of the cases observed, and as many as a third in one of the stations examined, the caution was delivered to suspects in such a garbled manner as to be virtually incomprehensible. Sometimes it was not given at all.'[81]

The new caution warning of the inferences which may be drawn from silence makes it harder to decide whether or not to speak. The Justice[82] study of the caution given under the Criminal Evidence Order in Northern Ireland, which is similar to the new caution, found that only 5% of suspects could understand its significance. The caution initially proposed to reflect the changes to the right to silence in the CJPOA contained 58 words. Critics argued it was likely to confuse suspects and it had to be shortened. But the new caution 'You do not have to say anything. But it may harm your defence if you do not mention when questioned something which you later rely on in court. Anything you do say may be given in evidence' poses greater problems of understanding and it is likely to generate confusion and to increase the pressure to speak.

Whether or not there is a formal right to silence, most people feel a social pressure to speak when asked questions and it takes considerable resolution to remain silent in the face of sustained questioning. Even if one has a right not to speak, this does not prevent questions being asked and exposure to questioning can undermine the will to remain silent. However, while increasing awareness of rights through education would influence the ability of citizens to exercise a rational choice, it would not neutralise the pressures to speak which are built into conversational discourse. As Hepworth and Turner note in their examination of confession, which they see as a routine feature of social relationships, 'it is not that we all suffer from a compulsion to confess but rather that we are subject to powerful norms not to remain silent.'[83] These pressures may be intensified when the interrogator is a figure of authority. Similarly, Irving observed in his study of police interrogation, that to remain silent when confronted with sustained questioning in a police interview room 'requires an abnormal exercise of will.'[84] Psychological experiments to analyse obedience, conducted by Milgram[85] have shown that the presence of an authority figure can have a powerful effect on an individual's actions and on his free will. One consequence is that the agent's sense of responsibility for his own actions may be impaired. The nature of confession in Western culture is intimately linked to the presence of an authority figure, whether in a religious or secular context. The idea of a duty to confess to officials and the belief in the remedial benefits of confessing, as Hepworth and Turner argue, are distinctive features of the Christian tradition which have survived secularisation.[86] The act of confessing affirms both the legitimacy of the interrogation and individual responsibility. Because silence may be construed as so abnormal in everyday interaction, it is not surprising that this common sense view may spill over into the legal context, so that silence in police interrogation or at trial, or when responding to accusations by third parties on equal terms, may be viewed with suspicion.[87] Gudjonsson's work has shown that individuals in such circumstances may come to doubt their own judgement and falsely confess.[88]

The PACE Codes have not adequately addressed this issue of the pressures to speak built into normal conversational practice and social interaction. Attention therefore needs to be given to how individuals manage to remain silent, while subject to these pressures. While police interrogation may be distinguished from everyday interaction, in terms of its structure, the unequal status of the parties, the fact that it is circumscribed by rules of evidence and procedure, it nonetheless retains the normal rules and conventions of everyday language. As Hepworth and Turner point out, language as a speech-exchange system consists of a series of obligations to speak when spoken to and not to interrupt others who are speaking.[89] They cite anthropological studies which show that for an outsider trying to participate in an alien society, a knowledge of when to remain silent may be as basic to the production of socially acceptable behaviour as a knowledge of what not to say.[90] A skilled interrogator can exploit these normal rules of discourse to trigger off a story which the speaker feels obliged to finish, for example, by encouraging discussion on an apparently unrelated topic, or by remaining silent after a response, which may encourage the respondent into saying more than he or she intended. Moston and Stephenson in their study of 641 suspects in three police stations also found a strong correlation between the extent of non-offence related conversations outside the police station and the number of subsequent admissions during interviews inside the police station.[91]

Legal discourse is hard to reconcile with the pre-established structure of conversational discourse. Legal discourse stresses the importance of voluntariness in the communication of knowledge and in deciding whether to remain silent, but it fails to take account of the strong social duty to speak built in to social interaction. Most people would feel that continuing silence would indicate boorishness or rudeness. While legal discourse is formally predicated on the requirement of voluntariness, to some extent common sense thinking has penetrated legal discourse in the rules developed regarding the treatment of silence in response to accusations by equals. The prerequisite of voluntariness is necessary to legitimate legal discourse and to reaffirm the values of honesty and individual responsibility, yet built into police interrogation are techniques of manipulation to encourage the suspect to speak. The development of sophisticated interrogation techniques will make it harder for the suspect to remain silent.[92] To some extent the experience of show trials in Stalinist Russia and of mass conversions, knowledge of the effects of isolation and persuasion on prisoners of war, has enhanced our understanding of the processes involved in inducing admissions without the use of direct physical sanctions. Psychological research has shown that people may falsely confess in the absence of a threat of physical violence. This conflict between voluntariness and pressure parallels a similar tension within religious confession. While Christian theology has stressed the need for spontaneous and voluntary confession, the acknowledgement of guilt and individual responsibility, as Hepworth and Turner[93] point out, at the same time various devices have been used to frighten or trick the individual into unburdening himself, such as the *confessional a surprise*, where the picture of Christ is transformed into a picture of the devil, to evoke a confession. Far from being spontaneous, the confession, they argue, is socially constructed and subject to rules and expectations of appropriate and relevant knowledge.

Although spontaneity and voluntariness are crucial to the integrity of confessions, as reflected in s 76 of PACE, the training of interrogators is precisely to encourage and produce speech. The suspect may have been arrested in the early hours of the morning or spent some time waiting for his solicitor to arrive, leaving him at a disadvantage while his interrogator is clearly in a position of strength, in familiar surroundings and in control of the interview. In the United States, manuals of interrogation instruct interrogators in the use of psychological techniques to encourage suspects to speak.[94] Walkley[95] has produced a handbook for the English market, expounding various interviewing strategies which may be used for successful interrogation. These American approaches to interviewing were influential during the 1980s, despite the shift of emphasis in PACE.

But the criterion of voluntariness underpinning the common law relating to confessions, and the notion of oppression in PACE, focus primarily on the impropriety of the police rather than the pressures inherent in an interrogation, or the use of techniques which are seen by interviewers as legitimate. Williamson and Moston[96] point to a number of reactions used by the police officer in negotiating the suspect's silence: he may curtail the interview or 'downgrade' by getting the suspect to talk about a noncontentious issue rather than the alleged offence, to establish rapport; he might also try repeating the question, or alternatively 'upgrade' by emphasising the evidence against the suspect to highlight his need to speak; he may comment on silence, reminding the suspect of the right to silence but at the same time pointing to the opportunity to speak, while avoiding language which might be construed as stressing the positive or negative consequences of speaking. Now that silence has more significance, police tactics may change: silence will be valuable so the careful framing of questions and the range of questions will be crucially important.

Gudjonsson and MacKeith[97] argue that for some suspects the experience of police interrogation may lead to psychiatric disorders, including post-traumatic neuroses. The stress arises from uncertainty about the future, the alien environment, isolation, and the presence of an authority figure. The suspect may display symptoms of anxiety and fear, hyperventilation and verbal incoherence. He may be taken to the police station in the middle of the night. During extended periods of detention, sleeping and eating patterns may also be affected. Consequently the ability to make a rational choice whether or not to speak may be affected.

If the suspect does speak, the reliability of his statement may be affected. Conditions such as claustrophobia may lead the suspect to grasp at any means to escape. A psychologist's report on Mark Braithwaite, one of the men wrongly convicted of the murder of P.C. Blakelock during the riot at Broadwater Farm in 1985, stated that he was convinced that Braithwaite had confessed following an acute anxiety attack due to claustrophobia which resulted from being enclosed in a police cell.[98]

The dynamics of the interrogation process therefore may be a key factor in waiver with consequent injustice, as we can see from the history of wrongful convictions. The pressure to speak also needs to be seen in the context of the role of the solicitor. As we saw earlier, legal representatives may be marginalised during interrogation, and in a relatively weak position to encourage the suspect to exercise his right to silence. Studies of legal advice show that advice to remain silent was rarely given before the CJPOA. In most cases suspects are advised to cooperate with the police,[99] not least because early co-operation with the police by admitting involvement may secure a caution in some cases. As McConville *et al* observe: 'Inaction on the part of most advisers has contributed to the transformation of the right to remain silent into a duty to submit to hostile

253

questioning precisely targeted upon provoking the suspect to respond to lines of interrogation which impute guilt.'[100]

In response to findings of impropriety and the poor quality of police interviewing and lack of supervision, a new approach to interviewing, investigative or ethical interviewing, is being introduced.[101] This was initiated by two Home Office Circulars which set out the principles of investigative interviewing and gave guidance on the appropriate skills training. It was based on discussion between the police, psychologists and lawyers. These principles and recommendations are reflected in new training courses and new training manuals, which are described by Williamson as providing an ethical foundation for the police in questioning suspects.[102] The effect is to shift the police role away from an adversarial to an inquisitorial role as a seeker of truth and to focus on obtaining high quality evidence and information, which can be used in the investigation, by thorough interrogation. The aim of investigative interviewing is to obtain accurate and reliable information from suspects, witnesses or victims in order to discover the truth about matters under police investigation. The guidelines stress that interviewing should be approached with an open mind. Information obtained from the interviewee should always be tested against what the officer already knows, or what can reasonably be established. The officer must act fairly. He or she is not bound to accept the first answer given and he has a right to put questions even if the suspect declines to comment.

Vulnerable suspects and witnesses should be treated with special consideration. It is envisaged that training will stress the need to record information accurately and to try to recognise those who at particular risk of making false confessions. Officers will be trained to explain the purpose of the interview to the suspect, and will be taught how to allow the suspect to give his account, how to bring the interview to an end, how to evaluate the interview and to learn from the experience of interviewing. Pilot studies have shown an improvement in interviewing skills following this training. The skills training is to be backed up by improved supervision of interviews and use of computerised interactive video training programmes. Eventually all officers will be trained in these techniques. But it may take some time for these skills to percolate into routine interviewing, particularly for those initially trained in American methods. So if these new training skills are put into practice the quality of interrogation should improve. But the emphasis will still be on the interviewee as a key source of information and encouraging him to speak; with the loss of the right to silence the suspect's account will become a key focus of the investigation and trial. Baldwin's study of interrogation noted the poor quality of interviewing, interviews were ill-planned and aimless, procedures were not properly explained to suspects, and many officers were determined to obtain a confession, presuming guilt prior to interview.[103] But Baldwin is sceptical regarding the impact of training as he found that often the most highly trained interviewers were the least effective.

The cumulative effect of permitting adverse inferences to be drawn from silence is to effectively shift the burden of proof. Statutory and common law infringements of the right had already whittled down the 'golden thread' of the *Woolmington* principle before the CJPOA. These infringements also illustrate the dangers of the 'slippery slope'. Each time inroads are made into the principle, a further contraction of a fundamental right becomes easier, as models and arguments become available for application to new areas, and resistance to abolition is weakened. A change at the pre-trial stage has implications for the trial stage, so a move towards advance disclosure in the 1987 Act can be seen retrospectively as a step towards dismantling the right to silence at trial.

As we have seen, the fact that the right to silence was so rarely exercised, combined with the growing list of exceptions and modifications, suggests that the fears of an 'abuse' of the right were without foundation. Yet curiously, the fact that the right was so rarely exercised was seen by some critics as a justification for curtailing it. Irving, for example, argued that if the right to silence was exercised by only a small number of suspects, then:

> it must be be relatively useless, and/or very hard to exercise. I do not care what the mixture is but on both counts I would not want anyone to be misled into thinking that this anachronistic abstraction acts as an effective practical safeguard for the average innocent suspect in custodial interrogation.[104]

From this he inferred that we should be looking elsewere for better safeguards. But he fails to take account of the problems facing the suspect in detention or the potential for the right to be revitalised. Zuckerman also argues that it might be preferable to abandon the privilege against self-incrimination, as it has already been eroded, and to develop instead the suspect's other rights.[105] The privilege is ineffectual in practice in protecting the suspect, he says, because it can be waived and this inevitably offers a challenge to the interrogator to persuade him to do so. The real protection to the citizen against random arrest and questioning, he claims, lies in the democratic political system, which restrains the power of the police and offers the citizen a variety of remedies for the abuse of that power. This is the direction in which English law is moving and strengthening the suspect's access to legal advice, he argues, gives greater protection from abuse to more people than the right to silence.

Zuckerman envisages that without the right to silence, the focus could be on fairness of interrogation procedures which would protect more suspects. By fairness he means mutual disclosure between defence and prosecution so that the suspect is informed of the allegations and evidence against him which the police possess: 'while the right to silence has little to commend itelf, it does not follow that it may be fairly abolished without introducing adequate countervailing measures.'[106] He argues that: 'There is nothing inherently wrong with requiring a suspect to answer the police suspicions during the interrogation. But there is a lot wrong in expecting a suspect to do so in a process which lacks the most fundamental ingredient of fairness: information about the case to be answered.'[107] The loss of the right to silence has to be compensated for by procedural safeguards. If the police refuse to provide the suspect with this information then the defence should be able to apply for evidence of silence in interrogation to be excluded at trial under s 78 of PACE.

While Zuckerman is right to warn of the dangers of relying on the privilege alone and the need to strengthen these curbs and remedies, nonetheless the right to silence did provide one important weapon in the armoury of the citizen and consideration should be given to means of making it more effective rather than resigning ourselves to its loss. If there is a gap between the formal right to silence and its exercise in practice, expressed in the fact that so many suspects waive their right, then efforts should be made to ensure that the right to silence is genuinely respected and that waivers are made knowingly and intelligently. This might be achieved by, for example, the promotion of greater public awareness of the right to silence, steps to ensure conformity to the requirements of the Codes of Practice as well as a fully independent police complaints procedure and substantially improved access to legal advice.

Notes

1. *Miranda v Arizona* 384 US 436 (1966).
2. [1976] 1 WLR 585.
3. *Woolmington v DPP* [1935] AC 462.
4. [1972] 2 QB 27.
5. [1987] 1 All ER 1. For discussion of *Hunt* see F. Bennion 'Statutory exceptions: a third knot in the golden thread' [1988] Crim LR 31, P. Mirfield, 'The Legacy of Hunt' [1988] Crim LR 19 and D. Birch [1988] 'Hunting the snark: the elusive statutory exception', Crim LR 221.
6. [1990] 1 WLR 1255.
7. A. Stein (1991) 'Criminal Defences and the Burden of Proof', Coexistence, 28, pp 133-147.
8. A. Ashworth and M. Blake [1996] 'The Presumption of Innocence in English Law', Crim LR 306.
9. *Ibid*, p 315.
10. *Ibid*, p 316.
11. M. Raphael (1990) 'The right to silence and economic crime', in S. Greer and R. Morgan (eds.) *The Right to Silence Debate*, Bristol, Centre for Criminal Justice, pp 60-66.
12. See *re Arrows Ltd No. 4: Hamilton v Naviede* [1995] 1 AC 75; *R v Saunders, R v Parnes, R v Ronson, R v v Lyons* [1996] Crim LR 420.

13. See *re Arrows Ltd No. 4: Hamilton v Naviede* [1995] 1 AC 75.
14. [1993] AC 1, [1992] 3 All ER 456.
15. [1993] AC 1, [1992] 3 All ER 456.
16. Report of the Royal Commission on Criminal Justice (1993) London, HMSO, Cmnd 2263, para. 4.30.
17. *Ibid*, para. 7.61.
18. *Saunders v UK* [1996] Times, 18 December.
19. *R v Saunders, R v Parnes, R v Ronson, R v Lyons* [1996] Crim LR 420.
20. [1996] Times, 18 December.
21. 10.5.94 No. 19187/91.
22. *Funke v France* (25 Feb 1993) Series A Vol 256-A.; see S. Nash and M. Furse [1995] 'Self-Incrimination, Corporate Misconduct, and the Convention on Human Rights', Crim LR 844.
23. [1996] Times, 18 December.
24. M. Raphael, *op.cit.*
25. Section 11 of the 1967 Criminal Justice Act was repealed by s 74 of the Criminal Procedure and Investigations Act 1996; disclosure of details of alibi is now governed by ss 5(7) and 5(8) of the 1996 Act.
26. M. Levi (1993) *Investigation, Prosecution and Trial of Serious Fraud*, RCCJ Research Study no. 14, London, HMSO.
27. E.W. Roskill (1986) *Improving the Presentation of Information to Juries in Fraud Trials*, London, HMSO.
28. A. Grosskurth [March 1994] 'Serious fraud: a dangerous precedent', Legal Action, 6. She also draws attention to the fact that the SFO does have a higher success rate in obtaining convictions than is often surmised from the failure of high profile cases and that there are cases, such as *Barlow Clowes,* where the pre-trial procedure worked well; juries may be able to follow the evidence if it is clearly presented.
29. (1977) Report of an Inquiry by the Hon. Sir Henry Fisher into the circumstances leading to the trial of three persons on charges arising out of the death of Maxwell Confait and the fire at 27 Doggett Road, London S.E.6, London, HMSO.
30. See *R v Keenan* [1989] 3 WLR 1193.
31. See *R v Dunn* [1990] Crim LR 572.
32. See *R v Parris* [1988] Times 2 November.
33. D. Feldman [1990] 'Regulating treatment of suspects in police stations: judicial interpretation of detention provisions in the Police and Criminal Evidence Act 1984', Crim LR 452.
34. See chapter 4 above.
35. I. Dennis [1989] 'Reconstructing the Law of Criminal Evidence', Current Legal Problems, 21.

36.   A breach of s 58 by delaying access to a solicitor will not of itself entail the exclusion of admissions made in the absence of legal advice. See *Alladice* (1988) 87 Cr App Rep 380.

37.   (1988) 88 Cr App Rep 338.

38.   [1990] Crim LR 572.

39.   (1990) 91 Cr App Rep 150.

40.   A. Sanders [January, 1991] 'Judicial creativity and suspects' rights', Legal Action, 7.

41.   See C. Pollard [1994] 'A Case for Disclosure?', Crim LR 42; [1996] 'Public safety, accountability and the courts', Crim LR 152.

42.   See *Kuruma Son of Kaniu v R* [1955] AC 177.

43.   A.J. Ashworth. [1977] 'Excluding Evidence as Protecting Rights', Crim LR 723 at 725.

44.   [1970] AC 304.

45.   [1975] QB 274.

46.   [1983] 1 WLR 350.

47.   (1985) 82 Cr App Rep 156.

48.   [1987] 2 All ER 65.

49.   (1991) 92 Cr App Rep 284.

50.   [1991] Crim LR 118.

51.   *R v Paris, Abdullah and Miller* (1993) 97 Cr App Rep 99.

52.   *Ibid.*

53.   [1987] 3 All ER 481. It has been argued that s 78 is too generous to the defence. Section 78 was intended to secure a fair trial rather than fair treatment of the accused, but judges have used it to exclude evidence obtained by police impropriety, even though it is clear that to admit such evidence would lead to an obviously guilty person being convicted. See M. Ockelton (1995) 'Rules of Evidence', in E. Attwooll and D. Goldenberg (eds.) *Criminal Justice*, Stuttgart, Steiner, pp 95-108.

54.   Cases may be found before and after PACE where confessions were excluded because a misleading view of the evidence was given by the police to the accused but this was based on an honest mistake. See *R v Kwabena Poku* [1978] Crim LR 488 and *R v McGovern* [1991] Crim LR 124.

55.   [1995] Crim LR 52.

56.   M. McConville, A. Sanders and R. Leng (1991) *The Case for the Prosecution*, London, Routledge.

57.   *Ibid*, p 78.

58.   *Ibid*, p 73.

59.   Only 4% of the sample in the Royal Commission on Criminal Procedure's study exercised the right to silence. In the study undertaken for the Home Office Working Group within the Metropolitan and West Yorkshire districts, the figures for complete silence were, respectively,

6% and 2.3%. In Williamson and Moston's study of 1017 cases it was found that 16% exercised their right to silence and of these, half answered some questions and the other half were completely silent. See T. Williamson and S. Moston (1990) 'The extent of silence in police interviews' in S. Greer and R. Morgan (eds) *op.cit.*, pp 36-43.

60.   See R. Leng (1993) *The Right to Silence in Police Interrogation*, RCCJ Research Study no. 10, London, HMSO and chapter 5 above.

61.   M. McConville and J. Hodgson (1994) *Standing Accused*, Oxford, Clarendon, p 108.

62.   *Ibid*, p 11.

63.   Over 70% in the Crown Court and over 90% in the magistrates' court.

64.   See General Council of the Bar Working Party Report (Seabrook Report) (1992) *The Efficient Disposal of Business in the Crown Court*. Support has also been received from the DPP and the Police.

65.   RCCJ Report, para. 7.42

66.   *Ibid*, para. 7.42, 7.47.

67.   *Ibid*, para. 7.51.

68.   [1783] 1 Leach 263.

69.   M. Zander and P. Henderson (1993) *The Crown Court Study*, RCCJ Research Study no. 19, London, HMSO.

70.   RCCJ Report, para. 7.43.

71.   J. Griffiths and R. Ayres (1967) 'A Postscript to the Miranda Project: Interrogation of Draft Protestors', 77 Yale Law Journal, 300.

72.   J. Medalie, L. Zeitz and P. Alexander (1968) 'Custodial police interrogations in our nation's capital: the attempt to implement *Miranda*', 66 Michigan Law Review, 1347.

73.   *Miranda v Arizona* 384 US 436 (1966).

74.   See *North Carolina v Butler* 441 US 369 (1979).

75.   J. Griffith and R. Ayres, *op.cit.*

76.   I. Clare and G. Gudjonsson (1993) *Devising and Piloting an Experimental Version of the Notice to Detained Persons*, RCCJ Research Study no.7, London, HMSO.

77.   G. Gudjonsson (1990) 'The "Notice to Detained Persons": How Easy is it to Understand?', Law Soc Gaz 87 (43), pp 24-7; (1991) 'The "Notice to Detained Persons", PACE Codes, and Reading Ease', Applied Cognitive Psychology 5, pp 89-95.

78.   G. Gudjonsson, I. Clare and P. Cross (1992) 'The revised PACE "Notice to Detained Persons": How Easy is it to Understand?' Journal of the Forensic Science Society, vol 32, pp 289-99.

79.   I. Clare and G. Gudjonsson (1993) *Devising and Piloting an Experimental Version of the Notice to Detained Persons*, RCCJ Research Study no.7, London, HMSO.

80. See D. Brown, T. Ellis and K. Larcombe (1992) *Changing the Code: Police Detention under the Revised Codes of Practice*, Home Office Research Study no.129, London HMSO.

81. J. Baldwin (1994) 'Police interrogation: what are the rules of the game?' in D. Morgan and G. Stephenson (eds.) *Suspicion and Silence*, London, Blackstone, pp 66-76, at p 67.

82. JUSTICE/CAJ (1994) *The Right of Silence Debate - the Northern Ireland Experience*, London.

83. M. Hepworth and B. Turner (1982) *Confession*, London, Routledge, p 32.

84. B. Irving and L. Hilgendorf (1980) *Police Interrogation: the Psychological Approach*, RCCP Research Study no. 2, London, HMSO; (1980) *Police Interrogation: the effects of the Police and Criminal Evidence Act 1984, a case study of current practice*, London, Police Foundation.

85. S. Milgram (1963) 'Behavioural study of obedience', Journal of Abnormal and Social Psychology, 67, 371; (1974) *Obedience and Authority: an experimental view*, London, Tavistock.

86. M.Hepworth and B. Turner, *op.cit.*

87. See chapter 1 above.

88. G. Gudjonsson (1992) *The Psychology of Interrogations, Confessions and Testimony*, Chichester, John Wiley; see chapter 10 below.

89. M. Hepworth and B.Turner, *op.cit.*

90. See K.H. Basso (1970) 'To give up on words: silence in Western Apache Culture', Southwestern Journal of Anthropology.

91. S. Moston and G. Stephenson (1994) 'Helping the Police with their Enquiries outside the Police Station', in D. Morgan and G. Stephenson, *op. cit.*, pp 50-65.

92. The methods used may vary. Walkley, for example, has promoted a strategic approach designed to encourage suspects to speak, while Kite of the Merseyside Police Training School favours an 'ethical' approach. See J. Walkley (1987) *Police Interrogation: A Handbook for Investigators*, The Police Review Publishing Co.

93. M. Hepworth and B. Turner, *op.cit.*

94. F. Inbau and J. Reid (1962) *Criminal Interrogations and Confessions*, Baltimore.

95. J.Walkley, *op.cit.*

96. T. Williamson and S. Moston, *op.cit.*

97. G. Gudjonsson and J. MacKeith (1982) 'False Confessions, Psychological Effects of Interrogation - a discussion paper' in A. Trankell (ed.) *Reconstructing the Past, The Role of Psychologists in Criminal Trials*, Stockholm, Norstedt; G. Gudjonsson (1992).

98. See *R v Silcott, Braithwaite and Raghip* [1991] Times, 9 December.

99.   M. McConville, J. Hodgson, L. Bridges and A. Pavlovic, *Standing Accused: The Organisation and Practices of Criminal Defence Lawyers in Britain*, Oxford, University Press.

100.   *Ibid*, p 111.

101.   Home Office Circulars 22/1992 and 7/1993.

102.   See T. Williamson (1994) 'Reflections on Current Police Practice,' in D. Morgan and G. Stephenson, *op. cit.*, pp 107-116; (1993) 'From interrogation to investigative interviewing: strategic trends in police questioning', Journal of Community and Applied Social Psychology, vol 3, pp 89-99; see also B. McGurk, J. Carr and D. McGurk (1993) *Investigative Interviewing Courses for Police Officers: an evaluation*, Police Research Series, no. 4.

103.   J. Baldwin, *op.cit.*.

104.   B. Irving, *The Guardian* (30 December 1988).

105.   A. Zuckerman (1989) *The Principles of Criminal Evidence*, Oxford, Clarendon, at p 307.

106.   A. Zuckerman (1994) 'Bias and Suggestibility: Is there an alternative to the right to silence?' in D. Morgan and G. Stephenson, *op.cit.*, pp 117-140 at p 136.

107.   *Ibid*, pp 136-7.

10 Miscarriages of justice

In the wake of the Guildford Four and Birmingham Six cases a Royal Commission was appointed to review the criminal justice system. The miscarriages of justice identified since the late 1980s have raised concern regarding a number of different stages of the criminal process, including police interrogation, expert evidence, problems with forensic evidence, the quality of defence work, errors by defence lawyers, disclosure and the problems within the appeal process. Some of the cases concern admissions allegedly overheard by cellmates in prison. The chances of mounting a successful campaign and attracting media interest are better for multiple defendants than for the single defendant trying to mount a campaign challenging his conviction from inside prison.[1]

Many of the wrongful convictions occurred prior to PACE, but PACE would not have protected those such as the Guildford Four and Birmingham Six, suspected of terrorist offences. While the Broadwater Three case arose before the PACE Codes had been fully implemented, the interrogations were conducted in a police station which was following the PACE Codes as part of a pilot study[2] and other miscarriages of justice have occurred since PACE has been in force. Many of these cases arose out of incidents leading to public outrage, where there was intense media coverage and considerable pressure for a conviction; the communities in question were seen as the source of a serious law and order problem and the prosecution's case was based on dubious confession evidence.

Even with improvements at the pre-trial and trial stages it is possible in any system that errors will occur and it is vital that there should be adequate procedures to deal with mistakes and in this context the Court of Appeal has been heavily criticised. On several occasions cases have been repeatedly referred to the Court of Appeal by the Home Secretary before a wrongful conviction has been quashed. In recent years attention has focused on the appropriate form a

'Miscarriage of Justice Tribunal' or Criminal Cases Review Commission might take. While these matters are very important, there is a danger of losing sight of problems which arise much earlier in the criminal justice process and much more attention needs to be paid to preventive measures. As well as false confessions which occur in the context of the police interview and which may be made without a lawyer present,[3] attention needs to be given to alleged admissions which occur outside the police station. There may be problems with the legal advice given so that the appropriate defence is not submitted at trial.[4]

Judith Ward was convicted for murder and causing an explosion when she was 25 and 43 by the time she was freed in June 1992.[5] The Home Secretary referred her case to the Court of Appeal in 1991 and the convictions were quashed in 1992. The Court of Appeal said that because she suffered from a personality disorder, no reliance could be placed on her confession. Medical evidence on her mental state had not been disclosed at trial and fresh medical evidence was submitted on appeal. The Court of Appeal also found that tests which favoured the defence had not been been disclosed by the Forensic Science Service and the police, prosecuting counsel and the DPP had also failed to disclose information. The Court of Appeal stressed the prosecution's duty to disclose information and that there would be few cases where that duty should not prevail, although the Court of Appeal subsequently modified its position on this.[6]

Stefan Kiszko also was convicted of murder because of the failure to disclose exculpatory evidence which was in the possession of the prosecution at the time of the trial, but not produced in court, namely the fact that semen was found in the sample from the clothing of the victim, yet he was infertile. The Court of Appeal quashed his conviction when it heard evidence not disclosed at trial.[7] In May 1994 the Court of Appeal quashed Eddie Browning's conviction for the murder of Maria Wilkes in 1988 because of police evidence which was not disclosed at trial. In the case of the Maguires the prosecution failed to disclose the notebooks of the forensic scientists.[8] The Maguires were convicted of possession of explosive substances in 1976 which were believed to be connected to the Guildford and London bombings. They applied for leave to appeal but leave was refused in 1977. Following the quashing of the Guildford Four conviction, the Maguires' case was referred back to the Court of Appeal and their conviction was quashed on the grounds that crucial scientific evidence, which would have indicated an innocent source of the nitroglycerine found on them and their premises, was not disclosed to the defence by the prosecution.[9] In June 1993 the Court of Appeal quashed the murder convictions of the Taylor sisters because of non-disclosure of evidence by the police and because of sensationalist reporting which undermined their right to a fair trial.[10]

Common features running through the miscarriages of justice are wrongful identifications, false confessions, the perjury of witnesses or co-defendants, problems with forensic evidence, police misconduct and planting of evidence, allegations of verbal confessions which were never made, ill-judged trial tactics and failure to disclose evidence. A new regime for disclosure is being introduced but the fear is that it will increase defence disclosure rather than prosecution or police disclosure.[11] In addition the poor quality of defence counsel was criticised in the Guildford Four case.

Evidence was fabricated in the cases of the Guildford Four, the Maguires, the Bridgewater Three and the Darvell brothers, as well as cases involving the West Midlands Police Serious Crime Squad and the Stoke Newington police. As well as intentional fabrication of evidence, there is the problem of false confession where the person may confess through bullying and hectoring or because of the person's mental state. Civil rights groups report receiving numerous claims of alleged miscarriages each year. Even allowing for a percentage of spurious claims, there appears to be a high number of claims worthy of investigation. The JUSTICE report on miscarriages of justice[12] identified problems at both pre-trial and trial stages, including poor defence work, police misconduct and poor quality police investigation, failure to call witnesses, underhand tactics of the prosecution and poor judicial summing up but which falls above the line necessary to ground an appeal. The appeal stage is also criticised because of the quantity and quality of legal advice and the Appeal Court's reluctance to intervene. Home Secretaries in the past have been reluctant to interfere with the courts' decisions; the police re-investigation may be inadequate and conducted by the same police force which dealt with the original inquiries.

A major cause of concern has been the failure to prosecute and convict many officers involved in miscarriages of justice and where prosecutions have been launched, the delay in bringing such prosecutions. One problem is that the time taken for miscarriages to be acknowledged also works against those wrongfully convicted. The charges against an officer and a forensic scientist involved in the Kiszko case were dropped because it was thought that they could not get a fair trial as the detective involved in the case had died. In the Birmingham Six case the Crown Prosecution Service did think that there was enough evidence to prosecute the police officers involved for perjury and conspiracy to pervert the course of justice, but the prosecution was stayed on the ground that there had been so much publicity on the case that the officers could not receive a fair trial.

False confessions

A suspect may be vulnerable to the risk of false confession because of his inability to cope with interrogation, as well as fears of being confined. Anxiety, fear and depression may make it difficult to make a rational choice whether or not to speak. If one does speak, one may say what one believes will hasten release. Even a false admission may offer the prospect of an early release in the short term in the form of bail. Guilt feelings about matters unconnected with the offence may also precipitate false admissions. In certain circumstances the suspect may genuinely come to believe that he has committed the crime and the individual subjected to group pressure may doubt his own judgement.[13]

Gudjonsson and MacKeith[14] distinguish three types of false confessions: voluntary, coerced-compliant and coerced-internalised confessions. The voluntary category embraces those people who, for various psychological reasons, confess spontaneously and who may respond to reports of crimes by regularly surrendering themselves to the police. They may be distinguished from those suspects who react badly to interrogation and confinement and confess in order to escape, while being fully aware that the confession is false, which Gudjonsson and MacKeith describe as 'coerced compliant' confessions. Compliant individuals are anxious to please and keen to avoid confrontation. Coerced-internalised confessions refer to cases where the confessants may actually believe what they are confessing is true and that they are guilty. These suspects may be highly suggestible and agree to leading questions, or actually believe they are guilty, perhaps because at the time of the alleged incidents they were under the influence of alcohol or drugs, or at the commencement of the interview they are clear that that they are innocent, but find that the interviewing process leads them to distrust their own judgement.

Gudjonsson is developing ways of testing suggestibility and compliance. Some people may answer 'yes' to questions without fully understanding them. Other individuals, suffering from certain personality disorders, may be prone to what he describes as 'confabulation', filling in gaps in their memory with imagined material.[15] Whether an individual will falsely confess will depend on a number of factors, including vulnerability and mental state at the time of interrogation and the way in which the suspect is treated by the interviewer. While PACE did seek to strengthen the position of suspects, by tape recording of interviews and the 'appropriate adult' requirement for juveniles and those with learning disabilities, it did not specifically address the wider problems of suggestibility or the desire to escape of non-vulnerable individuals.

A further category, the coerced-passive confession, is highlighted by McConville *et al.* Here the 'process of questioning induces suspects to adopt the *confession form* without necessarily adopting or even understanding the substance of what has been accepted or adopted...they may simply adopt words which amount to a confession without even appreciating that they have made an admission.'[16]

Psychologists' findings were used by the defence in the Broadwater Farm case to show how factors such as suggestibility, compliance and intellectual ability may lead to false admissions. The effect on rational decision-making may be exacerbated in contexts where the suspect is habituated to an authoritarian structure, for example, if he has been institutionalised and is routinely rewarded for co-operation. Problems may be faced by vulnerable individuals suffering from mental illness, personality disorders or those with learning disabilities.

Engin Raghip was aged 19 when interviewed for the Blakelock murder on the Broadwater Farm Estate in Tottenham. He was interrogated without a solicitor present and said that he had signed admissions because he was afraid following threats made by the police. In seeking leave to appeal he asked to admit fresh evidence on his mental age, which according to a psychiatrist, was 10 or 11, and on his suggestibility. The court dismissed these applications on the ground that the jury had seen and heard Raghip and could assess his suggestibility for themselves without needing the assistance of an expert. Silcott, Braithwaite and Raghip were convicted in 1986. The police claimed that Silcott had made an incriminating statement which he denied making and had not signed, and which was unsupported by forensic or identification evidence. At the first appeal the Court of Appeal upheld his conviction and it was not quashed until 1991. ESDA tests showed that crucial sections of Silcott's 'confession' had been added afterwards. He was convicted solely on confession evidence and denied access to a solicitor during interrogation. He refused to sign the interview notes and denied that he had ever admitted to murder. Raghip and Braithwaite his co-defendants said they had confessed only because of the pressure of the interrogation. After their initial appeals failed, the Home Secretary referred the case back to the Court of Appeal who finally quashed the conviction in 1991.[17] The court found that some parts of the records of the interview had been written at different times. During the investigation the police division involved was actually operating under the PACE rules.

The Court of Appeal said that when the judge is considering a submission under s 76(2)(b) of PACE regarding the defendant's mental state at the time of the interview, the decision should be based on medical evidence rather than the trial judge's own assessment of the defendant's performance during the interview. Moreover his decision should not be determined by whether or not the IQ of the accused falls above an arbitrary figure.

The weakening of the right to silence by the CJPOA is a regressive step for all suspects, placing them under further pressure to speak, or to risk adverse inferences being drawn from silence, while in the stressful context of detention. Under the Act suspects retain a formal choice whether or not to speak. But in practice, when they are cautioned regarding the possibility of adverse inferences from a late defence they are likely to believe that it would be better to speak. Trying to recall specific names of witnesses, times, places and events in these circumstances will increase the strain on defendants and raise special difficulties for suspects with a poor command of English, increasing the risk of unsafe confessions. The loss of the right to silence is most dangerous for vulnerable and younger suspects who may be more likely to make false statements to escape the pressure of police questions. As Owers notes:

> The assumption is that the opposite of silence is to tell the truth
> and that the people who are persuaded that remaining silent is

not in their best interests will then provide information which will allow the correct perpetrator to be identified. There is no evidence that this is the case.[18]

But vulnerable and naive people, the type of people who have in the past confessed to things they did not do, are likely to speak if subject to increased pressure, but what they say will not necessarily be the truth or lead to the right outcome.

Inevitably, there is a tension in interrogation between the interest of the police in crime control and the citizen's right not to incriminate himself. The fact that PACE allows for extensive periods of questioning, to a maximum of 96 hours, albeit with certain safeguards, reflects the assumption that delays will encourage the suspect to speak. While s 76 of PACE offers protection against oppressive conduct, it fails to deal with the issue of a person who is interviewed perfectly fairly and confesses voluntarily, but falsely. Where false confessions are made by individuals who are highly suggestible, the police lack the training to enable them to recognise this problem.

Confessions and vulnerability

The danger of convicting on the uncorroborated confession evidence of vulnerable individuals is vividly illustrated by the Confait case. Ronald Leighton was convicted for the murder of Maxwell Confait; Colin Lattimore was convicted of manslaughter and Leighton, Lattimore and Ahmet Salih were found guilty of arson with intent to endanger life, on the basis of confessions unsupported by any independent evidence.[19] It took three and half years and a vigorous campaign to exonerate them. Eventually their convictions were quashed on appeal.

Although the admissions were obtained from the boys in the absence of parents or legal advisers and the boys subsequently argued that they had been roughly treated, the confessions provided the basis for their prosecution and conviction. The confessions conflicted with the medical and forensic evidence and contained no information not already known to the police at the time of the interview. Colin Lattimore at the time was aged 18 but had the mental age of an 8 year old and was described by a medical expert as highly suggestible. Ronald Leighton was aged 15 and would be classified as 'borderline subnormal', having an IQ of 75. Ahmet Salih was at the time aged only 14. Colin claimed that he had confessed because he wanted to go home and the other boys claimed to have confessed simply to escape. Although the idea of confessing to involvement in a murder to avoid short-term detention might seem irrational, it indicates the effects of interrogation particularly on vulnerable suspects, unsure of how long they will be detained, and the difficulty of making a voluntary and intelligent decision to remain silent.

The case highlighted the vulnerability of suspects with learning disabilities and the campaign unearthed a number of similar cases. Mental illness, personality disorders, and physical conditions, such as diabetes or epilepsy, also may impair the judgement of suspects. Their understanding of what it means to remain silent may be affected. These problems will be exacerbated by permitting adverse inferences from silence. It was in the light of the problems encountered in the Confait case that the pressing need for special provision for vulnerable groups, embodied in clear directions for interrogating officers, became apparent. Gudjonsson defines psychological vulnerability as 'psychological characteristics or mental states which: (a) impair suspects' ability to understand their legal rights, (b) render suspects prone, in certain circumstances, to provide information which is unreliable or misleading.'[20]

Paragraph 11.14 of Code C of PACE specifies the treatment for persons at risk during interrogation:

> A juvenile or a person who is mentally disordered or mentally handicapped, whether suspected or not, must not be interviewed or asked to provide or sign a written statement in the absence of an appropriate adult unless paragraph 11.1 or Annex C applies.

These safeguards may be waived only in exceptional cases where delays are likely to lead to harm to others, hinder the recovery of property and alert others involved in the crime. The police should ask the appropriate adult to come to the police station if they believe the suspect to fall within these categories or to be a juvenile which is defined as under the age of 17.[21] The role of the appropriate adult is to protect the juvenile's rights, to advise him or her, and to ensure that the interview is conducted fairly. Paragraph 11.16 of Code C states that 'Where the appropriate adult is present at an interview, he should be informed that he is not expected to act simply as an observer; also that the purposes of his presence are, first, to advise the person being questioned and to observe whether or not the interview is being conducted fairly, and secondly, to facilitate communication with the person being interviewed.' The Code recognises the danger of unreliable evidence. It notes that:

> although juveniles or people who are mentally disordered or mentally handicapped are often capable of providing reliable evidence, they may, without knowing or wishing to do so, be particularly prone in certain circumstances, to provide information which is unreliable, misleading or incriminating. Special care should therefore always be exercised in questioning such a person, and the appropriate adult should be involved, if there is any doubt about a person's age, mental

state or capacity. Because of the risk of unreliable evidence it is also important to obtain corroboration of any facts admitted whenever possible.[22]

The appropriate adult will normally be a parent, guardian or social worker or other person responsible for his welfare such as a representative of the care authority or voluntary organisation or another responsible adult who is not a police officer. However, a study by Maguire[23] found that juveniles spent long periods in detention while waiting for an appropriate adult to arrive and similar problems may face other vulnerable groups. Brown, Ellis and Larcombe found that the police did not always inform the juvenile of his right to legal advice until the appropriate adult arrived so to avoid further delay the right to legal advice would be waived.[24] Evidence of improper pressure being put on juveniles to confess was found by Evans in his research for the Royal Commission.[25] The research was based on a study of 367 juveniles through the pre-court decision-making process in one police force. They found very high admission rates by juveniles even when the evidence was weak. Many juveniles were visibly afraid and distressed during detention and many confessed early on in the interview. Suspects rarely exercised their right to silence. They also received little assistance or guidance from the appropriate adults present. Three quarters of the appropriate adults did not contribute to the interview and those who did speak often did not support the suspects. They also found that a significant number of juveniles were cautioned even when they had denied the offence or had not clearly admitted their guilt. The Essex Social Services Department conducted research to see how the new Act and Codes were working in relation to the appropriate adult requirement, in the period from January 1986 to June 1987.[26] It found that the calls on social workers to act as appropriate adults were minimal. Moreover, many of the requests were made during office hours, by which time the suspect had already been in detention for a considerable time. In one quarter of the cases which they examined, the time between arrest and notification was over 5 hours. The average period of detention up to the time charged was 9.2 hours in 1987. What this study demonstrates is that the Act, which was designed to give special help to these groups, had the unintended consequences of increasing pressure on them by lengthening the time spent in detention. When appropriate adults are contacted, they may well be unsure of their precise role and passively rather than actively involved in the interviewing process.[27] But under the revised code the appropriate adult now 'shall be informed that he is not expected to act simply as an observer; and also that the purposes of his presence are, first, to advise the person being questioned and to observe whether or not the interview is being conducted properly and fairly, and secondly, to facilitate communication with the person being interviewed.'[28]

Evidence obtained in the absence of appropriate adults from juveniles and mentally disordered suspects has been excluded by the Court of Appeal.[29]

Because these groups are at particular risk of providing damaging statements, they need the full protection of the right to silence. The caution now warns of the adverse effects of a late defence but it may well be difficult for these groups to understand it or to make a rational choice whether or not to speak. Without the right to silence their disadvantages in police detention are exacerbated and problems of false admissions and unreliability may increase. But there is nothing in the revised Codes to compensate for the increased risks for vulnerable groups in the CJPOA. Lord Runciman has been very critical of the abolition of the right to silence and has argued that the increased powers of the police under the CJPOA will increase the risk of miscarriages of justice.[30] Under the Act vulnerable individuals will still be exposed to the risk of adverse inferences from silence during interrogation. Section 35, which covers silence at trial, stipulates that it cannot be activated if the accused is under 14 or his physical or mental condition makes it undesirable for him to give evidence, but there are no comparable provisions in sections 34, 36 and 37. The reference to 'a fact which *in the circumstances* existing at the time the accused could reasonably have been expected to mention' in s 34 means that the court may need to consider the suspect's age or mental capacity, according to the Court of Appeal in *Argent*,[31] but there is no reference to 'in the circumstances' in sections 36 and 37.

Special protection for suspects with learning disabilities is given in s 77 of PACE which provides that:

1)   Without prejudice to the general duty of the court at a trial on indictment to direct the jury on any matter on which it appears to the court appropriate to do so, where at such a trial -

      (a)   the case against the accused depends wholly or substantially on a confession by him; and

      (b)   the court is satisfied -
      (i)   that he is mentally handicapped; and
      (ii)   that the confession was not made in the presence of an independent person,

    the court shall warn the jury that there is special need for caution before convicting the accused in reliance on the confession, and shall explain that the need arises because of the circumstances mentioned in paragraphs (a) and (b) above.

Similarly, in summary trials the court should treat such a case as requiring caution before convicting the accused on his confession. The section only requires a warning and the use of caution; it does not prevent a conviction on that basis. Although mandatory corroboration warnings in relation to accomplice evidence and sexual offences were abolished by s 32 of the CJPOA, the warning in s 77 of PACE remains. However a corroboration requirement for confession evidence, rather than simply a warning, would offer a greater degree of protection. Where a confession is the bulwark of the prosecution case, then the jury is reduced to weighing the word of the police against that of the suspect.

The Runciman Commission recommended extending the protection of s 77 of PACE from mentally handicapped to mentally ill or mentally disordered suspects,[32] to bring the Act in line with the Codes where persons who may be mentally handicapped or mentally disordered are treated the same for the purposes of the Code.[33] The Commission stressed the need for clearer guidelines for officers regarding the criteria to be employed when considering the need for an appropriate adult.[34] It was not fully satisfied with the arrangements for the protection of vulnerable suspects in custody and stressed that better training was needed especially as the number of vulnerable suspects is likely to increase as more mentally disordered persons move into the community.

In *Bailey*[35] the Court of Appeal said that the trial judge should warn the jury under s 77 of the special need for caution before convicting the accused if the prosecution case depends substantially on the confession by a mentally handicapped person not made in the presence of an independent adult. A confession to a friend did not constitute a confession to an independent person. In *Morse*[36] the Court said that a person of low intelligence who is not capable of advising a juvenile cannot count as an appropriate adult. In *McGovern*[37] the court found that a confession made by a woman with an IQ of 73, without a solicitor present and in breach of the PACE Codes, should have been excluded at trial. The breach also rendered a second interview in which a solicitor was present inadmissible. In *MacKenzie*[38] the Court of Appeal said that where the prosecution case depends wholly on an unreliable confession from a defendant who suffers from a mental handicap, the judge should withdraw the case from the jury. In *Campbell*[39] the Court of Appeal held that whether the judge should warn the jury of the special need for caution in such cases depended on the comparative strength of the prosecution case in the absence of the confession. If the prosecution's case is just as strong without the confession, then a s 77 warning is not necessary.

One problem is the difficulty of recognising and identifying the condition of a suspect to see whether he falls within the ambit of these provisions, particularly in borderline cases. The use of these provisions appears to be limited. Gudjonsson, Clare, Rutter and Pearse assessed 173 suspects at the police station before they were interviewed by the police.[40] They monitored their mental state, intellectual functioning, reading ability, interrogative suggestibility, anxiety proneness and understanding of their legal rights. One aim of the research was to discover how easily suspects' intellectual deficits could be identified prior to questioning. They found that 35% of suspects had problems which might interfere with their coping ability or functioning during interrogation. The researchers considered that an appropriate adult was necessary in 15% of the sample, but the police in fact called on an appropriate adult in only 4% of cases. Suspects who were depressed and were actively suicidal were the ones most likely to be missed. There were also problems in identifying intellectual impairment if it did not interfere with social functioning. Some detainees would see this as a private matter to be concealed.

The majority of detainees had previous convictions so they had a reasonable understanding of their rights at the police station but only one third said they had read the Notice to Detained Persons. Many suspects in the study had low IQ scores. Taking into account the particular context of the study, Gudjonsson *et al* argue that it is unlikely that the average IQ of detainees is much over 85. So in practice the police are interviewing large numbers of suspects with low IQs, a sizeable proportion of whom are likely to suffer from a significant intellectual impairment. The police are able to identify the most disabled and vulnerable cases. Gudjonsson *et al* claim that earlier studies tend to under-estimate the incidence of significant intellectual impairment among suspects interviewed at police stations. They stress the need for proper training to identify vulnerable individuals, a review of the role of the appropriate adult and propose that detainees should be asked if they qualify for special help. At present police doctors who may be consulted may lack the necessary training to recognise mental disorders.

Other studies have found a gap between the numbers requiring an appropriate adult and the number of cases where an appropriate adult actually was contacted. Brown[41] found that the police officers in his study considered that only 1% of suspects required an appropriate adult by virtue of mental illness or mental handicap. This would seem to be lower than the number one would expect to find within the population of suspects as a whole. In *Moss*[42] the accused, who was just above the borderline, was kept in custody for 9 days and interviewed 9 times mostly without a solicitor present. At the fifth interview he made admissions in the absence of a solicitor and these formed the prosecution's case against him. On appeal the guilty verdict was found to be unsafe. His confession should have been excluded and simply giving a s 77 warning to the jury was insufficient. In *Lamont*[43] the defendant's conviction was quashed because the trial judge did not give a s 77 warning although the defendant had an IQ of 73 and there was little evidence apart from his confession. In *Kenny*[44] the Court of Appeal said that the court in determining whether a person falls within the ambit of s 77(3) of PACE for the purposes of excluding a confession, should consider every case on its own facts, rather than simply applying IQ test figures from previous cases.[45] There may also be problems where an individual does not speak English sufficiently well to grasp the significance of the question being asked and for example, may accept an accusation of murder, when he wishes to plead self-defence.

The Royal Commission on Criminal Justice recommended that the role and functions, qualifications and training of the appropriate adult should be reviewed by a Working Party.[46] Subsequently the Home Office Review Group made a number of recommendations, including a clear definition of the role of the appropriate adult, setting up appropriate adult panels, better training for professionals and guidance for police officers, the provision of more information at police stations and improving the advice in the PACE Codes on the kinds of persons who may fulfil the role of appropriate adult for particular classes of suspects. Appropriate adults should be entitled to confidential interviews with suspects, and the relationship between the suspect and appropriate adult should be governed by legal privilege.[47]

Confessions and corroboration

The danger of false confessions is particularly worrying in the absence of a corroborative requirement for confession evidence. The long history of wrongful convictions before and after PACE has shown the problems with confession evidence, beginning with the Confait case which generated demands for reform culminating in PACE. The Fisher Report[48] considered the issue of obtaining supporting evidence and recommended that there should be a 'supporting evidence' requirement, namely that a confession should be supported by other evidence in certain circumstances: where the Judges' Rules were breached; where the accused has learning disabilities, when a young person has confessed under police questioning in the absence of an independent adult, and in cases where a tape recording of a confession is unavailable. Efforts should be made by the police to obtain further evidence, to support or undermine a confession as part of their inquiries before reaching any firm conclusions. Where having done this, they are still left only with confession evidence, they should consider whether there are other possible suspects. By supporting evidence, the Fisher report meant evidence which would be relevant to the truth of the confession itself, such as special knowledge of the crime which could be known only to an individual present at the crime scene, as well as independent evidence linking him to the crime.

The demand for supporting and corroborative evidence received more support in the light of the experiences of the Guildford Four. This requirement should not be confined to the vulnerable groups referred to in the Fisher Report, but should apply to all confessions or, at the very least, to cases where the reliability of the confession has been shown to be jeopardised by breaches of the PACE Codes. When considering whether to prosecute, there should be a requirement for independent corroboration of a confession, such as witness testimony or forensic evidence. Since the Guildford Four case, there have been further cases involving appellants convicted on evidence of alleged confessions including those fabricated

273

by officers in the West Midlands Serious Crime Squad which cast doubt on several convictions involving those officers. Civil rights pressure groups such as the Legal Action Group have submitted evidence to the Royal Commission on the problems of relying on uncorroborated confession evidence and have argued that confessions should be admissible only if made in the presence of a solicitor.[49]

The majority of the Runciman Commission rejected a corroboration requirement for confession evidence because of the danger of wrongful acquittals and loss of public confidence in the criminal justice system which would result from this. The majority recommended that where a confession is credible and has passed the tests laid down in PACE, the jury should be able to consider it even in the absence of other evidence, but the judge should give a strong warning to the jury that it is dangerous to convict in the absence of supporting evidence. However, according to the majority of the Commission, there should be no strict requirement for supporting evidence.[50] The jury would be advised to look for supporting evidence, that is, evidence which convinces the jury that the contents of the confession are accurate, rather than independent evidence. A conviction would still be possible in the absence of such evidence. Others would argue that this is too weak and does not afford sufficient protection. The mere fact of a warning by the judge will be insufficient to deter the police from impropriety or to assist the jury in determining whether a confession is false.

The failure of the Royal Commission to recommend a corroboration requirement is surprising as the Commission recognised the real risk of false confession. The Commission acknowledged that people may falsely confess for a range of reasons, to protect others, to escape from custody, or because of guilt on an unrelated matter and that therefore the warning should be given in all cases of confession evidence and should draw attention to the additional danger of possible fabrication if it has not been tape recorded. But while the revelations of miscarriages of justice provided the *raison d'être* of the Commission, it did not take the opportunity to remedy the real problems in the system which generate miscarriages. It also rejected a requirement for confessions to be tape recorded or made in the presence of a solicitor before being admissible. Zuckerman[51] is very critical of the Royal Commission's report for failing to address the deeper causes of miscarriages and for focusing too much attention on the post-investigatory procedures when most problems lie in the investigatory process. Zuckerman sees the key problems as police bias and the suggestibility of suspects and witnesses: 'The police interrogator tends to approach his or her suspect, and sometimes even ordinary witnesses, with definite expectations which could inadvertently affect the information obtained from them.'[52] Yet little attention has been given to studying the effects of bias and suggestibility on the investigation of crime. 'Bias leads the investigator to seek evidence that supports his or her hypothesis and to overlook evidence that contradicts it.'[53] During interrogation the experienced interviewer will try to construct a case against the accused 'so as to fit the response obtained from the suspect'.[54] To counter bias and suggestibility, Zuckerman advocates involving the defence in the process of investigation. The extent of questioning of the suspect should be proportional to the amount of information given about the case against him.

A minority of the Royal Commission favoured a requirement of supporting evidence based on the *Turnbull* requirement in relation to identification evidence.[55] Under the *Turnbull* guidelines, if the quality of identification evidence is poor, the judge should withdraw the case from the jury and direct an acquittal, unless there is other evidence which supports the correctness of the identification. If the case goes to the jury, other evidence may be corroborative in the *Baskerville*[56] sense, but need not be so, if the jury is sure from the evidence that there is no mistaken identification. The judge should identify to the jury the evidence which he judges to be capable of supporting the identification and if there is some evidence which the jury might think supporting but it is not, the judge should tell the jury. But the *Turnbull* standard is arguably too weak and the stronger standard of corroboration in *Baskerville* is preferable, that is, 'independent testimony which affects the accused by connecting or tending to connect him with the crime. In other words, it must be evidence which implicates him, that is, which confirms in some material particular not only the evidence that the crime has been committed, but also that the prisoner committed it.'[57]

Moreover the research conducted for the Royal Commission supported the case for a corroboration requirement. McConville argued that the empirical evidence strongly favoured a move away from reliance upon extra-judicial confession evidence.[58] In 86.6% of confession cases in his sample the confession was supported by admissible evidence from an independent source. A corroboration requirement, even on the strong *Baskerville* standard, would not impose excessive burdens. The police would have needed to obtain significantly more evidence to meet such a requirement in less than 8% of prosecutions in his sample. In many cases the additional information required is already in the possession of the police and simply needs processing to convert it into evidence, for example, by laboratory examination. The effect of a corroboration requirement, he argues, would improve the evidence gathering of the police; without it the police may be less inclined to collect or preserve corroborating evidence. On the rule he advocates, no one could be convicted on the basis of confession evidence unless it was corroborated by independent evidence which pointed clearly to the guilt of the accused or linked the accused with the crime. He argues that 'the unqualified assumption that the introduction of a corroboration requirement means "lost convictions" is unsustainable; rather, such a rule would, among other consequences, merely confirm the result in cases which collapse under existing (lower) evidence thresholds and would additionally lead to the avoidance of some convictions based upon dubious foundations.'[59]

Current changes in the organisation of policing may mean that confessions are becoming less crucial to a conviction as the police are being encouraged to adopt a more proactive mode of work, with the focus on surveillance and intelligence-based detection and investigation.[60] In addition the managerial ethos is changing with a shift towards quality assessment in which good practice and strict observance of the requirements of PACE, will be factors to consider in assessing quality rather than clear-up rates alone. But this move away from reliance on confession evidence may be undermined by loss of the right to silence as the defendant's own account becomes the focus of the trial.

However, a corroboration requirement will not of itself guarantee no miscarriages of justice although it may reduce the risk. There is always the danger that the corroborating evidence itself could be fabricated or misleading or its status misconstrued. Moreover, in jurisdictions where there is a corroboration requirement very little may be required to support confessions as in Scotland, where some things may now be held as corroborative which would have been rejected in the past; there is increased use of self-corroborating evidence or special knowledge, even where the information in the confession is known by others.[61] The corroboration requirement has gradually been eroded in Scotland and there has been concern that special knowledge could be passed to the suspect by officers conducting the interview.

The appeal process

The experience of miscarriages of justice such as the Birmingham Six and the Guildford Four has highlighted problems with the appeals procedure and the narrowness of the grounds of appeal in preventing miscarriages of justice. The role of the Court of Appeal in handling alleged miscarriages of justice and its failure to deal with cases where the original evidence is in dispute, has been subject to widespread criticism. Part of the problem has been its reluctance to acknowledge failures on the part of the police and other parties and its own failings. The problems include access to the Court of Appeal, delays and the grounds of appeal.

Malleson[62] examined the appeal process for the Royal Commission and observed that while the court does have wide powers under the Criminal Appeal Act, it is reluctant to exercise them very often. This is due in part to its fear of usurping the jury, and its fear of the floodgates opening if it allows too many cases into the appeal system. It also has insufficient resources to investigate the circumstances surrounding the case and is in a poor position to assess the integrity of forensic experts, the police and other key bodies. She also found that many claims of miscarriages of justice do not even reach the Court of Appeal. These cases tend to be those which are unassisted, with little support or publicity. Only 15% of unassisted applications were granted leave to appeal compared to 45% of those who had legal assistance. But once they reach the Court of Appeal the outcome is still uncertain. While the Court of Appeal is now more willing to grant appeals, the results may be unpredictable.

The time loss rules designed as a penalty to deter frivolous appeals, argues Malleson, may also deter complainants from pursuing a case even though the rules rarely are applied, a fact of which many lawyers seemed aware. Solicitors may advice against appeal for fear of time loss. When the time loss rules were introduced in 1970, applications for leave to appeal dropped from 12,000 to 6,000 and have never recovered. The Royal Commission on Criminal Justice recommended that clearer information should be provided on the time loss rules by a Practice Direction from the Court of Appeal and that the maximum loss be 90 days.[63]

Some may feel they have been wrongly convicted because of poor legal advice and representation, so it will be difficult to ask the lawyer concerned to ground an appeal based on his own inadequacies. In the past there have been problems grounding an appeal in police impropriety because of the reluctance of the Court of Appeal to acknowledge this possibility. In the Birmingham Six case, for example, a key reason for the delay in quashing the conviction was the inability of the courts to accept the claims of physical abuse of the appellants by the police. By the time the Court of Appeal delivered its final judgement in the case, however, it was critical of the police and the scientific evidence.

Owers[64] cites a case where two sets of papers on the same application were sent for a decision on leave twice to the same judge by mistake. In one case leave was refused, in the other it was granted by the same judge dealing with the same papers. She advocates use of specialist judges with proper training and that legal aid should be given even after a single judge has refused and that the process should be expedited.

Plotnikoff and Woolfson[65] examined the particular problems facing potential appellants while in custody. They note that the services provided by lawyers to their clients following conviction and sentence are extremely variable. There is considerable ignorance of the powers of the Court of Appeal and the responsibilities of legal advisers. Few lawyers provided the client with a record of counsel's view of whether an appeal should be launched. Some prisoners decided against appealing on the basis of inaccurate information supplied by their advisers. In the study 1/4 of prisoners reported that they received no appeals advice from their lawyers during the 28 days following conviction or sentence. Information and advice given to prisoners was uneven in quantity and quality and rarely given in writing. There were particular problems for clients who did not speak English. Plotnikoff and Woolfson recommend that convicted or sentenced defendants who are legally represented should have the right to a 15-minute meeting with their lawyers at the Crown Court following the end of the case, to discuss counsel's view of the prospects for an appeal.

The Runciman Commission recommended that prisoners should be given advice in writing on any grounds for appeal and advice on whether an application for leave to the full court should be renewed and that this should be covered by legal aid.[66] The Commission also recommended that more resources should be given to prison governors to provide interpreters for non-English speakers and to facilitate communication with lawyers. Prisoners should be granted legal aid for solicitors to draft grounds of appeal, if the solicitor and counsel disagree on whether there are grounds of appeal.

If leave to appeal is refused there is an automatic right to re-apply but renewed applications assisted by counsel are three times more likely to be granted than unrepresented applications. If the full court refuses leave, then in the past the only option was to petition the Home Secretary to refer the case to the Court of Appeal under s 17 of the Criminal Appeal Act 1968 which itself raised problems. While the rationale underpinning these obstacles was to stop the floodgates, the Court of Appeal in practice does not have enough resources to deal with the small proportion of cases which reach it, which means lengthy delays. It also means that it is happier dealing with cases which raise technical or procedural problems which it can resolve quickly, where it can review the trial judge's directions, rather than appeals which require investigation of pre-trial mistakes by the police or by lawyers.

In the past the Court of Appeal has been reluctant to grant an appeal on the basis of counsel's conduct unless there has been 'flagrantly incompetent advocacy'.[67] However, in *Clinton*[68] the Court of Appeal said it could set aside a verdict in exceptional cases where the defendant is poorly advised by counsel.

Under s 2(1) of the 1968 Criminal Appeal Act the Court of Appeal should allow an appeal against conviction if it thinks that the verdict of the jury should be set aside, on the ground that under all the circumstances of the case it is unsafe or unsatisfactory, or that the judgment of the trial court should be set aside on the ground of a wrong decision of any question of law; or that there was a material irregularity in the course of the trial. But even where the point raised by the appellant might be decided in his favour, the Court may dismiss his appeal if it considers that no miscarriage of justice has occurred. In practice in most cases the Appeal Court has referred to cases being unsafe and unsatisfactory. Malleson's research showed that the most common ground of appeal was an alleged misdirection by the judge in summing up.[69]

Section 23(2) provides that the Court should hear fresh evidence if it would have been admissible at trial under the normal rules of admissibility and there is a reasonable explanation why it was not adduced at trial, and it appears to the Court of Appeal that it likely to be credible. If these criteria are met and it is likely that the evidence would have influenced the result of the trial, then the Court should offer a retrial. If a retrial is impracticable or undesirable for example, because of lapse of time, then the Court of Appeal should determine the matter. The Criminal Justice Act 1988 amends s 7 of the Criminal Appeal Act 1968. Before the CJA amendment, the Court could order a retrial only on the basis of fresh evidence. Following the amendment, the Court has the discretion to order a retrial whenever the interests of justice so require. This would include procedural irregularities or misdirection by the trial judge. The number of retrials has increased since 1991.

The House of Lords in *Stafford and Luvaglio v DPP*[70] in 1974 ruled on the construction of s 23 of the Criminal Appeal Act and specifically the approach to fresh evidence: the Court of Appeal should consider its own appraisal of fresh evidence, rather than the likely reaction of the jury to the new evidence. Since then the Appeal Court has considered the weight of the evidence instead of the effect that it might have on the jury. This has been widely criticised by the Runciman Commission and others, as the Appeal Court became in effect a trier of fact and usurped the function of the jury but without hearing the oral testimony of witnesses, or reviewing all the evidence at the original trial. Successful appeals based on fresh evidence are rare. In Malleson's sample of 102 successful appeals in 1992, only 4 were granted on the grounds of fresh evidence.[71]

In the Guildford Four case, Armstrong, Conlon, Hill and Richardson were convicted of murder in 1976. Their appeal was rejected. The case was referred to the Court of Appeal by the Home Secretary in 1989 and the Court quashed the conviction in 1989.[72] The Director of Public Prosecutions said that he no longer wished to support the convictions. Tests showed that the police claim that interviews had been recorded contemporaneously could not be sustained.

In the Birmingham Six case the fresh evidence submitted was heard and rejected at the 1987 appeal, but did not persuade the Court of Appeal until 1991. The Six were originally convicted for murder in 1975. Their first appeal was dismissed. The case was then referred back to the Court of Appeal in 1987 by the Home Secretary in the light of fresh scientific evidence and fresh evidence of maltreatment by the police following arrest. This appeal was also dismissed. Then the case was referred once again to the Court of Appeal by the Home Secretary in 1990 and heard in 1991 when their conviction was finally quashed.[73] The claim of maltreatment and of the falsity of the confessions had been made repeatedly from the outset but without success. Eventually the Court of Appeal was persuaded by the results of an ESDA test which showed that some of the notes of an 'interview' were not made contemporaneously and by the discovery that the Forensic Science Service had failed to disclose a possible innocent reason for what appeared to be traces of explosives on the defendants. In its judgement the Court criticised the police and the scientific evidence.

A substantial protection could be afforded to appellants if a statutory right to a retrial is granted, when the court considers the evidence so important that it would have had a significant effect on the jury. Alternatively, an independent body could be established to review difficult cases, to conduct an investigation into the evidence on which the conviction was based, rather than relying on the police to conduct that investigation. It could be empowered to refer cases back to the Court of Appeal, or to order a retrial. Legal aid could also be extended for the individual who wishes to challenge a wrongful conviction. While these measures would strengthen the chances of remedying a miscarriage of justice retrospectively, clearly the prime goal must be to prevent a miscarriage occurring in the first place, by strengthening the position of the suspect in interrogation.

The Royal Commission on Criminal Justice argued that the different grounds of appeal were confusing. The majority of the Commission recommended redrafting s 2 of the Criminal Appeal Act so that there is one ground of appeal, namely whether a conviction is or may be unsafe.[74] If it is unsafe, the conviction should be quashed. If it may be unsafe, the conviction should be quashed and a retrial should be ordered unless there are reasons which would make a retrial unsafe or impracticable. A minority favoured an additional ground of appeal, covering material errors of law or procedure at the trial.

The Commission also favoured a new approach to fresh evidence cases. The Court of Appeal has construed its powers in s 23 too narrowly and the Commission advocated that the Court should take a broader approach to the question of whether the evidence was available at trial and if it was, whether there is a reasonable explanation for the failure to adduce it then, or for any subsequent departure by a witness from the evidence given at the original trial.[75] The demand that evidence is likely to be credible, it argued, constituted too high a test. Instead the fresh evidence should be 'capable of belief'.[76] The Commission also argued that the Court of Appeal should recognise that juries may be in error or guided by emotion or misjudge the weight of certain forms of evidence and should be more willing to replace the jury's judgement with its own.[77] If there is no fresh evidence but the court, after reviewing the case, is satisfied that the verdict is or may be unsafe, the Court of Appeal should quash the conviction, notwithstanding that the jury reached their verdict having heard all the relevant evidence and without any error of law or material irregularity having occurred.[78]

The Criminal Appeal Act 1995 follows the recommendations of the Royal Commission and the Home Office Discussion Paper. It amends the grounds of appeal in the 1968 Act and abolishes the proviso to s 2(1).

Section 1 of the new Act requires leave to appeal on question of law alone unless the trial judge has certified that the case is fit for appeal. Section 2 of the 1968 Act is repealed and replaced as follows:

> Subject to the provisions of this Act, the Court of Appeal -
> (a)   shall allow an appeal against conviction if they think the conviction is unsafe; and
> (b)   shall dismiss an appeal in any other case.

The new Act does not include 'may be unsafe' as this was thought to be too confusing. The Court may still order a retrial where the interests of justice so require.

How it will work in practice is unclear but during the Parliamentary debates reference was made to the Act reflecting the recent practice of the Court of Appeal. It may be that the old construction will be used and it may be interpreted very narrowly.[79] Some argue that a separate ground of material irregularity should have been included as well. The Act has been criticised for failing to achieve the goals of the Royal Commission.

But the requirement for fresh evidence follows the RCCJ recommendation. The requirement in s 23 that the Court should exercise their power to receive fresh evidence if 'it appears to them that the evidence is likely to be credible' is replaced by a new requirement that the evidence is 'capable of belief.' The Act fails to deal with criticism of *Stafford and Luvaglio v DPP*.[80]

The Commission also proposed shifting the Home Secretary's powers under s 17 of the Criminal Appeal Act 1968 to refer a case back to the Court of Appeal to the Criminal Cases Review Authority[81] as these powers were rarely used and this proposal is implemented in the 1995 Criminal Appeal Act. In the period from 1981-1988 only 36 cases were referred to the Court by the Home Secretary and usually only if there was new evidence. So very few cases considered by C3 division of the Home Office were selected for referral. The cases which were referred tended to be those where fresh evidence had been discovered since the appeal. The Division was understaffed relative to the number of applications received. In the past applicants received very little information on why their cases were rejected or details of the statements taken during re-investigation.

In *Hickey*[82] the Divisonal Court decided that all applicants petitioning the Home Secretary to refer their convictions to the Court of Appeal, should be given reasons for the rejection and full disclosure of any new evidence or information that has come to light in re-investigations ordered by the Home Secretary in order to reach a decision. The court also considered the basis on which the Home Secretary should exercise his power to refer cases to appeal. The test should be wider than the one used in the past by the Home Secretary. He should ask himself could the new material reasonably cause the Court of Appeal to regard the verdict as unsafe? If the answer is yes, he should refer it to the Court of Appeal. The Divisonal Court emphasised the importance of openness in decision-making. Re-investigation material should normally be disclosed to the applicant before a decision is made on referral. This would give the applicant access to Home Office experts' reports, the statements of key witnesses and the basis of their evidence. Prior to *Hickey* the applicant might receive a one-page letter, in response to a large dossier of evidence, without the opportunity to challenge the facts behind the refusal.

In the past Home Secretaries have been reluctant to suggest to the Court of Appeal that the courts should have reached a different decision on the same set of facts. The Runciman Commission was critical of the Home Secretary's role and endorsed the view of the May Inquiry that 'the role assigned to the Home Secretary and his Department under the existing legislation is incompatible with

the constitutional separation of powers as between the courts and the executive...
it is neither necessary nor desirable that the Home Secretary should be directly
responsible for the consideration and investigation of alleged miscarriages of
justice as well as being responsible for law and order and for the police.'[83] The
Home Secretary's power to refer cases under s 17 should be reviewed, concluded
the Commission and a new body established, which would consider alleged
miscarriages of justice, supervise their investigation if further inquiries are
necessary and refer appropriate cases to the Court of Appeal.

Critics have argued that the Commission's recommendations do not provide
enough to strengthen the role of the Court of Appeal in ensuring compliance with
procedural rules[84] and do not address the errors which occurred in the major
miscarriages of justice. However, the Commission did propose the establishment
of a Criminal Cases Review Authority.

The Criminal Cases Review Commission

Most critics have agreed that a new review body or new powers are needed but
have differed on the precise form it should take. But it does need to be impartial
and independent with its own investigative staff and to be fully resourced. Some
critics favour a special tribunal or independent review body to deal with
miscarriages of justice, consisting of a broader range of personnel than judges.
Others favour changing and improving the powers of the Court of Appeal,
perhaps with expert assistance to give a full report on the case in question. The
May Report was critical of the Court of Appeal's tardiness in dealing with the
case of the Maguires and noted that neither the Court of Appeal, nor the Home
Office, had the power or expertise needed to investigate alleged miscarriages of
justice.[85] A new independent body was needed to deal with such cases.

The Royal Commission argued that the new body should be independent of
Government and the courts, comprised of lawyers and laypersons to deal with
allegations of miscarriages of justice. The applicant would approach the Authority
after his conviction is upheld by the Court of Appeal or if he fails to obtain leave
to appeal. It would supervise the investigation of the allegation and have the
power to require the police to follow up relevant lines of inquiry. If its
investigations suggest that there are grounds for thinking that a miscarriage of
justice has occurred, it would then refer it to the Court of Appeal, giving reasons
for referral. If the Authority thought there were no grounds to support such a
referral, it would then give its reasons to the applicant, who would have the right
to reapply. It would keep the applicant and prosecution properly informed during
the course of the investigation. The Court of Appeal would also have the power
to refer cases to the Authority for investigation, but the Authority itself would lie
outside the court structure. It would need to be properly resourced and would
report to the Home Secretary and through the Minister to Parliament. It should

be able to conduct interviews with prisoners and to commission expert advice, for example, on scientific evidence.

The only power remaining to the Home Secretary would be the ministerial responsibility for the exercise of the Royal Prerogative of Mercy but under a new regime it would seldom be necessary to use this. In *Bentley*[86] the Divisional Court affirmed that the court can review the exercise of this prerogative.

The Criminal Appeal Act 1995 sets out the powers and structure of the Criminal Cases Review Commission. It follows many of the recommendations of the Royal Commission on Criminal Justice. The new body takes over the Home Secretary's role in investigating alleged miscarriages of justice and in referring cases to the Court of Appeal. The members will be appointed by the Queen on the Prime Minister's advice. The body includes lawyers and non-lawyers. One third will be legally qualified, two thirds will have knowledge or experience of the criminal justice system. The appointments will be for a fixed term up to five years and renewable for a further five years. It is expected to receive more resources and a support staff to cope with an increased work load.

The body will not have its own investigating officers but will use police officers. Under s 19(1) the Commission may require an appropriate person from the original investigation, normally the Chief Constable, to appoint an investigating officer to carry out inquiries and to report to the Commission. The Commission can ask him to use an officer from from another force instead of his own. The Commission can veto the appointment but cannot specify what rank or force he should come from. It will not supervise the investigation but will direct it. The lack of day to day supervision has met with criticism. The fact that the police will carry out the investigations, and the investigating officer will be chosen by the Chief Constable of the police force where the alleged miscarriage of justice actually occurred, fails to address the fundamental problems which generated miscarriages. A fully independent body is seen by many as a precondition for success of the new body. However the Commission has a general power to undertake inquiries itself so it is possible that it may do so in exceptional cases.

The Commission takes over the Home Secretary's power under s 17 of the 1968 Act, so it may refer cases in relation to conviction or sentence. The criterion for referral will be: (i) whether there is a real possibility that the conviction would not be upheld by the Court if it were referred; (ii) this must be because of evidence or arguments not raised at trial or on appeal, and (iii) the appeal has been heard or leave to appeal refused. In exceptional cases it may consider referring a case even if the second and third conditions are not met.

The Act does not allocate a specific budget for the Commission's inquiries. It is also entitled to consider matters relating to sentencing which may well consume a large portion of its time and resources and weaken its effectiveness in dealing with miscarriages of justice. No additional provision is made for legal aid for persons whose cases are investigated by the Commission. The Commission can demand disclosure of documentary evidence from any public body, even regarding matters which are protected by secrecy or confidentiality. But it does not apply to government bodies already dealing with cases. Witnesses cannot be obliged to give evidence. The Commission is required to give its reasons to the applicant if it decides not to refer a case, following the decision in *Hickey*.[87] However it is not required to disclose all the information acquired during the investigation to the applicant.

While the new body is an improvement on the old regime in terms of resources and independence, problems remain. The Act does not deal with the problems of legal aid for those who have lost appeals, which may limit the effectiveness of the new system. The Act does not address the problems with the time loss rule or the need for appropriate training for judges hearing appeals and allegations of miscarriages of justice. The Commission lacks a proactive role identifying areas of the criminal justice system which require improvement and reform.

Malleson argues[88] that the Court of Appeal will play a crucial role in influencing the Commission's approach to referral. The Commission, she says, will 'improve the investigation of cases with strong fresh evidence but may fail to investigate or refer back cases which are based on the sole ground that the original evidence at trial was weak and the jury verdict was wrong'.[89] In the latter cases the Commission may think they are unlikely to succeed and not refer them. It will have greater resources and better staffing to ensure that allegations are properly investigated in the fresh evidence cases. The Commission is likely to learn quickly which cases succeed in the Court of Appeal and adjust its referral choices to meet this, so in practice it is likely to focus on fresh evidence cases instead of those which generate a lurking doubt about the safety of the conviction. So the Commission will approach the problem from the Court of Appeal's perspective and in deciding whether to refer, it will be influenced by the likely approach of the Court of Appeal. It is also unclear what criteria the Commission will use in deciding whether to initiate an investigation.

Conclusion

In the light of the above problems, there are a number of improvements which could be made. JUSTICE has proposed improvements in training to identify psychological attributes which may lead to false confessions as well as the establishment of the office of a Public Defender to assist defendants and defence lawyers and obtain information, with access to experts and forensic laboratories. A public defence service could also assist with appeals.

The costs in new measures preventing miscarriages of justice need to be set against the financial costs of compensating those wrongfully convicted and the human costs of their suffering and that of their families. Guiseppe Conlon died in prison before he could be cleared or his appeal heard. But while most attention has been paid to the appeals process the defects which led to miscarriages of justice occurred at an earlier stage of the criminal process, so attention needs to be focused on the pre-trial and trial stages as well as the appeal stage.

Confessions should not be admitted unless they are made in the presence of a solicitor, taped or their truth corroborated by independent evidence of other witnesses, although a video or audio recording will not of itself protect against false confessions where they are not coerced. The role of the appropriate adult could be improved with better training and provision.[90] There should be more legal aid to enable the defence to obtain independent scientific evidence. Terrorist suspects should be given the same rights as ordinary suspects. The appeal system needs to be improved in the ways identified above. Better means of rectifying miscarriages need to be established. Cases should not be excluded from investigation because there is no fresh information.

The protection of the accused should be boosted by access to an independent forensic service and an independent miscarriage of justice commission. Improvements in police disciplinary and complaints procedures would also contribute to strengthening the fight against wrongful convictions. Where they do occur, there should be proper and speedy compensation.

A crucial protection for the accused, the right to silence, has been lost. If the right to silence were to be restored ways of making it more effective could be considered, including the formulation of clearer guidelines on the limits of judicial comment, to strengthen the warning, to remind the jury of the danger of attaching evidential significance to silence and of the defendant's right to silence. The prohibition on comment by the prosecution should also be restored.

An effective right to silence, supported by proper provision for access to advice, should be seen as an essential feature of the criminal justice system, rather than being perceived simply as an obstacle to police efficiency or as an outdated relic of the past. A more positive approach would be to ensure that the right to silence is articulated in practice and restored to its proper place at the heart of the adversarial system. This would give more weight to the protective principle and to the right to a fair trial guaranteed by the European Convention on Human Rights.

Notes

1. See B. Woffinden (1990) *Miscarriages of Justice*, London, Coronet.
2. See *R v Silcott, Braithwaite and Raghip* [1991] Times, 9 December.
3. See chapter 4 above.
4. See *R v Ahluwalia* (1993) 96 Cr App Rep 133, *R v Humphreys*, [1995] NLJ 1032.
5. *R v Ward* (1993) 96 Cr App Rep 1.

6. See *R v Keane* [1994] 2 All ER 478, *R v Johnson, Davis and Rowe* [1993] Crim LR 689 and chapter 2 above.

7. *R v Kiszko* [1992] Times 18 February, 19 February.

8. *R v Maguire et al* (1992) 94 Cr App Rep 133.

9. *Ibid.*

10. [1993] Times, 1 June.

11. See chapter 2 above.

12. JUSTICE (1989) *Miscarriages of Justice*, London.

13. S.E. Asch (1951) 'Effects of group pressure upon the modification and distortion of judgements', in H. Guetzkow (ed.) *Groups, Leadership and Men*, Rutgers University Press; (1956) 'Studies of independence and conformity: a minority of one against a unanimous majority', Psychological Monographs, 70, 9.

14. G. Gudjonsson and J. MacKeith (1989) 'Retracted confessions', Medicine, Science and the Law, 28, 187; see also G. Gudjonsson (1992) *The Psychology of Interrogations, Confessions and Testimony*, Chichester, John Wiley

15. I. Clare and G. Gudjonsson (1993) 'Interrogative suggestibility, confabulation, and acquiescence in people with mild learning difficulties (mental handicap): implications for reliability during police interrogation', British Journal of Clinical Psychology, 32, pp 295-301.

16. M. McConville et al (1991) *The Case for the Prosecution*, London, Routledge, p 68.

17. See *R v Silcott, Braithwaite and Raghip* [1991] Times, 9 December.

18. A.Owers (1995) *Putting Wrongs to Right*, London, BIRW, pp 4-15 at p 6.

19. See Report of an Inquiry by the Hon. Sir Henry Fisher into the circumstances leading to the trial of three persons on charges arising out of the death of Maxwell Confait and the fire at 27 Doggett Road, London S.E.6. (1977) London HMSO, para. 2.26; C. Price, C. and J. Caplan (1977) *The Confait Confessions*, London, Marion Boyars.

20. G. Gudjonsson (1994) 'Psychological vulnerability: suspects at risk' in D. Morgan and G.Stephenson (eds.) *Suspicion and Silence*, London, Blackstone, pp 91-106, at p 94.

21. PACE s 37(15).

22. Notes for Guidance 11B.

23. M. Maguire (1988) 'The effects of the PACE Provisions on Detention and Questioning,' British Journal of Criminology, 19.

24. D. Brown, T. Ellis and R. Larcombe (1992) *Changing the Code: Police Detention under the Revised Codes of Practice*, Home Office Research Study, no.7, London, HMSO.

25. R. Evans (1993) *The Conduct of Police Interviews with Juveniles*, RCCJ Research Study no. 8, London, HMSO.

26. Essex Social Services Department Report (1987) Social Information Systems, Manchester.
27. *Ibid.*
28. Revised Code C 11.16.
29. See *R v Glaves* [1993] Crim LR 685.
30. (1994) Speech, JUSTICE Annual Conference.
31. *R v Argent* [1996] Times 19 December; see chapter 1 above.
32. Report of the Royal Commission on Criminal Justice (1993), para. 4.40, London, HMSO, Cmnd 2263.
33. Code C 1.4, Note 1G.
34. RCCJ Report, para. 3.84.
35. [1995] Times, 26 January.
36. [1991] Crim LR 195.
37. [1991] Crim LR 124.
38. (1992) 96 Cr App Rep 98.
39. [1994] Times, 13 July.
40. G. Gudjonsson, I. Clare, S. Rutter and J. Pearse (1993) *Persons at risk during Interviews in Police Custody: the Identification of Vulnerabilities*, RCCJ Research Study, no 12, London, HMSO.
41. D. Brown (1989) *Detention at the police station under the Police and Criminal Evidence Act 1984*, Home Office Research Study, London HMSO.
42. [1990] NLJ 665.
43. [1989] Crim LR 813.
44. [1993] Times, 27 July.
45. See also *R v Campbell* [1995] Crim LR 157.
46. RCCJ Report, para. 3.86.
47. (June 1995) Home Office Review Group Report, London, HMSO.
48. Sir Henry Fisher (1977) *op.cit.*, para. 2.26.
49. Legal Action Group, Submission to the Royal Commission on Criminal Justice.
50. RCCJ Report, para. 4.87.
51. A. Zuckerman (1994) 'Bias and Suggestibility: Is there an alternative to the right to silence?', in D. Morgan and G Stephenson (eds.) *op.cit.*, pp 117-140.
52. *Ibid*, p 122
53. *Ibid*, pp 126-7.
54 *Ibid*, pp 132-3
55. [1977] QB 224; [1976] 3 All ER 549.
56. [1916] 2 KB 658.
57. at 667.
58. M. McConville (1993) *Corroboration and Confession: the impact of a rule requiring that no conviction can be sustained on the basis of*

287

confession evidence alone, RCCJ Research Study no. 13, London, HMSO.

59.   *Ibid*, p 87.

60.   See M. Maguire and C. Norris (1993) *The Conduct and Supervision of Criminal Investigations*, RCCJ Research Study no.5, London, HMSO.

61.   See A. Grosskurth (October 1991) 'Scotland's pitfalls', Legal Action, 7.

62.   K. Malleson (1993) *Review of the Appeal Process*, RCCJ Research Study no. 17, London, HMSO.

63.   RCCJ, Report, paras. 10.19, 10.26.

64.   A.Owers, *op.cit.*

65.   J. Plotnikoff and R. Woolfson, (1993) *Information and advice for prisoners about grounds for appeal and the appeal process*, RCCJ Research Study no. 18, London, HMSO, at p 115.

66.   RCCJ Report, paras. 10.4, 10.17. 10.24.

67.   See *R v Ensor* [1989] 1 WLR 497.

68.   [1993] Crim LR 582.

69.   K. Malleson, *op.cit.*

70.   (1968) 53 Cr App Rep 1. In the Republic of Ireland the courts have rejected the subjective test of *Stafford and Luvaglio v DPP* in favour of an objective test in interpreting the Criminal Procedure Act 1993; see also Greg O'Neill, *Putting Wrongs to Right*, London, BIRW 1995, p 24-33.

71.   K. Malleson, *op.cit.*

72.   *R v Armstrong, Conlon, Hill and Richardson* (1989) Times, 20 October.

73.   *R v McIlkenny et al* (1991) 93 Cr App Rep 287.

74.   RCCJ Report, para. 10.32.

75.   *Ibid*, paras. 10.55,10.56.

76.   *Ibid*, para. 10.60.

77.   *Ibid*, para. 10.63.

78.   *Ibid*, para. 10.46.

79.   See R. Munday [1995] 'The Criminal Appeal Act 1995: (1) Appeals against Conviction', Crim LR 920.

80.   [1968] 53 Cr App Rep 1.

81.   RCCJ Report, para.11.11.

82.   *R v Secretary of State for the Home Department ex parte Hickey and others*, [1994] Times, 2 December.

83.   RCCJ Report, paras. 11.9, 11.10.

84.   See LAG (1993) *Preventing Miscarriages of Justice*, London.

85.   (1990) *Interim Report on the Maguire Case*, London, HMSO, HC 556; (1992) *Second Report on the Maguire Case*, London, HMSO, HC 296.

86.   *R v Home Secretary ex parte Bentley* [1993] Times 8 July.

87.   [1994] Times 2 December.

88.   K. Malleson [1995] 'The Criminal Cases Review Commission: How Will It Work?', Crim LR 929.

89.   *Ibid*, p 929.

90.   See R. Littlechild [1995] 'Reassessing the Role of the "Appropriate Adult"', Crim LR 540; J. M. Laing [1995] 'The Mentally Disordered Suspect at the Police Station', Crim LR 371.

Bibliography

Alldridge, P. [1992] 'Novel scientific techniques: DNA as a test case', Crim LR 687.

Amar, A.R. and Lettow, R.B. (March 1995) 'Fifth Amendment First Principles: The Self-Incrimination Clause', Michigan Law Rev, 93, 5, pp 857-928.

Asch, S.E. (1951) 'Effects of group pressure upon the modification and distortion of judgements', in H. Guetzkow, (ed.) *Groups, Leadership and Men*, Rutgers University Press;

___(1956) 'Studies of independence and conformity: a minority of one against a unanimous majority', Psychological Monographs, 70, 9.

Ashworth, A.J. [1977] 'Excluding Evidence as Protecting Rights', Crim LR 723.

___(1994) *The Criminal Process: an evaluative study*, Oxford University Press.

Ashworth, A.J. and Blake, M. [1996] 'The presumption of innocence in English Criminal Law', Crim LR 306.

Association of Chief Police Officers (1993) The Right of Silence, London.

___(1995) In Search of Criminal Justice, London.

Attwooll, E. and Goldberg, D. (eds.) (1995) *Criminal Justice*, Stuttgart, Steiner.

Baker Report (1984) Review of the Operation of the Northern Ireland (Emergency Provisions) Act 1978, London, HMSO, Cmnd 9222.

Balding, D.J. and Donnelly, P. [1994] 'The Prosecutor's Fallacy and DNA Evidence', Crim LR 711

Baldwin, J. (1992) Video-taping police interviews with suspects - an evaluation, Police Research Series Paper 1, Police Research Group Publications, London, Home Office.

___(1992) *The Role of Legal Representatives at the Police Station*, RCCJ Research Study no. 3, London, HMSO.

___(1992) Preparing the Record of Taped Interview, RCCJ Research Study no. 2, London, HMSO.

Baldwin, J. and McConville, M. (1980) *Confessions in Crown Court Trials*, RCCP Research Study no. 5, London, HMSO.

___(1981) *Courts, Prosecution and Conviction*, Oxford, Clarendon Press.

Baldwin, J. and Moloney, T. (1992) *Supervision of Police Investigations in Serious Criminal Cases*, RCCJ Research Study no. 4, London, HMSO

Barra McGrory, P.J. (1994) 'Solicitor's advice to the accused in the light of the Criminal Justice and Public Order Act 1994', London.

Bentham, J. (1825) *A Treatise on Judicial Evidence*, (ed.) E.Dumont, London.

___(1843) *Rationale of Judicial Evidence*, The Works of Jeremy Bentham, Bowring edition, Edinburgh, William Tait.

___(1987) 'Anarchical Fallacies', reprinted in J. Waldron (ed.) *Nonsense Upon Stilts, Bentham, Burke and Marx on the Rights of Man*, London, Methuen.

Block, B., Corbett, C. and Peay, J. (1993) *Ordered and Directed Acquittals in the Crown Court*, RCCJ Research Study no.15, London, HMSO.

___(1993) 'Ordered and directed acquittals in the Crown Court: A Time of Change, Crim LR 95.

Blom-Cooper, L. (1993) Report of the Independent Commissioner for the Holding Centres in Northern Ireland, London, HMSO.

Box, S. (1971) *Deviance, Reality and Society*, Holt, Rinehart and Winston.

Bridges, L. and Hodgson, J. [1995] 'Improving custodial legal advice', Crim LR 101.

Brown, D. (1989) *Detention at the Police Station under the Police and Criminal Evidence Act 1984*, Home Office Research Study, no. 104, HMSO.

Brown, D., Ellis, T. and Larcombe, K. (1992) *Changing the Code: Police Detention under the Revised PACE Codes of Practice*, Home Office Research Study, no. 129, HMSO.

Cape, E. [April, 1995] 'The right to silence: defending at the police station under the new regime', Legal Action, 12-14.

Churchland, P.M. (1979) *Scientific Realism and the Plasticity of Mind*, Cambridge, University Press.

___(1984) *Matter and Consciousness: A Contemporary Introduction to the Philosophy of Mind*, MIT Press.

Clare, I. and Gudjonsson, G. (1993) *Devising and Piloting an Experimental Version of the Notice to Detained Persons*, RCCJ Research Study no.7, London, HMSO.

Colville of Culross Q.C. (1987) Review of the Operation of the Prevention of Terrorism (Temporary Provisions) Act 1984, London, HMSO, Cmnd 264. Criminal Bar Association (1988) Comment of the Criminal Bar Association on the Consultation Paper.

Criminal Law Revision Committee (1972) *Eleventh Report, Evidence (General)* London, HMSO, Cmnd 4991.

Cross, A.R.N. (1970-1971) 'The Right to Silence and the Presumption of Innocence, Sacred Cow or Safeguard of Liberty', Journal of the Society of Public Teachers of Law.

___[1973] 'The Evidence Report: Sense or Nonsense - A Very Wicked Animal Defends the Eleventh Report of the Criminal Law Revision Committee', Crim LR 329.

Dennis, I. (1989) 'Reconstructing the Law of Criminal Evidence', Current Legal Problems, 21.

___(1993) 'Miscarriages of Justice and the Law of Confessions: Evidentiary Issues and Solutions', Public Law, 291.

___[1995] 'The Criminal Justice and Public Order Act 1994: The Evidence Provisions', Crim LR 4.

___(1995) 'Instrumental Protection, Human Right or Functional Necessity? Reassessing the Privilege against Self-Incrimination', Camb LJ 54(2) 342.

Descartes, R. (1911) *Meditations and Passions of the Soul*, in E.S. Haldane and G.R.T. Ross (eds.) *The Philosophical Works of Descartes*, Cambridge University Press.

Devlin, P. (1986) *Easing the Passing*, London, Bodley Head.

Dickson, B. (1989) 'The Prevention of Terrorism Act, 1989', NILQ, 40, 250.

Diplock Commission (1972) Report of a Committee to Consider Legal Procedures to Deal with Terrorist Activities in Northern Ireland, London, HMSO, Cmnd 5185.

Dworkin, R. (1977) *Taking Rights Seriously*, London, Duckworth.

___[November 8, 1984] 'Reagan's Justice', New York Review of Books.

___(1986) *Law's Empire*, Cambridge, Mass., Harvard University Press.

___(1993) *Life's Dominion*, London, Harper Collins.

___(1996) *Freedom's Law*, Oxford University Press.

Easton, S.M. (1991) 'The Evidential and Methodological Problems of Genetic Fingerprinting', Explorations in Knowledge, XVIII 1, 39.

___[1991] 'Bodily Samples and the Privilege against Self-Incrimination', Crim LR 18.

Ehrman, H. (1970) *The Case That Will Not Die*, London, W.H.Allen.

Essex Social Services Department (1987) Report on the PACE Appropriate Adult Requirement, 1986-1987, Manchester, Social Information Systems.

Evans, R. (1993) *The Conduct of Police Interviews with Juveniles*, RCCJ Research Study no.8, London, HMSO.

Fairweather, F. and Levenson, H. (November 1990) 'The new PACE Codes of Practice,' Legal Action, 21.

Feldman, D. [1990] 'Regulating Treatment of Suspects in Police Stations: Judicial Interpretation of Detention Provisions in the Police and Criminal Evidence Act 1984', Crim LR 452.

Fenwick, H. [1995] 'Curtailing the Right to Silence. Access to Legal Advice and Section 78', Crim LR 132.

Feyerabend, P.K. (1974) *Against Method*, London, New Left Books.

___(1979) *Science in a Free Society*, London, New Left Books.

Fisher, H. (1977) Report of an Inquiry by the Hon. Sir Henry Fisher into the circumstances leading to the trial of three persons on charges arising out of the death of Maxwell Confait and the fire at 27 Doggett Road, London S.E.6, London, HMSO.

Friendly, H. (1968) 'The Fifth Amendment Tomorrow: the case for constitutional change', University of Cincinatti Law Review, 37, 676.

Galligan, D. (1988) 'The Right to Silence Reconsidered', Current Legal Problems, 69.

Gardiner Report (1975) Report of a Committee to Consider, in the Context of Civil Liberties and Human Rights, Measures to deal with Terrorism in Northern Ireland, HMSO, Cmnd 5847.

Gearty, C. and Kimbell, J. (1995) *Terrorism and the Rule of Law*, London, King's College.

General Council of the Bar of England and Wales (1973) Evidence in Criminal Cases, Memorandum on the Eleventh Report of the CLRC Evidence (General).

___(1992) Working Party Report, The Efficient Disposal of Business in the Crown Court.

Gifford, T. (1984) *Supergrasses: the Use of Accomplice Evidence in Northern Ireland*, London, Cobden Trust.

Greenawalt, K. (1974) 'Perspectives on the Right of Silence', in Hood, R. (ed.) *Crime, Criminology and Public Policy*, London, Heinemann, 235.

Greer, S. (1986) 'Supergrasses and the Legal System in Britain and Northern Ireland', LQR 198.

___[1987] 'The rise and fall of the Northern Ireland Supergrass System', Crim LR 663.

___(1995) *Supergrasses: A Study in Anti-Terrorist Law Enforcement in Northern Ireland*, Oxford, Clarendon Press.

Greer, S. and Morgan, R. (eds.) (1990) *The Right to Silence Debate*, Bristol Centre for Criminal Justice.

Greer, S. and White, A. (1986) *Abolishing the Diplock Courts*, London, The Cobden Trust.

Griffiths, J. and Ayres, R. (1967) 'A Postscript to the Miranda Project: Interrogation of Draft Protestors', 77 Yale Law Journal, 305.

Gross, A. C. (1990) *The Rhetoric of Science*, Harvard University Press.

Grosskurth, A. (October 1991) 'Scotland's pitfalls', Legal Action, 7.

___(May 1992) 'With Science on their Side' Legal Action, 7.

___(March, 1994) 'Serious fraud: a dangerous precedent', Legal Action, 6.

Gudjonsson, G. (1989) 'Retracted confessions', Medicine, Science and the Law, 28, 187.

___(28 November 1991) 'Understanding the Notice to Detained Persons', Law Soc Gaz.

___(1991) 'The "Notice to Detained Persons": How Easy is it to Understand?', Law Soc Gaz 87, pp 24-7.

___(1991) 'The "Notice to Detained Persons", PACE Codes and Reading Ease', Applied Cognitive Psychology, 5, pp 89-95.

___(1992) *The Psychology of Interrogations, Confessions and Testimony*, Chichester, John Wiley.

___(1994) 'Psychological vulnerability: suspects at risk' in D. Morgan, and G. Stephenson (eds.) *Suspicion and Silence*, London, Blackstone, pp 91-106.

Gudjonsson, G., Clare, I. and Cross, P. (1992) 'The revised PACE "Notice to Detained Persons": How Easy is it to Understand?', Journal of the Forensic Science Society, 32, pp 289-99.

Gudjonsson, G., Clare, I. Rutter, S. and Pearse, J. (1993) *Persons at Risk During Interviews in Police Custody: the Identification of Vulnerabilities*, RCCJ Research Study no. 12, London, HMSO.

Gudjonsson, J. and MacKeith, J.A.C. (1982) 'False Confessions: Psychological Effects of Interrogation - A Discussion Paper', in A.Trankell (ed.) *Reconstructing the Past, The Role of Psychologists in Criminal Trials*, Stockholm, Norstedt.

Guest, S. (1985) 'The Scope of the Hearsay Rule', LQR 10, 385.

Hadfield, B. (1990) 'Direct Rule, Delegated Legislation and the Role of Parliament', in J. Hayes and P. O'Higgins (eds.) *Lessons from Northern Ireland*, Belfast, SLS Publications.

Haldane Society (1992) *Upholding the Law? Northern Ireland: Criminal Justice under the Emergency Powers in the 1990s*, London.

Hall, P. (1988) 'The Prevention of Terrorism Acts', in A.Jennings (ed.) *Justice under Fire, The Abuse of Civil Liberties in Northern Ireland*, London, Pluto.

Hepworth, M. and Turner, B. (1982) *Confession*, Routledge.

Hill, C. (1974) *Change and Continuity in Seventeenth Century England*, London, Weidenfeld and Nicolson.

Hogan, G.and Walker, C. (1989) *Political Violence and the Law in Ireland*, Manchester University Press.

Home Office Circulars (1995) 16/95; (1993) 7/93; (1992) 22/1992.

Home Office (1995) A Consultation Document on Disclosure, London, HMSO, Cmnd 2864.

Hor, M. [1993] 'The privilege against self-incrimination and fairness', Singapore Journal of Legal Studies, 35.

___[1995] 'The presumption of innocence; a constitutional discourse for Singapore' Singapore Journal of Legal Studies, 365.

Hurd, Douglas (30 July, 1987) Lecture, Police Foundation.

___(25th October, 1988) Speech, Bow Group.

Inbau, F. and Reid, J. (1962) *Criminal Interrogations and Confessions*, Baltimore.

Irving, B. (1980) *Police Interrogation,the Effects of the Police and Criminal Evidence Act 1984, A Case Study of Current Practice*, London, Police Foundation.

Irving, B. and Hilgendorf, L. (1980) *Police Interrogation: the Psychological Approach*, RCCP Research Study no.2., London, HMSO.

Jackson, J. (1988) 'The Northern Ireland (Emergency Provisions) Act 1987', NILQ, 39, 235.

___[1989] 'Recent developments in criminal evidence', NILQ 105.

___[1990] 'Recent development in Northern Ireland', in S. Greer, and R. Morgan (eds.) *The Right to Silence Debate*, Bristol Centre for Criminal Justice.

___[1991] 'Curtailing the Right of Silence: Lessons from Northern Ireland', Crim LR 404.

___[1995] 'The value of jury trial', in E. Attwooll and D. Goldberg (eds.) *Criminal Justice*, Stuttgart, Franz Steiner, 79.

___[1995] *Putting Wrongs to Right*, London, British Irish Rights Watch

Jackson, J.D. and Doran, S. (1990) 'Judicial Fact-Finding in the Diplock Court in Northern Ireland', University of Manchester.

___(1992) 'Miscarriages of justice: the role of the Court of Appeal', SACHR Seventeenth Report, 267, London, HMSO.

___(1995) *Judge Without Jury: Diplock Trials in the Adversary System*, Oxford University Press.

___[1995] 'Interpreting the Silence Provisions: the Northern Ireland Cases', Crim LR 587.

Jeffreys, A.J., Wilson, V. and Thein, S.L. (1985) 'Hypervariable "Mini-satellite" Regions in Human DNA', Nature, 314, 66.

___(1985) 'Individual Specific "Fingerprints" of Human DNA', Nature, 616, 76.

Joyce, M. (July 21, 1990) 'High Profile: DNA in Court Again', New Scientist.

Justice (1967) *The Interrogation of Suspects*, London, Stevens.

___(1989) *Miscarriages of Justice*, London.

___(1994) *The Right of Silence Debate - the Northern Ireland Experience*, London.

Kassin, S.M. and Wrightsman, L.S. (1985) 'Confession evidence', in S. Kassin and L.S. Wrightsman (eds.) *The Psychology of Evidence and Trial Procedure*, Sage.

Laing, J.M. [1995] 'The Mentally Disordered Suspect at the Police Station', Crim LR 371.

Law Commission (1990) *Corroboration of Evidence in Criminal Trials*, Working Paper No. 115.

___(1991) *Corroboration of Evidence in Criminal Trials*, no. 202, London HMSO.

___(1995) *Evidence in Criminal Proceedings: Hearsay and Related Topics*, no. 138, London, HMSO.

Law Society (1988) Submission to the Home Office Working Group on the Right to Silence.

___(October, 1994) 'Changes in the Law Relating to Silence: Advice to Practicioners from the Criminal Law Committee of the Law Society', Criminal Practicioners Newsletter.

Legal Action Group (November, 1988) Response of the Legal Action Group to the Home Office Working Group on the Right to Silence Consultation Paper, London.

___(January 1990) Report of the Working Group on the Right to Silence, Response of the Legal Action Group.

___(1993) *Preventing Miscarriages of Justice*, London.

Legal Aid Board (1995) Annual Report 1994/5, London, HMSO.

Leng, R. (1993) *The Right to Silence in Police Interrogation*, RCCJ Research Study no.10, London, HMSO.

___[1995] 'Losing Sight of the Defendant: The Government's Proposals on Pre-Trial Disclosure', Crim LR 704.

Levi, M. (1993) *Investigation, Prosecution and Trial of Serious Fraud*, RCCJ Research Study, no. 14, London, HMSO.

Littlechild, R. [1995] 'Reassessing the role of the "Appropriate Adult"', Crim LR 540.

Lord Chancellor's Department (1995) *Legal Aid Targetting Need: the future of publicly funded help in solving legal problems and disputes in England and Wales*, London, HMSO,Cmnd 2854.

MacEntee, P. and McGuinness, D. (1989) 'The Criminal Justice Act 1984 and the Right to Silence', Annex B, Fourteenth Report of the Standing Advisory Commission on Human Rights, 63.

Maguire, M. (1988) 'The effects of the PACE provisions on detention and questioning', British Journal of Criminology, 19.

Maguire, M. and Norris, C. (1993) *The Conduct and Supervision of Criminal Investigations*, RCCJ Research Study no. 5, London, HMSO.

Malleson, K. (1993) *A Review of the Appeal Process*, RCCJ Research Study no. 17. London, HMSO.

___[1995] 'The Criminal Cases Review Commission: How Will it Work?', Crim LR 929.

May Report (1990) *Inquiry into the Circumstances surrounding the convictions arising out of the bomb attacks in Guildford and Woolwich in 1974, Interim Report on the Maguire Case*, HC 556 of 1989-90.

___(1993) *Inquiry into the Circumstances surrounding the convictions arising out of the bomb attacks in Guildford and Woolwich in 1974, Second Report*, HC 296 of 1992-3.

McCabe S. and Purves, R. (1974) *The Shadow Jury at Work*, Oxford, Blackwell.

McConville, M. (11th December, 1987) 'Silence in Court', NLJ, 1169.

___[1992] 'Videotaping interrogations', Crim LR 532.

___(1993) *Corroboration and Confessions: The Impact of a Rule Requiring that no Conviction can be sustained on the Basis of Confession Evidence Alone*, RCCJ Research Study no. 13, London, HMSO.

___(September 1993) 'An error of judgment', Legal Action, 6.

McConville, M. and Hodgson, J. (1993) *Custodial Legal Advice and the Right to Silence*, RCCJ Research Study no.16, London, HMSO.

McConville, M., Hodgson, J., Bridges, L. and Pavlovic, A. (1994) *Standing Accused: The Organisation and Practices of Criminal Defence Lawyers in Britain*, Oxford, Clarendon Press.

McGurk, B., Carr, J. and McGurk, D. (1993) *Investigative Interviewing Courses for Police Officers: an Evaluation*, Police Research Series, no.4.

Medalie, J., Zeitz, L. and Alexander, P. (1968) 'Custodial Police Interrogations in our nation's capital', 66, Michigan Law Review, 1347.

Meng Heong Yeo [1983] 'Diminishing the Right to Silence: the Singapore experience', Crim LR 89.

Milgram, S. [1963] 'Behavioural study of obedience', Journal of Abnormal and Social Psychology, 67, 371.

___(1974) *Obedience to Authority: an experimental view*, London, Tavistock.

Mirfield, P. [1995] '"Corroboration" after the 1994 Act', Crim LR 448.

___[1995] 'Two Side-Effects of Sections 34 to 37 of the Criminal Justice and Public Order Act 1994', Crim LR 612.

Mitchell, B. [1983] 'Confessions and police interrogation of suspects', Crim LR 596.

Morgan, D. and Stephenson, G. (eds.) (1994) *Suspicion and Silence*, London Blackstone.

Moston, S. and Stephenson, G. (1993) *The Questioning and Interviewing of Suspects Outside the Police Station*, RCCJ Research Study no. 22, London, HMSO.

Moston, S., Stephenson, G. and Williamson, T. (1992) 'The Effects of Case Characteristics on Suspect Behaviour during Questioning' British Journal of Criminology, 32, pp 23-30.

___(1993) 'The Incidence, Antecedents and Consequences of the Use of the Right to Silence during Police Questioning', Criminal Behaviour and Mental Health, 3, pp 30-47.

Munday, R. [1995] 'The Criminal Appeal Act 1995: (1) Appeals against Conviction', Crim LR 920.

___[1996] 'Inferences from Silence and European Human Rights Law', Crim LR 370.

Norman, C. (1989) 'Maine case deals blow to DNA Fingerprinting', Science, 1156.

Ockelton, M. (1995) 'Rules of evidence' in E. Attwooll and D. Goldberg (eds.).

O'Neill, G. (1995) *Putting Wrongs to Right*, London BIRW, 24.

Owers, A. (1995) *Putting Wrongs to Right*, London, BIRW, 4.

Packer, H.L. (1968) *The Limits of the Criminal Sanction*, Stanford University Press.

Pattenden, R. [1995] 'Inferences from Silence', Crim LR 602.

Peirce, G. (1996) *A Hostage to Fortune? Do We Need Permanent Counter-Terrorism Laws?* London British Irish Rights Watch

Plotnikoff, J. and Woolfson, R. (1993) *Information and Advice for Prisoners about Grounds for Appeal and the Appeal Process*, RCCJ Research Study no.18, London, HMSO.

Police Complaints Authority (1995) The First Ten Years, London, HMSO.

Pollard, C. [1994] 'A Case for Disclosure', Crim LR 42.

___[1996] 'Public safety, accountability and the courts', Crim LR 152.

Price, C. and Caplan, J. (1977) *The Confait Confessions*, London, Marion Boyars.

Raphael, M. (1990) 'The Right to Silence and Economic Crime', in S. Greer and R. Morgan (eds.) pp 60-66.

Redmayne, M. [1995] 'Doubts and Burdens: DNA Evidence, Probability and the Courts', Crim LR 464.

Roberts, D. [1995] 'Legal advice, the Unrepresented Suspect and the Courts: Inferences from Silence under the Criminal Justice and Public Order Act 1994', Crim LR 483.

Roberts, P. and Willmore, C. (1993) *The Role of Forensic Evidence in Criminal Proceedings*, RCCJ Research Study, no. 11, London, HMSO.

Roskill, E.W. (1986) *Improving the Presentation of Information to Juries in Fraud Trials*, London, HMSO.

Royal Commission on Criminal Justice (1993) Report, London, HMSO, Cmnd 2263.

Royal Commission on Criminal Procedure (1981) Report, London, HMSO, Cmnd 8092.

Royal Ulster Constabulary (1987) The Chief Constable's Annual Report.

Ruddell, G. (1990) 'A Summary of Recent Judicial Decisions in Northern Ireland', in S. Greer and R. Morgan (eds.), 53.

Ryle, G. (1966) *The Concept of Mind*, Penguin.

Sanders, A. [1988] 'Rights, Remedies and the Police and Criminal Evidence Act', Crim LR 802.

___[1990] 'Access to Legal Advice and Police Malpractice', Crim LR 494.

___(January, 1991) 'Judicial creativity and suspects' rights', Legal Action, 7.

Sanders, A., Bridges, L., Mulvaney, A. and Crozier, G. (1989) *Advice and Assistance at Police Stations and the 24 Hour Duty Solicitors Scheme*, London, Lord Chancellor's Department.

Sanders, A. and Young, R.(1994) *Criminal Justice*, London, Butterworths.

Shackleton Report (1978) Review of the Operation of the Prevention of Terrorism (Temporary Provisions) Act, 1974 and 1976, London, HMSO, Cmnd 7324.

Smith, D.J. and Gray, P. (1983) *Police and People in London* IV, London, Policy Studies Institute.

Smith, G. (November, 1996) 'Playing politics with the law', Legal Action 8.

Smith, G. and Miller, R. (September 1995) 'Redressing the balance', Legal Action, 10.

Softley, P. (1980) *Police Interrogation: an Observational Study in Four Police Stations*, RCCP Research Study no. 4, HMSO.

Standing Advisory Commission on Human Rights, Fourteenth Report of the Standing Advisory Commission on Human Rights for the Period 1 November 1987 - 31 March 1989, London, HMSO, Cmnd 394.

Stein, A. (1991) 'Criminal Defences and the Burden of Proof', Coexistence, 28, pp 133-47.

Stephen, Sir James Fitzjames (1883) *A History of the Criminal Law of England*, Macmillan.

___(1948) *Digest of the Law of Evidence* 12th edition, Macmillan.

Steventon, B. (1993) *The Ability to Challenge DNA Evidence*, RCCJ Research Study no. 9, London, HMSO.

Stuntz, W.J. (1988) 'Self-Incrimination and Excuse', Columbia Law Review, 88, 1227.

___[1989] 'The American Exclusionary Rule and Defendants' Changing Rights', Crim LR 117.

___(1995) 'Lawyers, Deception and Evidence Gathering', 79 Va L Rev 1903.

Sufian, J. (February, 1991) 'DNA in the Courtroom', Legal Action 7.

___(1991) 'Forensic use of DNA Tests', 303 BMJ, 4.

Taylor, Lord (1994) Tom Sargant Memorial Lecture, 144 NLJ 12.

Temkin, J. [1993] 'Sexual History Evidence - the Ravishment of Section 2', Crim LR 3.

Thomson Committee (1975) Criminal Procedure in Scotland (Second Report) London, HMSO, Cmnd 6218.

Thornton, P., Scrivener, A. and Mallallieu, A. (1992) *Justice on Trial*, London, Civil Liberties Trust.

Treacy, S. [1994] The Right of Silence and the Courts, including the European Convention on Human Rights, London.

Twining, W. (1985) *Theories of Evidence: Bentham and Wigmore*, London, Weidenfeld and Nicolson.

Van Kampen, P. and Nijboer, H. (November 1994) 'DNA Fingerprinting in the Dutch Code of Criminal Procedure', Expert Evidence, Vol 3, no. 2, 70.

Walker, C. (1992) *The Prevention of Terrorism in British Law*, Manchester, University Press

Walker, C. *et. al.* (1996) *A Hostage to Fortune? Do We Need Permanent Counter-Terrorism Laws?*, London, BIRW.

Walkley, J. (1987) *Police Interrogation: A Handbook for Investigators*, The Police Review Publishing Co.

Walsh, D.P.J. (1983) *The Use and Abuse of Emergency Legislation in Northern Ireland*, London, The Cobden Press.

Wigmore, J.H. (1961) *Evidence in Trials At Common Law*, Vol. VIII, McNaughten rev. ed.

Williams, G. (1987) 'The Tactic of Silence', NLJ, 1107.

Williamson, T. (1993) 'From Interrogation to Investigative Interviewing: Strategic Trends in Police Questioning', Journal of Community and Applied Social Psychology, 3, pp 89-99.

___(1994) 'Reflections on current police practice' in D. Morgan, and G. Stephenson (eds.) pp 107-16.

Williamson, T. and Moston, S. (1990) 'The extent of silence in Police Interviews', in S. Greer and R. Morgan (eds.) pp 36-43.

Willis, C. et. al. (1987) *The Tape Recording of Police Interviews with Suspects*, Home Office Research Study, no. 97, London, HMSO.

Winter, J. [1995] Human Rights and the Peace Process, International Journal of Discrimination and the Law, Vol. 1, no.1, pp 63-6.

___[1996] 'Why the Northern Ireland Peace Process has Failed: The Human Rights Perspective', International Journal of Discrimination and the Law, Vol 2, no.2, pp 39-51.

Wittgenstein, L. (1958) *Philosophical Investigations*, Oxford, Blackwell.

Woffinden B. (1990) *Miscarriages of Justice*, London, Coronet.

Wolchover, D. and Heaton-Armstrong, A. (1990) 'The questioning Code Revised and the Flaws which Exist', 140 NLJ 320, 369, 407.

___(1990) 'Last fence for the new PACE Codes', Counsel, 15.

Working Group on the Right of Silence (September, 1988) Consultation Paper, Home Office.

___(1989) Report of the Working Group on the Right of Silence, Home Office, C Division, London, July 13, 1989.

Young, S.J. [1991] 'DNA Evidence - beyond reasonable doubt?', Crim LR 264.

Zander, M. (1978) 'The Right of Silence in the Police Station and the Caution' in P. Glazebrook (ed.) *Reshaping the Criminal Law*, London, Stevens.

___[1979] 'The Investigation of Crime: a Study of Contested Cases at the Old Bailey', Crim LR 203.

___[1993] Note of Dissent, RCCJ Report, London, HMSO, Cmnd 2263, pp 221-35.

___(November, 1993) 'An error of judgment?', Legal Action 6.

___(1995) 'Reform of the Criminal Justice System: The Report of the Runciman Royal Commission', in E. Attwooll and D. Goldberg, (eds.) pp 9-26.

Zander, M. and Henderson, P. (1993) *The Crown Court Study*, RCCJ Research Study, no. 19, London, HMSO.

Zuckerman, A. (1989) *The Principles of Criminal Evidence*, Oxford, Clarendon.

___[1989] 'Trial by Unfair Means - the Report of the Working Group on the Right to Silence', Crim LR 855.

___(1990) 'The Privilege against Self-Incrimination and Procedural Fairness', in S. Greer and R, Morgan (eds.) 28-30.

___(1994) 'Bias and Suggestibility: Is There an Alternative to the Right to Silence?' in D. Morgan and G. Stephenson (eds.) pp 117-140.

Table of statutes

Bail Act 1976
Children and Young Persons Act 1933
Companies Act 1985
Criminal Appeals Act 1995
Criminal Evidence Act 1898
Criminal Justice Act 1967
Criminal Justice Act 1982
Criminal Justice Act 1984
Criminal Justice Act 1987
Criminal Justice Act 1988
Criminal Justice and Public Order Act 1994
Criminal Procedure Code (Amendment) Act 1976
Criminal Procedure (Insanity and Unfitness to Plead) Act 1991
Criminal Procedure and Investigations Act 1996
Financial Services Act 1987
Magistrates' Courts Act 1980
Northern Ireland (Emergency Provisions) Act 1987
Official Secrets Act 1911
Police and Criminal Evidence Act 1984
Police and Magistrates' Courts Act 1994
Prevention of Crime Act 1953
Prevention of Terrorism (Temporary Provisions) Act 1989
Sexual Offences (Amendment) Act 1976

Table of cases

North Carolina v Butler 441 US 369 (1979)
Orozco v Texas 394 US 24 (1968)
Parkes v R [1976] 1 WLR 1252
People v Castro, 545 NYS 2d 985 (Sup Ct Bronx County, 1989)
People v Doyle [1977] IR 336
Practice Note (Crown Court:Defendant's Evidence) [1995] Times, 12 April,
    [1995] 1 WLR 657, [1995] 2 All ER 499
Re Arrows Ltd. [no.4]: Hamilton v Naviede [1995] 1 AC 75
R v Absalom [1988] Crim LR 748, (1989) 88 Cr App Rep 32
R v Ackinlose [1996] Crim LR 747
R v Adams [1957] Crim LR 365
R v Alath, R v Brightman [1990]1 WLR 1255
R v Ahluwalia (1993) 96 Cr App Rep 133
R v Alladice (1988) 87 Cr App Rep 380
R v Anderson [1993] Crim LR 447
R v Argent [1996] Times, 19 December
R v Armstrong, Conlon, Hill and Richardson (1989) Times, 20 October
R v Bailey [1995] Times, 26 January
R v Bailey and Smith [1993] Times, 22 March
R v Baskerville [1916] 2 KB 658
R v Bathurst [1968] 2 QB 107
R v Beales [1991] Crim LR 118
R v Berry [1993] Crim LR 973
R v Bishop [1975] QB 274
R v Britzman [1983] 1 WLR 350
R v Bryce (1991) Cr App Rep 320, [1992] 4 All ER 567, (1992) 95 Cr App Rep
    320
R v Burke (1985) 82 Cr App Rep 156
R v Campbell [1994] Times, 13 July, [1995] Crim LR 157
R v Canale [1990] 2 All ER 187
R v Chance [1988] 3 All ER 225
R v Chandler [1976] 1 WLR 585
R v Christie [1914] AC 545
R v Christou (1992) QB 979
R v Chung (1991) 92 Cr App Rep 314
R v Clinton [1993] Crim LR 582
R v Condron and Condron (1996) 161 JP 1
R v Cooke [1995] Crim LR 497
R v Cowan, R v Gayle, R v Ricciardi [1995] 4 All ER 939
R v Cramp [1880] 14 Cox CC 390
R v Davidson [1988] Crim LR 422
R v Deen [1994] Times, 10 January

R v Director of SFO ex p Smith [1991] 3 All ER 452, (1992) 3 WLR 66
R v Delaney [1988] 88 Cr App Rep 338, [1988] 2 All ER 135
R v Devine C.A. May 13 [1992]
R v Dunford (1990) 91 Cr App Rep 150, [1991] Crim LR 370
R v Dunn [1990] Crim LR 572, (1990) 91 Cr App Rep 237
R v Edwards [1975] 2 QB 27
R v Edwards (1991) 2 All ER 266
R v Elson [1994] Times, 30 June
R v Emmerson (1991) 92 Cr App Rep 284
R v Ensor [1989] 1 WLR 497
R v Everett [1986] Crim LR 826
R v Everitt, R v Riley (1990) 91 Cr App Rep 208
R v Foster [1975] RTR 553
R v Fullerton [1994] Crim LR 63
R v Fulling [1987] 1 QB 426
R v Furnival [7 February 1990] Independent
R v Gilbert (1977) 66 Cr App Rep 237
R v Glaves [1993] Crim LR 685
R v Gordon [1994] Times, 27 May, [1995] Crim LR 413
R v Graham [1983] 7 NIJB 36
R v Harris (1987) 84 Cr App Rep 32
R v Hassan [1970] 1 QB 423
R v Henry [1990] Crim LR 574
R v Hoare (1966) 50 Cr App Rep 166
R v Horne [1990] Crim LR 188
R v Hughes [1993] Times, 12 November
R v Humphreys [1995] NLJ 1032
R v Hunt [1987] 1 All ER 1
R v Hunt [1992] Crim LR 582
R v Jackson [1955] 1 WLR 591
R v Johnson, Davis and Rowe [1993] Crim LR 689
R v Joseph [1993] Crim LR 206.
R v Keane [1994] 2 All ER 478
R v Keeling [1942] 1 All ER 507
R v Keenan [1989] Crim LR 720
R v Kelt [1993] Times, 15 December, [1994] 2 All ER 780, [1994] 1 WLR 765
R v Kenny [1993] Times, 27 July
R v Kinsella, December 1993, Belfast Crown Court.
R v Kiszko [1992] Times, 18 February, [1992] Times, 19 February
R v Kwabena Poku [1978] Crim LR 488
R v Lamont [1989] Crim LR 813
R v Leckey [1944] KB 80

R v Secretary of State for the Home Department ex p Gallagher [1994] Times, 28 February

R v Secretary of State for the Home Department, ex p Hickey [1994] Times, 2 December

R v Silcott, Braithwaite and Raghip [1991] Times, 9 December

R v Smith [1985] Crim LR 590

R v Smurthwaite, R v Gill [1993] Times, 5 October, (1994) 98 Cr App Rep 437

R v Smythe [20 October 1989]

R v Sparrow [1973] 1 WLR 488

R v Stafford and Luvaglio (1968) 53 Cr App Rep 1

R v Steenson [1986] 17 NIJB 36

R v Sullivan (1966) 51 Cr App Rep 102

R v Taylor [1993] Times, 1 June

R v Turnbull [1976] 3 All ER 549, [1977] QB 244

R v Walsh [1989] Crim LR 822

R v Ward (Judith) (1993) 96 Cr App Rep 1, [1993] 2 All ER 577

R v Ward (Wayne) (1994) 98 Cr App Rep 337

R v Warickshall [1783] 1 Leach 263

R v Waugh [1950] AC 203

R v Weekes [1993] Crim LR 211

R v Weeks [1995] Crim LR 52

R v Whitehead [1929] 1 KB 99

R v Wickham, Ferrara and Bean (1971) 55 Cr App Rep 199

R v Williams and Smith (1994) Times, 27 January

R v Woon [1964] 109 Crim LR 529

Rhode Island v Innis 446 US 291 (1980)

Rice v Connolly [1966] 2 QB 414

Rochin v California 342 US 165 (1952)

Saunders v UK [1996] Times, 18 December

Schmerber v California [1965] 384 US 757

Selvey v DPP [1970] AC 304

Smith v Director of SFO [1992] 3 All ER 45, [1993] AC 1

South Dakota v Neville, 312 NW 2d 723 (SD 1981), 459 US 533 (1983)

State (McCarthy) v Lennon [1936] IR 485

State v Rambo 69 Kan 77 Pac 563 (1904)

State v Schwartz 447, NW 422 Minn (1989)

United States v Dionisio 410 US 1 (1973)

United States v Frye 293 F 1013 (DC Cir, 1923)

United States v Two Bulls 9025 F 2d 1127 (1991)

Wong Kam-Ming v R [1979] AC 247

Woolmington v DPP [1935] AC 462

Index

Confait case, 39, 123, 145, 179, 267-8

Confessions, 4, 16, 22, 44-7, 81, 109-10, 119-22, 143, 150, 165, 170, 173, 180, 183-4, 199-200, 244-6, 253-4, 264-76, 285

Corbett, C., 144

Corroboration
meaning of, 83
of confessions, 47, 173, 184, 273-6, 285
corroboration rules, 46, 83, 148-50, 270-1
silence as corroboration, 61-3, 65, 135, 147-50, 219, 242

Credibility, 43, 63, 145, 151, 156, 170

Crime control, xi, 39, 85-6, 163, 166, 185, 189, 198, 204, 267

Criminal Appeal Act 1968, 278-80

Criminal Appeal Act 1995, 280-1, 283

Criminal Cases Review Commission, 97, 262, 282-4

Criminal Evidence Act 1898, 19-23, 25, 38, 147, 244

Criminal Evidence (Northern Ireland) Order, ix, xii, 14, 25, 60-72, 78, 84-97, 137, 156, 168-9, 219, 250

Criminal Justice Act 1967, 48, 52,

Criminal Justice Act 1987, 48, 238-9, 242

Criminal Justice Act 1988, 150, 278-9

Criminal Justice Act 1991, 150

Criminal Justice and Public Order Act 1994, vii-ix, 3, 6, 10-19, 23-9, 37-8, 47-8, 53, 60-8, 106, 114-5, 120, 123-4, 127, 133-6, 145,

147-8, 152, 154, 156, 165, 168, 182-3, 192, 213, 215-6, 228, 236, 248, 250, 253, 266-7, 270-1

Criminal Law Revision Committee, viii-x, xii, 14, 37, 39-41, 47-8, 56, 106, 109, 133, 135-6, 147, 152, 163, 189, 198

Criminal Procedure and Investigations Act 1996, 52-3, 179, 242

Cross, R., viii, 151-2, 201-2

Crown Prosecution Service, 49-50, 144, 178, 264

Crozier, G., 137

Dennis, I., ix, 31, 145, 174-7, 180, 182, 243

Diplock Commission, 78-9

Disciplinary principle, 5, 123, 125-6, 174-5, 177, 243

DNA
Database, 52, 216, 223-4, 226, 228
Profiling, 180, 207, 214-6, 218-31

Donnelly, P., 224-5

Doran, S., 80-1, 171

Drug Trafficking Offences Act 1986, 238

Dworkin, R., 187-9

Ellis, T., 114, 119-20

Emergency powers, 69-70, 72-9

Emergency Provisions Act, 47, 62, 70, 79, 81, 94, 98

Entrapment, 175

ESDA test, 175, 279

European Convention on Human Rights, 16, 28, 74, 107, 176, 190-1, 219, 223, 240-1, 285